W9-BMK-515

THE GERMAN CONCEPTION OF HISTORY

The German Conception

of History

THE NATIONAL TRADITION OF HISTORICAL

THOUGHT FROM HERDER TO THE PRESENT

By Georg G. Iggers

Wesleyan University Press

MIDDLETOWN, CONNECTICUT

Library of Congress catalog number: 68 - 17147

Manufactured in the United States of America

First printing May 1968; second printing October 1969

To James Luther Adams

Contents

Preface   ix

Chapter I   Introduction   3

II   The Origins of German Historicism:
THE TRANSFORMATION OF GERMAN HISTORICAL
THOUGHT FROM HERDER'S COSMOPOLITAN
CULTURE-ORIENTED NATIONALISM TO THE
STATE-CENTERED EXCLUSIVE NATIONALISM
OF THE WARS OF LIBERATION   29

III   The Theoretical Foundations of German
Historicism I: Wilhelm von Humboldt   44

IV   The Theoretical Foundations of German
Historicism II: Leopold von Ranke   63

V   The High Point of Historical Optimism—
The "Prussian School"   90

VI   The "Crisis of Historicism" I:
THE PHILOSOPHIC CRITIQUE: COHEN,
DILTHEY, WINDELBAND, RICKERT, WEBER   124

VII   The "Crisis of Historicism" II:
ERNST TROELTSCH AND FRIEDRICH MEINECKE   174

VIII   The Decline of the German "Idea"
of History:
THE IMPACT OF TWO WORLD WARS AND
TOTALITARIANISM ON GERMAN HISTORICAL
THOUGHT   229

IX   Conclusion   269

Notes   287

Suggested Readings   349

Index   357

Preface

Despite the great impact of German historical thought and scholarship on the development of the cultural sciences throughout the world, as well as on political and social thought in Germany, no comprehensive study of German historiography or German historical thought has appeared in English during the past fifty years. In Germany a great number of monographs have been published on individual historians, but only two general works have appeared in recent years, each written from a point of view very different from that of the present author. Of these, one, *Geist und Geschichte vom deutschen Humanismus bis zur Gegenwart,* was written by an Austrian advocate of a Greater Germany, Heinrich Ritter von Srbik, an historian still steeped in the tradition of German Idealism; the other, *Studien über die deutsche Geschichtswissenschaft,* consists of a collection of essays by East German Marxist historians edited by Joachim Streisand.

Like the two above-mentioned studies, this work is not primarily intended as a history of German historiography. Rather it seeks to present an interpretative, critical analysis of the theoretical presuppositions and political values of German historians in the major national tradition of German historiography from Wilhelm von Humboldt and Leopold von Ranke to Friedrich Meinecke and Gerhard Ritter. Ranke's ideal of absolute scholarly detachment proved to be unobtainable by any historian in the tradition and undesirable to many. Instead, the scholarship of these historians continued to be closely interwoven with a *Weltanschauung* and a set of political values that remained relatively static in the face of changing intellectual and social conditions. The book traces the dissolution of the tradition in terms of its own inner contradictions and under the impact of political events. It is hoped that this volume may be of use at a moment when German historians are seriously re-examining their national history as well as the methodological and philosophic assumptions of their classical historians in the light of the political catastrophes of the twentieth century. It should also be of particular interest to historians and social theorists outside of Germany in countries such as the United States, France, and Italy. There, in recent years, the theoretical assumptions of "German historicism," especially as interpreted by Wilhelm Dilthey and Max Weber, have received considerable attention.

This book is an outgrowth of a broader and yet uncompleted work on the idea of progress the twofold purpose of which is to deal historically with the role of ideas of progress and decline in modern historical and political thought and theoretically with the validity of these ideas. A grant from the John Simon Guggenheim Memorial Foundation permitted me to devote myself full-time to this topic in Paris during the academic year 1960-1961. As I became increasingly concerned with the German critics of the idea of progress, I moved across the Rhine to Göttingen, where with the help of a fellowship from the Rockefeller Foundation I was able to complete the basic research for the present volume. I gratefully acknowledge these grants as well as a grant-in-aid from the Newberry Library in Chicago in the fall of 1964, which enabled me to complete the manuscript. Further grants from the Research Foundation of the State University of New York and the University of Buffalo Foundation allowed me to spend the summer of 1966 in Göttingen in order to rewrite the section of the manuscript dealing with German historiography since 1945. Two supplementary grants came from Dillard University during the academic year 1960-1961 and from Roosevelt University during my stay at the Newberry Library. I also wish to express my gratitude to the staffs of the *Niedersächsische Staats-und-Universitätsbibliothek* in Göttingen and of the Newberry Library with its excellent collection of German historiography, and particularly to Lawrence Towner, the director of the Newberry Library.

I am indebted to a large number of individuals for their advice and comments. I especially wish to thank my wife for her many suggestions and her encouragement. Professors Manfred Schlenke, Louis Gottschalk, Harold T. Parker, Gerald Feldman, Gerhard Masur, and Günter Birtsch read the entire manuscript. I am particularly grateful for Professor Feldman's extensive criticisms and detailed suggestions. Dieter Groh and Maarten Brands read the introduction; Jurgen Herbst, the chapter on Humboldt; Ernst Schulin, the chapter on Ranke; Peter Krausser, the section on Wilhelm Dilthey; Georg Kotowski and James L. Adams, the chapter on Ernst Troeltsch and Friedrich Meinecke. John L. Snell, Rudolf von Thadden, Gerhard Ritter, Eberhard Kessel, Dietrich Gerhard, K. D. Bracher, Maarten Brands, Bedřich Loewenstein, Werner Berthold, Pieter Geyl, George Kren, Jorg Wollenberg, Ernst Hinrichs, Christoph Schröder, and Klaus Epstein read and commented on versions of Chapter VIII. Others, including Fritz Fischer, Werner Conze, Fritz Wagner, Geoffrey Barraclough, Hermann Heimpel, Hermann Wein, Reinhold Wittram, and Eberhard Kolb, permitted me to interview them on the problems of the study.

I am dedicating this book to James Luther Adams, who in my days as a graduate student first introduced me to some of the problems discussed in this book and who over the years has closely followed my work and often offered valuable advice. I believe that the dedication is particularly fitting because James Luther Adams, like the best of the men discussed in this volume, has combined scholarly integrity with an active commitment to the great political and ethical problems of the day.

There are two obvious omissions in this book. There is no discussion of the historiography of the Nazi Period or of that of East Germany since 1945. As explained above, this book is not intended as a comprehensive study. The classical national tradition of German historicism undoubtedly contributed to the atmosphere that facilitated the rise of an authoritarian regime and many of the historians in this tradition, but by no means all found it easy to come to terms with the Nazis. Nevertheless, the tradition differed basically from the *völkisch* ideology of official Nazi historiography. Helmut Heiber in his voluminous *Walter Frank und sein Reichsinstitut für Geschichte* (Stuttgart, 1966) and Karl Ferdinand Werner in his brief book *Das NS—Geschichtsbild und die deutsche Geschichtswissenschaft* (Stuttgart, 1967)

have begun to investigate the role of the historian in the Nazi regime.
The failure to discuss historiography in East Germany is not intended
as non-recognition of the historians of the D.D.R., but results from the
fact that the tradition of historiography discussed in this book came to
a fairly abrupt end there in the years after the war.

GEORG G. IGGERS

Buffalo, New York
August 30, 1967

THE GERMAN CONCEPTION OF HISTORY

Introduction

In few countries in modern times have professional historians been as consciously guided in their practice by a conception of history as in nineteenth- and twentieth-century Germany. This was true under circumstances where, except for the Hitler years, historians were free of the intellectual regimentation which prevails in totalitarian regimes.

With much more justification than in France, Britain, or the United States, we may speak of one main tradition of German historiography. This tradition, broad and varied in its manifestations, was given a degree of unity by its common roots in the philosophy of German Idealism. One of its founding fathers was Leopold von Ranke, but he was by no means the only one. Another, perhaps equally important in the translation of German Idealist philosophy for historical practice and of greater influence upon German historians in the mid-nineteenth century, was Wilhelm von Humboldt.

What gave the tradition its distinguishing characteristics was not its critical analysis of documents, so closely associated with the name of Ranke. The critical method and the devotion to factual accuracy were not peculiar to Ranke or the nineteenth-century German historians. To an extent, they were developed by an earlier generation of historians, philologists, classicists, and Bible-scholars. Moreover, they were easily exported and adapted by historians in other countries who wrote under the impact of very different outlooks. The critical method became the common property of honest historical scholars

3

everywhere. What distinguished the writings of the historians in the main tradition of German historiography was rather their basic theoretical convictions in regard to the nature of history and the character of political power.

This historical faith determined historical practice as well as the problems that historians posed. For the most part it centered upon the conflict of the great powers and determined the methods they employed: their heavy emphasis on diplomatic documents to the neglect of social and economic history and of sociological methods and statistics. This faith also gave the works of these historians a political orientation, not in the narrow sense of party partisanship—for within the broad tradition we find conservatives, liberals, democrats, and socialists of every description—but in the central role they assigned to the state and in their confidence in its beneficial effects.

There were, to be sure, important thinkers who were not part of this tradition, historians such as Jacob Burckhardt, Julius von Ficker, Johann von Döllinger, Max Lehmann, and Franz Schnabel, and philosophers such as Arthur Schopenhauer and Friedrich Nietzsche. Other scholars, such as Lorenz von Stein and Karl Lamprecht, stood at the margins of this tradition in their attempts to discover great social and economic forces operative in history. Nevertheless, the basic philosophic assumptions upon which the tradition rested were accepted not only by the majority of German historians, but also by scholars in other disciplines. The philosophy and methodology of historicism permeated all the German humanistic and cultural sciences, so that linguistics, philology, economics, art, law, philosophy, and theology became historically oriented studies.

Historicism has too many meanings to be useful as a term without careful delimitation.[1] In Chapter II, we shall discuss the term at greater length. In this book, when we speak of historicism, we shall generally refer to the main tradition of German historiography and historical thought which has dominated historical writing, the cultural sciences, and political theory in Germany from Wilhelm von Humboldt and Leopold von Ranke until the recent past. It should nevertheless be emphasized that historicism as a movement of thought was not restricted to Germany, but that since the eighteenth century this historical outlook has dominated cultural thought in Europe generally.[2]

The core of the historicist outlook lies in the assumption that there is a fundamental difference between the phenomena of nature and those of history, which requires an approach in the social and cultural sciences fundamentally different from those of the natural sciences. Nature, it is held, is the scene of the eternally recurring, of phenomena themselves devoid of conscious purpose; history comprises unique and unduplicable human acts, filled with volition and intent. The world of man is in a state of incessant flux, although within it there are centers of stability (personalities, institutions, nations, epochs), each possessing an inner structure, a character, and each in constant metamorphosis in accord with its own internal principles of development. History thus becomes the only guide to an understanding of things human. There is no constant human nature; rather the character of each man reveals itself only in his development. The abstract, classificatory methods of the natural sciences are therefore inadequate models for the study of human world. History requires methods which take into account that the historian is confronted by concrete persons and groups who once were alive and possessed unique personalities that called for intuitive understanding by the historian. These methods must take into account that not only the historian's subject matter but he himself stands within the stream of time, and that the methods and logic by which he seeks objective knowledge are themselves timebound.

Friedrich Meinecke, Ernst Troeltsch, and others have recognized that the historical outlook was the outcome of broad currents of European thought in the seventeenth and eighteenth centuries. However, they have maintained that only in Germany did historicism attain its full development. Historicism liberated modern thought from the two-thousand-year domination of the theory of natural law, and the conception of the universe in terms of "timeless, absolutely valid truths which correspond to the rational order dominant thoughout the universe" was replaced with an understanding of the fullness and diversity of man's historical experience. This recognition, Meinecke believes, constituted Germany's greatest contribution to Western thought since the Reformation and "the highest stage in the understanding of things human attained by man."[3] Western European thought, Troeltsch and Meinecke maintained, nevertheless continued to be committed to natural law patterns of thought into the nineteenth and twentieth centuries.[4] This difference in philosophic outlook, they claimed, lay at the basis of the deep divergence in cultural and political development which they observed between Germany and "Western Europe" after the French Revolution.

This juxtaposition of German historicism and Western natural law, however, undoubtedly distorts the realities of the intellectual situation in the nineteenth and twentieth centuries. For the break with natural-law patterns, which Troeltsch and Meinecke observed in Germany, occurred in Western Europe as well. Here, too, romanticism and the reaction against the French Revolution were accompanied by a new interest in historical studies. Moreover, the impact of German literature, philosophy, and historical studies left deep impacts in France, England, and elsewhere.[5]

The relation between history and political science was reversed generally in Europe. The historian no longer looked to political philosophy for the principles of rational politics, as in the Enlightenment, rather, the political theorist turned to history. Not only conservative writers, such as Burke and Carlyle, but liberal theorists as well (Constant, Thierry, Michelet, Macaulay, and Acton) sought the roots of French or English liberty in the remote national past rather than in the rights of man.[6] Even the positivistic sociology of Auguste Comte or Herbert Spencer, which later German critics regarded as the antithesis of German historicism, viewed society in terms of historical growth.

It is undoubtedly true, nevertheless, that historicism received its most radical expression in Germany. This radicalism unquestionably reflected the peculiar role which historicism played in German political thought. For far from representing a purely cultural phenomenon devoid of all political connotations, as Meinecke maintained in the face of his disillusionment with the course of German politics in the 1930's[7], historicism from the beginning was permeated with political ideas.[8] Carlo Antoni has shown how closely the emergence of the historicist outlook in the eighteenth century was bound up with the attempts of political theorists to defend local rights and privileges against the encroachment of the centralizing Enlightenment state. This held particularly true in areas such as the Swiss cantons and the German petty states, where the modern bureaucratic state was not yet firmly established.[9] Antoni has suggested that historicism can serve as the common denominator for a Europe-wide "reaction and revolt of national traditions against French Reason and the Age of Enlightenment," as expressed in the application of an abstract math-

ematical mentality to culture and politics.[10] But it was in Germany
that the conflict between national traditions and French ideas was
particularly intense. Germany lacked the heritage of a great literature which England, Spain, and Italy possessed.

The literary revival in Germany in the late eighteenth century
involved the attempt to free national literature from the influence of
French neo-classic patterns, and was far more conscious than the
romantic stirrings elsewhere. But, most important, German political
nationalism arose in the struggle against the French domination of
Germany in the aftermath of the wars of the French Revolution and
the Napoleonic victories, a struggle which intensified the anti-
Enlightenment bias of German political thought. The tradition of
historical thought with which we are dealing in this book was a child
of the German national revival and the Wars of Liberation. The
liberal historians in the tradition sought to derive their liberalism
from the spirit of reform which guided the great bureaucrats. Men
such as Stein, Humboldt, Gneisenau, and Scharnhorst, sought by
edicts from above to create an efficient, modernized monarchy, able
to mobilize the human resources of the nation and willing to provide
the conditions in which personal liberty, juridical security, and a
degree of popular participation in public affairs would be balanced
with a respect for traditional organs of authority. In the Spirit of
1813 they saw a saner German counterpart to the ideas of 1789. The
radically equalitarian demands of the French Revolution and its challenge to all tradition, they feared, laid the road open to the systematic tyranny of the state over man, such as exercised by a Robespierre or a Napoleon.

Three sets of ideas occupy a central role in the theoretical position of the German national tradition of historiography with which
we are concerned in this book: a concept of the state, a philosophy
of value, and a theory of knowledge. None of these three concepts is
entirely peculiar to German historiography, but all three have found
an extreme formulation in German historical thought.[11]

1. *The state as an end in itself and the concept of the
Machtstaat.* Historicism in Germany, as elsewhere, viewed the state
as the product of historical forces. In Germany, as in Great Britain
or France, the culture-oriented historiography of the eighteenth century exemplified by Voltaire or Gibbon gave way to a nation-

centered politically oriented approach to the past. However, German historians looked back to political traditions which were very different from those of French or British historians. To be sure, the historians with whom we deal idealized neither the Holy Roman Empire nor the remnants of medieval corporatism. Rather, their model is the enlightened *Obrigkeitsstaat,* best represented by the Hohenzollern monarchy of the Prussian Reform Era. Their conception of the state thus contains an aristocratic and bureaucratic bias together with an appreciation of the position of the cultured, propertied middle classes as pillars of society. The state for them is neither the nation in Michelet's sense nor is it embodied in the history of parliamentary institutions in the British meaning. They maintain a much sharper distinction between government and governed than do their French and British counterparts. In Ranke's words: "No matter how we define state and society, there always remains the contrast between the authorities and the subject, between the mass of the governed and the small number of governors"[12]

In place of the utilitarian concept of state, as an instrument of the interests and welfare of its population, German historiography emphatically places the idealistic concept of the state as an "individual," an end in itself, governed by its own principles of life. States have more than merely empirical existence, Ranke observes; they each represent a higher spiritual principle, "so to say an idea of God. . . . It would be foolish to consider them as so many institutions existing for the protection of individuals who have joined together, let us say, to safeguard their property."[13]

2. *Antinormativität, the rejection of the concept of thinking in normative terms.* Closely related to the concept of the state, as an individual and an end in itself, is a certain philosophy of value. By definition, any form of historicism has to recognize that all values arise within the concrete setting of an historical situation. The tradition of historicism with which we are dealing, however, goes a step further by assuming that whatever arises in history is per se valuable. No individual, no institution, no historical deed can be judged by standards external to the situation in which it arises, but rather must be judged in terms of its own inherent values. There are thus no rational standards of value applicable to a diversity of human institutions. Instead, all values are culture-bound, but all cultural phe-

nomena are emanations of divine will and represent true values. In the realm of political values, the foundations are thus laid for an ethical theory of the doctrine of state. If Machiavelli viewed the striving for power in amoral terms, German historicism raises it to an ethical principle. It must be the uppermost task of the state, Ranke observes, to achieve the highest measure of independence and strength among the competing powers of the world, so that the state will be able to fully develop its innate tendencies. To this end all domestic affairs must be subordinated.[14]

The critics of the doctrine of reason of state, Meinecke declares, overlook that "morality has not only a universal but also an individual side to it and the seeming immorality of the state's egoism for power can be morally justified from this perspective. For nothing can be immoral which comes from the innermost, individual character of a being."[15] The state can thus not sin when it follows its own higher interests, generally interpreted in power-political terms, for in pursuing these interests it furthers high ethical aims. Only in a strong state, Humboldt and Droysen assure us, are freedom, law, and cultural creativity secure. The state is thus not sheer power, but the institutional embodiment of morality. International conflicts are never merely a struggle of power, but beyond this a conflict of moral principles. Victory in war, Ranke agrees with Hegel, generally represents the victory of the higher moral energies.[16]

The identification of national power with freedom and culture is by no means unique to German historicism. Nevertheless, there is missing in the German tradition the conscious attempt so frequent in nineteenth-century nationalism in Italy, France, America, and Britain, which identifies national aspirations with universal human values.[17] Beginning with Ranke, historians in the German tradition stress the intransferability of political institutions.[18] Germany has little to learn from France; it must rather strive to develop institutions fully in its own traditions. Every state is unique, embodying a particular and inimitable spirit and ethics. German nationalism is thus much more historically oriented, far more devoid of an idea which transcends the political or ethnic nation.[19] The historicism of Johann Gottfried Herder in the eighteenth century had initiated a keen awareness of the variety of human values; in the nineteenth century it increasingly tended to lead to a negation of universal human values.[20]

3. *Anti-Begrifflichkeit, the rejection of conceptualized thinking.* In the theory of knowledge as well, the break with the natural law belief in the rational substructure of human existence is carried to a greater extreme than in other forms of historicism. The uniqueness of individualities in history restricted the applicability of rational methods in the study of social and cultural phenomena. The spontaneity and dynamism of life refused to be reduced to common denominators. From Humboldt and Schleiermacher on, German historians and cultural scientists have tended to stress the very limited value of concepts and generalizations in history and the cultural sciences *(Geisteswissenschaften).*[21] Conceptualization, they assert, empties the reality of history of its vital quality. History, the area of willed human actions, requires understanding. But this understanding *(Verstehen)* is possible only if we cast ourselves into the individual character of our historical subject matter. This process is not accomplished by abstract reasoning, but by direct confrontation with the subject we wish to understand and by contemplation *(Anschauung)* of its individuality, free of the limitations of conceptual thought. All historical understanding, Humboldt, Ranke, and Dilthey agree, requires an element of intuition *(Ahnung).*

This rejection of abstract reason by German historicists does not, however, mean a rejection of all rationality in scientific inquiry. On the contrary, as we shall see, historicism is predominantly a scholarly movement which seeks rational understanding of human reality. Recognizing the emotional qualities of all human behavior, it seeks to develop a logic that takes into account the irrational aspects of human life. The same deep faith in the ultimate unity of life in God, which marks the political and ethical thought of historicism, also marks its theory of knowledge. From Humboldt to Meinecke, German historians are aware that all historical study takes place in an historical framework, but they are also confident that scholarly study leads to objective knowledge of historical reality. This leads to the professionalization of historical research and the development of canons of critical scholarship. In practice, German historical scholarship is never able to free itself from conceptualized thinking. It works with a concept of the state which is much more static, far less aware of cultural diversities than that employed by historians outside the tradition. Nor were the German historians able to free themselves of value judgments, to let history speak through them (as Ranke

demanded) to the extent that they postulated in theory. They dog-
matically ruled out the possibility of a common human substructure
subject to rational inquiry by insisting that history was the sphere of
the unique. Little place was left for comparative studies of cultures
or for the analysis of constant structural characteristics of societies.
This is in sharp contrast with attempts elsewhere (Fustel de
Coulanges, Alexis de Tocqueville, Jacob Burckhardt, Lord Acton,
Frederick Turner) or in Germany (Lorenz von Stein, Marx and
Engels, Karl Lamprecht, Max Weber, Otto Hintze) to combine a
recognition of the diversity of institutions with a search for the constant or typically recurring elements in historical change, as well as
for patterns of development.

These philosophic notions of history were to dominate German
historiography for more than a century. As we shall see in the next
chapter, they had roots in the cosmopolitan, culture-oriented historicism of the eighteenth century and in the classical *Humanitätsideal*
of Herder, Goethe, and Kant. They acquired their nationalistic and
power-oriented form in the period of stress and strain of the Napoleonic invasions, and became a part of the national heritage in the
enthusiasm which accompanied the Wars of Liberation. They were
integrated into the political faith of a generation who, in the decades
of the Restoration, strove against the forces of absolutism for national unity and the establishment of liberal institutions cleansed of
alien French ideas and loyal to German traditions. Among conservative historians, these philosophic notions were reinforced by Ranke's
activities as a historian, publicist, and teacher.

In the years immediately preceding 1848, a more liberal generation of young historians, skeptical of Ranke's conservative leanings
and looking for Prussian leadership in German unification, turned
back to Humboldt, Fichte, and Hegel for inspiration. The failure of
the 1848 Revolution further convinced the same historians of the
primacy of state action and of the ethical rightness of political
power. The year 1871 seemed to them to be the culmination and
justification of historical development. German nationalism had become inextricably interwoven with the "German" idea of history,
which in turn now became closely and equally associated with the
Bismarckian solution to the German question. Conservatives, liberals, and to an extent even democrats, shared in the common religion
of history. Germany's entry into the area of world politics found

historians firmly convinced that Ranke's conception of the great powers could be extended to the world scene. World War I once more united most historians from left to right in a fervent defense of the "German idea of history" against "Western natural-law doctrine."

Thus, German historians moved in a world of their own, which remained remarkably unchanged in the midst of the great transformations of the nineteenth and early twentieth centuries. Their intellectual capital to a large extent remained that of the glorious days of the Wars of Liberation. They were remarkably inattentive to the great social and economic changes brought about by industrialization. History to them remained primarily the interplay of the great powers, and diplomatic and political documents continued to offer the prime sources for historical study. Where historians did acknowledge the emergence of the masses as a political factor, as Heinrich von Sybel did in his study of the French Revolution, they assumed that the principles of international politics and warfare had remained essentially unchanged since the emergence of the modern absolutist state. Sociology was viewed with suspicion. Even the great tradition of economic history, which came into being with Gustav Schmoller, subordinated economic to political and power-political factors. Similarly, at the turn of the twentieth century, the circle of social and political reformers around Friedrich Naumann, which included eminent men such as Max Weber, Ernst Troeltsch, and Friedrich Meinecke, saw the primary solution for the domestic social and economic problems of an industrial society in an expansive foreign policy. They championed democratization of government primarily as a means of strengthening the nation in the international power struggle.

Despite their rejection of the classic idea of progress, German historians and social thinkers still remained remarkably optimistic regarding the future of the modern world at a time when a cultural malaise had become apparent among liberal thinkers in the Western countries. Burckhardt's and Nietzsche's words of warning, whatever their impact upon broad masses of young Germans, mostly fell upon deaf ears among the leading German historians. In 1914, with very few exceptions, German historians and social philosophers were unable to understand the completely changed character of warfare and international realities. They were prisoners of an idea. This idea, with its roots in the nineteenth century, influenced their judgment of the political realities of the twentieth century. Only the terrible calamities of Nazism and World War II led to a serious and wide-spread re-examination of the basic philosophic assumptions of the national tradition of historiographical thought.

This book has a twofold task: one historical, the other theoretical. As an historical study, it will attempt to trace the emergence, transformation, and decline of the main orientation of German historical thought and historiographical practice from Wilhelm von Humboldt and Leopold von Ranke to Friedrich Meinecke and Gerhard Ritter. The study proceeds on the assumption that this line of thought represented a continuous tradition. In the spirit of that tradition, we will seek to portray this line of thought as a unique event in the history of ideas. The book is not intended as an exhaustive history of German historical thought in the nineteenth or twentieth century. Rather, it proposes to reconstruct the basic conceptual structure of the tradition and to follow the dialogue which took place within this framework. Insofar as the tradition extended to cultural scientists and political theorists, as well as to historians, we must necessarily consider thinkers other than historians who played a decisive role in this dialogue.

In another sense, however, this study consciously violates the spirit of German historicism, for it not only seeks to understand but to judge. It rejects the historicist precept that every historical individuality must be measured only by its own inherent standards. Rather, it proceeds on the antihistoricist assumption that there are tenets of logic and ethics common to all mankind. A main purpose of the study is to analyze the basic theoretical propositions of the German historicist tradition. Within these propositions, it claims to find two types of basic contradictions which led to the dissolution of the tradition. On the philosophic level it sees this contradiction in the historicist attempt to base a positive faith in a meaningful universe on historical relativism. The early representatives of the German historicist tradition were still deeply steeped in the belief that this was a moral world, that man possessed worth and dignity, and that an objective understanding of history and reality was possible. As we observed, they insisted at the same time that all values were unique and historical, that all philosophy was national, and all understanding individual. They insisted upon the radical diversity of men and of human cultures. What preserved them from ethical and epistemological relativism was their deep faith in a metaphysical reality beyond the historical world. They were convinced that each of the diverse cultures merely reflected the many aspects of this reality.

Many, including Ranke and the majority of the Prussian historians, remained wedded to a Lutheran religiosity which, in its optimism, seemed to lack any profound understanding of the propensity of political institutions to abuse power. Others in German Idealistic tradition still saw in history the fulfillment of a great rational process. The increasing orientation toward the natural sciences in the course of the nineteenth century did not destroy this faith. For basic to German idealism and to the optimism of German historicism was not the concept that reality was idea, but that the world was a meaningful process. Nor did the philosophic discussions of the Neo-Kantians regarding the nature of history and of historical knowledge decisively shatter this faith—at least among the historians—even if they cast doubt on it.[22] Only the cataclysmic events of the twentieth century set the stage for a serious and widespread re-examination of historicist principles.

There is a second more general question which interests us, that of the relation of historicism to political theory. Particularly interesting is to what extent historicist concepts were compatible with liberal and democratic political theory. German historicism was indeed a revolt against aspects of the Enlightenment, but by no means as radical a reaction against political liberalism as has often been assumed. Historicism, as we shall see, had its conservative wing, represented by Ranke, Treitschke in his later years, Below, Marcks, and others. But for the most part the historians in the national tradition considered themselves liberals. Indeed, the main currents of nineteenth- and early twentieth-century liberalism in Germany stood within the historicist tradition. Nevertheless, on the plane of social and political ideas, the historicism of the liberal German historians was marked by profound inconsistencies. Its narrow conception of the state, modeled on the Restoration Prussian monarchy, prevented German historians from adequately taking into account the broad social, economic, and cultural forces operating in history.

Historiography in Germany thus preserved an aristocratic bias far longer than in Western countries. History, at least until

Meinecke's *Weltbürgertum und Nationalstaat,* with some notable exceptions, was mostly history in a narrow political sense, relating the actions of statesmen, of generals, and of diplomats, and leaving almost entirely out of account the institutional and material framework in which these decisions were made. Although Meinecke introduced a concern with the political relevance of ideas, his *Ideengeschichte* centered exclusively around the intellectual biographies of great personalities and consciously ignored the social setting within which political ideas arise and function. Nor was the peculiar synthesis of freedom and authority, which the German historians proposed, a convincing or a lasting one. The German historians in the historicist tradition rejected the doctrine of natural law. As we noted, they insisted that the state should not be judged by external ethical standards or by utilitarian norms of the freedom and welfare of its citizens, but that its conduct must always be guided and judged in terms of its power-political interests and that, therefore, the demands of foreign policy always must have preference over domestic considerations. In contrast to classical social contract theory, they insisted, and probably rightly so, that freedom can be achieved only within and through the state. However, they believed that the freedoms they sought, and which were essentially those of liberals generally, the rights of the person (freedom of expression, rule of law, and the presence of representative institutions through which public opinion could cooperate in the making of political decisions), could be achieved within the framework of the traditional state. They tended to believe that the Hohenzollern monarchy, with its aristocratic and authoritarian aspects and its unique bureaucratic ethos, guaranteed a better bulwark for the defense of individual liberties and juridical security than a democracy in which policy would be more responsive to the whims of public opinion than to considerations of reasons of state. What they wanted, therefore, was a *Rechtsstaat* best achieved, they thought, in a constitutional monarchy which provided organs of popular representation but maintained important prerogatives of executive rule, especially regarding foreign affairs and a military free of parliamentary control. This position was held even by such early twentieth-century critics of the Wilhelminian state as Friedrich Meinecke, Ernst Troeltsch, Max Weber, Hans Delbrück, and Friedrich Naumann. They sought to link the masses more closely to the monarchy through social reforms and a more democratic suffrage.

The political faith of historicism rested upon a metaphysical optimism which in retrospect seems incredibly naive. German historians liked to stress that they understood the realities of power more fully than their Western counterparts who remained closer to natural-law traditions; also that the German idea of freedom better recognized the social character of freedom in an industrial age, and the relation of freedom to the total social and political life of a nation. "There is no pure idea of political freedom," Ernst Troeltsch commented in a war lecture on the "German Idea of Freedom." Rather, the concept of political freedom, like all political concepts, has developed from the total spiritual and political life of a nation. In contrast, "the ideas of 1789" conceived freedom in terms of the "isolated individual and his always identical rationality."[23]

Confident in the meaningfulness of the historical process, German historians and political theorists from Wilhelm von Humboldt to Friedrich Meinecke almost a century later were willing to view the state as an ethical institution whose interests in the long run were in harmony with freedom and morality. But once the belief in a divine purpose in social existence declined with the increasing secularization of thought in the nineteenth century and the triumph of naturalism, the philosophic foundations of the historicist faith in the harmony of power and morality lost their credibility. The concept of the *Rechtsstaat* developed by late nineteenth- and early twentieth-century liberal legal philosophers, as exemplified by Hans Kelsen, was fundamentally different from the classical liberal conception of government by "established and promulgated law," as formulated, for example, by John Locke. For legal positivists like Hans Kelsen, it mattered that the state follow established law and recognize a sphere of private life, but the question of the just or unjust content of the law became irrelevant. As Professor Hollowell has observed, classical integral liberalism has held that the state existed "to preserve human dignity and individual autonomy, to attain values that are inherent in individuals as human beings." For the late nineteenth-century German advocates of the *Rechtsstaat* "procedure and the manner of enactment replaced justice as the criterion of law."[24] The ethical restrictions on the power of the state were thus removed. Although historians for the most part remained loyal to the idealistic heritage of the nineteenth century, Treitschke's frank assertion that the state is sheer power, along with various subsequent expressions of what

Meinecke has called a "biological ethics of force," were in a sense logical consequences of the theoretical premises of historicism.

Historicism prided itself on its openness to historical reality. For its adherents, the great strength of the classical German tradition of historiography rested in its complete freedom from ideology. For Meinecke, German historicism represented the highest point in the understanding of things human because it freed historical thought from normative concepts. Instead, it sought to grasp historical reality in its living individuality without forcing it into the strait jacket of concepts. Nevertheless, German historicism, as a theory of history, possessed many of the characteristics of an ideology. Far from seeking to understand each historical situation from within, the German historians in the national tradition generally committed the sin of which they accused Western historians: imposing concepts or norms on historical reality. It is perhaps inescapable that the historian approaches history from a standpoint that reflects the imprint of his personality and of the social and cultural framework within which he writes. What distinguished German historicism was nevertheless the rigidity of this standpoint, the refusal of its historians to see their timebound political and social conceptions and norms in historical perspective. But in a more narrowly political sense, too, in many ways historicism functioned as an ideology.

Historicism, as we already suggested, was closely tied to the political and social outlook of a class, the academic *Bildungsbürgertum.* Far from attaining the impartiality and *Überparteilichkeit* (standing above parties) which Ranke proposed as an ideal of scientific historiography, German historians in this tradition from Ranke to Meinecke and Ritter were all deeply committed politically. Wittingly, and to some extent unwittingly, historicism provided a theoretical foundation for the established political and social structure of nineteenth-century Prussia and Germany. There is a great degree of truth to Georg Lukacz's observation (written from a Marxist point of view) that "the axiom of German historiography, 'Men make history,' is only the reverse historiographical and methodological side" of the coin of Prussian-bureaucratic absolutism.[25] The contradiction in the German historical conception of ethics and freedom thus appears to reflect contradictions within the fabric of German society and politics themselves.

A study of German historiography therefore can not fully divorce itself from an analysis of the basic theoretical concepts of German historians nor from an awareness of the institutional framework within which nineteenth- and twentieth-century historical thought and writing took place in Germany. We shall not, however, undertake to write a social history of ideas in this book. There is already an extensive literature on the relation of ideas to institutions in Germany. A good deal of this literature revolves around the problem of the political and cultural divergence of Germany from the West, a problem which has become central to almost every significant examination of conscience in Germany since World War I.

Within this literature, written from divergent standpoints by historians, social theorists, and cultural critics standing within German traditions, those seeking a way to liberal-democratic values and institutions, and Marxists, there is a broad area of consensus. Germany, it is generally agreed, entered the age of the democratic masses and of modern industry at a time when aristocratic institutions and attitudes were still much more intact in Germany than in the Western European countries, not to speak of the United States. Marxist and non-Marxist historians alike stress the importance of the decline of the middle class in Germany after the sixteenth century, which Hajo Holborn describes as "in many ways more bourgeois than the eighteenth."[26]

Germany lacked the great bourgeois families of commerce or finance which in France, Great Britain, or the Netherlands were able to exert a degree of political influence. To a much greater extent than in the West, the manufactories which came into existence in the age of mercantilism were state-owned. Artisans and shopkeepers, still closely attached to a precapitalistic, corporative outlook, occupied a more influential role among the urban classes than in Western countries. On the other hand, the predominant social and economic position of the land-owning aristocracy remained generally intact in the absolutistic territorial states. The process toward bureaucratic, absolutistic centralization took place in the seventeenth- and eighteenth-century German principalities, as it did elsewhere in Europe. The difference, however, was that the open confrontation which occurred between aristocracy and monarchy in France during the *Frondes,* or in Bohemia and Moravia in the Winter War, did not come about in Prussia. Here a political compromise emerged between nobility and crown.

The sixteenth and early seventeenth centuries, which saw a decline in trade in the Western areas of Germany, witnessed an increasing economic prosperity among the large scale *Junker* land-owning nobility east of the Elbe, and an accompanying re-establishment of manorial rights at a time when the seignioral system was disintegrating in the West. As in Mecklenburg, Pomerania, and elsewhere, these developments in East Elbian Prussia were accompanied by the emergence of an aristocratic *Ständestaat,* in which the manorial lords entrenched themselves by occupying interlocking positions of economic, political, and social dominance. The Thirty Years' War ushered in a reversal of this trend. The economic decline of the *Junkers* was accompanied by a rise in princely power. In Prussia, as elsewhere in Europe, the aristocracy progressively lost its political functions but was confirmed in its social privileges, and was able to maintain its control over local government and retain its manorial privileges to a much larger extent than in France. East Elbian towns, on the other hand, retained few of their local privileges but were almost thoroughly subordinated to the Hohenzollern bureaucracy. Where territorial princes were less successful than in Prussia in consolidating their power (as in Saxony or Brunswick), territorial or state-wide diets, in which the aristocracy played a dominant role, continued to exist. As Leonard Krieger observed, the Hohenzollerns went much further "beyond the standard division of labor between political power and social privilege to incorporate the aristocracy into the authoritarian military and civil posts of the state itself" than did the Bourbons or the Habsburgs.[27] It is true that merit tended to replace birth as a prerequisite for office and advancement. Nevertheless, the aristocratic character of the bureaucracy was maintained to a larger extent than in France or Austria. Frederick II indeed sought to strengthen it, and a new bureaucratic nobility, in part recruited from the middle classes, was integrated with the hereditary East Elbian aristocracy through intermarriage, and encouraged to acquire manorial estates.

On a political plane, Enlightenment demands for social reconstruction expressed themselves in a very different form in German states from those in France. The Prussian aristocracy, integrated into the bureaucratic structure and secure in its local privileges, sought to a much lesser extent than its French counterparts to challenge the centralized structure of the monarchy. Nor did the judicial system represent a check on royal absolutism in Prussia as the *parlements* did in France. Rather, the spirit of reform sought to free the bureaucracy from arbitrary royal interference, and establish rule by law and established procedure. Among the middle classes, too, the academically trained civil servant *(Beamte),* the professors, *Gymnasium* teachers, and pastors, possessed a greater influence upon public life and a relatively higher social status than their counterparts in more commercially oriented Western urban settings. There existed no movement for radical social reorganization, but only demands for reforms within the framework of the old system. Recurrent through the writings of the German Enlightenment are demands for individual freedom, intellectual and religious tolerance, due process of law, and economic liberty. Freedom is more often defined in terms of individual spiritual growth rather than in terms of political participation.

As Hajo Holborn observed, "The entire intellectual *(geistige)* movement of the eighteenth century aimed almost exclusively at the education of individual man and subordinated all political demands to this goal."[28] The state itself was regarded as a positive good, an institution in which, in many ways, the ideals of the Enlightenment had already been attained, a framework where full development of individuality and culture could take place.[29] The young Wilhelm von Humboldt's definition of freedom in terms of "the highest and most proportionate development of one's resources into one whole"[30] was thus compatible with his later assertion that only within a strong nation was the development of freedom possible.

The early enthusiasm with which many Germans received the initial moderate phases of the French Revolution was soon dissipated by the Jacobin Reign of Terror, and was transformed into intense hostility under the impact of the French occupation of the western sections of Germany and the introduction of the Napoleonic political system. Many of the aspirations of German liberals were fulfilled in the years after 1806 by the reforms introduced into the Prussian monarchy by Stein, Hardenberg, Scharnhorst, and Humboldt after the defeats of Jena and Auerstädt. In many ways these reforms resembled those introduced in France between 1789 and 1791. A large degree of economic liberty was granted, the privilege of the guilds and corporations was broken, the peasants were emancipated. The administrative structure was streamlined. A conscious effort was

made to link the citizens to the state more closely through the introduction of municipal self-administration, the announcement of plans
for the ultimate creation of diets for the provinces and the monarchy,
and the creation of a militia drawn from popular conscription. At the
same time, the reforms left intact the authority of the monarchy and
the central position of the aristocracy in the bureaucracy.

Hans Rosenberg even suggests that the Reform Era marks the
victory of "bureaucratic absolutism" over "monarchical autocracy."
What took place in Prussia was a "revolution from above." The
initiative for reforms in Prussia in 1807, as in France in 1788 and
1789, came from a ministerial bureaucracy. In an acute crisis, this
bureaucracy sought to reconstruct the state more rationally by assail-
ing the most obsolete claims of the titled aristocracy. Here, however,
the similarity ended. In France, as Rosenberg observes, the opposition of the nobility to the curtailment of their privileges and the
restructuring of government "was broken by the political emancipation of the Third Estate. In Prussia, however, throughout the confused and confusing years of Reform, the struggle for predominance
remained almost altogether the internal affair of the upper ten thousand."[31] The struggle against Napoleonic domination confused the
issues of liberal political reforms with those of awakening nationalism. Far from preparing the way for a more radical popular revolt,
as in France, the reforms by the aristocratic bureaucrats led to broad
middle- and lower-class support for the Hohenzollern monarchy in
its struggle for a supposed national cause against foreign absolutism.
Further, it sharpened the ideological differences between Prussian
liberalism and the heritage of the French Revolution.

Out of the Wars of Liberation arose the myth of the Spirit of
1813 cultivated by Prussian-oriented historians from Droysen to
Meinecke and central to the political beliefs of the German historicist tradition. From this perspective, the reformed Prussian monarchy marked a high point in the history of human freedom, a society in which the individual was fully free, but at the same time was
integrated into a social whole. Here was the core of the "German
conception of freedom," of the ideas of 1813, which German historians contrasted sharply with the atomistic view of society supposedly
inherent in the ideas of 1789.

Although German liberal aspirations were disappointed in the
period of reaction which set in after 1815, and especially after 1819,

no radical alienation occurred between the German middle classes and the Prussian state. Democratic radicalism found expression in the Young German literature and in Left Hegelian philosophical and theological writings. But these ideas were restricted to a relatively small number of intellectuals who were not part of the academic establishment, as well as to some artisans. Many advocates of radicalism, moreover, went into exile. The liberal critics of Prussian political conditions, both inside Prussia and increasingly elsewhere in Germany, still regarded the Prussian monarchy as capable of returning to the ideals of 1813, and of completing the task of creating a liberal national state in harmony with German traditions. Indeed, the basic reforms of the Stein period remained intact. The *Beamtenstaat* remained a good deal freer from arbitrary monarchical intervention than it had been in the eighteenth century. Municipal self-administration, peasant emancipation, and economic liberty were maintained. The scope of the latter during these years was even enlarged by the *Zollverein*. Still not satisfied were the demands of the liberals for increased constitutionalization, for an end to arbitrary restrictions of individual liberties, especially for censorship, and for positive steps toward national unification.

Few of the liberal historians of the *Vormärz* advocated a parliamentary monarchy as it already existed in Great Britain. Historians, such as Dahlmann and Droysen, who played a significant role in 1848 in the "classical liberal" caucus of the Frankfurt National Assembly, rather sought to preserve the prerogatives of a constitutional monarchy and a bureaucracy which consulted representative institutions without being entirely bound by them and respected civil liberties without necessarily guaranteeing them in writing. We may leave open the question whether parliamentary government was already foredoomed to failure in Germany in 1848 or in Prussia in 1862. The incipient industrialization of Germany and the largely illusionary fear of plebeian revolt, occasioned by the revolutions of 1792, 1830, and 1848 in France and by the isolated incidents of industrial unrest in Germany in the 1840's, undoubtedly contributed to the hesitation of middle-class liberals to resort to revolutionary violence. The riots in Frankfurt in 1848, after the Malmö Armistice, had underlined the extent to which the German liberals believed that they were forced to rely upon Prussian arms as a bulwark against the radical left. The events in Bohemia, Posen, and Schleswig made clear the dependence of the liberals on Prussian and Austrian arms in order to fulfill their national aims. The defeat of the Prussian liberals by Bismarck, between 1862 and 1867, led to a reconciliation of large segments of middle-class liberalism with the monarchy, which now fulfilled the economic, national, and many of the political aspirations of the Prussian liberals.

On the surface, the ideals of 1813, the constitutional, national *Rechtsstaat* with representative institutions, had been achieved. "The Bismarckian synthesis, as consolidated after 1871," Hans Rosenberg observes, "brought peace, great national prestige, and an almost spectacular long-term upswing of material growth, highly competent and honest public administration, with a profound respect for law and order, a substantial measure of personal rights, civil liberties, and social security, and a flourishing intellectual and artistic life to the German people."[32] Among the Prussian-oriented historians only relatively few observers, such as Hermann Baumgarten and Theodor Mommsen, began to perceive the tenuous character of liberal and popular institutions in a society where political power in an age of industrialism rested in the hands of an elite committed to seignioral, militaristic, bureaucratic, and authoritarian traditions. As Theodor Mommsen correctly saw, the authoritarian structure of the German state, its incomplete parliamentarization, its attachment to military and aristocratic values of obedience, prevented the emergence of a spirit of political responsibility among the German people at a time when the emergence of mass political movements within the constitutional framework of the Bismarckian state made such responsible citizenship increasingly necessary. In contrast to Western and Northern European countries, Germany preserved the political influence and social prestige of the landed and military aristocracy during a period when industrialization, with its concommitant social effects, had proceeded much further than in Western countries such as France. Historicism doubtlessly maintained itself in a form relatively unchanged from its classical foundations partly because important aspects of the institutional framework from which it had arisen and which it had served to defend remained relatively unchanged.

The failure of German historical theory to adopt itself to changing social-intellectual realities reflected the institutional basis of the historical profession itself. From the late eighteenth century on, historical scholarship in Germany was centered at the universities. In

Europe and the United States, this generally became the case only later in the nineteenth century. The historian, as has often been pointed out, was an employee of the state, a *Staatsbeamter*. It is questionable, however, whether this status restricted his opportunities to express himself. On the contrary, as a severe critic of the German historicist tradition and of the Prussian state, Eckart Kehr, has recognized, his status as a civil servant in fact gave the university professor a high degree of protection against political pressures.[33] Indeed, until Bismarck's compromise with the liberals in 1867, the historians in the national tradition mostly were in opposition to the *status quo.*

It is perhaps more important for an understanding of the historians' failure to re-examine their historiographical practices and political conceptions that the historians considered themselves a part of the *Bildungsbürgertum,* the bourgeoisie of culture and education. For the most part they identified themselves with the aspirations of this class.[34] Thus, in 1848, they shared the desire for liberalization and national unification, but also the fear of social upheaval which might result from a radical challenge to the established order. Although, with few exceptions, they opposed Bismarck's highhanded policies during the Prussian constitutional crisis from 1862 to 1867, they were able to accept the compromise with Bismarck in 1867, and to see their liberal and national aspirations largely fulfilled in the German Empire.

Highly decisive for the relative lack of development of German historiographical theory was the manner in which the academic profession was recruited. No basic reform of the German university system had taken place since the establishment of the University of Berlin in 1810. Only in very recent years have there been attempts at such reforms, which have so far had very limited success. The academic profession remained a closed caste. The *Ordinarius* retained not only an extremely high degree of control over the teaching and research activities of his subordinates, but in concert with his colleagues was able to restrict admission to the profession. The painful process of *Habilitation,* by which a candidate to be admitted to university teaching had to be adopted by an *Ordinarius* under whose direction he composed his *Habilitationsschrift*[35] effectively, especially after 1871, restricted the admission of historians whose outlook or background did not conform with the academic establishment. The men who broke with basic tenets of the historicist faith, such as Karl Lamprecht, or became deeply skeptical of it, as did Friedrich Meinecke in his later years, generally did so only after they themselves had become *Ordinarien.* Revisionists, as in the case of Erich Eyck, either were not professional historians or, like Arthur Rosenberg, were admitted to university teaching (to a *Dozentur*) early in life. For the most part they were never called to a chair or saw their careers blocked, as in the case of Veit Valentin. The system of recruitment has remained essentially intact since 1945.[36] The historicist faith itself has, however, come under critical examination. The creation of new chairs, especially in areas marginal to history, such as political science and contemporary history *(Zeitgeschichte),* and freer from the intellectual and ideological traditions of the German historical profession, has for the first time enabled larger numbers of historians critical of the classical national tradition of historiography to pursue university careers.

It is therefore not surprising that the theoretical assumptions rooted in German idealistic philosophy, upon which historicism rested, continued to play a role in German political historiography long after these theories had been abandoned or at least seriously questioned by philosophers and cultural scientists. The hold of classical historicist notions on philosophy and the social sciences (as we shall see in Chapter VI) had been effectively challenged before World War I. The cataclysmic events of the twentieth century were required to end the almost exclusive domination by classical historicism over German academic historiography (see chapter VIII). As a political theory, historicism, in rejecting the rationalistic conception of reality inherent in natural law philosophy, had not rejected political liberty. Rather, it assumed that liberal demands for individual liberties, popular participation, and juridical security could be attained within the framework of the traditional, authoritarian *Obrigkeitsstaat.* As a philosophic theory of value, historicism maintained a similar compromise between apparent opposites. It rejected the possibility of rational ethics, of rights and values not bound to a specific historical situation but derived from the structure of human nature common to all men. Nevertheless, the theory of value of classical German historicism differed profoundly from the expressions of later advocates of philosophical irrationalism. These political decisionists of the 1920's (e.g., Carl Schmitt, Martin Heidegger,

Ernst Jünger)[37] reduced all political value positions to subjective decisions or biological functions in a struggle for national survival.

Classical historicism at no time asserted that the universe was devoid of rational or ethical purpose, but expressed its faith that the apparent expressions of irrationality, individual spontaneity, and will were manifestations of an underlying ethical order. This faith assumed the existence of a God who at each moment in history, actively, created the mysterious balance which linked each sovereign monad to the total whole. The rise of a naturalistic world view in the nineteenth century, which accompanied the mechanization of life, made this faith steadily less convincing. The introduction of the historicist outlook into social and humanistic studies in the nineteenth century contributed to the destruction of the idealistic assumptions of historicist philosophy. By studying each institution, each idea or ideal as a one-time event linked to a specific historical and cultural setting, historicism prepared the way for the relativization of all value. Moreover, it led to the position that the *Geisteswissenschaften,* the natural sciences, must themselves be *"wertfreie Wissenschaften"* (value-free sciences) which study values as cultural phenomena devoid of any innate or transcendent validity. The "crisis of historicism" of which Troeltsch spoke revolved around the increasing realization by social theorists and philosophers that the rigorous application of historical method ultimately led to the destruction of all certain knowledge about man and to the relativization of all firm values, an apparently inescapable dilemma resulting from man's inability to transcend the flux of history.

If the historicist approach remained relatively intact in German historiography into the post-World War I period, in contrast to the social sciences, this undoubtedly reflected the deep emotional commitment of historians not only to the German idealistic tradition but also to the Prussian state. Social theorists of the twentieth century were confronted by the shambles of the idealistic tradition. The historians, on the other hand, lived amidst political realities in which a good deal of the traditional institutional structure had remained intact. World War I led Friedrich Meinecke to re-examine the optimistic notions regarding the harmony of ethics and power. Walter Götz in the 1920's called for a thorough re-examination of the political presuppositions of German historiography. Otto Hintze sought to introduce a broad, comparative, sociological note into the state-oriented historiography of the German school. For the majority of German historians, however, defeat and war-guilt theses seemed to provide new incentives to defend the Bismarckian solution and the rightness of German intellectual traditions. The Nazi experience, variously interpreted by German historians both as a repudiation and as a radicalization of these traditions, nevertheless led a great deal of the German academic profession to question seriously, for the first time, the age-old association of liberty with the traditional authoritarian state.

World War II finally destroyed much of the institutional framework within which historicism had arisen. The Bismarckian state was broken apart. Prussia was dissolved as a political unit. East Elbia was either lost to Germany entirely or underwent profound social transformation. The new international realities no longer permitted Germany to play the role of a major power. In Eastern Germany, historiography became a function of a new authoritarian state based upon very different ideological foundations. In Western Germany, democratically as well as conservatively oriented historians, at least in the first two decades after the war, were obliged by the new constellation of realities to identify German political interests with those of the Western democracies. The ideological dichotomy of Germany and Western Europe had lost a good deal of its political foundation. Doubtlessly, the disillusion with the past, the postwar prosperity, the emergence of a consumer-oriented society, and the stability of parliamentary government in the Federal Republic all contributed to the consolidation of an ethos in closer harmony with the realities of a modern mass society. Although older patterns of historical thought and historiographical practice have remained alive in Germany, the traumatic experience of Nazi dictatorship and defeat, and the less traumatic transformation of German realities in postwar Germany, have led to a crisis of conscience among German historians and a re-examination of traditional methodological conceptions and political values.

The present work begins with the divergence of German historical thought from the main patterns of European thought at the turn of the eighteenth to the nineteenth century. It ends on a mildly hopeful note in regard to the return of broad segments of German opinion to the main streams of Western thought. The final part of Chapter VIII will assess to what extent a revision of basic historical concepts has taken place in Germany since 1945. The German historiographical situation is too complex to reduce it to a common denominator; the classical historical tradition is still very much alive today. For the first time, however, a significant number of historians, particularly in works on the recent past, have written from the standpoint of democratic commitments. Also for the first time, a larger number of historians have sought to come to grips with the realities of a technological mass society, and to integrate the methods of the historian with those of the political scientist and the sociologist.

A return to generally Western traditions of thought in the midtwentieth century no longer means a return to Enlightenment conceptions of natural law. The image of the "West" portrayed by German historians especially since World War I (e.g., Troeltsch) was hopelessly antiquated and failed to recognize the extent to which romanticism, the progress of the natural sciences, the mechanization of life and thought in the nineteenth century, had eroded the Enlightenment heritage. By different paths, main currents of German and other European thought had converged upon a similar point. Historical relativism was not restricted to Germany. Much of modern thought reflected a profound awareness of the apparent ethical meaninglessness of the world, the irrationality of man, and the absurdity of history. Historical reason thus participated in the destruction of faith in reason and purpose in human affairs. If the book treats historicism historically, as a movement of thought, the first section of the concluding chapter seeks to deal with the historicist and relativistic critique of natural law on theoretical grounds. The question is cautiously raised whether there are no elements of the Enlightenment notion of a constant, rational element in man and history which survive this critique, and continue to retain a degree of validity and relevance for historical and political thought.

[CHAPTER II]

The Origins of German Historicism

THE TRANSFORMATION OF GERMAN HISTORICAL
THOUGHT FROM HERDER'S COSMOPOLITAN CUL-
TURE-ORIENTED NATIONALISM TO THE STATE-
CENTERED EXCLUSIVE NATIONALISM OF THE
WARS OF LIBERATION.

It is difficult to set even an approximate date for the beginnings
of historicism. If we mean by historicism an approach to history
which seeks to re-create the past *wie es eigentlich gewesen* and to
recapture the unique qualities of an historical situation, then a great
deal of narrative history written from a secular standpoint has been
historicist in outlook since Classical Antiquity. The idea that historical research, with its concern for detail and individuality, basically
differed from the generalizing and classificatory approach of the natural sciences was well known long before the eighteenth century.
Aristotle already had observed that historical statements deal with
"singulars" rather than with "universals."[1]

The basic elements of historical method were well established in
the eighteenth century and recognized even by the rationalists. Since
the age of humanism, scholarship, especially as carried on in the
academies of the seventeenth and eighteenth centuries, had recognized criteria for the critical analysis of sources. It is true that there
was not yet a well-established tradition of critical inquiry and that
the great "pragmatic" historians of the Enlightenment, men such as
Voltaire and Gibbon, tended to construct grandiose syntheses based
upon inadequate evidence. The scholars, on the other hand, accumulated data with insufficient attention to the continuity and development of institutions.[2] But the careful re-creation of individual reality
is by no means in contradiction with natural law theory. To "understand" is not yet to "condone" or to "accept." It is possible to

29

portray an individual in his individuality with his unique values, and yet measure him by standards of right and wrong applicable to a broader humanity.

If, however, like Friedrich Meinecke, we understand historicism not merely as an approach to history, but as a comprehensive philosophy of life which views all social reality as a historical stream where no two instances are comparable and which assumes that value standards and logical categories, too, are totally immersed in the stream of history, then historicism is a creation of the eighteenth century. More specifically, it is the German reaction against certain Enlightenment patterns of thought, especially the doctrine of natural law. The first two great theoretical formulations of the historicist position in the eighteenth century are very probably Giambattista Vico's *New Science*,[3] first published in 1725, and Johann Gottfried Herder's *Also a Philosophy of History* of 1774.[4] Vico had already stressed that the study of social reality requires methods fundamentally different from those of the natural sciences because society, unlike nature, cannot be reduced to the "insensible motion of bodies"; rather, it consists of the conscious acts and volitions of individuals which take place in the stream of time. Men and societies can be understood only when approached historically. To be sure, Vico's aim in studying history was not to study history for its own sake. For him the history of mankind, far from showing the total diversity of man, still appeared as a clue to general truths about mankind. Every historical epoch has its place in the recurrent cycles (*corso* and *ricorso*) which make up the upward spiral of history. Only in Herder's early work of 1774 do we find the historicist position formulated in its radical form: the conception that every age must be viewed in terms of its own immediate values; that there is no progress or decline in history, but only value-filled diversity.

We have sought in the Introduction to distinguish a specific, predominantly German tradition of historiography and historical thought in the nineteenth and twentieth centuries from broader currents of thought in Europe generally, which may have been described as forms of historicism. We shall not attempt to study the origins of historicism as a European phenomenon, but in this chapter shall restrict ourselves to the more modest task of following the transformation of German historical thought from the cosmopolitan culture-oriented nationalism of Herder in the late eighteenth century to the nationalistic and power-oriented assumptions of much of German historiography in the nineteenth and twentieth centuries.

A history of the emergence of the historicist outlook in seventeenth- and eighteenth-century European thought still needs to be written. Meinecke proposed something of the sort in *The Origins of Historicism* wherein he sought to trace the rise of historicism as a "general Western movement" which had its culmination in German thought. But Meinecke's book is only marginally related to the emergence of a historical approach to cultural and social reality in the eighteenth century and his concept of historicism has relatively little to do with history. What Meinecke describes as the emergence of historicism, in the course of the eighteenth century, is rather the steady recognition of the limitations of intellect in the understanding of human reality. For Meinecke, the chief obstacle to historical understanding was the doctrine of natural law. Before the life quality of history in its individuality and spontaneity could be understood, the two-thousand-year-old hold of the Stoic-Christian natural law faith in a static, rational world order had to be broken. In its place the recognition had to be established that the human psyche *(Seele)* occupied the central point in history and that this psyche was "determined not by reason or understanding but by will."[5] Meinecke's book thus becomes a hymn to the beneficent triumph of unreason in modern consciousness.

Ironically, Descartes stands at the beginning of Meinecke's account of the emancipation of modern thought from a rational conception of reality. It was Descartes, Meinecke notes, who reoriented European philosophy from the analysis of the supposedly objective reality of the external world to the examination of human consciousness. The Enlightenment historians—Voltaire, Montesquieu, Gibbon, and Hume—through their universalistic interest, contributed to an understanding of the variety of human institutions; the Pietists, and the Pre-Romantics to an understanding of the intertwining of emotion and intellect; the traditionalists to an awareness of the extent to which there is reason in the apparent unreason of inherited institutions and ideas. The triumph of soul over intellect in Meinecke's book does not, however, lead to the dissolution of knowledge and values, but rather to the Neo-Platonic conception that behind the apparent irrationality and turbulence of the historical world there stands a realm of great perennial ideas. These ideas are neither abstract nor universally valid, but embody the perennial essences of the fleeting individualities that comprise the historical world. They can be grasped only by the total soul, never by cold reason. The relativistic dilemmas of historicism are thus overcome for Meinecke, and historicism becomes the basis for the recognition of real truths and values. In Goethe, whose relation to history Meinecke recognizes as a very ambiguous one,[6] Meinecke sees the culmination of historicist thought. It was Goethe who most fully perceived in each individuality not merely a set of fleeting phenomena, but a concrete manifestation of an individualized eternal idea. He understood that reason expresses itself never abstractly, but only within concrete, historical individuals.

There are several disturbing contradictions between Meinecke's theoretical Assumptions in *The Origins of Historicism* and his application of these ideas. On the one hand, Meinecke argues that history is an open process, and every particular must be understood in terms of its own unique worth rather than as a part of a greater predetermined pattern. But the history of ideas presented by Meinecke has almost a Hegelian ring. Leibniz, Gottfried Arnold, Voltaire, and Edmund Burke all are reduced to steppingstones in the process by which European consciousness reaches its fulfillment in Goethe's idea of individuality. It is also striking that Meinecke, who so emphatically stressed the interrelatedness of thought and life, so completely isolated the history of ideas from the historical and social settings in which these ideas arose and operated. So thoroughly disillusioned with the course of German politics since World War I, Meinecke now interpreted historicism as a purely cultural movement devoid of political implications. The transition of historical thought from eighteenth-century European forms (traced by Meinecke in *The Origins of Historicism*) to the peculiarly German tradition of political thought (which he had already described almost thirty years earlier in *Cosmopolitanism and Nation State*)[7] remained tenuous and unclear.

Carlo Antoni has given a much more comprehensive and differentiated picture of the interrelation of ideas, institutions, and political forces in eighteenth-century historical thought.[8] There was no one form of historicism, Antoni maintains, but a variety of historicisms "all profoundly different in accordance with the national traditions to which they belonged" and the political aspirations they sought to fulfill.[9] In Great Britain, France, Italy, Switzerland, and also in Germany, there arose in the eighteenth century a new interest in the past. There was a peculiarly modern attitude toward history, absent in classic, medieval, and Renaissance thought, "regarding the positive value of history understood as human progress in its immanent, worldly, and secular reality."[10] What distinguished this new outlook from major Enlightenment patterns of thought was its rejection of a mechanistic world view; its belief that history, far from being a collection of abuses and superstitions, was itself the key to the understanding of man as a social and political being. In this sense, Antoni believed, Giambattista Vico and Edmund Burke, as well as Justus Möser and Johann Gottfried Herder, stood in the historicist tradition. Inherent in this emphasis upon an organic continuity between past and present was the rejection of the attempts by Enlightenment despotism or the French Revolution to reconstruct government and society along bureaucratic centralistic lines, disregarding the diversity of traditional institutions. But the conflict between the modern state, enlightened conceptions of liberty, and traditional institutions was obviously much less severe in Great Britain than on the Continent. It distinguished the conservatism of Burke, who recognized the elements of change and progress in historical institutions, from the reactionary glorification of the medieval or even the primitive Germanic past among certain Swiss and German thinkers.[11]

A great deal of social and political thought in the nineteenth century recognized that man could only be understood in terms of his historical existence.[12] What distinguished the German tradition of history with which we are dealing so radically from other expressions of historicism in the eighteenth and nineteenth centuries was its emphasis upon the uniqueness and irrationality of values transmitted by history. At the heart of this emphasis is what Meinecke has called the concept of individuality.

However, the concept of individuality, which Meinecke considers to be so central to historicism, seems to be far less broadly European and have more peculiarly German roots than Meinecke suggests. Ernst Troeltsch has pointed at the peculiar twist which Luther gave to the theory of natural law. Subsequently, this turn, according to Troeltsch, profoundly distinguished Lutheran from Catholic and Calvinist ethics. In the place of a concept of a rational law of Nature, Luther substituted an irrational law of Nature. Luther argued in accordance with St. Paul's admonition that "there is no power but of God: the powers that be are ordained of God." Every state represented the will of God, and thus required the complete obedience of the Christian in all matters temporal. Reason therefore expressed itself not in abstract moral commandments, but in historical institutions. The positive authorities were the concrete manifestations of natural law. Luther's political and social ethics are thus conservative.[13] His concept of society lacked any real concern with change.

A much more dynamic theory of individuality appears in the monadology of Leibniz in whom Meinecke sees one of the important sources of historicism. In the place of the Newtonian concept of Nature as a mechanism with interchangeable parts, governed by abstract laws reducible to mathematical formulae, Leibniz presented the vision of a cosmos filled with self-contained units, monads, each unique, deriving its energy from within and developing in accordance with its own inner laws of change, yet in harmony with the whole.

The sharp distinction between reason and unreason drawn by Descartes disappears for Leibniz. "Not only through the *lumen naturale* of reason but also through instinct" we find innate truths.[14] Similarly, the sharp line drawn in French and English thought, between the sciences and the humanities lessens. The term *Wissenschaft* as used since Leibniz encompasses a much broader scope than the French or English term "science." Leibniz's plan for scientific academies provided not only for the study of nature, but for the liberal arts as well.[15] In Germany Leibniz's ideas, systematized and popularized by his disciple Christian von Wolff—a man now almost forgotten but for several decades the dominant philosophical figure in Germany—left their impact upon the intellectual climate of the German Enlightenment. This also held true of the anti-intellectualism of the Pietist revival. Gottfried Arnold and Johann Georg Hamann stressed the interrelation of reason and passion, and Hamann saw in history "the cyphers, hidden signs" and "hieroglyphs" of God.[16] A similar faith that divine wisdom expressed itself in the unique institutions of history was to be seen in the traditionalism of Justus Möser. Nevertheless, these were only isolated elements of a theory of history. It was Herder who, in *Also a Philosophy of History,* first offered an extensive presentation of historicist principles in Germany in an extreme form from which he retreated in his later works.[17]

Basic to Herder's position are two concepts which remain fundamental to the entire affirmative tradition of German historicism with which we are dealing. The first of these concepts involves the idea of individuality. Herder, in contrast to natural law philosophy assumes that all values and all cognitions are historic and individual. "In a certain sense, every human perfection is national, secular, and most closely considered, individual."[18] History, he insists, is constant movement. Nevertheless, within the flux of history, there are certain centers with at least relative stability: the nations. They possess a morphology; they are alive; they grow. They are not rational in character, but dynamic and vital; things in themselves, not means. It is the historian's task to understand them. Nations have the characteristics of persons: they have a spirit and they have a life span. They are not a collection of individuals, but are organisms.[19]

This concept of individuality involves a theory of value and knowledge, and contains at least certain implications for political theory. It assumes that there are no universally valid values, that ethics cannot be based upon precepts of reason or upon the assumption of a common human nature. Rather, all values come out of the spirit of nations. Herder, as a matter of fact, not only protested against the application of the standards of the Enlightenment to other civilizations or ages but, in contrast to later nineteenth-century writers, warned against a Europocentric approach to history.[20] His concept of the nation as the source of all truth implied that there were no objective criteria of truth. Again, this was an extreme position which he modified later, but it was inherent in the historicist position. Strictly speaking, there could be no objective approach to history, Herder insisted. Not only could man not transcend the process of history, but insofar as history was an organic stream, it had to be approached by methods other than those of what Herder called the "mechanistic" spirit of modern philosophy.[21] Reason could not understand life, but only create lifeless concepts. Verbal description could not re-create living reality. History could only be understood through empathy.[22] Indeed, the borderline between truth and error, good and evil, became a very difficult one to draw. Herder wondered whether there was such a thing as prejudice. He held that what we call prejudice, and what may be only the expression of the national spirit at an early stage of its development, may "be good . . . because it makes the nation happy and gives it cohesion." Conversely, objectivity and rationality may be signs of national disintegration, of "disease" and "intimation of death."[23] Although, in the area of politics, Herder shared the demands of his contemporaries for a liberalization of the state and greeted the coming of the French Revolution with sympathetic interest,[24] his view of history certainly undermined the theoretical basis upon which the tradition of classic liberalism was based. Herder's theories of truth and value were incompatible with the philosophy of natural law or the theory of the social contract.[25]

The second central concept of Herder's philosophy of history was that history was a benevolent process, an idea which was basic to all affirmative historicist traditions with which we are presently concerned. German historians in this century have tended to stress that historicism involved the negation of the idea of progress. This was true only to the extent that the historicist position denied that there was any unilinear advance in history or that history developed according to a scheme. In another sense, however, German historicism was much more optimistic about the meaningfulness of history than were even adherents of the classical idea of progress. Theories of progress may assume either that human advancement is inevitable and that the process of history is determined in an upward direction (Hegel, Saint-Simon, Marx, Comte), or that man can be perfected, that progress is possible if man applies rationality to human institutions. Either position, particularly the second (the two positions do not necessarily exclude each other) implies that there is irrationality in the existing world; that there is a conflict between the world as it *should be,* and one day may be, and the world as it is. In this sense, the idea of progress still adheres to the tradition of natural law. German historicism on the other hand, assumes that all that has grown naturally or historically is good. "Every nation has its center of happiness within it."[26] History is the source of real value.

To be sure, there are the seeds of relativism in this concept, for it assumes that all knowledge and all values are related to concrete cultural and historical settings. Such a supposition could lead to the anarchy of values.[27] The historicism of Herder rests upon the firm belief that there is a divine purpose in history, that "Providence guides the path of development onward."[28] All of Nature and of history reflect God. Herder compares history to a stream rushing to the ocean or to a growing tree. History is indeed meaningful, the "scene of a guiding intention on earth, although we do not perceive this ultimate purpose at once.[29] Basically, mankind is still one, according to Herder. However, the meaning of history is not found in the direction of events toward a rational end, but in the multiplicity of ways in which the human mind expresses itself in the diversity of nations.

Truth, value, and beauty are not one, but many. They are found only in history and manifest themselves only in the national spirit. True poetry and true art for Herder are thus always national and historical. He set to work to compile and translate his great anthologies of folk poetry. For him, as for much of nineteenth-century Germany, history became the cornerstone of true culture. Implied in this concept is the assumption that all meaningful philosophy must become history of philosophy, and all theology the history of theology.

In *Also a Philosophy of History,* Herder had laid the foundations for a historicism which spread far beyond the German boundaries. Herder's theory directly contributed to the reawakening of historical interest. His writings were translated into the Slavic languages, as well as into French and English. His ideas merged with the broad stream of Romantic philosophy to challenge Enlightenment doctrines throughout Europe; yet historicist doctrine by no means had been fully developed. Herder had presented the most coherent theory of historicism, but several important concepts that later played a significant role in the German historical tradition of the nineteenth century were still missing in his writings or had not been fully developed by him.

Moreover, historicism was by no means the dominant intellectual attitude in Germany in the late eighteenth century; nor was it the sole challenger of the Enlightenment faith in human rationality. We have already cited the strong currents of pietism and traditionalism. Important in the transition from natural law doctrine to historicism were two trends of thought which in many ways were still committed to Enlightenment ideals, but nevertheless contributed to the modification and completion of historicist doctrine. These were the *Humanitätsideal* which further defined the idea of the individual, and German idealistic philosophy which elaborated upon the idea of identity, a central element in historicist faith. The *Humanitätsideal* is difficult to define because it is so intimately interwoven with the personalities of the small group of eminent, creative thinkers who gave it expression: Goethe, Herder, Winckelmann, Schiller, and Wilhelm von Humboldt, each of whom left a different and personal imprint.[30] It derives a good deal of its original inspiration from Winckelmann's studies of classical Greek art and from Herder's *Ideas for the Philosophy of History of Humanity,* written in his more mature years.

These writers agree with the Enlightenment that there is a common humanity, a certain nobility and dignity present in seed form in all men. "The purpose of our existence," Herder comments, "is to develop this incipient element of humanity *(Humanität)* fully within us. . . . Our ability to reason is to be developed to reason; our finer senses are to be cultivated for art; our instincts are to achieve genuine freedom and beauty; our energies are to be turned to the love of man."[31] Still, if the Enlightenment stresses the common characteristics of man and his rationality, the *Humanitätsideal* stresses the diversity of man and the interrelation of all aspects of his personality, of rationality and irrationality, into a harmonious whole. Every individual is different, and the task incumbent upon each one is to develop his own unique personality to the fullest.[32] Hence the idealization of the Greeks. "Mankind as a whole," writes Wilhelm von Humboldt, "exists only in the never attainable totality of all individualities that come into existence one after another."[33] Peculiarly absent from the group's admiration of the Greeks, however, is an appreciation of the great value which the Greeks had placed on politics. Freedom for these German thinkers was, first of all, an inner, spiritual matter rather than a political concept, as it was for much of Enlightenment thought. For Goethe and Humboldt the individual person constitutes the prime unit of which humanity is composed; for Herder the nations, too, possess the characteristics of individuality to a greater extent than individual persons. Nevertheless, Herder's concept of nationality assumes a basic equality of worth among all nations as contributors to the richness of the human spirit. In this sense, he is cosmopolitan in spirit no less than Goethe.

The concept of individuality contained within the *Humanitätsideal* differs from Enlightenment theories of the individual in still another important way, particularly from those ideas which had been developed by associationist psychology (e.g., Locke, Condillac, Hume, and others) or utilitarianism (Bentham, James Mill). For Wilhelm von Humboldt the individual is not found in the empirical person we perceive, but in the higher idea he represents.

The purpose of man's life is thus emphatically not "happiness," but rather the fulfillment of this idea. Wilhelm von Humboldt argues against state action in behalf of the welfare of the citizens since such action misunderstands the "dignity of man."[34] Kant similarly had written in his *Idea of a Universal History from a Cosmopolitan Viewpoint* that Nature is not concerned with man's "living well," but only with his "living in dignity."[35] The rejection of "happiness" as an end of life was common to the whole tradition of historicist thought from Humboldt and Ranke to Meinecke. "Eudaemonism" became a pejorative term by which German historians tried to dissociate their own idealistic position from most of English and French historical thought.[36] In the concept of the individual as the expression of an idea lies the link between the theory that every individual possesses "individuality" and that each collective group, too, is an "individuality." Groups and individuals share in the expression of ideas. It was therefore not very difficult for Humboldt, who at first had recognized that only individual persons possess the characteristics of individuality, to admit this applies to states and nations as well.

The Enlightenment concept of natural law underwent further revision in German philosophic discussion after Kant. Fichte, Schelling, and Hegel all accepted the theory of the basic uniqueness of individuals and nations in history. At the same time, they also accepted the Enlightenment faith in a rational universe. They attempted to solve this dilemma by seeing in reason not an abstract norm divorced from abstract reality, but rather something immanent within reality. Kant had already suggested in the *Idea of a Universal History from a Cosmopolitan Viewpoint* that reason was operative in history. He had assumed that "all the natural potentialities of any creature are destined to develop once fully and to the end for which they are intended,"[37] and that the history of the world similarly saw the steady growth of rationality. Hegel had described history as the development by which the rational idea immanent in the world takes on concrete form.[38] But the actors in this process are the individuals whom Hegel terms "the Peoples."[39] Each people, in developing its own unique character, simultaneously plays its role in the world process. Although Hegel's conception of progress thus brings individuality into harmony with the overall process, it nevertheless significantly violates the historicist theory of the radical autonomy of the individual. In the Hegelian system, the individual becomes a means within a larger process. Historicism, however, stresses that the spontaneity of the individual must be preserved. His growth cannot be forced into a scheme.

Nevertheless, an important aspect of the German Idealist view of history as a rational process is incorporated into historicist thought. Humboldt acknowledges that collective groups, too, possess the characteristics of individuality, as he steadily moves from the position of the *Humanitätsideal* to that of historicism. He believes that although every individuality and its idea are radically unique, they directly form part of a divine design in a "mysterious" way which we cannot perceive.[40] "World history," he wrote in 1825, "is unthinkable without a cosmic plan governing it."[41] Similarly, Ranke sees in the state an entity "real-and-spiritual-at-once *(real-geistig)*." With Hegel he is convinced that, in pursuing its own power-political interests, the state acts in accordance with a higher order that governs the world. As he has Friedrich say in the *Political Dialogue:* "But seriously, you will be able to name few significant wars for which it could not be proved that genuine moral energy achieved the final victory."[42]

However, the most important factor in the transition from an Enlightenment to an historicist outlook was doubtless the impact of political events upon the German intellect between 1792 and 1815. The educated German public, with few exceptions, had hailed the French Revolution. The tremendous disappointment which had set in in Germany after the revolution reached its terroristic phase, led to a widespread re-examination of natural law doctrine. The reaction against the ideology of the revolution was intensified by the Napoleonic domination of Germany. This strengthened national feeling, and in the public mind identified Enlightenment values with a hated French culture. German opinion, for the most part, did not want a restoration of prerevolutionary political and social conditions. The defeat of Prussia in 1806 initiated a period of extensive reforms in that kingdom. But reformers, such as Baron von Stein, Hardenberg, and Humboldt, searched for liberal institutions peculiarly suited to German traditions.

In three important ways the German attitude toward history changed in these years:

1. The Enlightenment faith in universally applicable ethical and political values, which had been already challenged before the Revolution, was now completely shattered. Except for a few isolated

thinkers who like the Freiburg historian Carl Rotteck remained faithful to the principles of 1789, German educated opinion now agreed that all values and rights were of historic and national origin and that alien institutions could not be transplanted to German soil. Moreover, they saw in history, rather than in abstract rationality, the key to all truth and value. Within this broad consensus there were, of course, many nuances from traditionalists like Savigny and Haller who emphasized the extreme diversity and spontaneity in history to German Idealist philosophers such as Fichte and Hegel who viewed history as a rational process.

2. The concept of the nation had changed fundamentally.[43] Herder's nationalism was still cosmopolitan in spirit. Each nation contributes to the richness of human life. Nationalism links the nations to each other rather than separates them. Herder optimistically believes that the nationalization of political life contributes to international peace. "Cabinets may betray each other. . . . But fatherlands will not move against each other. They will rest peacefully by each other's side and stand by each other like members of a family. Fatherlands at war with each other would be the worst barbarism of the human language."[44] In 1806, Fichte in his *Addresses to the German Nation* could distinguish the Germans as an original nation that, unlike others (e.g., the French), had not lost touch with the original genius transmitted through its speech. The French had then become a superficial nation, who, as Humboldt wrote in 1814, lacked "the striving for the divine."[45] Nationalism no longer united, it divided. In Ernst Moritz Arndt's poetic definition of the war winter of 1812-1813, the German fatherland was to be found "where every Frenchman is called foe, and every German is called friend."[46]

3. Finally, the state occupies a very different role. Herder wrote in 1784 that it is "inconceivable that man is made for the state." He considered the state an artificial institution, and held it to be generally detrimental to human happiness.[47] Humboldt argued for the limitation of state powers in very similar terms in 1792. The activities which mattered, he wrote, were carried on by civil society. The state, which he and Herder held to be a mechanical device without real ties to society, restricted the free development of the individual wherever it exceeded its minimum function of preserving order.

Along with Herder or Schiller, he viewed Germany as a cultural rather than a political nation. But by 1813 he came to identify "nation, people and state."[48] Similarly, Fichte who wrote in 1794 that "the aim of all government" is "to make government superfluous,"[49] by 1800 in his *The Closed Commercial State*[50] bestowed extensive economic functions on the state. In his *Addresses to the German Nation* of 1806, he raised the state to the role of the moral and religious educator of the German nation.[51] Moreover, the state was increasingly viewed in power-political terms. Humboldt did so in his famous "Memorandum on a German Constitution" of 1813. Fichte, in his Machiavelli essay of 1807, warned that in the relation between states "there is neither law nor right except the right of the stronger." This condition placed the prince, who was responsible for the interests of the people, "in a higher ethical order whose material substance is contained in the words, *'Salus et decus populi suprema lex esto.'* "[52]

This assumption implies that, in following its own interests, the state acts not only in accordance with a higher morality than that represented by private morality, but also in harmony with the basic purpose of history. In its most extreme form, this theory of the identity of *raison d'état* and cosmic plan probably appears in Hegel's *Philosophy of Law* (1820). "Each nation as an existing individuality is guided by its particular principles," Hegel writes, "and only as a particular individuality can each national spirit win objectivity and self-consciousness; but the fortunes and deeds of States in their relation to one another reveal the dialectic of the finite nature of these spirits. Out of this dialectic rises the universal Spirit, pronouncing its judgments," the highest judgment, "for the history of the World is the world's court of justice."[53] This conception that the struggles of the individual nations are part of a cosmic, rational dialectic violates historicist principles. Nevertheless, even Ranke, who rejected any schematization of history, accepted the idea that generally the victors in a conflict represent the morally superior nation.

Historicism, in the course of the revolutionary and Napoleonic Wars, had thus not only increased its hold upon the educated public, but also had changed its character. An aesthetic, culturally oriented approach to nationality increasingly gave place to the ideal of the national state. The concept of individuality, which Goethe and Humboldt still applied to the uniqueness of persons, now primarily referred to collective groups. The historical optimism of Herder, which saw a hidden meaning in the flow of history, had been fortified by an even more optimistic idea of identity: the assumption that states, in pursuing their own power-political interests, act in accord with a higher morality. A third idea, absent in earlier historicism, now occupies a central place in historicist doctrine: the concept of the primacy of the state in the nation and in society. In the course of Wars of Liberation and even more so after 1815, the political interests of the nation were increasingly identified with the power-political interests of the Prussian state. Together, these three concepts were to provide the foundations for the theoretical assumptions of much of German historiography in the nineteenth and twentieth centuries.

CHAPTER III

The Theoretical Foundations of German
Historicism I: Wilhelm von Humboldt

1.

WILHELM VON HUMBOLDT'S personality was unique and many-sided,[1] so that his intellectual development was not typical of changes taking place in the German intellectual climate of his time. But there are certainly aspects of Humboldt's life and thought which are highly indicative of these transformations. An aristocrat, cosmopolitan in outlook, a friend of Goethe and especially of Schiller with whom he exchanged over a thousand letters,[2] Humboldt on the eve of the invasion of Germany by revolutionary France shared fully in the *Humanitätsideal*. An active statesman in the Prussian reform administrations of Stein and Hardenberg after 1809, Humboldt participated in the new liberalism, which in the struggle against Napoleon affirmed national values against the principles of 1789. He no longer viewed the German nation as primarily a cultural community, but as one of political power.[3] Throughout Humboldt's life there is a thread of continuity with the cosmopolitan, humanistic orientation of his younger years, as well as a clear shift of emphasis toward the new national values.

Humboldt's first political writings were stimulated by the French Revolution. He had visited Paris during the crucial months of 1789[4] and had assessed the developments in France more soberly than many other Germans. They, like his friend Friedrich Gentz, had first welcomed the upheaval with almost unbounded enthusiasm, only to turn as strongly against it. On the surface, his *Ideas on an Attempt to Define the Limits of the State's Sphere of Action* of 1791, often considered the classic work on German Liberalism, proposes a state very similar to that of orthodox liberalism since Locke. The state is not an end in itself, but "a subordinated means, to which the true end, man, must not be sacrificed."[5] Its purpose is the protection of the fullest freedom of all individuals; its functions are to be reduced to the absolute minimum needed to protect the rights of the individual against violation from within and to guarantee his security against threats from without.[6] Rejecting the totalitarian argument that the state must further the happiness of its citizens, Humboldt denies the state all positive functions, including a role in education, religion, or the improvement of morals.[7] These and other functions might be required in society, he admits, but they should be the work of free, voluntary associations, not of the state. The state must not be identified with civil society *(Nationalverein),* Humboldt warns. The state is marked by coercion and the concentration of power; civil society, on the other hand, consists of a pluralism of groups, freely chosen by the individuals and subject to change.[8] Not the state, but the voluntary institutions of a free society preserve and foster cultural values, according to Humboldt. The line dividing state and civil society therefore needs to be a clear one, with the state forbidden from interference in the private lives of its citizens. This assumes a state, governed by standing laws which guarantee the rights of the private individual against official interference.

But the theoretical foundations upon which Humboldt bases his concept of the state were very different from those of classical liberalism. The latter had sought a theoretical justification for individual liberties in a doctrine of natural law. It saw the sources of man's humanity in his ability to think and thus to grasp the rational structure of the universe and of ethics. Classical liberalism viewed rights in terms of abstract, universal principles. It saw those characteristics as essentially human which were universal and uniform among men. But for Humboldt, as for Goethe, Schiller, or Herder, who also shared in the *Humanitätsideal* of German classicism, it was essential to man's humanity that he develop his own unique individuality to its fullest. They shared the Enlightenment belief that man possessed a special dignity, but this dignity, they held, had to be understood in dynamic terms of individual growth. However, while they recognized that man's dignity and end were prescribed by the nature of things or reason, they did not think that reason dictated clear rules for this development. Rather, man's growth had to be governed by the inner nature of his peculiar individuality. Freedom from state interference was necessary because "man's highest purpose—the one prescribed by eternal immutable reason, not by changing inclinations, (was) the highest and most proportioned development of his resources into one whole."[9] Yet this development was possible only when the state did not interfere with man's natural development. The individual was a living organism; the state a mechanical tool which, through legislation, would impose external restraints upon natural growth.[10] Man did not exist in a vacuum, Humboldt acknowledged, and in contrast to the state society was natural and necessary for the individual as he unfolded his "unique individuality" (Eigentümlichkeit).[11] Humboldt assumed that there was a basic harmony among individualities in growth and did not see in society as such, as distinct from the state, a significant source of constraint. Indeed, if the functions of the state were restricted to a minimum, then in his opinion the "highest ideal of the co-existence of human beings" could be attained; namely, that in which "every being develops not only out of himself and for his own sake."[12]

Such a concept of individuality appears hardly compatible with the concept of equality in the classical sense. Indeed, certain important elements of classic liberal political theory are missing. There is nowhere any proposal for government by consent, nor for any system of checks and balances to control the power of the state. Indeed, because Humboldt conceives the state as unified and possessing "absolute power"[13] and rejects the representative principle, he argues that the state's functions must be limited to the bare minimum of preserving security. Because of the coercive character of the state, the positive social functions must be left to voluntary associations. Were the state to carry on positive functions, Humboldt maintains, it would require the consent of every individual, something very different from the majority will of its representatives.[14]

The Limits of the State constitutes a theoretical repudiation of the paternalistic welfare state, primarily that of the absolutistic Polizeistaat of eighteenth-century enlightened depotism, but in principle also of the revolutionary state. In no sense does the book contain a rejection of monarchy as such, or even of absolute monarchy. As Siegfried Kaehler has pointed out in his political biography of Wilhelm von Humboldt,[15] Humboldt's endorsement of the French Revolution never goes beyond the idea of liberty. Already in 1789, he viewed with misgivings the egalitarian aspects of the revolution. In his diary, he condemns the decisions of the night of August 4th, abolishing feudal rights in France, "when a number of nobles, most of them poor, gave away what belonged to the wealthy." As he tells an enthusiastic supporter of the Revolution:

> I said that the deputies had no authority to renounce (these privileges), that the surrender of these privileges had come too quickly and had no useful but only harmful consequences since they nourished chimerical ideas of equality.[16]

Perhaps most strikingly in discord with classic liberal ideals is Humboldt's glorification of war in the *Limits of the State*. Kant, too, had paid homage to the positive aspects of war.[17] War and antagonism had stimulated human activities and hastened the development toward a civil society on rational foundations in which war would be abolished. But for Humboldt war is a desirable end in itself, a permanent feature of human societies, "one of the most wholesome manifestations that plays a role in the education of the human race." He regretfully saw war assume a less and less important place in the modern world, and believed there is no substitute for it. War "alone gives to the total structure the strength and the diversity without which facility would be weakness and unity would be void."[18] Standing armies must be abolished not to dampen the warlike spirit but to spread it through the nation, to "inspire the citizen with spirit of true war."[19]

Doubtless, this positive attitude toward war is related to Humboldt's anti-eudaemonism, his rejection of personal welfare as the highest ethical good. This attack against "eudaemonism" is central to the thought of all the significant writers of the German historical tradition from Humboldt to Meinecke and of German Idealists from Kant to the Hegelians. "Happiness and pleasure," Humboldt observes, "are far removed from the dignity of man. Man most enjoys those moments in which he experiences the highest degree of strength and inner unity. But at these times he is also closest to profound misery."[20] For Humboldt the highest ethical good is still found in the development of the individuality and uniqueness of each man. But the higher values, which replace personal happiness as the highest good, could be easily interpreted, as they later were by German writers of the historicist and German Idealist tradition, in terms of the subordination of the welfare of the greatest possible number of individuals to the historic destiny of the community.

In that case, could the limited state, advocated by Humboldt in the *Limits of the State,* actually be established? This raises the question whether man possesses meaningful choices in his political behavior or must act exclusively within the framework of historical institutions. In the final chapter of his book on the application of theory to reality, Humboldt deals with this question, and develops a theory of social change. Classical liberalism holds that society could be effectively changed by the application of theory to social reality. Without entirely discounting the role of ideas, Humboldt emphasizes the limitations of such an approach. Change could take place only within a concrete historical and social situation, he argues; hence the application of theories to societies is possible only within very narrow limits. Every situation *(Lage)* in which men find themselves has a definite inner structure or form that can not be transformed into any self-chosen one. Change is possible, however, but it requires a prior transformation of opinions and attitudes. One could, without disturbing the existing order of things, prepare for transformations by acting on the minds and characters of men and giving them a direction no longer in accord with the *status quo.* Any other approach would disturb the natural course of human development.[21] and have disastrous consequences.

This stress upon the role of "pure theory" in legislation sharply distinguishes Humboldt from the historicist position of a Savigny. Despite his recognition of historical realities, Humboldt affirms:

> that natural and general law is the only foundation of all positive law, and that one always has to come back to natural law, and that therefore—to cite a principle of law which serves as the source of all other principles of law—no one can ever in any way obtain a right through the energy or the ability of another person without that person's consent.[22]

Humboldt's affirmation that such a transcendent law exists signified, of course, his recognition that not all institutions function in accord with this transhistorical norm. This was already implied in the mere fact that Humboldt wrote a book on the theory of a nonexisting state. But did this recognition of a "natural and universal law" not stand in contradiction with Humboldt's belief that the individual should be judged only by measures proper to him, and not by external abstract norms? Humboldt thus agrees with the French revolutionaries that the state must bring the "real condition of things" as close to the "right and true theory" as possible. But this "approximation" is possible only insofar as "true necessity" does not hinder its course. The possibility of change, however, rests on the assumption that "men (were) sufficiently receptive of that liberty which the theory (taught), and that this liberty could bring about those wholesome consequences which always accompanied liberty when there were no obstacles in its way." But the "possibility" of applying the theory is always limited by "Necessity" *(Nothwendigkeit).* Doubtlessly keeping in mind the developments in France, Humboldt warns that to ignore "necessity" in effecting social reforms would lead to the destruction of the very values these reforms are intended to bring about.[23]

What is left of theory and of "universal, natural law" in view of the force of "necessity?" Apparently very little. The state "must always let its actions be determined by necessity." This principle was not conceived in terms of historical determinism; rather, necessity was defined in terms of the "unique individuality" of men.[24] Necessity, the respect for the uniqueness of the individual, determines the theoretical demand for the limited state. The recognition of the uniqueness and diversity of men forbids the state to undertake "positive" action to achieve "useful" ends, since what is useful to an individual is always subject to speculation and can not be determined from the outside. Necessity is thus in harmony with freedom. No "other principle [could] be reconcile[d] with respect for the individuality of independent beings and the concern for freedom which derive[d] from this respect."[25] Then what remains of theory, of "eternally immutable reason," of the "natural, universal laws of nature" is merely the recognition of the total diversity of men. The theory of the state, confronted by the necessities of the real situation, hangs in mid-air as an abstraction, incapable of realization.

Humboldt is quite aware of all this. In describing the "theoretical principles" of political power, he proceeds from the "nature of man," viewing man "in the form most characteristic of him," not yet determined by any concrete relationships. "But man nowhere exists like that,"[26] he adds. The implementations of the theory require a degree of maturity for freedom. "Albeit, this maturity is nowhere perfect and in my opinion will remain foreign to the sensual, extroverted individual."[27] Thus, Humboldt asks his readers to refrain from all comparisons with reality, "despite all the general observations of these pages."[28] As he wrote to Schiller: "This treatise has no relation to present-day circumstances."[29] This may explain in part why this classic of German liberalism was never published in its entirety during Humboldt's lifetime, but appeared only in 1851, long after his death.[30]

2.

Humboldt's defense of the liberal state in *The Limits of the State,* however, includes two basic assumptions which in their modified form are still reminiscent of classic liberal theory. Humboldt maintains that there is a "pure theory" of the state, one based upon the principle of "eternal reason" and thus opposed to the existing "positive" state. This holds true even if for him, in contrast to classic liberal thought, the chasm between the ideal and the existing state are unbridgeable. Moreover, he finds a human dignity common to all men. In his other writings, Humboldt carefully attempts to free himself from all abstract or universal principles and more closely approaches an organicist concept of society and history.

This had been already true of his critique of the new French Constitution which he had written in August 1791, a year before the *Limits of the State.*[31] It had been a great error of the Constituent Assembly, he holds, to attempt to base a constitution upon "pure reason." Only that could develop harmoniously in men or in the state as "a sum of active and passive human energies" which has its origin within and is not imposed from without. Constitutions can not be drafted on men as sprigs on trees. "Where time and nature have not done the spade work, one might as well bind blossoms with threads. The first noonday sun will wilt them."[32] He does not urge the wise legislator to work out the "pure theory" of the intended reform in detail, as he does in the *Limits of the State,* but asks him to free himself from abstract considerations, to determine the actual direction of change, and then modify this direction by degrees. While reforms are possible within narrow limits, human institutions are only to a very small extent the result of deliberate human action. Indeed, as he comments, "when we offer philosophic or political reason for political institutions, we will, in actuality, always find historical explanations."[33]

In the fragment "On the law of the Development of Human Energies (1791)," Humboldt sets the limits of reason and abstract law even more narrowly. Even if we possess the key to the universe, "a rational truth that pointed to the necessity of a uniform law," this knowledge gives us no real insight into the nature of things. For living Nature, in contrast to "lifeless," physical nature, can be grasped only through an act of understanding, of intuitively experiencing its innermost character. Indeed "understanding" of the lifeless, physical world is not really possible. We can establish uniformities in its behavior, but these relate only to its external appearance, not to its inner essence, which we can grasp in others who are analogous to us in being alive. We can know living things only through the energies they express which reflect their particular individualities. The more we succeed in reducing phenomena to abstract concepts, the further we move away from the understanding of real living forces and of individual essences.[35]

In other essays of the 1790's, Humboldt develops further his concept of individuality and its implications for ethics and education.[36] In "On the Spirit of Mankind,"[37] written in 1797, he stresses that every man must have a goal, a "first and an absolute yardstick,"[38] but this ultimate value must be related to his inner nature. The final goal common to all men is the "dignity of men," but there is no set pattern by which this can be attained. However, this "absolute yardstick," which man finds only in himself, does not relate to "momentary pleasure or for that matter to his happiness." It is a "notable characteristic of man's nature to be able to scorn pleasure and to do without happiness." This yardstick is to be found in a man's "inner value, in his higher, more perfect self."[39] Humboldt, in distinguishing between the essential and incidental elements of individual character, already approaches his later view that each individual represents an idea. Still noticeably missing is the view that collective groups, other than mankind as a whole, possess individual character or represent ideas. This concept was to become important to Humboldt's later political writings.

3.

Until 1809, Humboldt's relation to politics had been that of an outsider. Even as Prussian envoy and minister plenepotentiary in Rome, between 1802 and 1809, Humboldt had primarily devoted himself to aesthetic and scholarly tasks. Since 1792, he had written no essay on political questions, and even in the *Limits of the State* he had approached politics as a theoretical problem without direct relation to reality. As one of his political biographers observes, his primary concern in the *Limits of the State* is not with the question of the needs and functions of the state, but an aesthetic interest in the development of the individual personality.[40]

This relationship changed abruptly, when Humboldt was called to Berlin in 1809 upon Baron von Stein's recommendation that he reorganize the Prussian system of education. From 1809, until the reaction which set in with the Carlsbad Decrees in 1819, Humboldt served the Prussian state in active, policy-making roles; for example, as envoy to Austria from 1810 until the end of the Congress of Vienna; as minister charged with the task of preparing a draft for the Prussian constitution in 1819; as one of the statesmen who, under the leadership of Stein and Hardenberg, attempted to reform the Prussian state along liberal lines after the humiliating defeat at Napoleon's hands in 1806. He succeeded in reshaping the Prussian schools in accord with his *Humänitatsideal*. In the primary schools, he modified the then existing pedagogy, which he considered mechanical and rationalistic, and substituted Pestalozzian methods that took into account the inner needs and interests of the individual child. In the *Gymnasien,* he replaced preoccupation with Latin philology with emphasis upon the study of the Greeks. Influenced by Winckelmann's perhaps one-sided interpretation of Greek art, Humboldt believed with Goethe that the Greeks had succeeded in approximating the ideal of the harmoniously proportioned and totally developed individuality. He was instrumental in founding the University of Berlin in 1810, with its principles of freedom of research and teaching which were to set a pattern for all German universities.[41] He unsuccessfully attempted to reduce the function of the centralized state in matters of education by urging the transfer of state school funds to the local communities. Humboldt's very assumption of the responsibilities of minister of education, of course, constituted a recognition of functions of the state which he had previously denied.

While it may be going too far to see in Humboldt's turn to the state, as one historian has done, the decisive victory of the "individuality of supra-individual forces over the individual who has lost his sovereignty to the living forces of history that surround him,"[42] Humboldt's concept of the relation of the individual to the state and the nation underwent a radical change. In his political memoranda, Humboldt continues to view the organization of the state not merely in terms of the needs of the state, but also in terms of the education of its citizens as individuals. For this reason, he stresses the need to transfer state powers to voluntary associations in which individuals can grow through participation. But under the emotional impact of the new political nationalism in the era of the Wars of Liberation, Humboldt began to recognize the state as a metaphysical reality. The state has an existence independent of the needs of the individual, and the nation is interwoven with the state. This new orientation appears most clearly in his "Memorandum on the German Constitution" of December 1813.[43] Nation, state, and people are one, he observes.

> In the way in which nature united individuals into nations and sorted mankind into nations, there lay contained a deep and mysterious means by which the individual, who is nothing by himself, and the race (Geschlecht), which has meaning only in individuals, kept on the true road of the proportionate and gradual development of their energies.[44]

Germany was not merely a spiritual unit, Humboldt now urged; as he and Goethe had once believed, Germany required no political bonds, but rested upon a community of "manners and customs, language and literature." What made Germany a whole was the "memory of rights and liberties enjoyed in common, of glory won in battle and dangers faced together, the memory of close bonds which linked the fathers and which are now alive only in the nostalgic longings of the grandchildren."[45] This unity required political expression. Fearful of overly great centralization, Humboldt saw a confederation as the solution of the problem of national unification most in harmony with German's history and character, although a confederation dominated by Prussia and Austria. However, this German state needed to be strong against the outside, not merely to provide protection in an unstable world, but also because political power was a prerequisite for the cultural development of Germany.

> Germany must be free and strong, not only to be able to defend herself against this or that neighbor, or for that matter, against any enemy, but because only a nation which is also strong toward the outside can preserve the spirit within from which all domestic blessings flow. Germany must be free and strong, even if she is never put to a test, so that she may possess the self-assurance required for her to pursue her development as a nation unhampered and that she may be able to maintain permanently the position which she occupies in the midst of the European nations, a position which is so beneficial to these nations.[46]

Power, largely conceived in military terms, now appeared to Humboldt as a positive good. This was not inconsonant with his earlier observations on the positive effects of war upon character. As he wrote in 1817, in a recommendation on the army budget:

> The usefulness of a strong army ready for battle begins long before the day war is declared. Throughout periods of peace such an army assures internal security, strengthens the influence of the state in all its dealings with foreign powers, and exercises an influence on the character of the nation.[47]

This emphasis upon the dependence of the individual on the nation finds its most extreme expressions in passages in his correspondence during the war years. Because of their casual character, perhaps they need to be received with some caution. Thus, he writes his wife:

> Believe me. There are only two good and benevolent forces (*Potenzen*) in this world, God and the nation (*Volk*). Everything in between is useless and we are of use only to the degree that we are close to the nation (*Volk*).

Again he states:

> All national energy, life and spontaneity rests in the nation (*Volk*).

> One can accomplish nothing without the nation and needs it con-
> stantly. Man is nothing but by virtue of the power of the whole and
> only as long as he strives to be in accord with it.[48]

This concept of the nation or people as an individual with an individual character led him to propose a harsh treatment of France at
the Congress of Vienna. He based his demands not only on the
political interests of Prussia or of Germany, but on his condemnation
of the French national character, the absence of a "striving for the
divine which the French lack not only as a nation but virtually
without exception also as individuals."[49]

From this new emphasis upon historic and collective forces, the
draft recommendation Humboldt prepared for a Prussian Constitution[50] is interesting, for it indicates a new type of liberalism which no
longer recognized the individual as the basic unit in politics and as
the purpose for which the state exists. The draft did guarantee the
basic rights of the individual to be secure in his person and in his
property, due process of law, freedom of conscience, and freedom of
the press. It also provided for representation. The draft conceived the
constitution not merely as serving the "objective" purpose of the
state and providing more efficient government, but also as fulfilling
the "subjective" needs of the citizens. Through political participation, they would grow morally and spiritually. Society was no longer
seen as a composite of individuals, but as an organic whole of corporations representing social functions. The corporations, it is true,
were adapted to the demands of modern Prussian life and primarily
were viewed as organs of political representation.

Humboldt wished to maintain the economic freedom established
by the reform edicts. The political role of the nobility was to be
preserved only to the extent that the nobles still fulfilled an actual
function. Humboldt idealized corporate institutions far less than
Stein. Extensive administrative functions were to be transferred from
the central government to the communities and the provinces in
order to stimulate local participation in public affairs. The proposed
estates general for the monarchy were to have powers similar to
those possessed by the parliaments created by the French Charter or
by the Southwestern German constitutions granted in the 1820's, and
they were to resemble these parliaments in their organization. But
the language of this document, which certainly envisaged a much
higher degree of popular participation than did these other constitu-

tional documents, was much further removed than they were from the principles of 1789. The author of the *Limits of the State* now saw the individual acquire his rights of citizenship no longer by virtue of being an individual, but only on the basis of meeting the qualifications for acceptance into a corporation.[51]

4.

There is little radically new in the three important essays which Humboldt wrote on the nature of history after 1814. His views of history, in terms of growth and life, his stress that the act of under-standing requires the total personality and not merely the rational faculties of the observer, and his belief in the uniqueness of the individual, were all present. However, the emphasis had changed. The residues of belief in a common human nature and in common human rights derived from reason (basic elements of the theoretical foundations of the political liberalism of Humboldt's *Limits of the State*), now had receded almost completely in the background. His theoretical rejection of rational ethics and of objective criteria of knowledge was now almost absolute. History remains the only source of knowledge about man, but since man is irrational and history the scene of his actions, history must be approached by a method which takes into account this irrationality.

Three aspects of Humboldt's essays of this period are of particular interest: (a) the extent to which he pursues the irrational forces of life and history; (b) his theory of ideas[52] by which he seeks to find a metaphysical foundation for his doctrine of individuality and discover meaning and a common basis of existence in a pluralistic world; (c) his theory of understanding or *Verstehen*[53] through which he attempts to do justice to the irrational nature of history, as well as of man.

The first aspect, the irrational character of history, forms the topic of Humboldt's "Reflections on World History,"[54] a bitter critique of the idea of progress and all attempts at systematic philosophies of history, including those of Kant. It is folly to seek meaningful direction in history, Humboldt argues. Attempts to do so only do violence to the events of history by forcing them into schemes and robbing them of their individuality. They treat mankind too intellectually, cutting the close relation of man's history with the forces of

nature. There is indeed coherence *(Zusammenhang)* in history, but
of an organic rather than an intellectual kind. Mankind, Humboldt
suggests, resembles a plant, an analogy which was not entirely fortu-
nate since a plant possesses an internal structure which Humboldt
apparently denies to the history of man. The individual person's
relation to the nation is comparable to a leaf's relation to the tree.
Mankind consists of a ladder of individualities from the individual
through the collective bodies to the race as a whole. Each individuality (whether individual person or nation) receives its unique character not in slow stages, but by sudden spontaneous generation. The
birth of an individuality is also the beginning of its decline. The
individuality dies, but its spirit survives. Thus, it is "the most important thing in world history to preserve this spirit as it endures,
changes form, and in some cases becomes extinct."[55]

There is indeed a purpose to world history, but it is not to be
found in a progressive perfection of man. We must not expect man
to attain an abstractly conceived end, Humboldt warns; rather, we
must hope that the "creative power of nature and ideas remains
inexhaustible."[56] Mankind as a "whole" existed only "in the never
attainable totality of all the individualities which in the course of
time become **real**."[57] The intent of history is that all energies express
themselves and develop clear expressions of their individual characters. There is no higher purpose. Individual lives are not parts of a
superpattern. "The fates of human generations roll past like the
streams which flow from the mountains to the sea."[58]

In sharp contrast to German Idealist philosophers or even to
Herder, Humboldt denies any meaningful development in history.
Here the analogy with the plant seemingly ends. For every individual
at his spontaneous birth contains something radically new. Again the
genius, "a great mind or a mighty will," might suddenly give rise to
something "new and never experienced," completely incapable of
"mechanical" explanation.[59] Certain uniformities do exist in nature
and even in man, Humboldt admits. Without them, no statistics
would be possible. But the element of freedom and the continuous
creation of novelty make any historical prediction impossible. Indeed, history is chaos. Man, possessing intellect, might carry certain
ideas from nation to nation and develop them, "but suddenly," he
warns, "his noblest creations are destroyed again by natural events or
barbarism," for "it is evident that fate does not respect the creations

of the spirit. This is the mercilessness of world history." In studying wars and revolutions the historian does not need to ask about their purposes, but only about their origins which often were "physical or animalistic" in character. Basic in human history is the vitalistic "urge to produce and to reproduce."[60] The historian who primarily approaches world history from the standpoint of the growth of cultures or civilization misunderstands the extent to which man is not a being of reason and understanding, but a product of nature.[61]

This brings us to the second aspect of Humboldt's essays. If history is all flux, the individualities remain as a stable element and through them history gains meaning. In his essay "On the Task of the Writer of History, (1822)"[62] Humboldt further develops the thought, already expressed in earlier writings, that the individualities are merely the concrete, historical expressions of an underlying metaphysical reality, the ethical ideas.

Yet the term "ideas" must not mislead us, for they are not clear concepts. They are not to be understood in the Platonic sense as pure forms which could find their repeated imitations or approximations in the physical world. Each idea represents the essence or character of an actually existing individuality. In this sense, ideas are conceived as eternal and would survive their physical manifestations. But ideas certainly are not universal in the sense of a Platonic triangle or of the Platonic concept of justice, able to manifest themselves in very different historical situations. Each idea is related to something real in the physical world. Humboldt probably never should have used the term "idea" in this way, for he refers to something thoroughly nonrational; namely, to those elements in natural and historical reality which cannot be explained in terms of rational factors. The doctrine of ideas, as formulated by Humboldt, involves the recognition of the basically irrational character of human history and human life. Indeed, Humboldt's concept of individuality carries within it elements of the nihilistic notion that history is nothing but a mass of individuals with individual wills.

This doctrine of ideas seems to point at a hopeless chaos of values. Actually, of course, Humboldt was neither a nihilist nor even a thoroughgoing relativist. By seeking the idea in the existing, limited individualities, Humboldt reflects his faith that there is meaning in the midst of flux; that all fits into a divine mystery; that "world history was inconceivable without a cosmic plan governing it."[63]

Each idea reflects one aspect of infinity. Although it is impossible for man to understand the "plans of this cosmic government" *(Welt-regierung),* he can intuitively gain glimpses of it *(erahnden)* through the ideas.[64]

Thus, despite his insistence upon flux and chaos in history, Humboldt preserves his faith that in a higher sense history is a meaningful drama. Humboldt makes two assumptions fundamental to the optimism that distinguishes the *Historismus* of the nineteenth century from the radical relativization of values with which historicism has been identified in twentieth-century Germany. He assumes that individuals have an inner structure and character, that they are not merely a bundle of passions. He therefore admonishes: "One must seek the Best and the Highest that the subject has attained in all his diverse activities. This we link together into one Whole, a Whole that we consider to constitute its unique and essential character. Everything that does not fit into this character, we may consider to be incidental."[65] He also assumes that the great diversities in history all fitted in some mysterious way into a harmonious whole; that if left to their free course all historical tendencies were good; and that, in this best of all possible worlds, evil consisted of the attempt to divert the natural tendencies of history.

The third aspect to be found in Humboldt's essays—recognition of the role of the irrational in history, joined to a faith in an ultimate meaning in the flux of human events—poses special problems for the historian. Humboldt was the first nineteenth-century writer to work out a theory of knowledge which took these insights into account.

A first important methodological consideration arose for Humboldt from the fact that in approaching history the historian is dealing with "living," not with "dead" matter. Here, similar to later writers, Humboldt makes a distinction between the methods applicable to the "natural sciences" and those proper to the "historical sciences." However, Humboldt never conceives physical nature to be entirely dead or nonhistorical. The living can never be approached as something static that might be viewed under fixed conditions at one given point of time. To comprehend a living being, we must see it as a totality and understand its inner essence. For Humboldt this cannot be achieved by mere external description, but requires harmonious use of "rational observation" *(beobachtender Verstand)* and "poetic imagination" *(dichtende Einbildungskraft).*[66]

But as Humboldt developed his theory of individuality into a metaphysical doctrine of ideas, these conditions for historical understanding, which he presented at the turn of the century in "The Eighteenth Century," no longer sufficed. Now, in "On the Tasks of the Writer of History," he sees history as the only guide to an approximate understanding of the "totality of being."[67]

The task of the historian, as presented in the latter essay, is to depict what has happened *(Darstellung des Geschehenen)*. Toward that end he must begin with a simple description. But what has happened *(das Geschehene)*, Humboldt hastens to point out, is "only in part accessible to the senses. The rest has to be felt *(empfunden)*, inferred *(geschlossen)*, or divined *(errathen)*." Only fragments are apparent to the observer. "What binds these fragments, what puts the individual piece in its true light and gives form to the whole remains beyond the reach of direct observation." Facts are not enough. "The truth of all that happens requires the addition of that above mentioned invisible element of every fact and this the writer of history must add."[68]

The role Humboldt now assigns to the historian is a much more ambitious one than previously outlined in his earlier essay. It involves more than merely grasping the character of an individual personality or of a nation. Through the study of the individual, the historian now could gain general knowledge, once the task of the philosopher. But if the historian's intent (the search of ultimate truth) now resembled that of the traditional philosopher, his method, the only one by which such truth could be approached, had to remain that of the historian, according to Humboldt.[69] The historical sense requires "a feeling for the real" in its "flux" and "time-boundness," yet it also involves the search for meaning.

The historian, Humboldt stresses, does not merely arrange facts meaninglessly; he attempts to discover links, to understand the events in a larger context. This distinguishes him from a mere pedant. "The historian worthy of the name must present every event as part of a whole."[70] He recognizes on one hand, the "inner spiritual freedom" of every individuality and, on the other, the dependence of every event on preceding and accompanying causes. He perceives that "reality, not withstanding its apparent haphazardness, is governed by necessity." But to impose concepts upon the actual events is to violate this historical reality; not to go beyond the bare facts is to forego meaning. Not merely the understanding of a wider context, but the understanding of a concrete, individual historical situation requires more than the mere presentation of facts.

This interrelation of facts and ideas demands a twofold methodological approach. The first requirement, Humboldt counsels, is an "exact, impartial, critical examination of the events."[71] Here is the core of the critical method, the establishment of facts, the weighing of evidence through the empirical and rational approach to sources, documents, and the like. But in the search for meaning, for the "links within the matter under investigation," this approach does not suffice. The idea must be comprehended, and the act of comprehension *(Begreifen)* requires resources other than those of purely conscious perception. In his search of the idea, the historian resembles the artist; only he is not permitted the latter's free use of phantasy, but is much more closely bound to reality. The critical, empirical approach to this reality has to be supplemented by "intuiting that which cannot be reached by this means," but by intuition *(Ahnden)* which proceeds from the concrete facts.[72] This intuition for Humboldt implies that the "ideas" which express themselves in concrete reality, can be comprehended only approximately and dimly. But it also assumes that meaningful relationships exist. For man's intuitive understanding *(Ahnden)* or rational comprehension *(Begreifen)* of such truth

> presupposes within the comprehendent something analogous to what later will actually be comprehended, a pre-existing, original agreement between subject and object. Comprehension involves not merely development of subjectivity nor taking from an object, but both simultaneously. . . . When two persons are separated by a gulf, no bridge of understanding can lead from one to the other. In order to understand one another, one must in a sense already have understood each other to begin with.[73]

However, this theory of understanding assumes a common bond not entirely compatible with Humboldt's view of the radical uniqueness of individuals, a contradiction of which he was never fully aware.

"On the Tasks of the Writer of History" was Humboldt's last great contribution to historical theory. Two years later, Ranke's *His-*

tories of the Romanic and Germanic Peoples appeared with the famous methodological appendix, "In Criticism of Recent Historians." But the basic metaphysical and epistemological assumptions of the great tradition of German historicism from Ranke to Meinecke had been already formulated by Humboldt. With his essay "On the Tasks of the Writer of History," the philosophical theory of German historicism was complete. The break with *Aufklärung* and *Humanitätsideal* was now very real. Humboldt had always seen in history a vital, dynamic force which could not be directed by rational planning. He had never shared the faith of the *philosophes* in the possibility of reorganizing society along rational lines. Nevertheless, he had been firmly convinced that the basic unit in society is the individual. His concept of liberty had been cosmopolitan rather than national.

In the three decades that separated the essay "On the Limits of the State" from "The Tasks of the Writer of History," Humboldt came to recognize the primacy of collective forces and he identified these with nationality. Humboldt recognized the central role of the state within the nation, and he developed a theory of knowledge aimed at the understanding of the irrational, vital forces of history and of the unique, metaphysical reality of these forces. These theories, the doctrine of ideas, the individualizing approach, the concept of the central role of politics in history, formed the basic elements of the philosophy of history of German historiography and historical thought from Ranke to Meinecke.

CHAPTER IV

The Theoretical Foundations of German Historicism II: Leopold von Ranke

1.

Two misconceptions have marked the image of Ranke held by American historians, since history in the 1880's became an academic discipline on purportedly Rankean principles. Ranke has been viewed as the prototype of the nontheoretical and, for many, the politically neutral historian. When his conservative prejudices have been recognized, he has nevertheless been given credit for the fact that these prejudices were not reflected in his historical narrative.[1]

Graduate study in history developed in American universities at a time when philosophic naturalism and positivism dominated the intellectual scene. In their endeavor to give academic respectability to historical study, a few writers who had been influenced by Comte and Buckle, e.g., Andrew D. White, John Fiske, Henry and Brooks Adams, identified scientific history with the application to the historical process of general laws similar to those of the natural sciences. A far greater number of writers were conscious of the distinctions between historical narration which deals with unique situations and discourse in the natural sciences which aims at general and typical truths. Accordingly, they sought to explain the scientific character of historical writing and its method of establishing facts objectively, free from philosophical considerations. For this new school of historians Ranke was the "father of scientific history"[2] who, as H. B. Adams at Johns Hopkins University observed at the time, "determined to hold strictly to the facts of history, to preach no sermon, to point no moral, to adorn no tale, but to tell the simple historic truth." His sole ambition was to narrate things as they really were *("wie es eigentlich gewesen").*[3]

Ranke was thus identified in America with a concept of historical science that eliminated not only philosophical but also theoretical considerations. He was understood to have conceived historical science primarily as a technique that applied critical methods to the evaluation of sources. If carried out conscientiously, this approach by necessity would recognize only monographic studies as scientific. As Professor Emerton commented, after he proclaimed Ranke the founder of "the doctrine of the true historical method": "If one must choose between a school of history whose main characteristic is the spirit, and one which rests upon the greatest attainable number of recorded facts, we cannot long hesitate. . . . Training has taken the place of brilliancy and the whole world is today reaping the benefit."[4] Similarly, George B. Adams told the American Historical Association, in a presidential address in 1908 in which he attempted to defend "our first leader" against the onslaught of the social scientists, that theoretical questions must be left to "poets, philosophers, and theologians."[5] The image of the nonphilosophical Ranke, concerned only with facts, rejecting all theory, was taken over by the "New Historians" who had repudiated the older "scientific" tradition and stressed the interaction of social factors in human history. Frederick Turner and J. H. Robinson attacked the Ranke whom the "scientific" school had created. The image of the naturalistic Ranke survived. Only a few years ago, as prominent a historian as Walter P. Webb observed that Ranke "was contemporary with Lyell and Wallace, Darwin and Renan, who were applying the analytical and critical method with startling results in their respective fields. He turned the lecture room into a laboratory, using documents instead of 'bushels of clams.' "[6]

To an extent, Ranke's individualizing method did prepare the way for the type of unreflective, professional history-writing which marked not only American historiography at the end of the century, but had already manifested itself in many German historical and legal studies in the second part of the nineteenth century.[7] Still, despite Ranke's concern with the critical examination of sources, perhaps no German historian of the nineteenth century (with the possible exception of Droysen) paid as much attention to the theoretical foundations of his historical practice as did Ranke. Moreover, no one succeeded as completely in integrating his concept of the historical process and his theory of knowledge with his political views. The philosophic context of Ranke's methodological consideration received little understanding in America, particularly at a time when his basic metaphysical and religious assumptions had become questionable, even in German thought. Indeed, little was left of Ranke's heritage for broad groups of pedantic historians on both sides of the Atlantic, except a souless positivism which Ranke had always repudiated.

2.

One can question whether the new critical treatment of sources or the introduction of the seminar method into historical instructions was Ranke's main contribution to German historiography. Ranke was not the first historian to apply the so-called "new" critical methods to the examination of historical sources. Friedrich August Wolf (1759-1824) and August Böckh (1785-1867) had applied rigorous philological criticism to the examination of classical texts. Herbert Butterfield, in a recent chapter on the Göttingen School, has traced the eighteenth-century background of modern historiographical method.[8] When Ranke applied critical methods to modern historical texts, he was consciously indebted to Barthold Georg Niebuhr's critical approach to Roman history. Perhaps more significant for historical thought, if not also for historical practice, was Ranke's development of the basic philosophical concepts of the Historical School during his editorship of the *Historisch-Politische Zeitschrift (Historical-Political Review)* from 1832 to 1836.

Ranke published his first book, the *Histories of the Romanic and Germanic Peoples from 1494 to 1514,* in 1824. In its famous technical appendix, "In Criticism of Modern Historians," he applied the critical principles of G. B. Niebuhr to the discussion of modern sources. By that time, the line between a philosophical and an Historical School, which Savigny had defined so neatly, had already divided the University of Berlin into two hostile camps. The one centered around Hegel; the other included a broad group of jurists. Friedrich Carl von Savigny and Karl Friedrich Eichhorn, the founders of the Historical School, belonged to this second group as did Niebuhr, the philologists Böckh, Bopp, and Lachmann, and the theologian Schleiermacher. What divided the two schools was their different concept of truth and reality. Was the diversity in the phenomenal world merely a manifestation of an underlying rational principle, as Hegel maintained? If so, then truth could be attained only by reducing this diversity to rational concepts. Or was this diversity reality itself, and was any attempt to reduce it to a conceptual scheme a violation of the fullness and individuality inherent in life?

Both schools shared in the conviction that behind the phenomena of historical study there was a metaphysical reality, and that the aim of all study must be the apprehension of this reality. Niebuhr, Savigny, and Ranke agreed with Hegel that true philosophy and true history were basically one. They differed from Hegel in their conviction that this fundamental reality could be approached only through historical study, for it was much more complex, vitalistic, and elusive and possessed much greater room for spontaneity and uniqueness than Hegel's panlogistic concept of the universe would permit. In brief, only history offered answers to the fundamental questions of philosophy. "History," Savigny and Eichhorn observe in the Introduction to the first volume of the *Zeitschrift für geschichtliche Rechtswissenschaft (Journal for Historical Jurisprudence)*, "is by no means a mere collection of examples but is the only way to true knowledge *(Erkenntnis)* of our own condition *(Zustand)*." This, Savigny stresses, does not mean the superiority of the past over the present.[9] Rather, the Historical School recognizes the value and autonomy of every age, and only stresses that the living connection, which links the present to the past, be recognized. In the area of law, this means that there is no abstract, philosophic law, no law of nature which can be codified; instead, every law is inseparably interwoven with the total historical development of a people. The jurist must eliminate those aspects of the law which have atrophied and no longer constitute a living part of the present.[10] If Savigny thus recognizes the elements of change within tradition, at the same time he denies the possibility of progress. For history is neither static, nor is any epoch a steppingstone in a linear process of fulfillment. Rather, every age represents an end and a value in itself.

The issues between the two schools were well illustrated in the bitter controversy which developed between Leopold Ranke and

Heinrich Leo, after the latter, a young disciple of Hegel, had reviewed Ranke's first book and its Appendix.[11] It was not Ranke's insistence upon methodological accuracy, however, which Leo challenged, but his view of history. Indeed, Leo based his criticism on grounds that Ranke would have accepted. He merely rejected the justice of these criticisms. Ranke's style was poor, Leo complained; he had introduced sentimentality into his narration, and lacked critical judgment in the use of his sources.[12] The real controversy in the critical exchanges between the two men centered around their treatment of Machiavelli, and this involved two fundamental problems of a philosophic nature: (1) was it legitimate to apply ethical standards to the assessment of historical characters and (2) should historical personalities be studied for their own sake or in terms of their role in world history? Ranke, attempting to refrain from passing moral judgment upon Machiavelli, viewed the Florentine in terms of his time. He did recognize that there was something "shocking" *(Entsetzliches)* in Machiavelli's teachings. However, Ranke held that *The Prince* had not been intended as a "general textbook" for practical politics. Rather, Machiavelli's teachings were directed at a specific historic situation.[13] Ranke shuddered at the idea of using them as general precepts of political action, as readers had done for centuries. But as the means used for a specific situation, he urged that they be understood. As pointed out in Ranke's Preface to the *Histories of the Romanic and Germanic Peoples,* the task of history is not "to judge the past" but the more humble one, "merely to show what really happened *(wie es eigentlich gewesen).*"[14] We must "be just," Ranke argues. "He (Machiavelli) sought Italy's salvation. But conditions seemed so desperate to him that he was bold enough to prescribe poison . . . Cruel means" alone could save "an Italy corrupted to the core."[15]

For Leo, on the other hand, the Florentine historian must be judged both by moral standards and as a world-historical person. In the Introduction to his translation of Machiavelli's letters, Leo describes him as an amoral person who looked at good and evil as an outside observer and pursued the most perverted sensual pleasures without real personal engagement, "a mind torn loose from all that is eternal."[16] Machiavelli, Leo continues, knew that as one flatters French, Burgundian, or German princes with the hope of expelling the Turks from Europe, so Italian princes were flattered with the vision of cleansing the fatherland.[17] Machiavelli's patriotism was a mere device to obtain personal ends. But all of this is unimportant, Leo concludes, compared to the man's "world historical significance" as the midwife of the new age of the modern state to whose basic principle he gave expression, without himself being conscious of his great task.[18]

Hence Ranke's supposed criteria for judging the value of historical works solely in terms of the degree to which they represented "naked truth" appeared faulty to Leo. For truth, he holds, is found not in the representation of every detail, but in a context that takes growth into account. The true landscape painting is not one in which the painter has counted every blade of grass which changed before he had time to finish the painting, but one that places the living scene in front of the observer "without in the least sticking pedantically to details." And history is like that. "Truth in history is the process of life and of the spirit. Historiographical truth consists exclusively in describing this process which is manifested in the events. This description need not betray the index finger of the philosopher although the true historian and the philosopher meet at every step."[19]

However, to identify his concept of naked truth with "the silly notion of copying and making anatomical slides"[20] seems to Ranke a caricature of his procedure. Ranke believes that he, no less than Leo, sought general truth, but he argues that it can be apprehended only through the particular. By absorbing himself in the particular, he attempts to represent "the general straight away and without much circumlocution." Only in its outward appearance is the individual phenomenon particular; within it, as Leibniz had already recognized, the individual event contains something deeper, "a general truth, significance, spirit." This general truth cannot be grasped through extensive reasoning, but only in a more direct way, in a manner closer to that of the poet or the artist. "In and by means of the event, I have tried to portray the event's course and spirit and to define its characteristic traits. . . . I know how little I have succeeded. But he should not scold me," Ranke continues in reply to Leo, "whose thinking is restricted to perpetuating the generalizing formulas of the (Hegelian) school. I shall not scold him either. We are traveling on entirely different roads."[21]

But if reality consists of a multiplicity of individual natures which can not be reduced to a common denominator, history seems to lose its meaning. While Ranke finds a common denominator in God, he rejects Hegel's pantheism which identifies God with the total process of history. His is a Christian panentheism which sees God distinct from the world, but omnipotent in it. Hence Ranke defends his observation that "each time at the decisive moment something enters which we call chance *(Zufall)* or fate *(Geschick)* but which is God's finger"[22] from Leo's charge of sentimentality and superstition. The presence of God alone prevents the alternative between the total determinism of fate and the "materialist notion that all is contingent." God alone offers the bond of unity for Ranke—and for that matter for the Historical School in general—in a world where values and truths are related to historic individualities, rather than to universal human norms. Inherent in this type of historicism which Ranke espouses is always the threat that, if Christian faith is shaken, history will lose its meaning and present man with the anarchy of values.

Despite Ranke's defense, Leo is not entirely incorrect in charging that the *Histories of the Romanic and Germanic Peoples* resemble a heap of unassorted details. The historicist positions avowed by Ranke in his replies to Leo have found relatively little application in this work. Ranke has done little, in fact, to seek the general within the particular. One great idea gives the work a degree of inner unity, the concept of the Romanic and Germanic Peoples as a historic unity distinct from nations that compose them and distinct from Europe or Christendom as a whole. The book attempts to treat the emergence of the modern international system of the great powers in the two crucial decades between 1494 and 1514. As a recent American critic observes: "The use of the plural in the title was indicative of the uncorrelated multitude of events and developments, mostly matters of war and foreign policy, in which the book abounded. It resembled a wild garden before the gardener brought order, clarity, and form into its profuse growth."[23] Nor did the *Ottoman and Spanish Empires in the 16th and 17th Centuries* (1827) or *The Serbian Revolution* (1829) exhibit any philosophic undertones or intent. Only when Ranke turned to the political issues of the day in the 1830's did he further develop the philosophic view of history which he had vaguely indicated in his reply to Leo.

3.

Ranke systematically approached the theoretical problems underlying his historical practice only during the four years of his editor-
ship of the *Historisch-Politische Zeitschrift,* between 1832 and 1836.
Otherwise, he offered little of a theoretical nature, except for random
remarks strewn through his histories and correspondence. One notable exception was the brief introduction to the lectures "About the
Epochs of Modern History," which he read to King Maximilian of
Bavaria in 1854.[24] But in the essays of the *Historisch-Politische
Zeitschrift,* as well as his lecture notes[25] and his inaugural address,
"On the Affinities and Differences Between History and Politics,"[26]
from that period, Ranke developed the most systematic and coherent
exposition of historicist principles in nineteenth-century historiography. For the most part it was in direct defense of Prussian institutions of the Restoration period and of his own predilections.

The *Historisch-Politische Zeitschrift* was founded under the initiative of Count von Bernstorff, the then foreign minister. In founding
it, von Bernstorff had had two purposes in mind. He wished to
provide an organ for the defense of the policies of an enlightened
Prussian bureaucracy against its numerous liberal critics on the left.
But he also wished to distinguish the positions of the Prussian government from that of the reactionary right. In the fall of 1831 this
latter group, which included distinguished men such as Radowitz,
von Raumer, and the Gerlachs, had founded the *Berliner Politisches
Wochenblatt* (Berlin Political Weekly) to propagate the feudal doctrines of the late Karl Ludwig von Haller.[27] The men associated with
this weekly publication considered enlightened despotism a forerunner of liberalism. They distrusted the Prussian bureaucracy. Their
ideal of government was a pre-absolutistic Mecklenburg type of constitution in which political power was preserved or restored to the
aristocratic and noble classes within society. Von Bernstorff and the
men he consulted in this enterprise, particularly Savigny and Johann
Albrecht Eichhorn,[28] von Bernstorff's principal adviser, as well as
the Hamburg publisher Perthes, represented a more enlightened position. They recognized the rising role of the middle classes and the
need for Prussia to assume active leadership in satisfying the national
and economic demands of this class. At the same time, von Bernstorff and his friends wished to do this within the framework of the

existing political structure of Prussia and Germany through the agency of a benevolent and relatively progressive Prussian bureaucracy and with a minimum of concessions to political liberalism. These men, accustomed to royal absolutism and used to obedience rather than to deliberation, probably underestimated the force of liberal and national feeling, as well as the entrenched opposition of the vested interests of the old regime.

Ranke's own political inclinations fitted well into this program. He had been relatively unaffected by the nationalist enthusiasm of the Wars of Liberation. His deep Lutheran piety was not narrow in a confessional sense. Nevertheless, it strengthened his respect for the established wordly authorities, the *Obrigkeit,* as part of God's design. He was not yet as doctrinaire in his conservative views as he would become in later years. Although he had been a close friend of Savigny, Niebuhr, and Schleiermacher since his arrival at the University of Berlin in 1825, he had been much closer to the liberal circle around Varnhagen von Ense during the first three years of his stay in Berlin than he liked to admit later.[29] Having been granted the complete freedom of expression in the review which he had requested, including the privilege not to have to submit the journal to censorship, Ranke conceived his task as one of keeping equal distance between the extremes of the *Berliner Politisches Wochenblatt* and of liberalism. Later, he commented on this episode: "I had been so bold as to undertake to defend a third orientation midway between the points of view that confronted each other in every public and private discussion. This new orientation, which adhered to a *status quo* which rests on the past, aimed at opening up a future in which one would be able to do justice to new ideas, too, as long as they contained truth."[30] Whether Ranke made his distance from the reactionaries clear is doubtful. In the *Historisch-Politische Zeitschrift,* his criticisms almost entirely were directed at the liberals. Ranke seems to have disappointed Perthes, who withdrew his sponsorship from the journal after the appearance of the first volume in 1832.[31] Instead, Ranke found himself encouraged by the very conservative Ancillon who succeeded von Bernstorff as foreign minister during that year.[32]

Thus almost all that appeared in the *Historisch-Politische Zeitschrift* related to the critique of liberalism and of its theoretical foundations. But Ranke did not content himself with stressing the need of an historical approach for an understanding of the empirical functioning of political forces. Rather, in his contributions to the review, as well as in lectures on the methods and scope of historical study written at this time, he stresses the role of history as a guide to philosophical truth. Through history he seeks to uncover the metaphysical realities underlying the state which could provide the basis of a conservative theory of politics.

Three notions recur throughout his essays and lectures of the period and give them a high degree of unity. The first is the argument against the application of abstract principles to politics, and the identification of "theory" with liberalism and the ideas of the French Revolution. The second is the idea that, although all existence can be understood only in terms of its history, behind the ephemeral appearance of every particular phenomenon there is concealed a general truth. A final idea is that the states existing in history are the concrete expressions of underlying ideas.

1. Ranke's warning in the Introduction to the *Historisch-Politische Zeitschrift* that political and social institutions must not be approached from the standpoint of abstract theory, but be viewed in terms of their concrete existence, is understandable on methodological grounds as an almost indisputable maxim of historical study. So is his demand that political and social values must be understood within the context of the institutions within which they operate. "It is so seldom," he observes, "that an undertaking or an institution is examined in terms of the conditions proper to it, usually one is satisfied with applying the measuring stick of theory."[33] The historian as historian must suspend judgment. "A pure judgment is possible only if one judges any person in terms of that person's own standpoint and of his inherent aims."[34] But it is harder to follow Ranke when he, like Herder, Humboldt, and Savigny before him, holds that the principles and ideals that have guided societies or individuals possess objective value. Ranke does not regard them as value-free historical data which have no ethical significance for the scholar. For him all products of history and everything that operates within the context of a historical society are concrete, objective values. Such a position involves an extreme optimism regarding history and nature which Ranke shared with other adherents of the Historical School and with many thinkers in the Romantic tradition. It assumes that there is no real evil in nature. But in stressing that all historical phenomena possesses objective value it contains the seeds

of a radical ethical relativism.

Once we assume, as Ranke did, that all institutions or ideas that have roots in history are valuable, a basis for judging political decisions is established. Not that the historian can measure political decisions by abstract, universal ethical standards, but he can unearth the extent to which such acts followed the historical lines of development of a state. "True politics," Ranke observes, "constantly keeps in mind what constitutes practical interests, what is necessary, and what can be carried out." Such politics does "not surrender its part at any moment for the sake of possibly deceptive prospects. Rather such politics aims at tranquil progress *(Fortgang)* and gradual but certain development."[35] This type of true politics proceeds on the basis of positively existing and dominant trends. It eschews innovation and planned reform. For nothing is more urgent for our time "than to remind ourselves of the difference between regular *(gesetzmässig)* progress and impatient, disruptive innovation, between intelligent preservation (of existing institutions) and the onesided defense of antiquated forms which have become lifeless."

Even if Ranke knew that statesmen could not be guided by ethical doctrine in following the practical and necessary interests of the state, he was nevertheless sublimely confident that the statesman's pursuit of such historic necessities would not conflict with the "immutable, eternal principles." For "men of insight knew at all periods of history what was good and great, what was permitted and right, what constituted progress and what decay. In its broad outlines it is inscribed within the human breast. Simple reflection suffices for us to understand it."[36]

It is an obvious conclusion from this concept of historical growth that liberal institutions, developed abroad, were not applicable in Germany. For, as Ranke observes: ". . . every people has its own politics."[37] The task of Germans is to create a genuinely German state which corresponds to the spirit of the nation.[38] France had shown the ill effects of drafting foreign, British, and especially North American political ideas onto her traditional institutions.[39] The danger of the French Revolution had lain less in the strength of French arms than in the spread of "doctrines of seemingly universal validity."[40] Behind the diversity of states and national character, Ranke sees a divine purpose: through the diverse nations, God gave expression to the "idea of mankind." The idea of the state finds its expression in the various states. If there were only one possible and right form of the state, then the only meaningful form of government would be a universal monarchy. However, this is not the case. The task of every great people, "the condition of its existence (was) to provide the human spirit with a new form of expression, to articulate this expression in its own new forms and to reveal it anew. This is the task God has given it." Everything great in Germany since the French Enlightenment, had been achieved not in imitation, but in opposition to French forms and ideas.[41]

This position is not very different from Humboldt's. Even certain political demands made by Ranke for his immediate time were similar. With Humboldt he saw the danger of creating a unitary German state wherein provinces and states would lose their individual character.[42] Closer bonds needed to be drawn, particularly in regard to defense and commercial relations and notably the control of the press, without creating a uniformity of institutions. For Germany existed in diversity. "Who will ever be able to define in concepts or put into words what is German?"[43] "It is as if they wished to depict the genus but destroy the species. The genus appears only in the species. It possesses no other way of manifesting itself." To destroy the differences would be to kill the living reality.[44] Ranke differs from Humboldt in his far less critical identification of the then existing German governments with the historical trends. Hence his portrayal of Germany as forming "one family" with its legitimate princes.[45] Unlike either Haller on the right or liberals such as Stein or Humboldt, Ranke does not question the centralizing reforms of the eighteenth-century enlightened despots in Germany. He accepts unconditionally the bureaucratic structure of Prussia, and observes that the military power upon which Prussia's prestige rests "requires that its needs be met without any reductions or interruptions; it requires unity and strict subordination."[46] He opposes a constitution for Prussia, and argues against a Prussian Parliament representing the estates *(Ständeversammlung)*[47] for which Stein and Humboldt had called.

Completely missing from his essays is the demand for greater local self-administration, characteristic of liberal and even conservative political programs of the time. Ranke nowhere acknowledges the rights of individuals against the state which Humboldt and Haller had defended from opposing political positions. Absent in his concept of Prussia is both the conservative view of "liberties" *(Libertäten)* and the liberal idea of the integrity of the individual. Although Ranke recognizes that the Carlsbad Decrees, adopted by the German states in 1819 to suppress "demagogic" agitation, following the murder of Kotzebue, were emergency measures too stringent to be maintained as permanent legislation, he nevertheless justifies press censorship. Certainly, he admits scholars must have full freedom to investigate truth, but the communication of scientific truth must be distinguished from that of political opinions. The political press, when left uncontrolled, has circulated not only "doctrines and ideas," but has stirred up passions and represented diverse interests "so that immediately strong opposition is organized against the supreme authority, creating a conflict of parties. It is questionable, he continues, whether this situation which points at a pluralistic society is in accord with the "general welfare." The defenders of freedom of the press "would have to prove that such a condition is at all desirable for the lives of nations; that it is also useful and beneficial to young states still in the process of formation."[48]

These diverging concepts regarding the structure of the Prussian state, held by men like Haller, Ranke, or Wilhelm von Humboldt, point at a basic dilemma inherent in the historicist orientation. It had been a fundamental assumption of the Historical School that political and other values could be clearly and indisputably recognized within the historical context in which they operated. The ethics to be followed by the Prussian state was determined by Prussia's nature and history as a state. This implied, of course, that every state or nation was an organic body with one tradition. If this tradition could be identified, then one could separate the extraneous elements from the state. But what happened if within the same social group there were several, diverging traditions? The naive assumption that the dominant political forces were the sole ones with roots in history, and hence the only ones that could claim to be legitimate, proved to be much more problematic than Ranke realized. No significant thinker held this position unconditionally. Ranke drew the distinction between legitimate and illegitimate rulers common to conservative thought. In recognizing the reality of change, he admitted that there were elements in existing states which were antiquated and lifeless.[49] Moreover, one government might combine two conflicting forces. In Ranke's opinion, this had been the case in the *Charte* of the French

Restoration which had wedded the two irreconcilable principles of monarchy and constitutional government.[50]

What Ranke did not recognize was that the historian could trace the historical background of the values and institutions of a society and that he could describe the conflicting forces in a society at a given moment; however, when he identified certain forces as those which alone represented the historical direction of the nation, he was making an arbitrary choice. Even if he could exclude revolutionary attempts to remodel society as inorganic and unhistorical, he would still be confronting a pluralism of traditions and of interests. The pious distinction made by the writers in the tradition of the Historical School since Burke, between deliberate attempts at directing social change and natural, organic growth, is a doubtful one. In the face of the conflicting interests, traditions, and values which exist in any society, the statesman is forced to guide the state consciously in a definite direction. He can not merely follow the direction of history, as Ranke had hopefully assumed, but must decide whether to champion the maintenance of Prussian state power, the restoration or preservation of feudal privileges, or the extension of representative institutions.

2. As we have already observed, Ranke's empiricism has often been misunderstood, and not only in the United States. Empiricism refers to a methodological position, as well as to a philosophical concept of reality. The empiricist insists that knowledge can be gained only through sense data and through inductions resulting from these data. Empiricism generally implies a philosophically nominalist position. For the most part, empiricists hold that phenomena alone are real or that knowledge cannot go beyond phenomena. In the philosophic sense, Ranke was no empiricist. His position was much closer to philosophic realism.[51] Just as he saw a deeper reality behind historical phenomena, so he saw in phenomena merely the concrete expressions of metaphysical forces. In the methodological sense, Ranke was an empiricist only to a limited degree. Despite his insistence upon the objective, critical observation of the particular event as the beginning of all historical study, Ranke never found in such data the only means of obtaining knowledge. Rather, the intuitive understanding of these data was to open up the possibility of attaining glimpses of the reality underlying the ephemeral appearance of

the world of senses. Ranke's desires for objectivity must be therefore understood not merely as a call for the exclusion of one's own subjective desires and prejudices from historical cognition. Ranke agreed with the empiricists that the object of the historian's research must be to establish what had actually been *(wie es eigentlich gewesen)*, but for him this historical reality was not exhausted by historical events. Rather, Ranke assumed that there was an objective order behind these events. "The historian is merely the organ of the general spirit which speaks through him and takes on real form *(sich selber vergegenwärtigt)*."[52] His impartiality *(Unpartheilichkeit)* consisted less in not approaching the great "struggles of might and ideas" without an opinion of his own, but "only in this, that he recognizes the positions occupied by the active forces (in history) and does justice to the relationships peculiar to each. He sees these (forces) appear in their particular selves, confront each other and struggle. In such conflicts the events and fates that dominate the world are carried out."[53] In fact, Ranke is not very far removed from Hegel.[54] What distinguishes the two men sharply is Ranke's insistence that knowledge of the objective order can be gained only through thorough study of the individual event, which must never be approached with abstract concepts, and his conviction that the plan of the universe is beyond man's grasp, that man can only intuitively suspect *(ahnden)* its outlines. "For although every spirit *(geistiges Wesen)* stands in relationship to God, the human spirit is not identical with God." As Ranke quotes St. Augustine: "The Human spirit gives witness of the Light but is not the Light. The true Light is the Word, which is God and has created all."[55]

In the lectures which he delivered in 1831 on the "idea of Universal History," Ranke developed his thoughts regarding the methods and intent of historiography. History as a science shares with philosophy the task to grasp "the core of Existence"; it resembles art in its manner of "reproducing life that has vanished." It differs from art in referring to a "real" rather than an "ideal," to a subject matter which requires an empirical approach. Historical thinking requires elements of both philosophical and artistic thought directed toward a "real" subject matter.[56]

The most significant difference between philosophy and history is in approach. The philosopher approaches reality from the perspective of general concepts. He attempts to subsume all of life under a "unifying concept" *(Einheitsbegriff),* to schematize life and history. The historian proceeds from the "condition of existence" *(Bedingung der Existenz).*[57] For the philosopher the individual matters only as a part of the whole; for the historian the individual is of interest. Both sciences have disputed the sole truth of their approach. The historians have questioned the possibility of nonhistorical truth. They have considered philosophical cognition to be timebound.

> (History) does not want to recognize philosophy as something Absolute *(Unbedingt)* but only as an appearance in time. History assumes that the history of philosophy is the most exact form of philosophy; that absolute truth cognizable by mankind is found in the theories which appear in various ages, no matter how contradictory these theories may be. History goes one step further and assumes that philosophy, especially when it attempts to define doctrines is merely the expression in linguistic form of national cognition *(nazionalen Erkenntnis).* The historian denies that philosophy has any absolute validity.[58]

Ranke is quite aware of the radically relativistic possibilities inherent here in the historical approach. But he does not draw radically relativistic conclusions. As he writes: "When the philosopher regards history from the perspective of his field, he looks for the infinite only in progress, development and totality. The historian, on the other hand, finds an infinity in every existence, an eternal element coming from God in every being, and this eternal element is its principle of life. For this reason," Ranke notes, "the historian inclines to turn to the individual. He makes the particular interest count. He recognizes the beneficent and enduring. He opposes disintegrating change. He acknowledges a portion of truth even in error."

But can we be convinced that existence really has a divine basis? "It is not necessary to prove elaborately the presence of an eternal element within the individual," Ranke replies. For our endeavors rest on this religious foundation. We believe that nothing can exist without God or live without Him. Although we have emancipated ourselves from certain narrow theological notions, we nevertheless acknowledge that all our efforts derive from a higher, a religious source."[59] But Ranke never asks himself what remains, once the religious foundations in which he believes so fervently have been destroyed by doubt?

From this belief in the metaphysical foundations of historical reality, Ranke draws several methodological demands. The first is the "pure love of truth." Because we acknowledge "a higher reality" in the event, the situation, or the person that we wish to understand, we must have respect for what actually happened. But this does not mean "that we should stop with the appearances." For "then we would grasp only something external although our own principle directs us to what is within."[60] From this arises the need for a thorough, penetrating study based upon sources, without which we are incapable of historical cognition. For historical understanding is not a mechanical act of which everyone is equally capable. Here the differences between Ranke's epistemology and that of empiricism becomes very clear. For the "essence" *(Wesen)* and "content" *(Inhalt)* of the appearances which the historian studies are spiritual unities *(geistige Einheiten)* which can be grasped only by spiritual apperception *(geistige Apperception)*.[61] But apperception is not an empirical act of description or explanation. Rather, it involves a degree of genius present to an extent in everyone, but in very unequal degree.[62] There follow the remaining demands for a universal interest on the part of the historian, a concern with establishing causal relationships, impartiality, and the search of the total context. Ranke regards it as "certain" that behind the outward appearance of the historical events, persons, and institutions studied, there is always a totality *(Totalität, Totales),* an integrated, spiritual reality.

> The whole *(Totale)* is as certain as is its every outward expression at every moment. We must dedicate our full attention to it. . . . (If we are studying) a people, we are not interested in all the individual details through which it expresses itself as a living thing. Rather its idea speaks to us through its development as a whole, its deeds, its institutions, its literature.[63]

The task of understanding must always begin with thorough immersion in the subject matter, "exact research, step by step apprehension, and study of the documents." Having been immersed in the subject matter, we may then approach the spiritual essence through an act of intuition *(Divination).* Certainly, man knows too little to be able to unfathom the meaning of world history.

"I consider it impossible to solve the problem completely," Ranke observes. "Only God knows world history. We only perceive its contradictions. As an Indian poet put it, its 'harmony is known only to the gods but unknown to man'. We can only approach it intuitively and from a distance. Nevertheless we can perceive unity, continuity *(Fortgang)* and development."[64] "Thus," Ranke concludes, "our paths as historians lead us to the problems of philosophy. If philosophy were what it should be and history were perfectly clear and complete, the two disciplines would be in complete agreement."[65]

3. On the basis of this concept of history, Ranke is able to construct a metaphysics of politics. This view of history is striking in its radical optimism. Although Ranke rejects the Hegelian notion that historical development can be explained in rational terms, he is no less confident that history is a meaningful process. In one sense, his optimism goes considerably further than that of Hegel. For Hegel sees in all history, past and present, the signs of man's irrationality and imperfection which has not yet been overcome. For Ranke, however, "every epoch is immediate to God."[66] This optimism expresses itself in several ways. History for Ranke is meaningful. Despite his recognition that man at any time could only see small perspectives of the total reality, Ranke was never bothered by the doubts of objective knowledge which troubled later historians. Admittedly, on the basis of religious faith, he assumes that there were meaningful units *(geistige Einheiten)* in history, something which did not follow from empirical inquiry. He further assumes that these meaningful units, individuals, institutions, states, and nations, are not merely ethically neutral, but as expressions of the will of God represent positive values. From this he draws the conclusion that states are such meaningful units, ends in themselves, and that in following their vital interests, they can only do good.

The belief held by Ranke that there is an ethical order in the universe which applies to the political realm, too, coincides with the faith of most of the Judaeo-Christian tradition. But what is almost entirely missing in Ranke, despite his pronounced Christianity, and for that matter is absent in most Romantic thought, is the recognition of an element of evil in man and in human institutions.[67] The biblical prophets, as well as Stoic, Christian, and Enlightenment natural law thinkers, have always seen a dualism between the ethical law and the positive reality. This conflict requires the active intervention of ethical man in order to bring human institutions in harmony with the demands of justice, even if the limitations of human nature permits only an approximation of this ideal. For Ranke there is operative within the political world an automatic harmony which restores the rightful order if it has been disturbed. Thus, in the famous essay, "The Great Powers," he describes a balance of power among the great states as a central instrument in the European order, incapable of destruction by the urges of hegemony of any great power. "It is true that the commotions in the world now and again destroy this system of law and order," as French ambitions had done. "But after they have subsided, this system is reconstituted, and all efforts aim at making it perfect once more."[68] The struggle of the powers is not merely a meaningless clash of power.

> World history does not present such a chaotic tumult, warring, and planless succession of states and peoples as appears at first sight. Nor does history deal only with the often dubious advancement of civilization. There are forces and indeed spiritual, life-giving, creative forces, nay life itself and there are moral energies, whose development we see. They cannot be defined or put in abstract terms, but one can behold them and observe them. One can develop a sympathy for their existence. They unfold, capture the world, appear in manifold expressions, dispute with and check and overpower one another. In their interaction and succession, in their life, in their decline or rejuvenation, which then encompasses an ever greater fullness, higher importance and wider extent, lies the secret of world history.[69]

This leads Ranke to the concept of the spiritual character of power, a theme recurring throughout his writings, but most systematically developed in the "Political Dialogue" in the *Historisch-Politische Zeitschrift*. The state must not be conceived as the state in the abstract, but as the concretely existing, specific state in its historical development. The state is not merely an empirical concentration of power; it possesses a "positive spiritual content," an idea which cannot be expressed in general, abstract terms because it relates specifically to the particular state. This "idea that inspires and dominates the whole"[70] shapes the state into an organic unit, completely different from all other states. "There is an element which makes a state not a subdivision of general categories, but a living thing, an individual, a unique self."[71] This uniqueness, of course, prevents the successful transplantation of alien institutions or ideas. The state is real in its concrete particular existence; at the same time, it contains in its fundamental idea an element which is general, which transcends the transitory reality of the concrete state, but which can express itself only in the concrete state. The state, in Ranke's terms, is thus "real-and-spiritual" *(real-geistig)* in its "unimagined uniqueness."[72] Thus every independent state has special tendencies of its own, determined by the idea derived from God. In the states themselves, Ranke writes, "instead of the passing conglomerations which the contractual theory of the state creates like cloud formations, I perceive spiritual substances, original creations of the human mind—I might say, thoughts of God."[73]

Two important implications follow from the above: the spiritualization of power and struggle, and the subordination of the interests of the individual to the state. The activities of the state are determined by its idea, according to Ranke. This idea finds itself in conflict and ultimately involves the clash of military power. The state originated through struggle; its existence and development are inextricably connected with struggle. "The world, as we know, has been parceled out. To be somebody, you have to rise by your own efforts. You must achieve genuine independence. Your rights will not be voluntarily ceded to you. You must fight for them." But is it not brute force alone that matters then, Karl asks Friedrich in the *Political Dialogue.* No, Friedrich replies. The foundations of the European community are there and remain, although this community requires "moral energy" to attain "universal significance." As confident as Hegel in the victory of good through the struggle of arms in the course of history, Ranke has Friedrich observe: "But seriously, you will be able to name few significant wars for which it could not be proved that genuine moral energy achieved the final victory."[74] In one important sense, Ranke's state is limited in its ambition: his recognition of a European community and of the role of all the great powers to maintain this community and contribute to the fullness and variety of the European family.

Thus, for Ranke, a state can only develop fully to the extent that it is independent of other states. Considerations of foreign policy and military strength are primary to the state. Its "supreme law" must be to subordinate its internal life to these needs.[75] Opinions in regard to the internal structure of the state must fall behind considerations of foreign policy. Differences of domestic politics must be transcended in public discussion, as they were before the French Revolution, and "politics again relegated to the field of power and foreign affairs where it belongs."[76]

The individual is thus clearly subordinated to the needs of the state. States as ideas of God are ends in themselves. "It would be ridiculous to explain them as so many institutions for the safeguarding of interests of individuals who may have banded together for the protection of their private property."[77] Individuals have their existence only in the state. In the good *(rechten)* state "purely private life" does not exist for the individual citizen. "Our activities belong primarily to our community."[78]

Liberty in the sense in which liberals or democrats have traditionally understood the term therefore needs redefinition for Ranke. For Friedrich, in the *Political Dialogue,* man is wholly a "political creature" whose personality is formed and develops in relation to the community. The state is a "spiritual unity" whose fundamental idea "permeates every individual, so that he feels in himself some of its spiritual force, that he considers himself a member of the whole with love for it, and that the feeling of belonging to the community is stronger than the feeling of provincial, local, or individual isolation."[79] In this sense, the state resembles a family, and "what belongs together by nature does not need a social contract. Among parents and children, among brothers and members of the same family, no compact is needed."[80] Hence there is also no need for written guarantees of individual rights. In every healthy state liberty is identical with obedience. "Compulsion will be transformed on a higher level into voluntary individual initiative. Duty will become liberty." Once this is attained, the state can achieve what must always be the supreme aim of its domestic policy: social cohesion on the basis of the voluntary cooperation of its citizens.[81]

In its organization the good state was understood by Ranke as a monarchy in which "the right man is placed in the right place."[82] To demand participation of the governed in the affairs of government, or to consider the governing class as a group alien to those they rule, is to misunderstand the role of the division of labor in a society. The rulers represent a "selection of the most skillful in the whole nation, who have cultivated their ability for this task."[83]

Underlying Ranke's monarchical conviction is the optimistic idea that, left to herself, "nature, which is always complete, guarantees that these (capable men) are always there. All that matters is to find them."[84] Considering "the human inclination to abuse power," Karl asks whether the power of the government should not be limited. To Friedrich, who admits that this form of government can degenerate in a thousand ways, this seems unnecessary. The state will not only abstain from regulating those spheres of life in which "nothing is more desired than spontaneity of expression," but it seems obvious to Friedrich that this type of government is "founded in the nature of things, required by the idea of our monarchies."[85]

One cannot help sensing a very deep contradiction in Ranke's argumentation in the *Political Dialogue*. On the one hand, Ranke's purpose is to describe not the "best state," but "merely to understand the one before our eyes."[86] On the other hand, he is constantly seeking the good state, the natural state. If all the existing states are of divine origin, should not, as Carl asks, "all states be equally perfect?" In other words, should not the North American Republic, the French July Monarchy, as the product of historical forces, be of equal value with the Prussian Monarchy. If Ranke were consistent in his demand that the historian or political thinker should find the state in history rather than apply abstract criteria to it, he should have had Friedrich reply to Carl in the affirmative. Instead, he now distinguishes between the "idea" of the state "to which we ascribe divine origin" and "its realization, its concrete form in the world."[87] Thus there are healthy and sick states. By the former type, which he compares to a body "in possession of all its powers and all its limbs," he obviously does not mean the libertarian state that limits the sphere of political power.

Indeed, Ranke's study of the state seems to have little to do with the concretely existing historical states. He tends not to study states in terms of their functions, the operation of power within them, or the conflict of interests. As Professor Theodore H. Von Laue observes, for Ranke practical politics involves the training of civil servants and the experts of government.[88] Political theory deals with "the state," but the state is an abstract, standing separate and above the actual activities of real governments. Conceived as a metaphysical reality, it could be used to demand the supremacy of the monarchy over the individual. Narrowly conceived in political and military terms, divorced from the total pattern of social, economic, and intellectual forces, Ranke's concept of the state seems to apply to the absolute monarchies of the sixteenth, seventeenth, and eighteenth centuries much more closely than to states in general.

Certainly, Ranke is justified in rejecting the metaphysics of individual rights. But in its place, he substitutes a metaphysics of state rights. Despite his emphasis upon the individual character of states as the products of history, in practice all of his states are surprisingly alike. As Ernst Schulin points out, in a recent study on the place of the Orient in Hegel's and Ranke's concept of world history, Ranke seems far less capable of describing the individual characteristics of a people than Hegel.[89] In practice, all Ranke's states are guided by the abstract demands of a *raison d'etat* relatively uneffected by internal developments. In this close identification of the state with foreign policy, Ranke's concept of the state appears more abstract and rigid than those of Savigny or Wilhelm von Humboldt. Viewing political power in this manner, Ranke also has little understanding for the new forces that operated in European society since the French Revolution.

After 1836, Ranke wrote little relating to historical or political theory, except for random remarks scattered throughout his writings. Two notable exceptions remain: the lecture to King Maximilian in 1854 wherein he rejected the existence of linear, moral progress and spoke of the immediacy of all epochs before God, and the "Political Memoranda"[90] in which he counseled King Friedrich Wilhelm IV of Prussia on revolutionary events between 1848 and 1851. These memorandums show little change in Ranke's political views,[91] although he now considered a constitution to be inevitable. Afraid of the danger of social upheaval, which he saw hidden behind universal suffrage that had been granted in 1848, he urged the introduction of a limited suffrage and the maintenance of ultimate political control in royal hands. The Prussian Army alone had prevented the revolution from succeeding. King and Army for him were the only stable forces in Germany. "Only when destructive parliamentary majorities will have won control of the army will the revolution have finally triumphed in Germany. Only then will a constituent assembly exercise the same rights as the French Assembly did it in 1789."[92] Behind ministerial responsibility, there lurked the threat of rule by "artisans and day laborers."[93] Afraid of the spread of French ideas, he still saw the need for a common German press law.[94] He was unwilling to support the extension of political rights; nevertheless, he recognized the social obligations of the state. Not from humanitarian or moral considerations, but from the standpoint of the military needs of the Prussian state that needed workers to serve in its army, Ranke advocated the right to work.

> It is conceivable that the state might employ in peace time under military discipline at least those workers fit for military service. Just as once the military was transformed from an inchoate mass of volunteers into a disciplined army, the activities of unskilled laborers now need to be organized. One can form labor brigades for those public works that still need to be undertaken, such as building projects, flood control, soil reclamation, etc. On the other hand, only limited political rights can be granted to the non-political classes.[95]

Ranke followed Bismarck's policies with little enthusiasm. Even after 1849, he still hoped for a strengthened *Bund* under joint Prussian and Austrian leadership which would permit political diversity, and not threaten the traditional pluralism that he considered so important to the cultural development of German nationality. Bismarck's concession to the liberals disturbed him even more deeply, although he never opposed it openly. When he hailed Bismarck after his break with the National Liberals in 1879, it was not because he saw in him the founder of the German Empire, but rather the man who defended Europe from social revolution.[96]

Despite the lack of theoretical formulations after 1836, Ranke's prolific historical writings nevertheless reflect the ideas presented in the essays of the period from 1831 to 1836. Although he closely relied upon the documents, his histories are not highly specialized monographs. He seeks to trace dominant trends that he, however, generally defines in narrowly political terms. Using official sources, Ranke tends to judge events from the standpoint of governments. Thus, as Eduard Fueter has pointed out, in the discussion of the English Revolutions in the seventeenth century, he appears to ignore the great economic transformations without which the events of the time cannot be understood, because these changes were not recorded in diplomatic papers.[97]

Rudolf Vierhaus has disputed this view. In a recent study, Vierhaus has sought to defend Ranke against the frequent accusations that he neglected the role of the social and economic forces in history and had no understanding for the great emerging social forces of the nineteenth century.[98] Ranke, Vierhaus argues, had no narrow political concept of society for which only the cultured elite composing the *Obrigkeit* were significant. "Any reading of his works leaves . . . the impression that Ranke did not ignore *(wegretouchiert)* the masses but took them seriously as an important factor of historical movement." Ranke "wrote no line without being conscious that historical life is not only determined by the thoughts and deeds of the few great men but just as much by the interests, needs, abilities, fears and desires of the many."[99] Vierhaus rightly points out that Ranke was not entirely blind to social and class conflict. Nevertheless, Vierhaus's documentation does not really change the traditional image of Ranke. Indeed, in the 1830's, in his diary Ranke himself suggested that a world history be written which would emphasize the growth of population and stress economic and cultural activities; colonization, knightdom, the building of churches, art, and religion in the Middle Ages; agriculture and public works in the eighteenth century and the "tremendous development of industry and highways" in the nineteenth century. However, this was an isolated remark.[100]

As Hans Schleier notes, the attempts to recount the instances of Ranke's preoccupation with economic and social questions only underline how marginal these problems were to Ranke's historiography, and how little he understood the social forces of the nineteenth century.[101] Vierhaus himself admits how poorly informed Ranke was about the economic conditions of the working class and how little understanding he had for the social questions of his time.[102] Ranke, analagous to many of his contemporaries, saw the vision of an amorphous mass threatening all culture and civilization, and he failed to appreciate the significance of industry. He saw many social changes, of which the rise of the "third estate" was the most important to take place. The central social problem for Ranke was, Vierhaus admits, a political one, that of fitting the bourgeoisie into the framework of the old state, at the same time excluding the masses who lacked all prerequisites for political responsibility.[103] Ranke's concept of the state remained a static one. The continental monarchical great power, as it had arisen in the struggle between princes and estates and the religious civil wars between the sixteenth and the eighteenth centuries, remained for him the model by which the states that existed in history were to be judged.[104] This concept of the state reflected Ranke's attachment to legitimacy, his religiosity, and the impact of the political thought of German Idealism on his thinking. But this viewpoint of the state remained inadequate for an understanding of the preabsolutistic state or of the political forces that emerged in the nineteenth century.

It is to his credit that in an age of rising nationalistic sentiment in historiography, Ranke did not sacrifice his belief in a European community. For him, state and nation were never identical, although he recognized the tendency of nations to form states and realized the strength which nineteenth-century states had gained from the rise of national feeling. Ranke studied all major states, which he described as the Germano-Romanic world, in terms of their interaction within this broader European context.

Paradoxically, Ranke's fame in Germany grew at a time—the period after the 1848 Revolution—when to most historians he belonged to a past age. Despite his political convictions, or perhaps because of them, his historiography remained relatively aloof from the issues of the day. Heinrich von Sybel criticized his lack of moral involvement,[105] and Heinrich von Treitschke noted his aristocratic disdain for the masses who seemed not to exist in his histories which centered around courts and chanceries.[106] Nevertheless, in at least three important ways, Ranke seemed bound to this time and left an impact upon his contemporaries. This was true, first of all, in his critical use of documents, which for the most part tended to be diplomatic ones. Second, the new generation of nationalistic historians, including Sybel and Treitschke, were to follow him in their emphasis of the central role of the state and especially of foreign affairs in history. Thus, despite their criticisms of Ranke, the new historians absorbed much of his concept which saw the struggle of the great powers at the center of history. Even if the state for the newer generation of National Liberals embodied popular and national forces, essentially it still conceived state power in the bureaucratic and military tradition of eighteenth-century Prussia. Finally,

Ranke, like Hegel, viewed the state as an ethical good. This spiritual-ization of power helped to pave the way for the advocacy by historians of a *Realpolitik* which Ranke himself would have followed only with reservations. The decades after 1890 witnessed what has been called a Ranke Renaissance, an attempt to expand to the world scene the Rankean concept of the interplay and balance of the great powers. Less successful was the endeavor to free historiography of its political commitments, and return to the supposed objectivity and *Überparteilichkeit* of Ranke's historiography. This aspect we shall discuss later in this book.[107]

The High Point of Historical
Optimism—the "Prussian School"

1.

RANKE taught at the University of Berlin until 1871. He died in 1886 at the ripe age of ninety-one. Only slowly in the course of the century did his fame undisputably establish him as the great German historian of the age. But while his disciples respectfully acknowledged his important contributions to critical method, they increasingly regarded him as a monument, albeit a living one, who belonged to a bygone age. Ranke's political ideals remained those of a moderate conservative of the Restoration period. In the main he accepted the better aspects of the prerevolutionary political structure: the enlightened bureaucratic state, and the European political community dominated by the balance of interests among the five great legitimate monarchies. He was not fully unaware of the stirrings of national sentiment as a result of the revolutionary and Napoleonic wars. Ranke regarded them as elements that strengthened the traditional order by emotionally committing the populations to their dynasties rather than as the beginning of a new force requiring thorough going changes in the domestic and international affairs of the European nations. For him the task of the historian was to contemplate the play of historic forces, although perhaps not as dispassionately as his critics have claimed, and to leave the responsibilities of governing to the statesmen. They could find wisdom and guidance in the impartial picture of historical change uncovered by the historian.[1]

But Ranke unquestionably underestimated the social and economic transformation of the times and misunderstood the demonic character of nationalism. For two generations of historians, who were deeply involved in the struggle for liberalization and national unification, Ranke's ideal of historical objectivity seemed to express a regrettable degree of moral indifference.[2] Increasingly committed to the careful application of critical methods to the analysis of sources, these younger writers nevertheless regarded the study of the past not as an end in itself, but as a means to achieve the political and ethical requirements of the moment—the liberal national state. Almost all of the important German historians were politically active. In the period before 1848, Karl Rotteck and Karl Welcker were parliamentarians; F. C. Dahlmann and Georg Gervinus were among the Göttingen Seven who were expelled from the University of Göttingen in 1837, after they protested King Ernst August's suspension of the Hanover Constitution. Friedrich Christoph Dahlmann, Gustav Droysen, Karl Welcker, Georg Waitz, Georg Gervinus, Max Duncker, and Rudolf Haym were members of the Frankfurt Parliament during the 1848 Revolution. Ludwig Häusser was a member of the Baden legislature and Theodor Mommsen was the editor of a political newspaper in Schleswig-Holstein.[3]

When, in 1857, the transfer of the conduct of government from the mentally ill King Frederick William IV of Prussia to his brother, Prince William, marked the end of the postrevolutionary period of Reaction, some of these men founded the *Preussische Jahrbücher (Prussian Annals)* to demand the unification of Germany under the leadership of a reformed, constitutional Prussia. In this they were supported in contributions to the journal by younger historians such as Heinrich Sybel, Heinrich Treitschke, Hermann Baumgarten, and the philosopher Wilhelm Dilthey.[4] Never before had German historians played such an active part in the course of German events as in the decisive years between 1830 and 1871 which saw the struggle for national unification. The history of Germany and that of German liberalism cannot be written without devoting considerable space to the central role played by the historians.

However, the unification of Germany was achieved at the expense of important liberal principles, particularly those of parliamentary control of foreign and military affairs and of ministerial responsibility. In the new *Reich* a generous degree of autocracy was combined with constitutional forms that granted very limited controls to a parliament of which only one chamber was elected by popular vote. Students of German history have seen in the compromises of German liberals with the national principle and Prussian power the core of the "tragedy of German liberalism"[5] and the German failure to develop responsible constitutional government. In 1848, German moderate liberals, even democrats, had been willing to rely upon Prussian arms in order to wrest the predominantly German duchies of Schleswig-Holstein from Danish rule. They particularly sought to prevent the application of a liberal Danish Constitution to Schleswig, and looked to Prussia to maintain predominantly Polish Posen as part of the German Confederation. Despite their dislike of Prussian reaction, slightly more radical men among the liberals, such as Georg Gervinus and the Southwest German liberal Karl Welcker, saw in the Prussian Army the only effective protection against the much more serious threat of social revolution.[6] The failure of the Revolution of 1848 had disillusioned these liberals on the possibility of achieving unification through the consent of all German states, including Austria. Therefore, they now turned to a "little German solution" to be accomplished with the aid of Prussian military and diplomatic strength. But only a progressive, liberal Prussia, they thought, could accomplish this task. When Bismarck in violation of the Prussian Constitution implemented the army reform in 1862, despite the opposition of the lower chamber, the men around the *Preussische Jahrbücher* protested. By 1866, after the Prussian victories over Denmark and Austria, all, with the sole exception of Gervinus, had made their peace with Bismarck.

What happened in 1848 and between 1862 and 1867? Various explanations have been offered for the failure of German liberalism. It has been suggested that the tragedy of German liberalism rested in the surrender by German liberals, including liberal historians, of their liberal principles to nationalist sentiment and military power. From the standpoint of classical liberalism, as understood in Western countries, such a compromise of principles undoubtedly took place. Historians, still closely attached to German national traditions, have argued against this interpretation, for they believed that there was no alternative to the Bismarckian state. Walter Bussmann points out that in the absence of a liberal state the liberal historians "first had to create the state which they wished to liberate." A third possibility is that the historians neither sacrificed their principles nor bowed to inescapable necessity. Rather, their conception of liberty was already so different from that of Western liberals before 1848 that, when they subordinated libertarian to nationalistic principles in 1848 and later, they acted not in violation but in accordance with their liberal principles. As Leonard Krieger has suggested, their peculiar idea of liberty, founded upon older national assumptions, saw princely authority and state power not as the polar antithesis of political freedom, but as its historic associate.[7]

Despite individual differences, all the aforementioned historians shared relatively similar political beliefs and belonged to that current of political thought identified by German historians as "moderate" or "classical" liberalism.[8] Organized in Frankfurt as the "Casino" (named after the hotel at which they met), they were a loosely grouped party dominated by university professors. Their group provided the leadership of the "little-German" movement and prepared the road to the formation of the National Liberal party in the 1860's. They shared many of the basic political demands of Western liberalism and opposed royal absolutism. They called for a constitution, for the *Rechtsstaat,* a state based upon law. Moreover, they demanded organs of representative government elected by districts rather than representing traditional estates. They advocated equality before the law and favored the abolition of legal inequalities which remained, such as the restrictions upon Jews.[9] Furthermore, they considered freedom of the press and of inquiry a cornerstone of the free state and regarded the rights of the individual person as important. Parenthetically, it is worth noting that neither Dahlmann nor Droysen had favored a written declaration of rights when they were members of the Constitutional Commission of the Frankfurt Parliament. Analagous to liberals in England and France at the middle of the century, they generally opposed universal suffrage and regarded socialism and democracy with a great deal of suspicion, although both Mommsen and Gervinus had some sympathy for the idea of popular sovereignty.[10] As in the case of English and French liberals, they saw in constitutional monarchy the best protection of the rule of law against the despotism of the masses. Unlike their Western colleagues, they were less convinced of the need for parliamentary supremacy in such a monarchy. They shared the political and economic interests of the middle classes.

Probably the professorial liberals, members of the professional middle class of learning, the so-called *Bildungsbürgertum,* tended to champion these demands more wholeheartedly after 1848 than broad segments of the *Besitzbürgertum,* the rising commercial, financial, and industrial middle class, the bourgeoisie of property.[11] For the reaction of 1849 did not bring a return to the old order. The Prussian monarchy not only promulgated a constitution, but on the whole followed liberal economic lines. As the *Preussische Jahrbücher* noted in 1866: "Political economy never found itself in conflict with Bismarck in questions of principle as abstract political or constitutional theory did."[12] To an extent the security offered by the strong monarchy against the rising, although unjustified, fear of unrest among the working class compensated the middle classes for the lack of effective power given to parliament.

What distinguished German "classical liberals" much more sharply from Western classic liberalism than their political programs were their conceptions of the state and of historical development. Unlike Western liberals, they rejected not only the theory of natural law, which had already become problematic for most English and French thinkers, but also the doctrine of the primacy of the individual. In their place, they put the primacy of historical forces. For Western liberal thought, even when it had freed itself from the fiction of the original social contract, the state remained an instrument for the achievement of the welfare of the individual. For a man like J. S. Mill it remained a necessary evil whose functions should be limited to the utmost in order to permit the greatest play of individual forces.

German "moderate liberals" never shared this skepticism in regard to the state. They not only viewed the state as a natural product of historical forces, but considered it a positive good, an ethical value without which culture and morality were impossible. In viewing the state as the product of history, they nevertheless saw history in terms very different from the conservatives of the Historical School. They shared with Western liberals the belief that existing states were still imperfect, but capable of being perfected. In Western ideas of progress, however, the roots of natural law theory were still visible. John Stuart Mill, Edgar Quinet, even Herbert Spencer assumed that there were rational ethical and political norms toward which men could strive deliberately. German "moderate liberals" were much more aware than Savigny or Ranke had been of the demands of the present. They intended to further these demands actively, but they thought that the direction of development of universal truths was determined much less by the rational cognition or by the ethical desires of men than by the tendencies of development inherent in every society.

In this sense, there was a good deal of Hegel as well as of the Historical School in German liberal theory. None of the German liberal historians considered themselves Hegelian, not even Droysen who was, perhaps, most deeply indebted to Hegel. All rejected Hegel's systematic philosophy, his schematization of history. But, more or less consciously, they nevertheless accepted his concept of the ethical character of the state and the meaningful development of history.[13] Thus they were considerably more optimistic basically than the Western theorists of unilinear progress whom they criticized. Western liberal theorists had to assume that there were elements of irrationality in modern political life as well as abuses of power; that might and right were often in conflict. They therefore tended to view political power with caution, seeing in it not the manifestation of a divine plan, but an instrument in the hands of human beings who, unless checked, would be tempted to abuse their power.

Although the German historians accused the Western thinkers of failing to understand the reality of power in political society, Western conceptions of the state, in terms of conflicting individual and group interests, undoubtedly reflected a much more realistic understanding of political power as it actually operated. Indeed, they clearly recognized the demonic character of power. Precisely because so many Western thinkers, under the continuing influence of natural law patterns of thought, tended to distinguish the state as it is from the state as it ought to be, they were able to approach the state much more empirically and dispassionately. In a sense, they often failed to stress sufficiently the interrelation of men in society and the limits which tradition set to political reform. But even this failing was more characteristic of the doctrinaire liberalism of certain eighteenth-century *philosophes* than of the much more pragmatic approach of nineteenth-century English or American movements.

German moderate liberals were in a much more difficult position to formulate a consistent political theory than Western classical liberals, Hegelians, or advocates of historical right. Unlike Savigny, or to a lesser extent Ranke, men such as Droysen and Sybel were unable to accept existing institutions as good, merely because they were the products of history; nor were they able to accept them as the necessary products of historical development. Analagous to Thomas Jefferson or John Stuart Mill, they sought "just" institutions and called upon the historian for strong ethical convictions which would be meaningful, only if there existed the possibility of implementing them. Thus the German political historians, recognizing the force and logic of historical development, sought to reconcile ethics with power and freedom with necessity. They stressed the role of the great individual in social change, the heroic personality of an Alexander the Great or a Napoleon. But they stressed that the genius of these heroes largely consisted of their unusual ability to understand the trend of history and seize the specific opportunities of the moment. They identified the state with power, but saw in power not mere force, rather, it was an instrument to further the ethical aims of the state. These aims might be hidden and their attainment involve the apparent use of evil. But this evil was only what Hegel had called the "cunning of reason *(List der Vernunft)*" by which the spirit inherent in history moved forward to a more perfect and rational state. As Treitschke observed, in describing Napoleon's seizure of power on the 18th of Brumaire 1799: "We know now that the deed of that day was a poorly prepared *coup d'état,* executed without skill or assurance and with an inexcusable amount of brutality and lies. That it nevertheless succeeded is the surest proof for its historic necessity and greatness."[14] Success was therefore its own ethical justification. But this stress upon power was still different in spirit from the positivism of later realists who saw in history a mere struggle for national or racial survival. All the German political historians of this period, including Treitschke, believed that there was a higher purpose to this struggle; that history led to a society wherein man would be freer and happier. However, they were willing to sacrifice the individual to the process.

2.

It is common to distinguish between pre-1848 liberalism in Southwestern Germany and in the North. In the states of the Southwest, which had formed a part of Napoleon's Confederation of the Rhine, French revolutionary ideas had taken firmer roots than in

Prussia. In their reforms Stein, Hardenberg, and Humboldt paid greater lip service to English rather than to Gallic models. In the smaller states, the political influence of the rising middle classes was kept less in check by a landed nobility which formed the backbone of the cadres of the Prussian Army and bureaucracy. In the years after 1815, moreover, the promise of representative institutions, unfulfilled in Prussia, became a reality in Bavaria, Baden, and Württemberg. The liberal movement in these medium-sized constitutional states have been described as Francophile in spirit in their affirmation of natural law. Prussian liberalism, more closely oriented to England, stressed the historic roots of law.

This distinction has been probably given too much importance.[15] Karl von Rotteck, perhaps the only historian of note in the South who was outspokenly favorable in his judgment of the French Revolution during the period of the Moderate as well as the Jacobin Revolution, affirmed the natural law theory. French thought had many sides to it, and Rotteck's colleague at Freiburg, Karl Theodor Welcker, combined his admiration of Montesquieu's recognition of the historical and geographical factors determining constitutions with his preference for British institutions. England was a model for a broad segment of Southern German thought, too, but much political sympathy for England radically misunderstood the British concept of the state. French revolutionary thought, it was held, saw the state as a mechanical device created on abstract, nonhistorical principles in order to protect the rights of individuals who were viewed as atoms without a close tie to society. The British Constitution, on the other hand, was viewed by German historians as the product of centuries of evolution linking the individual to the community. Certainly, both ideas were oversimplifications. The ideal of democracy, contained in Rousseau's *Social Contract* and to a degree practiced by the Revolution, assumed the supremacy of the nation over the individual. The British development increasingly led to a state limited in its functions and leaving a previously unknown degree of freedom not only to traditional corporations, but to private associations and individuals. The line between state and individual was far more clearly defined in the Britain of the Reform Era of the 1820's and 1830's than in the France of Robespierre. A much truer source of German liberal ideas lay in German concepts of corporative *(ständische)* liberties which had guided Stein and Humboldt.[16]

For the German public, however, the French Revolution represented not only the rule of the masses, but paradoxically also the
application of the theory of natural law to politics: the supremacy of
reason over history and of the rights of the individual over the demands of society. Thus, to the extent that the ideal of unity began to
overshadow that of freedom, German liberalism increasingly turned
away from French ideals and became sharply critical not only of the
Revolution, but hostile to the French nation.[17] This turn of events
began long before the frustrations of 1848; in fact, almost at the
beginning of the German liberal movement for national unification.
It involved not only the subordination of individual freedom to German unity, but also that of right and justice to national interest and
power.

Karl von Rotteck alone placed ethics over power. Rotteck, however, born in 1775, twenty years before Ranke, belonged to another
age. An ethusiastic supporter of the French Revolution, Rotteck
nevertheless dedicated his *Universal History,* of which the first volume appeared in 1812, to the "struggle for right and self-
determination" against Napoleon, a struggle which Rotteck continued against post-Napoleonic reaction. He frankly admitted that his
purpose in the *Universal History* was not the scientific exposition of
the past, but a pragmatic one of propagating ethical politics.[18] In
1818 he exchanged his chair of history at the University of Freiburg
im Breisgau for that of political science and natural law. As in the
case of his fellow-historian and parliamentarian, Karl Welcker, he
lost his post in 1832 as a result of his active fight within and outside
the Baden Parliament for liberal reforms. With Welcker, he edited
the *Staatslexikon,* an encyclopedia of politics which became a standard work in the middle-class households of the 1830's and 1840's.
Convinced of the reality of a "law of reason," applicable to existing
political institutions, Rotteck viewed history as the steady progress
toward a just society. In his opinion, constitutional government corresponded "completely in theory and at least approximately in practice" to a "purely rational system of public law *(Staatsrecht)*." The
constitution he proposed resembled those advocated by classical
liberal theorists since Locke. Government constituted a contract, he
argued. Sovereignty resided in the people who governed through their
representatives.

In contrast to Rousseau, Rotteck stressed the need for a distribution of powers within the government, and the guarantee of individual rights. The ministers were to be responsible to parliament. With Rousseau he optimistically assumed that the "general will" as interpreter of what was right would act in harmony with the will and welfare of the individuals, but he subordinated the democratic state to a higher law. In this sense, his conception of the rational state, as an instrument of law using rightful means alone, differed from those of revolutionary movements which were willing to make the end justify the means.[19] Rotteck thus acted in harmony with his convictions when he arose at the Badenweil *Fest* (a demonstration held by liberal nationalist students and professors in Baden in June 1832, a few days after students from all over Germany had demonstrated at the Hambach *Fest* for German unity) and warned against placing national belonging as the highest value. Unity must not be achieved at the cost of civil liberties. "Rather freedom without unity, than unity without freedom," he asserted.[20] Unification accomplished through Prussian or Austrian dynastic leadership, rather than through popular pressure, was of dubious value, he warned.

In sharp contrast, another South German, the Swabian publicist and member of the liberal opposition, Paul Achatius Pfizer, admonished in the same year in his *The Goal and Tasks of German Liberalism*[21] that national unity must not be subordinated to political freedom. "The majority of the people who think recognize the need of civil liberties," he complained, "but they do not acknowledge the even greater necessity for national independence which should never be freely sacrificed to the former."[22] It was questionable, he observed, whether "greater personal freedom" in the constitutional German states would advance the cause of unity. On the other hand, once unity was achieved, freedom would follow. The preservation of liberty required the protection of a strong, unified nation.[23]

Freedom, Pfizer stressed, cannot be understood as an abstract, human value. Rather, it is always intertwined with nationality. Every nation has a peculiar mission *(Lebensaufgabe)*. National distinctions will never cease. The contrast between Germany, "the home of soul *(Gemüth)* and thought *(Gedanken)*" and France, "the land of movement and superficiality" will remain eternally. "Nationality and personal freedom must henceforth go hand in hand."[24] National unification required a German Constitution which could be truly national, only if it provided for a parliamentary body that represented the entire German nation. German liberals must call for freedom of the press. However, these rights are not derived from "general principles of reason and the philosophy of law, or from the demands of the spirit of the time and the level of culture which Germany has reached today, but from reasons which are to be found entirely in positive law and in concretely existing presuppositions."

Specifically, Pfizer based this right upon the historical constitution of the Holy Roman Empire which he held the princes of the Rhine Confederation had had no right to abrogate in 1806, until it had been replaced by a new constitution acceptable to the peoples of Germany.[25] "Political rationalism," he complained, "which with its concepts of law fights against the laws of nature and sees the necessary character of all the ambitions of our time in the abandonment of the path of history, the rejection of the concrete, and disdain for the actually existing conditions, assumes that man has infinitely more power to create and is much more independent from what positively is, than he really is." True freedom consisted not "in spitefully opposing the force of circumstance, of things as they are, with one-sided abstractions, but in recognizing which way the finger of destiny points in world history and acting in accordance with it so that the weight of necessity may be made light and its yoke gentle."[26]

If freedom consisted of recognizing and following the path of historical necessity, then the relation between political behavior and ethics had to be viewed from a different standpoint than the one of traditional morality. For the course of history could not be judged by abstract principles; nor could such principles determine the course of political action which the historical situation required. Indeed, the mere possession of political power might constitute a moral and political right. "The right of the stronger is also a right," Pfizer notes, in arguing for the predominant position of Prussia in Germany.[27]

In a somewhat similar manner, Friedrich Christoph Dahlmann in his *Politics, Reduced to the Ground and Measure of Existing Conditions,* published in 1835, recognized that considerations of political interest must precede those of right and justice in the decisions of a state. A North German born in 1785 in Wismar on the Baltic, professor at Kiel after 1813, Dahlmann became at an early stage in his career an active spokesman of the rights of the German Schleswig-Holsteiners against the Danish monarchy.[28] Dahlmann was much more conservative in his political demands than Pfizer. Distrustful of popular sovereignty, Dahlmann nevertheless was a main proponent of the British Constitution as a model for Germany. His advocacy of constitutional government was linked, however, to a theory of the state as an organic unity playing a given role in a great historical drama, a conception which was certainly alien even to Burke. To be sure, British political theorists, including the liberals, had been very much aware of the historic sources of English liberty. But this was a far step from considering the state a "personality united in body and spirit"[29] to which "man faithful to his higher purpose *(Bestimmung)* must bring every sacrifice of purpose and person, only not the sacrifice of this, his higher purpose itself."[30] Although the state was not identical with the "divine order" *(göttliche Ordnung),* there was nothing in Dahlmann's opinion which "approximate(d) the divine order more closely on earth than the political order."[31] The state, he admitted, was not an end in itself, but served a "higher order." Dahlmann believed "in a great common work of mankind, to which the states contributed only preparatory labors, also in an external completion of things human at the end of history." In brief, he believed in progress.[32] This condition was accompanied by a mystery which the historian or political scientist could observe but not explain; namely, the contradiction between individual and political ethics, between what was "good, corresponding to the moral laws of the individuals," and what was "right *(recht),* corresponding to the commandments of the state."[33] For the state had to conduct not only domestic politics, but also international relations. Reminiscent of Hegel, Dahlmann implied that conflict among sovereign states was necessary for the fulfillment of the divine plan. "He who wants a world state or a state encompassing mankind . . . takes away from mankind organized in states the prospect of reaching the highest stage of cultural development in which the state, which had its origin in the family, perfects itself in the family of states."[34] Because of the role of the state within the "higher order" of things and the mysterious dualism of ethics, "the state is, of course, concerned with creating conditions of law and justice, but this is not the ultimate purpose of the state."[35]

One could therefore not speak of universally applicable political principles or of good forms of government. Political theories, the attempts to explain what the state is, Dahlmann points out, are engulfed by the "stream of time." Political science at most can indicate what is wrong and sick within a political society; never what is right.[36] The state can be approached only from the standpoint of history. Hence Lafayette's attempt to define the rights of men appeared absurd in Dahlmann's eyes.[37] Nevertheless, Dahlmann did not fail to distinguish between "good" and "bad" states. The "good state," although supreme over the individual, restricts individual action and property only to the minimum degree required by "public welfare."[38] This state seems strikingly similar to the British monarchy or, at least, to Dahlmann's conception of it. He recognizes royal prerogatives to an extent to which they no longer existed in the nineteenth century. Indeed, despite Dahlmann's insistence upon an historical approach to political values, his histories of the English and French Revolutions[39] in which he propagates his constitutional views, have been criticized by later historians who consider them more doctrinaire than those of English and French liberal historians.[40]

In a vein similar to Pfizer and Dahlmann, Georg Gervinus, Dahlmann's one-time colleague at Göttingen and lifelong friend, despite their diverging political views, argued in his lectures on "Politics on Historical Foundations," delivered in Heidelberg in 1846-1847, that "we must be just as concerned with the acquisition of power as we are with the possession of freedom."[41] Thus in 1848 all three were willing to turn to Prussian aid in order to maintain German supremacy in the Prussian-controlled parts of Poland. As Dahlmann wrote at the time: "Those who counsel nations against the cult of an unconditional humanism are quite right. A nation has not only a right, but even a duty, to be egoistic."[42] For Gervinus's position was indeed consistent with the theoretical views of history which he had already developed in 1837 in his *Foundations of Historical Science*.[43] Here, Gervinus had carefully distinguished the method of the philosopher from that of the historian. The historian, he warned, should not read an aim or a direction into the historical process, as Kant or Herder had done.[44] Unlike the poet or the philosopher, he should begin with the real historical world.[45] Once he immersed himself in the subject matter of his study, Gervinus agreed with Humboldt, he would comprehend the ideas underlying this reality. Amidst the apparent chaos of events, he would intuitively grasp *(ahnen)* the outlines of the plan that governed the world.[46]

But despite Gervinus's implicit rejection of Hegel, his doctrine of ideas bore closer affinity to the latter's conception of historical development than to the doctrine of individuality contained in Humboldt's essay on "The Tasks of the Historian," with which Gervinus identified his views.[47] Gervinus did not interpret the ideas as Humboldt had done; namely, that which summed up the uniqueness and essential character of a person or of an institution, and could not be defined in general terms or seen as part of a unified, total pattern. The ideas for him were rather the great tendencies which gave order and direction to the "chaotic mass" of events. Gervinus did carefully guard himself against seeking one coordinating idea by which history might be transformed into a system. The question of the origin and end of man was admittedly not within the realm of the historian's inquiry. The historian sought to grasp the direction of specific historic movements. This task was of immense importance for the politician, for man could not determine the course of events. Freedom, he insisted, existed only within the framework of the great historical forces, the ideas. The great individuals were the men who, especially in the earlier periods of development, bodily represented the ideas and advanced them.

> When he seeks to find these ideas within the events, the thoughtful historian merely does what thoughtful men generally do. For the latter must learn that when they intervene in public affairs they must sensibly associate themselves with the moving ideas of their time. For only where we act in harmony with these ideas will our actions prosper. When we oppose these ideas, our endeavors will be fruitless.[48]

This, of course, implied that ethical values are not considered as standards by which historical institutions may be measured, but that the dominant trends in history themselves reflect ethical values and that there is no basic conflict between morality and success.

3.

Despite individual differences, all of the German "political" historians of the mid-nineteenth century shared certain basic concepts regarding the nature of society and of the historical process. As a recent student of the German liberals in the Frankfurt Parliament of

1848 has pointed out, they all assumed that there existed a "pre-established harmony" between a man's personal freedom and his membership in a community.[49] In criticizing eighteenth-century French liberal thought, they perceived correctly that freedom in the abstract is meaningless and must be defined in terms of concrete social institutions. Yet they did not wish to render account of the threats to individual liberty emanating from the state or from society. They thought it possible to minimize the conflicts between society and the individual by conceiving freedom in a Lutheran tradition as something essentially spiritual and nonpolitical in character, and by considering liberty of conscience as the most important freedom.[50] A second point of common faith was the assumption that politics, law, and morality all had a "common source," that "morality was steadily becoming more political and politics more moral."[51] Underlying these assumptions was the firm conviction that there was a plan in history; that human societies were moving with irresistible force toward a state wherein the remnants of a conflict between ethics and power, individual rights and social cohesion, would be minimized; a process in which the nationalities would play a decisive part as organized political groups.

Johann Gustav Droysen (1808-1884), the founder of the so-called "Prussian School" of historians, not only wrote history upon these assumptions, but alone among his colleagues in his *Outline of the Principles of History (Grundriss der Historik)*[52] and his accompanying lectures on system and method in history[53] attempted to analyze extensively the theoretical presuppositions of historical practice. Despite certain shifts in emphasis in the course of his writings, particularly his increasing recognition of the role of force in politics after the disappointments of 1848, there is a remarkable unity in Droysen's thought. As in the case of the other "political" historians we have discussed, the events of 1848 affected his development much less profoundly than has been assumed by some critics. His basic political conception, particularly his recognition of the primacy of the state over individual interests or ethical considerations, remained unchanged since the beginning of his career in the 1830's.

None of the historians we have discussed was a Hegelian. They all recognized that historical method was incompatible with an abstract philosophical approach.[54] Nevertheless, the young Droysen perceived "God's almighty government" in a way which reminds us more of Hegel, whom he accused of heathenism, than of Christian theology. "I am so permeated with God's almighty reign that I believe that not even a hair can fall from any head without His willing it," he wrote to publisher Friedrich Perthes in 1836. More humble than Hegel, he recognized that "the finitude of our understanding prevents us from penetrating this marvelous mystery."

> . . . we believe that in everything, down to the smallest detail, God's eternal guidance operates powerfully but full of care. Man and his free will, the laws of nature and their disruptions, the seemingly arbitrary play of chance . . . all this is nothing but a tool of the great, universal necessity in which we believe. To follow the traces of this Necessity, to live in accordance with it, to submit humbly to it is the only worthy content of our knowledge and the only secure foundation for our actions.

Ranke's and Schlosser's approach to history were therefore not truly historical in Droysen's opinion. If Schlosser had tended to dissolve history into a compendium of moral judgments or individual acts, Ranke, Droysen thought, had gone little beyond collecting facts. Leo's approach would have been his own, Droysen wrote to Perthes, if Leo had not been so one-sided in following the "lines of development *(Richtung der Entwicklung)*" without giving sufficient attention to the phenomena.[55] A decade later, he similarly avowed his faith "that a divine hand carries us, that it guides the fates of great and small alike," and he saw the only higher task of historical science in "justifying this faith." We can speak of history as a science, Droysen held, because it "sees and finds a direction, a goal, and a plan amidst the wildly rushing waves."[56] Although he later claimed Humboldt as a principal source of inspiration for his *Outline of the Principles of History,*[57] he believed that history reflected one great guiding thought rather than a plurality of ideas and tendencies. In the manner of a dialectical process, thought challenged and transformed nature and became part of it, and in "negating" created new ideals and prepared new negations.[58]

This confidence in a higher purpose permeates Droysen's histories. In his *History of Alexander the Great* of 1833, followed by two volumes on the history of Hellenism, Alexander's heroic personality appears as the tool of a great historic purpose, the unification of the ancient pagan world which prepared the foundations for the spread of Christianity. The parallel to the later German situation is apparent when Droysen bestows the task of leadership upon the Macedonian military monarchy, not on the culturally more active Greek city-states. Only with the help of Macedonian generals could Greek culture spread throughout the Orient.[59] The *Wars of Liberation,* first delivered as lectures in 1842-43, trace the development of the modern idea of freedom in the course of the American and French Revolutions, but most important in the Prussian Reform Movement. The *History of Prussian Politics,* begun in 1855 and never completed, attempts to pursue the very questionable thesis that since the fifteenth century the Prussian rulers, conscious of Prussia's German mission, followed a consistent line of conduct. Prussia, Droysen declares, could best serve German unity by following her own interests, which are also Germany's, and build upon her own strength.

But the historical mission of Prussia, Droysen agrees, does not mean that the Prussian Government, as it existed in 1843, was the divinely ordained state. The idea of a "divine order" *(göttliche Weltordnung),* of "God's rule of the world" *(Gottes Weltregierung),* which recur through all of Droysen's writings implies that there is constant development, that not the institutions of the past, but those in the line of historical development are legitimate.[60] Prussia, more than any other state, rested upon a developing rather than a static principle. The development of this principle to a very high degree had been the work of the House of Hohenzollern. The reforms after 1806, not the restoration of 1815, marked the renewal of Prussia.[61]

Thus a real distinction exists for Droysen, at least until 1848, between ethical and unethical rule; between governments which depend upon mere power *(Macht)* and those that rest upon ethical foundations. The latter alone are true states. In Droysen's opinion, states require the consent of the men they govern. The great achievement of the age of revolutions had been the emergence of the state through the identification of the peoples with their governments. In 1844, Prussia wavered as to whether "she should become a state or a power *(Macht),* German or European, civic *(staatsbürgerlich)* or dynastic."[62] Droysen therefore rejects Ranke's concept of the European system of the great powers. The true state, Droysen believes, is linked to its people. Its foreign policy is determined by national interest, and conducted openly in the presence of public opinion rather than by secret diplomacy. Its purpose lays in domestic rather than in foreign policy, in developing the "free, responsible, ethical, political life of its citizens." If the state were to be linked to its people, Prussia must cease to be European and become German.[63] Its primary aim must be the unification of Germany, not the balance of power. But this does not mean that Prussia should renounce its power. Political reform would rather give the Prussian state a more popular basis and thus strengthen it. Germany should be powerful without thirsting for power. The United States provides the prime example of a state which became powerful because it was not primarily interested in power.[64]

Droysen does not advocate a parliamentary state in the British sense, guarantying basic individual rights. He recognizes that the trend of the past two centuries points to the establishment of a *Rechtsstaat,* a state based upon law, in which the relations between the princes and their peoples are clearly defined. All this is good. The rule of law under constitutional government is needed, Droysen admits, but he also warns that "law *(Recht)* is much, infinitely much, but not everything."[65] The great error of "vulgar liberalism," Droysen wrote in 1847, had been its insistence upon government based on popular sovereignty and bound by written guarantees of individual rights. Government by the will of the people does not require "the sum of all individual wills"; nor is it the main purpose of constitutional government "to be the people's defense against the crown and perhaps provide for the ultimate right to refuse taxes." The "true essence of constitutionalism" rather consists of "the state removing from its competence all that does not properly belong to it." The state must recognize the right of other spheres of society *(sittliche Kreise),* ethical circles, in order to develop fully. It must "encompass the movement and dynamic interaction" of these other spheres within its own functions, and thus carry historical development onward. "For historical development," Droysen concludes, "is the only common factor in all human relations."

This, of course, reflects a remarkable optimism regarding the nature of power, shared by few if any of his colleagues. It is remindful of the naive faith of a utopian socialist such as Saint Simon who hoped to institute a sane society through appeals to the good will of the ruling dynasty. Restrictions of power are not necessary, according to Droysen; power would restrict itself. The omnipotent state must be rejected. Enlightenment thought favors such a state, Droysen holds. The high point of Enlightenment absolutism had been represented by the Jacobins and by Napoleon in their refusal to respect the existence and independence of spheres of cultural activity outside the state. Droysen's views of the benevolence of power rests upon his optimism in regard to historical development. The insights of individuals, "themselves the result of the progressive development of history," are being constantly transformed into the institutions and common attitudes of the total community. From this Droysen concludes that the strength of a constitution depends upon the strength of its government which, in turn, relies upon the government's recognition of its "true task." A strong government therefore offers a more effective guarantee of law and individual freedom than a written constitution.[66]

It is not surprising that Droysen joined Dahlmann in Frankfurt in opposing a written declaration of rights. Less convincing, and slightly smacking of intellectual dishonesty and an unwillingness to admit that nationality for him was more important than freedom, were Droysen's arguments against the proposed Danish Constitution. In defense of the traditional estates, he invoked the principle of historic right, which elsewhere he had steadily rejected in favor of the rights of historical development.[67] His opposition to a representative body for all of Prussia had been based upon very different grounds from his attack upon the Danish Constitution. Droysen feared that the transformation of Prussia into a constitutional state might delay the unification of Germany. The events of 1848 had taught him that only a powerful Prussian state could bring about unification. Perceiving that Germany could not be united from Frankfurt, he now saw the only solution in a powerful Prussian state. "German unity could not be created by 'Liberty' or by 'national resolutions,' " he observed. "The creation of German unity required the presence of a power which could challenge the other powers."[68] What mattered now was whether Prussia was strong, not whether she carried out reforms within. Prussia's interests were identical with those of Germany. Politics, after the disappointments of 1848, must be purely concerned with power. "I don't give a damn whether we have jury trials or if our communes are represented on the basis of universal suffrage," he wrote to an acquaintance in 1851.[69] But then, despite his earlier admiration of Baron von Stein's reforms, he had never considered these institutions of great importance to a free society. Indeed, it is questionable whether the events of 1848 brought about as profound a change in Droysen's thinking as historians generally have maintained. It is true that Droysen once had distinguished more sharply between the state as it was and as it ought to be, when he contrasted the state as an ethical entity with the state as power. Now he stressed that the state is power. But he still saw in the power of the state the manifestation of an ethical reality that must be sharply distinguished from mere "brute force" *(rohe Gewalt).*

4.

Later historians often tended to see Droysen's *Outline of the Principles of History* somewhat one-sidedly from the viewpoint of their time. For them Droysen, in his attempt to distinguish the methods of historical inquiry from those of the natural sciences, stood in a line of thought from Humboldt to Dilthey.[70] In the *Outline of the Principles of History,* and particularly in his review of Buckle's *History of Civilization in England,*[71] Droysen sought to demonstrate the inapplicability of the methods of the natural sciences to historical study. This interpretation of Droysen's thought is undoubtedly correct, but it tends to underplay a very important point of agreement which existed between Droysen and the Western positivism he rejected. As the title of his *Lectures on the Encyclopedia and Methodology of History*[72] indicated, he intended to develop a system of history as well as to discuss its epistemological foundations. Despite his profound methodological differences with Buckle, Droysen agreed with Buckle that history is not primarily concerned with individual truths at the total expense of generalizations. He shared with Buckle in the faith that history is a meaningful, lawful, and progressive process which the historian could understand to a high degree.

In sharp contrast to Western positivists, Droysen, as Humboldt, Ranke, and Gervinus before him, believed that historical study requires understanding of its subject matter rather than causal explanation. For in history, in contrast to nature, he argued, we are not dealing with dead matter, governed by the "mechanics of atoms," but with "acts of volition," each having its origin in an individual ego or in the common ego of a community.[73] This subject matter determined the methods employed by history.[74] Understanding was possible for Droysen because of man's dual, spiritual-physical nature[75] which Humboldt and Ranke already had recognized. Every external act of man reflects an internal process. From these external, empirically observable expressions we can grasp the essence or meaning of an event, even if no external expression ever reflected this essence completely.[76] "In one word, there is nothing that moves the human spirit or that has found expression through the senses which cannot be understood," he wrote.[77] All tools made by men, as well as all institutions created by him, such as law, governments, churches, reflect the human spirit and therefore can be understood. On the other hand, understanding is possible neither in philosophy nor in the natural sciences. Philosophical and theological speculation can attain abstract cognition *(Erkennen),* but not real understanding *(eigentliches Verstehen).* Similarly, we can classify Nature, explain natural phenomena by laws, but not understand them.[78]

There is, however, a fundamental difference in Droysen's concept of *Verstehen* (understanding) and that of Ranke and Humboldt. The subject matter itself, history consisting of human actions, they agree, determines the method of inquiry. But this subject matter is differently understood by Droysen. For Humboldt and Ranke the important units of history are individualities. Historical study is concerned with understanding these individualities. For Droysen history is a whole and must be understood as such; the acts of volition are parts of a total pattern. History and Nature are both scenes of ceaseless movement *(rastlose Bewegung).* What distinguishes the two realms is that this movement in Nature takes the form of periodic repetition, while in history it is ceaseless progress *(rastlose Steigerung).*[79] The subject matter of history is the ethical world *(der Kosmos der sittlichen Welt).* At any one moment, this world consists of a tremendous "maze of transactions *(Geschäften),* circumstances, interests, conflicts, passions, etc." which can be viewed from many aspects: technological, judicial, religious, or political.

> . . . historical science is just as little a photographic reproduction of all this reality as natural science is a collection of all details in the physical world. Both sciences are ways in which the human spirit views things, the forms in which this spirit cognizantly *(wissend)* grasps and takes possession of the ethical, natural world. To view the ethical world in growth and becoming, in its movement, is to view it historically.[80]

Droysen criticizes Buckle not for believing that there is progress in history, but because Buckle's naturalistic approach to history is irreconcilable with meaningful progress. In Nature there can only be recurrence, Droysen argues; there is no place for purpose.[81]

Behind Droysen's concept of *Verstehen* there is a tremendous optimism in regard to man's ability to know. *Verstehen,* "the most perfect form of cognition which is humanly possible," is an intuitive act and does not proceed according to abstract logic. It involves all aspects of men, his "whole spiritual-physical nature," not merely his ability to reason through a situation. It is rather "like an act of creation, like a spark of light between two electrophoric bodies, like the act of conception." Historical understanding resembles our comprehension of a conversation when we hear or grasp not merely individual words or even sentences, but are able to take in the context because that which is spoken reflects such a total context.[82] The concept of *Verstehen,* as understood in German historical thought, implies that there are very definite limits to human understanding. For one thing, *Verstehen* suggests that understanding is a highly subjective and personal activity. There is therefore no general method for the attainment of truth or any objective criterion for testing truth. We can understand only out of our own special situation and we confront not truth as such, but the personality of concrete human beings or communities with their own subjective limitations. This follows from the doctrine of ideas utilized by Humboldt and Ranke. What saved both Ranke and Humboldt from subjectivism was their firm belief that the objects of our understanding in their radical diversity still reflect the will of God and represent aspects of a many-sided reality.

By the end of the century, this faith in an underlying reality was shaken. Max Weber no longer believed in it; for Dilthey it had at least become problematic. We could still speak of types of values, of *Weltanschauungen,* but the question of value or truth in any transcendent sense became meaningless. For Droysen, on the other hand, the *Verstehen* approach still made objective knowledge possible because he believed firmly that he lived in a meaningful and integrated world. Cognition is always limited and colored by our personal limitations and by belonging to a state, a national group, or a religion, he admits. But for him these groups, which influence and limit our cognition, are the products of an objective reality. His knowledge, he recognizes, is "the relative truth of my position *(Standpunkt),* as my fatherland, my political and religious convictions, and my serious study have permitted me to attain it." Such truth he considers preferable to an "emasculated objectivity" which, uncommitted to any standpoint, can only attain sterile generalities.

> Of course, I shall not want to solve the great tasks of historical presentation from my arbitrary subjectivity or my small and petty personality. But when I look at the past from the standpoint of my people, state, and religion, I stand high above my own ego. I think, as it were, from a higher Ego, in which the slags of my own petty person have melted away.[83]

Such a view, which conceives all knowledge as colored by man belonging to an historical group, would have been highly relativistic if Droysen had not been convinced that there were objective forces at work in history, and that to an extent at least the historian could transcend his narrow situation to gain a glimpse of these forces. That this was possible, is implied in Droysen's discussion of the four steps necessary for understanding. First, all historical inquiry must begin with a critical reconstruction of the facts, although it must be kept in mind that an historical event, such as a battle, does not consist of hard facts but of acts of will.[84]

A second step in interpretation consists of a study of the conditions under which these actions took place. A third, more significant step is the psychological interpretation which attempts to reconstruct the acts of volition. But this does not yet constitute understanding. To attain understanding we must proceed to the fourth step, "interpretation of the ideas which fill the gap left by psychological interpretation." These ideas are not abstract thought; rather, they are the ethical forces *(sittliche Mächte)* which manifest themselves in such concrete social institutions as the family, the church, society, or the state.[85] These moral forces make man the human being that he is, Droysen observes. History is basically nothing, but the story of the progress of these forces.[86] Moreover, these forces, not the deliberate actions of individuals, create the concrete institutions which appear in history.

> Historical research knows that personalities are the media, but only the media, through which these things work, that the giftedness of

individuals, their wishes and desires, their innermost self *(eigenste Totalität)* are only the stages, the links in the restless growth *(Werden)* of things, that—as the expression goes—things go their way independently of the good or evil volitions of those through whom they accomplish their end *(durch welche sie sich vollziehen)*.[87]

The historian is thus primarily concerned with understanding the great social forces operating in history.[88] For "all human existence and activity is merely the expression and outward manifestation of these ethical forces."[89] What matters to the historian is only that which is of "historical" rather than of personal importance. He must know when "private transactions" *(Geschäfte)* become "history" *(Geschichte)*. For the historical significance of King George Podiebrad of Bohemia does not consist

> in what he did in his day by day transactions but in the influence which his actions had on the overall development of history. We do not want to make his personal acquaintance, but want to investigate and elucidate his historical significance.[90]

Related to Droysen's concept of history as an integrated system is his historical optimism. There cannot be any real conflict between ethics and society because society constitutes the concrete expression of ethical ideas. These ideas, on the other hand, cannot develop in the abstract, but only within the framework of social institutions. Droysen distinguishes three types of ethical communities, each unfolding in four stages. Man differs from the animals insofar as his natural drives lead him into communities of spirit *(seelische Gemeinschaft)*.[91] Such natural communities are the family, the neighborhood, the tribe, and the nation *(Volk)*. They fulfill natural, biological needs, but at the same time have a higher spiritual significance. Less closely knit are the "communities of ideals" *(ideale Gemeinsamkeiten);* namely, language, the arts, the sciences, and religion. To maintain harmony among conflicting interests, "practical communities," institutions of social control, are required. Droysen distinguishes four such practical communities: the spheres of society, welfare (the economy), law, and power (the state).[92] The individual is ethical to the extent that he identifies himself with the community.[93] For this reason, there is no morality apart from society and no universal ethical principles. All ethics are historical in character.[94] "The ethical system of any period is only the formulation and synthesis of the state of knowledge attained at that period regarding the ethical forces." All ethical judgments are "relative truths, to be measured by what has been attained by that time."[95] This means, of course, that there is steady ethical progress.[96] Real evil does not exist. Evil merely expresses the finiteness of the human spirit at early stages of its development. "It belongs into the economy of historical movement but as 'something bound to diminish and disappear in the process of things.' "[97]

At the head of the hierarchy of social institutions stands the state. Droysen observes: "The state claims to be the sum, the total organism of all ethical communities, their common purpose."[98] But he is careful not to identify the ethical idea with the state alone, as Hegel had done, for man belongs to other ethical communities as well. "The great ethical communities in which man lives have a relationship to the state and serve to protect the state and enhance its honor. But by no means do they exist for the state, nor did they grow out of the state, nor are its limits theirs."[99] The state enables these ethical forces to function and develop freely. "The state as a public force," Droysen notes, "guarantees the security of all the ethical spheres within the state. These spheres sacrifice as much of their autonomy and self-determination as is necessary for the power to be able to defend and represent them." But, on the other hand, "power is greatest when the health, liberty, and movement of all ethical spheres is most fully developed."[100]

What Droysen clearly had in mind was a strong constitutional monarchy, such as the Prussia of the Constitution of 1850. The government was free from the pressure of parties and various interest groups which helped to determine the policies of a parliamentary state. Droysen was so confident of the forces of history that he could not conceive of the state misusing its powers. The state, in order to function effectively, had to be based upon power. "In the world of politics the law of force has the same validity as the law of gravity in the physical world."[101] But the state rested upon the great ethical communities. Convinced that the interests of the state are identical with the demands of ethics, Droysen regrets "the unfortunate notion that freedom had become worse off to the extent that the organization of power had progressed."[102] The power of the state guaranteed the freedom of the various spheres of society. The state alone is in a position to be an impersonal and impartial arbiter between these various spheres. Unable to see the dangers of unlimited power, Droysen could therefore not envisage the need for any effective restrictions on the power of the state. In his opinion, if the government follows the best interests of the state, it can not really do injury to the freedom of the various interests to express themselves. Hence it is immaterial whether the constitution provides for popular participation in government or not.

> It doesn't matter whether the estates, by whatever manner they have been convened, have the right to add their two cents' worth. Voicing their opinion whether through corporative or representative organs is much less important than one thinks. The essence of a constitution consists in whether and to what extent the state is aware that if it wants to increase its power it must act not in an autocratic fashion but must pursue its great real interests. It is immaterial whether it asserts these great interests on the basis of public discussion, representation, or circumspect administration.[103]

The power of the state cannot be limited by considerations of individual ethics. In following its "real interests," the state acts ethically, even if it seems to be functioning contrary to popular concept of personal morality. Power in contrast to raw "force" *(Gewalt)* is always ethical. If the soldier

> wounds and kills, desolates and burns because he has been ordered to do so, he acts not as an individual and in accordance with his individual opinions but in terms of the many relationships which together fill his Ego with content and which are intertwined in his conscience. He acts, so to speak, from a higher Ego. . . . The individual may often find this difficult. The conflict of duties may lead him to question what he may do and what he must not do. But he can feel secure in his conscience when he complies with his higher duty. He feels himself raised above his petty, individual Ego—as if he had been ennobled by a higher law—whenever he acts with full energy and dedication in the service of this higher general interest.[104]

5.

On a less ambitious scale, Heinrich von Sybel (1817-1895) in various essays and lectures attempted to deal with the same questions Droysen had treated in his lectures on the *Principles of History*.[105] The political positions of Sybel and Droysen were similar, even if during the constitutional crisis of the 1860's Sybel briefly stood a shade left of Droysen. In the so-called Preliminary Parliament at Frankfurt in 1848, Sybel had identified himself with the moderate liberal position, as he again did in the Prussian diets in the 1860's. A "liberal-conservative," as he labeled himself,[106] he consistently favored constitutional forms and the *Rechtsstaat* throughout his political career; yet, like Droysen, he opposed real parliamentary checks over the monarch and dreaded popular sovereignty. His early studies on Burke and the Whigs are therefore indicative of his attempt to define his own political position. So are his years of occupation with the *History of the Era of the French Revolution,* which reflects a much deeper concern for the role of social forces than may be found in any other work by an historian of the "political" orientation.[107]

Despite occasional shifts of emphasis, Sybel's views of historical method and the structure of historical reality are remarkably similar to those of Droysen. Sybel, too, emphasizes the difference in method between history and the natural sciences. The actions of men require "spiritual comprehension." The "means of exact control," which the scientist possesses for the verification of his observations, are available to the historian to a much lesser extent.[108] But despite these limitations, Sybel is convinced of the "possibility of certain knowledge" in history,[109] because all men are "human beings and are governed by the same laws of human nature" and every historical event is part of a total context.[110]

This confidence in the possibility of certain historical knowledge, and Sybel's deep conviction that there is a steady progress in human affairs, have made some German critics see a kinship between his historical thoughts and those of Western positivists.[111] To a very large extent, this kinship may apply to Droysen as well, despite his attack upon Buckle. But if Sybel believes that objective knowledge of history is possible, he believes no more than Droysen that an objective approach is necessary. Because we are part of the great context of history, our partial and subjective perspectives of history reflect an objective reality. For reasons very similar to those of Droysen, Sybel rejects Ranke's supposed "lack of warmth" and overly great concern with technical considerations and Schlosser's superficial moralizing.[112] After all, history can be only understood in relationship to actual life.

> For as certainly as no genuine historian can mature without ethical convictions, there are no genuine convictions which do not carry with them a definite relationship to the great questions of religion, politics, and nationality which move the world. The historian who seeks to withdraw to an elegant neutrality inescapably becomes soulless or affected.

Hence Sybel considers it "a considerable step forward" that for the past decades

> every historian who has had any significance in our literature has had his colors. There have been believers and atheists, Protestants and Catholics, liberals and conservatives, historians of all parties, but no longer any objective, impartial historians devoid of blood and nerves.[113]

It is the existence of a plan, the reality of progress which for Sybel, as for Droysen, eliminates fundamental conflicts between individual freedom and the state, between ethics and power. Freedom, Sybel notes is not mere freedom of constraint, "formal self-determination of the will without regard to the content of this will." In the German Idealist tradition, he rather views freedom as something positive, as "self-determination to attain culture and morality" *(Selbstbestimmung zur Bildung und Sitte),* as the "unfettered development of human nature." But freedom so conceived, Sybel stresses, is possible only within a community and under the guidance of the state as a moral institution. He therefore concludes "that the state has power over the individuals, that the latter owe obedience to the state and can achieve their own freedom only through this obedience."[114] The state is not the work of individual men. It and its laws are a "creation from above" *(eine Schöpfung von oben her).*[115] It is not a "mechanical tool," but a "living fellowship" *(lebendige Genossenschaft),* and "ethical potentiality" *(sittliche Potenz).* "The state is the realization of freedom through the power of the community" and its task is "synonymous with the perfection of human culture."[116] Hence the history of the state for Sybel, as for Hegel, represents the progress of the "ethical idea." Deeply convinced of man's steady advance, Sybel reminds his readers that if

> we examine the sixth, the sixteenth and the nineteenth century in terms of the density and productivity of the population, the purity of sexual morals, the respect for the individual human life, the security of civil society, the lessening severity of warfare, the striving for prosperity and education by all classes, we shall soon be convinced that one can nowhere speak of retrogression. Perhaps the modern period lacks here or there some of the brilliance of earlier times. But in the average sum of morality and humaneness, our time is superior to all earlier periods.[117]

Sybel was so confident of the mission of the state that he was willing, if necessary, to sacrifice civil liberties and ethical principles to its interests. He was more willing, perhaps, than Droysen to admit that real conflicts could occur between considerations of right and of might. What has grown historically, he notes, has a right to endure only if it is based upon "universal reason and the moral law." But, he continues cheerfully, only few political institutions lack this foundation completely.[118] It is not quite clear what he means by the laws of ethics and of Nature. A ruler apparently violates laws of Nature if he either attempts to tear himself loose from historical continuity (geschichtlich Gewordenen) or tries to block "the stream of new developments."[119] Even if the state's first need is power (Macht), it should use this power rightfully.[120] But when there is a conflict between might and right, the latter must yield. For "he who sides with the nature of things is always victorious; but he conquers only with difficulty if he has right against him." If necessary, Sybel holds, guarantees of rights, as well as civil liberties, must be sacrificed to the interests of the state.[121] Indeed, it is dangerous to limit the powers of the state formally.

> It is wrong to erect definite barriers to the activity of the state and to want to exclude the state from certain spheres of life. . . . The law of freedom does not require the state not to concern itself with certain aspects of human existence but requires rather that the state act within the meaning and in the interest of freedom.[122]

If the purpose of the state is not to be annihilated from the start, the state must have the right to determine the degree of political freedom that every individual shall have in terms of what the individual accomplishes for the total community *(Gesamtheit).*[123] But if the forces of history are those of progress, a line of action must be judged not in terms of abstract ethical norms, but in terms of success. Here, Sybel hastens to distinguish between apparent, momentary reward and "practical and enduring" attainment. However, success remains the "highest judge . . . the last and decisive court of appeals" *(die schlechthin entscheidende Instanz).* The genius who attains success through force and usurpation, Sybel concludes, must not be judged by the normal standards of morality.[124]

6.

It is therefore not surprising that the "moderately liberal" historians could make their peace with Bismarck as easily as they did during the constitutional crisis. None, with the possible exception of Gervinus (who did not make his peace), had democratic leanings. None was a liberal in the Western sense. All acknowledged the need of a strong state and rejected not only universal suffrage, but also any extensive controls by the legislature over the monarchy. Nevertheless, they sought a constitutional *Rechtsstaat* which would guarantee basic individual rights, effectively further the movement toward national unification, and generally follow progressive economic and social policies. They tended to be less opposed to the army reform bill itself, which had touched off the conflict between the Prussian Diet and the government, than they were alarmed by the violation of the Prussian Constitution. Perhaps most of all, they were concerned over the appointment of Bismarck as minister president because they viewed him as a representative of reactionary *Junker* interests.

All looked with suspicion upon the democratic forces around the newly founded Progress Party which, in 1861, emerged as the strongest party in the diet. It remained the center of the opposition to Bismarck in defense of the constitutional rights of the diet. Max Duncker favored the army reform bill in 1861 and even Bismarck's appointment the following year, although he had some mixed feelings about the man.[125] Droysen similarly was never really in the opposition.[126] Rudolf Haym, in an editorial explaining the compliance of the

Preussische Jahrbücher to Bismarck's decree of June 1st curbing the opposition press, admonished that "all of our institutions are based upon the principle that law *(Recht)* is the result of the collaboration of the government and the people,"[127] and that the "victorious will of the supreme power" must be inseparable from "right and morality." He regretted that Bismarck wished to save "old military Prussia . . . from a new Prussia, whose nucleus would be the bourgeoisie and whose center of gravity would be in parliament."[128] But, he conceded, "a nation is willing to tolerate much which is annoying and oppressive, even acts of abnormal violence, from a genius *(Genialität)* if his leadership proves itself by successes. . . . A nation is willing to sacrifice some of its domestic liberty if in return it is presented with an increase in power and prestige abroad." But the Prussian state had yet to "legitimate the repression which we all feel today"[129] by such accomplishments. Not all were willing to comply. Treitschke, infuriated by Haym's article, dissociated himself publicly from the *Preussische Jahrbücher.*[130] Sybel, although willing to compromise on the army issue and repelled by what he considered the doctrinaire position of the Progress Party, was increasingly driven by Bismarck's actions into opposition in defense of the constitution.[131] Urged by his friend Droysen, who admitted that he was "no great admirer of Herr von Bismarck," but recognized that "power is the first interest of the state,"[132] he replied in 1864, after the Prusso-Austrian conquest of Schleswig-Holstein: ". . . there is a limit to the sacrifice of right to might, a loosely drawn limit perhaps, but nevertheless an unshakable and absolutely firm one."[133]

After the Prussian defeat of Austria in 1866, the remaining opposition among the liberal historians disappeared. Neither Sybel nor the men around the *Preussische Jahrbücher* could doubt any longer that history was on the side of Bismarck. A majority of the liberal delegates in the Prussian Diet and the Reichstag of the new North German Confederation now formed a new National Liberal Party which made its peace with Bismarck and left the Progress Party relatively small and isolated. Hermann Baumgarten, in an extensive "Self Critique," chided German liberals for their failure to understand properly the importance of power, and for undermining the "ethical strength" of the people by their persistent attacks on the actions of the government as unconstitutional. "They are inflicting more serious harm to public morale and to the healthy development of the state then if they came to some sort of bearable terms with such a regime."[134] Treitschke revised his essay on "Liberty" and came back to the *Preussische Jahrbücher*. Although, in the earlier version written in 1861, Treitschke had recognized that "the state is not merely a means for promoting the interests *(Lebenszwecke)* of the citizens," and had argued that "there is no absolute limit to the power of the state," in his discussion of Mill's "On Liberty" he reflected upon the influence of Mill's essay, particularly its defense of intellectual freedom as vital to human progress.[135] In the version of 1864, he emphasized even more strongly the idea of the state as an end in itself, the limited character of all political freedom, and the meaninglessness of political equality.[136]

Only Gervinus saw the events of 1870 and 1871 with fears and misgivings. Disappointed by Prussian policy in the Schleswig-Holstein question in 1848 and Frederick Wilhelm IV's refusal of the German crown, Gervinus became irreconcilably critical of Hohenzollern leadership. The law governing European history, he observed in 1853, was one of "regular progress from the spiritual and civil liberty of individuals to that of the several and the many."[137] In our democratic mass age, the "great influence of individuals, whether rulers or private persons," was relegated to a secondary position.[138] Hence he observed with great concern in November 1870, that

> For him, who looks at the events of the day not with the eyes of the day but with the eyes of history, the (great martial events of 1870) seem pregnant with incalculable dangers, because they lead us on a path which runs completely counter to the character of our people, and what is even worse, counter to the character of the whole epoch.[139]

Droysen had said in 1866 that, once Germany became unified, the process of liberalization must begin.[140] This seemed to have been forgotten by 1871. Sybel, dismayed by the growth of socialism and by supposed Catholic strength, re-entered the *Landtag* in order to support Bismarck's domestic program. Only Treitschke and Mommsen began to sense the irreconcilability of national power and liberal principles, although in very different ways. Naturalistic views of power were replacing German Idealistic concept of power as an ethical force. August Ludwig von Rochau's *Foundations of Realpoli-*

tik had already appeared in 1853. There was little new in Rochau's assertion that "it is actually unreasonable to subordinate might to right. Only the stronger has and should have power." The main significance of Rochau's work was to introduce the term *Realpolitik* into the vocabulary of politics. Nevertheless, the book, as Treitschke related later, struck him like lightning, and he included it among the works which exerted the strongest influence upon his thinking.[141]

Both Treitschke and Baumgarten viewed power free from its idealization by the older men.[142] In his essay on freedom, Treitschke had already spoken of the "merciless race struggle in history," and had derided religion as "a subjective need of feeble human hearts."[143] In the 1870's and 1880's, politics increasingly appeared to him as a struggle for existence of nation against nation, of strong against weak. In the new Empire, he repeatedly became the spokesmen of a new conservatism opposing the Socialists and the "Pulpit Socialists" *(Kathedersozialisten)* around Gustav Schmoller, and the *Verein für Sozialpolitik* who advocated moderate social reforms within the framework of the existing German monarchy. "Millions must tend the fields and forge and plane so that a few thousands may explore, paint, and govern,"[144] he remarked. Treitschke gave support to nascent imperialist opinion and demanded a strong German world policy, colonies, and a navy. From a supporter of Jewish emancipation in his early days, he now turned anti-Semite.[145]

Theodor Mommsen, too, enthusiastically greeted the events of 1870-1871, and returned to parliament in the early 1870's as a National Liberal and an ardent supporter of Bismarck's *Kulturkampf* against the Catholic Church. Bismarck's introduction of protective tariffs in 1879, after the electoral victory of the Conservatives, appeared to him as a betrayal of National Liberal principles and of the National Liberal party. Re-elected to the Reichstag in 1881 as a candidate for the Secession party of liberals who had broken with the National Liberal party, he now began to see the dangers of a system in which popular representatives failed to have a decisive voice in the affairs of the nation. The National Liberals, it appeared to him now, had paid too high a price for unification and Bismarck had broken the spine of the nation. With regret Mommsen saw the increasing impotence of liberalism in the eyes of a generation which had grown up in admiration of Bismarck, and the domination of the political life of an industrial nation by semifeudal and military interests. In bitter disappointment, he commented in his will, written in 1899 four years before his death:

> I have never had or aimed at having a political position or political influence. But in my innermost self, and I mean with the best that is within me, I have always been a political animal and have wanted to be a citizen. But this is not possible in our nation in which the individual, even the best one, can never entirely transcend military subordination *(Dienst im Gliede)* and political fetishisms. This inner estrangement from the poeple to whom I belong has made me decide as far as possible not to appear before the German public for whom I have no respect.[146]

Another pessimistic note was introduced by Hermann Baumgarten. If, in 1870, he still complained that Germans always had underemphasized the role of power and overemphasized that of ideas,[147] by the 1880's he reassessed Bismarck's role in German history and was filled with deep concern for the future. He shared Mommsen's disappointment in Bismarck's retreat in the *Kulturkampf* and his break with liberal tariff policies. Even more keenly than Mommsen he saw hidden dangers behind the excessive glorification of power and nationality, the threat of a coming era of mass tyranny. He bitterly criticized Treitschke's *German History,* when it appeared in 1883,[148] and opposed both Treitschke's and Adolf Stoecker's expressions of anti-Semitism. To a much greater extent than Mommsen, his criticism of Bismarck's conservatism was coupled with the fear of popular government which had once been shared by most German "classical liberals." Analagous to Ranke before him, Baumgarten feared that Bismarck, by introducing universal suffrage, might have conjured spirits which he would be unable to control one day. "Only very few seem to suspect," he wrote to Sybel in 1890, "that universal suffrage is threatening not only the state but our whole culture, and is bringing about rule by the raw instincts of the masses in everything."[149]

Nevertheless, Mommsen and Baumgarten were relatively isolated in their uneasiness about the Bismarckian state, at least until the formation of the circle around Friedrich Naumann later in the 1890's. And the Naumann Circle, although deeply aware of the imperfections of the German monarchy, was still thoroughly convinced of the central role of power in the state and the future of Germany as a world power.

[C H A P T E R V I]

The "Crisis of Historicism" I

THE PHILOSOPHIC CRITIQUE: COHEN, DILTHEY, WINDELBAND, RICKERT, WEBER

1.

IN recent years intellectual historians, in increasing numbers, have diagnosed a profound crisis in European social thought in the quarter of a century which preceded the outbreak of World War I. Writers such as Stuart Hughes, Gerhard Masur, and Arnold Brecht[1] have seen the core of this crisis in the growing awareness on the part of social philosophers, social scientists, historians, and men of letters of the limitations of human knowledge and the subjective character of all cognition in regard to human behavior and social processes. Positivism, in the course of the nineteenth century, had progressively destroyed the traditional religious and metaphysical image of the world. But the positivists still assumed that the universe is an integrated system governed by mathematical laws, that the methods of the natural sciences would reveal the lawful structure of physical and social reality alike.

In the late nineteenth and early twentieth centuries, the positivistic picture of man and the universe itself came under attack from many corners. The new psychologists (Freud and Jung), the philosophers (Nietzsche, Dilthey, and Bergson), the poets and novelists (Baudelaire, Dostoevsky, and Proust), all revealed the basically irrational character of man. The historians and social scientists increasingly forsook their occupation with the problem of what constituted society or history; instead, they asked how a science of history or society was possible. They tended to regard all knowledge,

124

which went beyond constructions based upon empirical data, as colored by human subjectivity. The solution of any ultimate problems became impossible; the gulf between the world of Being and the world of Meaning apparently was complete.[2] The collapse of the Newtonian picture of the physical universe, at the turn of the century, and the construction of non-Euclidean systems of geometries further seemed to stress the limitations of human knowledge. Any interpretation of reality, other than one based upon strict induction, was doomed as poetry or imagination. The reliance upon empirical data alone, it was felt, would reveal a universe basically without meaning. In a sense, the attack upon positivism carried positivism to its own logical conclusions by destroying its remaining metaphysical assumptions.

This crisis in modern scientific and philosophic thought, brought about by the self-examination of consciousness, essentially marked the end of philosophy in the traditional sense. With the collapse of the metaphysical framework, only three tasks remained logically open for philosophic thought, none of them concerned with the search of truth or value in any ultimate way. The philosopher could turn to history and trace the changes in philosophical opinions over the ages or represent the dominant ideas of an age, a people, a tradition. Going beyond the mere historical description of ideas, he could still preserve something of the universal concern of the philosopher, as Dilthey had done. On the basis of comparative studies, he could classify the perennial issues and types of philosophic solutions of the life-riddle which have dominated the history of human thought. Again, philosophy could become pure logic and epistemology dealing with the conditions of human knowledge. Ernst Troeltsch observed that philosophy of history in the material sense, which discusses human history as a meaningful process, had given completely way to philosophy of history in a purely formal sense as the logic and epistemology of historical thought.[3]

This recognition of the limitations of human rationality, when carried to its logical conclusions, should have involved a radically relativistic position in regard to knowledge. Nevertheless, men such as Dilthey and Freud, who saw thought as an expression of life functions rather than as a rational process, were unwilling to draw the conclusion that objective knowledge of the physical or, for that matter, of the social and cultural world was impossible. Indeed, the attack against positivism at the turn of the century included in its vanguard Wilhelm Dilthey, Max Weber, and Sigmund Freud who shared the positivist regard for the empirical fact. In the spirit of positivism, they wished to free modern thought from its last remaining speculative assumptions. Even the revolutionary reformulations in physical theory, in the early 1900's, did not undermine the faith in science as a means of gaining knowledge of the world of Being. A serious crisis occurred in the realm of values in the insistence by social theorists, particularly in Germany, that values could be studied as facts, as part of a cultural-historical context, but that values did not exist in any ultimate sense, and science could not give any solution ot the question of values. Values, it was stressed, were based upon emotions, not cognition. Modern man was suddenly faced with the collapse of absolute values by the anarchy of convictions. Wilhelm Dilthey fearfully foresaw this as a consequence of his own thought.[4] Political decisions were theoretically reduced to matters of arbitrary or subjectivistic decision.[5] Whatever justification libertarian-humanitarian political ideals had sought in natural law or science were gone; nor could liberalism, democracy, or socialism find any basis of support in a theory of progress. For in a world which knew no absolute norms, progress in a rational direction was impossible. The real crisis in Western political thought, Arnold Brecht observed, was "not to be sought in the emergence of different ideologies, but in what preceded this event by about two decades—the rise of the theoretical opinion that no scientific choice between ultimate values can be made."[6]

From the vantage point of our time we look at the past, particularly before the outbreak of World War I, to find the roots of our cultural malaise. True, some of the roots are there. But we may be easily tempted to a one-sided view of this period, seeing it from the perspective of the great upheavals and catastrophes of the past half century. The role of ethical relativism, irrationalism, and cultural pessimism in social thought, at the turn of the century, has been probably overdramatized in some of the recent literature. It is doubtful whether modern relativism in regard to ethical and political values arose primarily as a result of the methodological discussions of that period. The famous distinction between the methods applicable to the cultural sciences and those of the natural sciences did not suddenly originate with Dilthey and Windelband, but went back to a line of thought which had its origins in the revolt of the German Historical School against the tradition of natural law. Perhaps much more important than the disenchantment with religion and metaphysics among positivistic writers, in the course of the nineteenth century, was the insistence of German historically oriented writers to approach ideas and values not in terms of absolute norms of truth or good, but as expressions of a specific age, culture, or people. What preserved Humboldt, Ranke, and Droysen from a radical relativism was their firm belief that the colorful variety of norms and institutions did not reflect a chaotic universe; rather, it revealed the many sides of a fundamental and meaningful unity that unfolded itself in history. This faith in the meaningfulness of history was shared by all the writers who engaged in the methodological discussion at the turn of the century: Wilhelm Dilthey, Wilhelm Windelband, and Heinrich Rickert, as well as Friedrich Meinecke and Ernst Troeltsch. Max Weber alone appears to have perceived the radical gulf between facts and values.

Today, when we look at the period from 1890 to 1914, we are particularly aware of the growing cultural pessimism and the currents of irrationalism. But the same years also witnessed the high point of modern optimism, an almost unbounded confidence in science and civilization. This was particularly true of Wilhelminian Germany.[7] The critiques of French and English positivistic theories of progress by German social thinkers should not mislead us. As we saw in Droysen's *Outline of the Principles of History,* the faith of the German historical tradition in historical development implied an optimism in regard to civilization and the future, at least as pronounced as that of more classical Western theories of progress or of social evolution. It implied a deep confidence in the forces of history, and in the peculiar contribution and mission of Germany in the modern world. Never, perhaps, was the confidence in the beneficent strength of civilization *(Kultur)* in its peculiarly German form as great. This civilization was conceived not merely in terms of Goethe, Kant, and Beethoven, but also included great scientific and technical achievements. None of the men engaged in the methodological discussion was a cultural pessimist. All were convinced of the destiny of Germany and the rightness of 1870-1871. Dilthey and Windelband were still good National Liberals. Men such as Max Weber, Ernst Troeltsch, and after 1900 Friedrich Meinecke, did indeed become keenly aware of the social injustices that existed in the Reich in the wake of industrialization. They also called attention to the dangerous political implications of an undemocratic constitution which permitted the semifeudal *Junker* interests an undue degree of influence in a modern technological society. Such a constitution left extensive room for the whims of the political dilettante, Wilhelm II.

Nevertheless, these men remained convinced of the basic rightness of German political development and the possibility of reforms within the traditional framework. They rallied behind Friedrich Naumann's attempt to "win the workers for the national state" not because they considered the creation of national harmony to be an end in itself, but because they saw in the reconciliation of the classes the *"conditio sine qua non* for the expansion of Germany as a world power."[8] In brief, just as earlier liberal historians had shared Western political ideals, Weber, Troeltsch, and Meinecke, along with philosophers Hermann Cohen and Paul Natorp, supported democratic and even moderately socialist concepts similar to those prevalent in Western countries. However, they subordinated these ideals to the power interests of the German state. Their belief in the harmony of individual interest and reason of state, of ethics and power, was shaken only in the course of World War I. Without a dissenting voice, all of the historians and theorists of this period went into the World War I firmly convinced of the value of the German national tradition.

Indeed, German historical thought in the decades after 1870 remained remarkably immune from the currents of pessimistic thought. The events of the 1860's had reinforced the faith of German historians in history as a meaningful process. All of German history seemed to point in the direction of the Second Reich. The growing prestige of the natural sciences and the popularization of naturalistic concepts of the universe had shattered the philosophic systems of German Idealism, but not its basic theories in regard to state or society. The triumph of the natural sciences had not undermined belief in history, but rather had reinforced faith in the progressive character of historical change.

The suspicion that modern civilization was approaching a profound crisis was shared by many thinkers and artists by 1870, but there were strikingly few historians among them. An important aspect of this new pessimism was the conviction that history was not a purposive process. Schopenhauer had already denied history the character of a science and maintained that no real wisdom could be obtained from the study of history.[9] Nietzsche had questioned the value of history for life.[10] Jakob Burckhardt in Switzerland seemed isolated among German-language historians in questioning the presence of a wise "economy" in world history. Both Ranke and Hegel had shared in this error, he warned. The historian could not trace meaningful development in history, or even study the past genetically. He had to be satisfied "with perceptions and crosscuts through history and in as many directions as possible." Only the "recurring, constant, typical" could be understood, and it is this which Burckhardt sought in the Italian Renaissance or the Age of Constantine.[11]

Nor did German historians in the years 1870 to 1914 reflect the fear that modern European civilization was in a crisis. Isolated voices of warning had been heard earlier. The philosopher Ernst von Lasaulx, still convinced that a divine law of organic development governed the multiplicity of historic institutions and ideas, in his *Philosophy of History* (1856)[12] voiced the belief that the culture of the West was nearing the end of another cycle. Similar to other conservative thinkers elsewhere, he saw the principal symptom of Western decline in the dissolution of Europe's religious consciousness. Together with the Russian Slavophile, Nikolai Danilevskii, a few years later, he held the hope that religious and cultural regeneration would come from the Slavic peoples. Few people read Lasaulx; a notable exception was Jakob Burckhardt.[13] Similarly, Droysen, in a moment of depression during the Crimean War, in 1854 diagnosed the growth of naturalism, materialism, and modern capitalism, with its rule of money and its resulting impoverishment of the masses, as a sign of the approaching collapse of European political dominance in the world.[14] Yet, in contrast to Burckhardt, German historians were amazingly unafraid of the developing technology and mass society, which had been a matter of deep concern to a small but important minority of English and French writers since early in the century. These included conservatives such as Joseph de Maistre and Thomas Carlyle, as well as liberals represented by John Stuart Mill and Alexis de Tocqueville.[15] Burckhardt greeted the events of 1870-1871 with deep dismay. Everything seemed to point to a world-wide Caesarism, to the triumph of the *terribles simplificateurs* who had been falling on Europe since 1789 like Tamerlane sweeping away traditions and replacing them with abstract utopias to which human lives and human values were sacrificed mercilessly.[16]

Another form of pessimism might have expressed itself in the awareness of a political crisis in post-1870 Germany. But, again, the dissidents were few. With scant exceptions, the historians were National Liberals. There was, however, a clear shift of emphasis from the pre-1870 years. More recently, historians have spoken of a Ranke Renaissance.[17] Gone was the liberal-ethical commitment of the Prussian historians of the pre-unification period. A new generation, which included Max Lenz, Hermann Oncken, Erich Marcks, Felix Rachfahl, and others, consciously sought to return to Ranke's ideal of objectivity and *"Uberparteilichkeit."* Historiography was to be freed from ethics. Heinrich von Srbik who had strong Greater German sympathies later saw in the "Ranke Renaissance" a "reattainment of scientific balance" lost by the liberal nationalistic historians.[18] The historian was again to be a detached observer of the great forces operating in history. Nevertheless, in basic ways, the political conception of the Neo-Rankean historians continued the tradition of the Prussian School. The central force in history remained the *Machtstaat*. Even more so than for the historians of the Prussian School, the emphasis shifted to the demands of foreign policy. The state's striving for power appeared not merely as an objective fact, but as an end in itself. The Neo-Rankeans extended Ranke's concept of the interplay of the great European powers to the colonial scene. The new historiography thus provided a theoretical foundation for *Weltpolitik* and imperialism. It is true that, after 1890, awareness of the social and political shortcomings of the Reich grew. No German historian of note, not even such critics as Gustav Schmoller, Friedrich Meinecke, or Karl Lamprecht, questioned the positive value of the nation and its need for political and military power and aggrandizement.

In two very different ways a critical attitude toward history did, however, manifest itself among German historians. The one was in the spread of a positivistic attitude. The other was in the reexamination of the methods and epistemological principles of history as a science, primarily carried out by philosophers and followed by practising historians with varying degrees of interest. Positivism, as a philosophic concept of history in the sense of Comte or Buckle, had no significant representative among German historians. Karl Lamprecht came closest to the positivist position in his hope to find laws of historical development through comparative studies, but in a way more reminiscent of Herder or Hegel or even Burckhardt than of French or English models.[19]

More important in German historical thought of the time was the attitude which placed fact above theory, and assumed that only the individually documented event was certain. There arose the turn toward extreme specialization, the scholar who knew more and more about less and less. Friedrich Meinecke observed a laboratory smell in much of German historiography after 1870.[20] The new specialist was the counterpart to the American historians of the time, whom we discussed; for them the essence of Ranke's method was the application of the critical apparatus freed from all philosophical concepts. Georg von Below regards the period from 1860 to 1878 as the nadir of German historiography, marked by a self-sufficient *(selbst-genügender)* empiricism.[21] Alfred Heuss describes how Theodor Mommsen, who wrote the first three volumes of his *Roman History* in the 1850's and the fifth volume much later, was unable to write the missing fourth volume in the changed scholarly setting. Always a careful critic of sources, confident that specialized research leads to knowledge, Mommsen found it difficult to return to the broad scope of his earlier volumes which he now regarded with great doubts.[22]

But no matter how widespread the new empiricism became in political and legal history, the determination to write general history, in the belief that history is a meaningful process, survived. Treitschke published the first volume of his *German History* in 1879, and Lamprecht's first volume appeared in 1891.[23] But more significant than these two works, each written with a very definite ax to grind, was the new research in economic and legal history. Here, too, the idealistic (and optimistic) view lived on. Lamprecht and even Treitschke already reflected the increasing awareness of social and cultural factors in the writing of political history. Both Gustav Schmoller (1838-1917) and Otto von Gierke (1841-1921) combined ethical conviction with the faith that history is the sole guide to the understanding of human and social behavior.

For Schmoller, as for the economists of the Historical School before him, economics is a normative science, a science of society *(Gesellschaftswissenschaft)* "which should study the relations not only between man and material goods but also between man and his fellows. The economic order was to be regarded as only one aspect and integral part of the entire social life and as such was to be evaluated from an ethical point of view."[24] Economics and social science aimed at the causal and systematic explanation of social phenomena. But only historical study could provide the theoretical foundations of such a science. Gustav von Schmoller did not believe in unilinear progress in history. The last chapter of his *Elements of a General Theory of Economics* nevertheless reflects his view that the course of history shows a slow but steady progress toward higher forms of economic organization, and toward an increasing fusion of mankind into one stream of development.[25] On the basis of this belief, he and his colleagues in the *Verein für Sozialpolitik* could trust in the ability of the German state to take leadership in achieving economic justice through a paternalistic policy of social reforms.

Similarly, Otto von Gierke, in the spirit of Savigny, regards law as part and parcel of man's communal life. Law in the abstract is meaningless. It exists only "in the concrete legal forms *(Rechtsbildungen)* of the associations *(Genossenschaften)* which appear and disappear in the stream of history" and primarily in the nation. The Historical School had not merely presented the world with a new speculative system, Gierke observes in his inaugural lecture on "Natural Law and German Law," but has "revealed a truth." An historical approach to law, Gierke insists, is not identical with legal positivism. In a sense, historical laws are concrete expressions of natural laws. Tacitus, may have been right in believing that German law, with its concern for the rights of individuals, was closer to natural law than Roman law.[26] The state, too, should not be viewed as a mere apparatus of power. Rather, it forms part of a living, organic community. In sharp contrast to Hegel or to the German "classical-liberal," previously discussed, Gierke sees the state as a complex organism of autonomous corporate bodies *(Genossenschaften)*.[27] But the prototypes of these bodies were in the medieval corporations, not in private, voluntary associations.

Gierke condemns the emphasis upon individual rights *(Individualrecht)* as characteristic of the Romanist tradition of law and alien to the historic, Germanic conception of groups. In the Germanic tradition, he claims, rights had always been seen in a social setting and corporate groups had been viewed not as associations of individuals based upon contract, but as "real collective persons" *(reale Gesamtpersonen),* each possessing a corporate constitution. He fought on two fronts: against the centralized, bureaucratic state, but also against "liberal individualism." On one hand, he attempted to limit the powers of the state wherein he saw merely one corporate group in the midst of many autonomous corporate groups which make up society. Similar in essence *(wesensgleich)* to other societies, it was limited in its functions. At the same time, Gierke appears ready to accept the state in an almost Hegelian fashion as the expression of reason, subject to no superior will. To be sure, he thought as Droysen, and to an extent even Hegel had before him, that reason dictates the autonomy of corporate life within the state. However, he did not think of the state in democratic terms, but considered the Hohenzollern monarchy to be normative for nineteenth-century Germany. As Wolfgang Friedmann observed: "Gierke was a genuine champion of corporate autonomy as well as a good German patriot of the Second Reich, and his theory is an unsuccessful attempt to reconcile . . . irreconcilables: to have it both ways."[28]

2.

The second way in which the critical attitude toward history manifested itself was in the re-examination of the methodological and epistemological foundations of historical study. But this re-examination by no means led to the radically relativistic position in regard to knowledge and ethics that has often been supposed. After the disillusionment of World War I, a new generation of thinkers was interested particularly in the relativistic implications of these earlier writings, and often isolated them from their total philosophical context. The overly close identification of Windelband and Rickert with Dilthey in recent popular or general treatments has further strengthened this impression.[29]

From its beginning, the epistemological discussion moved in two very different directions. On one hand, there was the Southwest German school of Neo-Kantians around Wilhelm Windelband and Heinrich Rickert. Their thought had a direct impact upon the methodological writings of historians and social scientists at the turn of the century, including Max Weber and Georg Simmel. On the other hand, there was Dilthey, who profoundly influenced this epistemological discussion only after World War I. At the time, however, he was taken seriously primarily by historians of literature and of art. Both Neo-Kantians and Dilthey shared in the Kantian concern to discover within consciousness the foundations which made science possible, in this case historical science. Both, however, conceived the nature of knowledge in very different terms. The Neo-Kantians recognized that the methods of the natural sciences were not freely applicable to the historical or cultural sciences. Nevertheless, they attempted to find categories for these studies as rational as those of the natural sciences, and to formulate concepts of causation applicable to the study of human and social behavior. They tried to find rational methods to apply to the irrational content with which these studies deal. Rickert, Windelband, and Weber all agreed that an objective, rational approach to history and society was possible. Dilthey, too, sought epistemological foundations for cultural studies, but he not only sacrificed the concept of causation; going further, he began to question the very possibility of a rational approach.

A very disturbing contradiction runs through all of Dilthey's writings, as if he wanted to have his cake and eat it, too. He conceived it as his life's work to write a "critique of historical reason," to study the "nature and conditions of historical consciousness."[30] On one hand, he attempted to provide historical and cultural studies with firm epistemological foundations, and throughout his life he maintained the firm conviction that this could be achieved. On the other hand, his examination of consciousness led him to the conclusion that all knowledge is radically subjective. It is perhaps his inability to solve this contradiction which largely explains that all his attempts to continue his *Introduction to the Geisteswissenschaften,* of which only a first volume was published in 1883, remained fragmentary.

Dilthey's intent in the *Introduction to the Geisteswissenschaften* is a strictly scientific one. As he explains in the Preface, the individual sciences *(Einzelwissenschaften)* had almost all emancipated themselves from metaphysics since the end of the Middle Ages. Only the sciences of history and society had remained subservient to metaphysics until well into the eighteenth century. Thereafter, they fell under the at least equally oppressive dominance of the natural sciences. The Historical School brought about "the emancipation of historical consciousness and historical science." But the Historical School was unable to counter effectively the positivistic use of the methods of the natural sciences in the study of society because it lacked a "philosophic basis" *(philosophische Grundlegung)* or lacked a well-defined theory of knowledge.[31] The "abstract school" had "neglected the relation of the abstract part *(Teilinhalt)* to the living whole." The Historical School, Dilthey believes, committed an equally serious sin when it rejected all abstractions.[32]

Once a philosophy of history, built upon metaphysical concepts, is ruled out, a substitute foundation must establish systematic relationships among propositions of the individual social and historical sciences. Comte and John Stuart Mill had attempted to respond to this problem by applying the concepts and methods of the natural sciences to these sciences, but in Dilthey's opinion in doing so they had mutilated historical reality. The foundation upon which these sciences rest must be found in consciousness. All sciences rest upon experience, Dilthey agreed with the empiricists and positivists. But experience is not merely a passive state in which the conscious mind receives sense data. For "all experience has its original connectedness *(Zusammenhang)* in the conditions of our consciousness in which it appears, in the totality of our nature."[33] This was not understood by Kant, Locke, or Hume. Their conceptions of experience only applied to our study of physical nature, for Nature we never really know. In Nature we only experience phenomena, "shadows" of a "hidden reality. On the other hand, we possess reality as it really is *(wie sie ist)* only through the facts *(Tatsachen)* of consciousness which are present in our inner experience."[34] The task of the social and historical sciences, better called the Geisteswissenschaften, is the analysis of these data of consciousness. The *Geisteswissenschaften* approach all historical and social reality from the viewpoint of the theory of knowledge. For these sciences must take into account that all thought, individual actions, and institutions are part of living totalities and processes, and can be understood only within their context. The various social sciences must relate all these expressions to their context. Hence all social sciences, Dilthey concludes, require a method which combines psychological and historical analysis. Intellect, analogous to volition and feeling, is merely one side of the process of life. An a priori thus does not exist, since all thought is part of a context. The questions of philosophy therefore can not be answered a priori, but only genetically by "evolutionary history *(Entwicklungsgeschichte)* which proceeds from the totality of our being."[35]

Different types of knowledge distinguish the natural sciences and the *Geisteswissenschaften*. With Droysen, Dilthey believes that we can know only the social and human world, never really the physical world. All our knowledge of the physical world is "relative," in the sense that we never actually grasp it directly, but merely observe external relationships. Dilthey agrees with Kant that the relationships which we perceive are not those that exist objectively in the physical world, but relationships which our mind imposes. However, in the *Geisteswissenschaften* real knowledge is possible. Here, our knowledge is not relative but direct. Its truth, however, does not consist of its correspondence to an outside reality. Rather, "that which I experience within me is there for me as a fact of consciousness because I become aware of it." This knowledge is experienced in its fullest sense. Only when we try to formulate our knowledge or communicate it to others does it become relative.[36]

So far, Dilthey assumes that objective knowledge is possible in the *Geisteswissenschaften*. He believes that through the various special social sciences *(Einzelwissenschaften des Geistes)* "historical-social reality" can be studied and known, and that these sciences can investigate and communicate knowledge about continuing relations in the historical world, such as religions, states, and arts; also processes of change involved in revolutions, epochs, or social movements. Dilthey's attempt to formulate an "epistemological foundation for the *Geisteswissenschaften,*" in essence a "critique of historical reason, of man's ability to know himself and the society and history he created,"[37] reflects his conviction that objective knowledge of man and of society are possible. Dilthey's very concept of the nature of this process of understanding seems to make the possibility of objective knowledge problematic and reduce all social science to mere subjectivism. For Dilthey's epistemology denies in effect that there is a separation between object and subject, and it reduces all thought to an expression of nonrational processes. Thus we perceive that he holds knowledge in the *Geisteswissenschaften* to be direct and not relative. In these sciences, unlike the natural sciences, the scholar is not confronted by phenomena or ideas *(Vorstellungen)* of the object under study, but he experiences the objects directly. The objects of his study are the data or facts of his consciousness. "The facts of our consciousness are nothing else but that of which we become conscious. Our hopes and aspirations, our wishes and desires, this inner world as such is the thing itself *(diese innere Welt ist als solche die Sache selber)*."[38] But thought for Dilthey is primarily a vital rather than a cognitive function. We can relate it to an individual "unit of life" *(Lebenseinheit)* or a cultural system, but in doing so we reduce it to an ideology; we deny or ignore its truth content. Moreover, rationality is no guide to truth. The unique *(Einmalige)* in history cannot be understood rationally. Analysis destroys the context of life, the "link between the Singular and the Universal" which can be grasped only by the "vision of the historian of genius" *(geniale Anschauung des Geschichtschreibers)*.[39]

The dilemma which Dilthey faces is essentially similar to that encountered by the entire Historical School which assumed that abstract knowledge was meaningless; that man could not grasp absolute truth or value, but in his cognition was limited to his position in history. The Historical School, however, found a solution which Dilthey rejects in the *Introduction to the Geisteswissenschaften* (although he returned to it in his later writings); namely, it assumes that there is an organic link between the individual and his society and that the society and nation are part of a larger context, either in the Hegelian sense as part of a great design or, in accord with Ranke and Humboldt, as one of the many manifestations of a fundamental reality. But for Dilthey there is something immeasurable in the individual which can not be related to society in any way. The organic analogy limped, therefore, and was as inapplicable to the study of society as were other abstract concepts.[40] In theory, Ranke and Humboldt would have agreed that *individuum est ineffabile*; in practice, they assumed the reality of social bodies as real historical individualities. For Dilthey (at least at this early stage of his writing) the notions of a *Volksseele* or *Volksgeist,* nation, or social organism, are "mystic" concepts unusable in history.[41] Social reality, rather is filled by a tremendous complexity of cultural systems and institutions, and every individual finds himself participating in a large number of these systems.[42] A group composed of individuals is never identical with those who formed it. Even if a man belongs to only one social group, there is something within him which does not enter into the group.[43] This is true even for as natural an institution as the family; for "the individual in his ultimate depth exists for himself."[44] And so, no matter how deeply the state may reach into the life of the individual, "the state links and subordinates the individuals only partly and relatively. There is something in them which is only in the hand of God."[45]

Hence all psychological studies of social groups or movements have their limit for Dilthey in the spontaneity of the individual person. There is always an element of human will which cannot be fitted into the natural order of things.[46] Neither could Dilthey turn to another solution; namely, that of natural law which, in its Stoic, Christian, and Enlightenment forms, had recognized a common element of rationality amidst the diversity of individuals. Dilthey, too, finds a certain uniformity in human nature;[47] not in man's cognitive faculties, but in his general makeup as a unit of life and volition. Indeed, if man discovers a meaningful context *(Zusammenhang)* in life (and as a living being, he has to find such an order in reality), according to Dilthey, he does so out of his highly personal life experiences.[48]

Thus a deep contradiction runs through the *Introduction to the Geisteswissenschaften.* Dilthey believes firmly that it is possible to study history and society scientifically, but also that all cognition is highly personal. On one hand, Dilthey does not entirely free himself from the faith of the Historical School in history as an objective process. On the other hand, he can no longer share the faith of Ranke or Droysen in a Divine Providence that operates in history. He considers such a faith to be metaphysical and devoid of scientific value. With the Historical School, he shares the conviction that history is a guide to knowledge of social and human realities. Interesting in this connection is his discussion of natural law. The positivistic conception of law erred, he believes, when it held that law could be arbitrarily created. Laws are not made, but found. In this sense they represent natural law, although not as an abstract law separated from a social and an historical context.[49] Even stronger is his belief in the steady intellectual advancement of man. Here, the impact of Auguste Comte is very visible. In over two-thirds of the first volume of the *Introduction in die Geisteswissenschaften,* Dilthey traces the steady emancipation of the human intellect from religion and metaphysics. This process provides a structure and unity to the history of Western civilization. In the development of scientific methodologies within the individual sciences Dilthey observes real "progress" *(Fortschritt).*[50] These sciences, he optimistically notes, are gradually approaching a solution of "those problems of sociology, of the philosophy of spirit or of history, which are at all accessible to a solution."[51] On the other hand, he considers any attempt to find meaning in history as fruitless. "Every formula by which we express the meaning of history is merely a reflection of our own agitated inner life."[52]

In his later essays and fragments, Dilthey attempts to solve the apparent contradiction between his belief in the possibility of objective knowledge and the subjective origin of all cognition by referring subject and object to a common stubstratum, Life. He believes that life appears to us in innumerable forms, but always demonstrates the same fundamental traits.[53] Understanding is possible in the *Geisteswissenschaften* because life "objectivates" itself in such institutions as the family, civil society, state and law, art, religion, and philosophy. As products of life and spirit, these institutions can be understood. They are not arbitrarily created by the subjective mind, but represent "objectivizations of life." Dilthey is aware of how closely he approaches Hegel's concept of the objective spirit. For Hegel these institutions were the concrete forms in which the absolute spirit, reason, unfolded itself progressively in history. But such a belief in the rationality of life and history is no longer tenable today, Dilthey holds. "Present day analysis of human existence" has revealed the irrationality of human life.

> We can thus not understand the objective spirit through reason *(aus der Vernunft)* but have to go back to the system of structural relations of the life units *(Strukturzusammenhang der Lebenseinheiten)* which has its continuity in communities. We cannot fit the objective spirit in a system of ideas *(ideale Konstruktion)* but must find the basis for its reality in history.[54]

For life in its objectivated form is structure. And the task of the systematic *Geisteswissenschaften* must be to analyze these basic structures.

An objective subject matter thus exists. There are concrete "cultural systems" (corresponding somewhat to Droysen's ethical communities) such as economics, art, religion, law, language, and so on, each a unit with common purposes and common institutions. Central among these institutions, giving them cohesion, is the organized power of the state. Dilthey agrees with Kant and Hegel that the state ultimately requires force and coercion, even brutality, because only the existence of the state makes culture possible.[55]

The question now remains how the scholar can discern these structures. Each structure is a system *(Wirkungszusammenhang)* governed by its own inner law[56]; yet all these autonomous systems are somehow in harmony with each other. They all reflect the spirit and values of a nation or of an age. No one social factor, e.g., the economy, brings about this "harmony" among the various cultural systems. Rather, all aspects of social life within a nation owe their similarity to "a common deep (source) which defies exhaustive description."[57] Every aspect of social and intellectual life receives the imprint of the special character of man of a specific nation at a specific time.[58] All social and cultural institutions are therefore for Dilthey, as they were for Hegel and Droysen, works of the spirit. As acts of the spirit, they are capable of being understood only through a subjective act of comprehension, through "experience, expression, and understanding" (Erleben, Ausdruck und Verstehen).[59] Nevertheless, the spiritual character of social institutions and the subjective nature of understanding in no way impair the objective reality of institutions, the real, objective coherence of history, and the possibility of objective knowledge in the cultural sciences. For Dilthey, as for Hegel or Ranke, history is a real process. It is not a construct of the subjective mind, even if Dilthey sees in history no longer the expression of "universal reason" as Hegel did, but of "life in its totality."[60] For Dilthey, as for Hegel, the historical world is still a whole (ein Ganzes),[61] even if within it other processes take place with their own laws of development.[62] Since history is a whole, a systematic study of history and of society is possible. Hegel, Dilthey notes, made the mistake of attempting to reduce "the diversity (Mannigfaltigkeit) of historical life" in all too rigid dialectical patterns. The other extreme of rejecting any attempts to use systematic concepts in historical study is "just as erroneous."[63] Dilthey, like Max Weber, seeks a systematic approach to the cultural sciences which takes into account the irrationality of life.

The primary task of the cultural sciences for Dilthey is, therefore, the analysis of structures. The cultural scientist cannot be concerned with the problem of the total direction of history, as Hegel or Comte were; nor does he see in history a multiplicity of unrelated events. Rather, he is concerned with structural relationships in history.[64] History, something objectively given, makes possible an objective study of the subject. It is true that the historian must select his topic of study; but the topic, in turn, determines what is relevant and what is irrelevant.[65] Basic to every historical structure is its system of values. The historian studies these values not in terms of their validity, but as something given and posited.[66]

Similarly, the *Geisteswissenschaften* can describe historical structures as something given, as integrated systems. They can show the basic values and philosophic outlook *(Weltanschauung)* which dominate them, and can compare and classify into types the *Weltanschauungen* of various culture systems or epochs. They can ascertain certain basic characteristics of the human mind. Beyond this, they cannot go. Indeed, the fundamental recognition of the *Geisteswissenschaften* is that thought is always a life function. Hence it cannot be approached from the standpoint of abstract truth, but only in terms of its relatedness to a life situation. The task of the *Geisteswissenschaften* is therefore a very different one from that of traditional philosophy which seeks ultimate truth. The *Geisteswissenschaften* merely attempt to relate ideas, works of art, political deeds, economic activities to the structures to which they belong, and to compare them with other structures. The spontaneity of the individual, described by Dilthey in the *Introduction to the Geisteswissenschaften,* shares in a large number of diverse cultural systems and groups and never is absorbed fully in any specific one. He recedes somewhere into the background in the much more organicist concept of society of Dilthey's later writings.

While this limited descriptive and classificatory knowledge is possible, according to Dilthey, any fundamental answer is impossible. The most impressive argument for the impotence of philosophy is the anarchy of philosophic systems which an historical study of Western thought reveals. The reason for this anarchy is the very relatedness of all thought to life. For "philosophy must seek the inner connectedness of its cognitions not in the world but in men . . . ."[67] "The *Weltanschauungen* are not products of thought. They do not originate from the mere will to know" but "from our conduct of life, from our life experience, from our total psychic structure" *(aus dem Lebensverhalten, der Lebenserfahrung, der Struktur unserer psychischen Totalität).*[68] Yet the process by which the *Weltanschauungen* originate is not arbitrary. Although each *Weltanschauung* is different, colored by different life experiences, a degree of regularity marks their genesis. The *Weltanschauungen* all arise from a common human need to solve the fundamental problems or "riddles" of life which confront the individual. Since "human nature is always the same, the principal features of life experiences are also the same," although the conditions under which we experience the basic situations of life are not identical.

All men are confronted with the reality of constant change, the "transitoriness of all things human" and the mystery of death.[69] Each individual out of his own situation attempts to solve these questions and to construct a world image *(Weltbild)*. Religion, art, and metaphysics represent these attempts to solve the riddle at their highest form. Each metaphysical system claims to be universally valid, but because these systems have their origin in specific situations of life, the conflict among them can never be solved.[70]

Thus there is an apparently insoluble antinomy between the "claim of every life or world view to universality and historical consciousness,"[71] which shows that philosophic systems change the same as mores, religions, and forms of government. The philosophic systems appear as historically conditioned, and thus illusory and subjective. But there is a solution, Dilthey rejoices, for these philosophies are not false but merely "symbols of the various sides of aliveness *(Lebendigkeit)*." The apparent contradictions between the philosophic systems springs from the "many-sidedness of aliveness." "The contradictions arise because the objective world pictures become autonomous in the consciousness of the scientists. By becoming autonomous, a system becomes metaphysics."[72] And thus our historical consciousness which had destroyed the belief in the validity of the philosophic systems has at the same time helped us to overcome the apparently insoluble contradiction between the claims of philosophies to general validity and the historic anarchy among them by showing the relatedness of these systems to life.[73]

Once we have understood the function of philosophic conceptions, the way is open for the scientific study of man. Dilthey is still convinced that objective scientific knowledge is possible on two levels in the *Geisteswissenschaften*. Although the social and human sciences are incapable of going beyond the study of life, they can understand the objective manifestations of life in the course of history. They are unable to solve problems involving questions of value, but they are able to show the relatedness of value in concrete social contexts and *Weltanschauungen*. Going beyond mere historical study, the *Geisteswissenschaften*, through a comparative approach, can unfathom the characteristics common to all human consciousness. They may thus transcend history by discovering the types of philosophic world images which recur perennially in man's eternal need to answer the riddle of life.

But has Dilthey really answered the question how knowledge is possible in the *Geisteswissenschaften?* For if cognition is essentially an intuitive act of experienceing life in its broader sense *(Erlebnis),* what guarantees are there that our insights are not merely subjective expressions of our needs and situations in the stream of history? Dilthey recognizes that "philosophy is a function in the purposive system *(Zweckzusammenhang)* of society,"[74] and that the methodology employed in philosophic investigation is always determined by the *Weltanschauung* of the investigator.[75] But would this not be equally true of the *Geisteswissenschaften?* Dilthey, of course, denies this. He believes that there is a method proper to the *Geisteswissenschaften* which gives these studies a scientific character and distinguishes them from the fruitless endeavors of philosophy. However, if such a method exists, then thought would no longer be directed by *Erlebnis,* but once again subjected to the logical categories. These Dilthey rejects as alien to the thought processes of human beings. The scholar, too, does not think along logical lines. Like all men he is a physio-psychic life unit, not a thinking machine. If Dilthey still believes in the possibility of objective knowledge on the basis of subjective life experience, it is because in German Idealistic tradition he still sees history as a process, and he assumes a basic harmony between the perspectivistic perceptions of the individual in the process and the total reality. "The first condition for the possibility of historical science," he writes, "lies in the fact that I myself am a historical being, that he who inquires into history is the same person who makes history."[76] It is not man's participation in transcendent reason, which Kant and the Neo-Kantians had assumed made it possible for man to understand the world and each other, but the fact that man himself is a part of Nature and of history.

Nevertheless, there is a note of despair in Dilthey's speech to his students and friends on his seventieth birthday in 1903, even if he concludes on the hopeful note that he sees the solution of the problems in sight.

I undertook to investigate the nature and conditions of historical consciousness—a critique of historical reason. This task led me to the most general of problems: a seemingly insoluble contradiction arises if we pursue historical consciousness to its last consequences. The finitude of every historical phenomenon, whether it be a religion, an ideal, or a philosophic system, hence the relativity of every sort of human conception about the connectedness of things, is the last word of the historical world view. All flows in process; nothing remains stable. On the other hand, there arises the need of thought and the striving of philosophy for universally valid cognition. The historical way of looking at things *(die geschichtliche Weltanschauung)* has liberated the human spirit from the last chains which natural science and philosophy have not yet torn asunder. But where are the means for overcoming the anarchy of convictions which threatens to break in on us?

I have worked all my life on problems which link themselves as a long chain to this problem. I see the goal. If I fall by the wayside, I hope that my younger companions and students will go on to the end of this road.[77]

3.

Analagous to Dilthey, the Neo-Kantians recognized the collapse of the great metaphysical systems, and sought to find a new basis for the natural as well as the human sciences. They, too, attempted to find this basis in human consciousness, but they viewed consciousness very differently from Dilthey. Despite the relativistic implications which later writers discovered in Neo-Kantian philosophy, Neo-Kantianism, as first formulated by the Marburg School around Hermann Cohen (1842-1918) and his disciple Paul Natorp (1854-1924), and then modified by the Baden or Southwest German School around Wilhelm Windelband (1848-1915) and Heinrich Rickert (1863-1936), reasserted the rationality of the human mind. This view reflected the great confidence of the late nineteenth century in science and scientific method.

What makes the laws of the natural sciences possible for Cohen, as for Kant, is not the lawful character of an objective nature, but the innate laws of the human mind which regulate the formation of our ideas. Going beyond Kant, Hermann Cohen rejects the notion of a noumenal world, the thing-in-itself, standing behind the world of phenomena. The laws of nature are not to be understood as categories by which the mind organizes the sense data it receives. Rather, these laws derive from pure thought alone, independently of sense data. In this context Cohen is far more radically idealistic than Kant, for he recognizes consciousness alone as real. But this idealism is very different from the subjective idealism of Berkeley. The consciousness that Cohen has in mind is not that of an individual subject, the type of consciousness studied by the psychologist. Rather, it is "consciousness as such," pure understanding, and within this transcendent consciousness the entire world is immanent. Cohen and his disciples by no means deny the existence of objective facts and events, but they understand these within the framework of the logical relations of consciousness.

If consciousness is logical and all reality exists within consciousness, then all reality is logical. What this amounts to for Cohen is that the laws of nature are laws of logic. In a way, logic is thus identical with the methodology of the natural sciences. Reality, then, fundamentally consists of a "web of logical relationships" which permit no place for an element of irrationality.[78]

Cohen recognizes a distinction between the methods of the natural sciences and those of the cultural or historical sciences. He hesitates, however, to name the latter *Geisteswissenschaften*. For, in contrast to Dilthey, the essence of *Geist* (spirit) for Cohen resides in cognition. "Spirit is human spirit in this sense . . . the spirit of methodical cognition, of the cognitive methods of science. The spirit of scientific cognition is the distinguishing mark of human reason. And human reason develops in scientific reasoning." In this context, the natural sciences, too, belong to the *Geisteswissenschaften*. What distinguishes the cultural and historical studies from the natural sciences is that the former deal not only with natural or logical relationships, but also with questions of value.

These studies therefore require two methods: "logic for definition, classification, and subdivision" along with the technical concepts required for a theory of cognition, and ethics for the analysis of the cultural content *(Kulturgehalt)*.[79] Ethics demands a method no less rigid than that of logic. Its approach to values is not psychological but transcendental. Ethical norms have their foundation not in experience, but in the structure of the mind. Hence the scholar cannot be satisfied with treating a *Weltanschauung* as a unique historical phenomenon which can be studied as something in itself not capable of being reduced to rational foundations. However, he must approach such a *Weltanschauung* from the standpoint of the absolute and timeless criteria of logic and ethics.[80]

Indeed, by implication, Cohen repudiates the traditional method of the historian who seeks to recreate the past *"wie es eigentlich gewesen,"* and refrains from ethical judgments or the establishment of general relationships. Cohen himself turned to a view of history which, despite his Kantian terminology, seems remarkably similar to Condorcet's idea of progress. History appears to him as the endless process by which man, through the use of reason, gains increasing control over nature and steadily approaches more closely the ideal of an ethical organization of society. This progress is not a cosmic process, as it was for Hegel. Rather, it results from the fact that human thought, because of the logical sturcture of consciousness, must arrive at a rational picture of the world and of society. This process by which the human mind and human society progressively approach the ideals set by reason is an eternal one, for the ideal can never be attained entirely.[81]

The ideal of politics and society which Cohen considers rational is essentially liberal-democratic and socially oriented. The "autonomous personality," demanded by the Kantian categorical imperative, requires a social setting. "The decisive criterion of the ethical spirit of a nation" may be found "in its conduct toward the working men's party."[82] Yet Cohen is remarkably free not only of a willingness to recognize the role of irrational forces in society, but of any pessimism in regard to modern culture or Wilhelminian Germany. He and many of his colleagues could therefore face World War I with complete confidence in Germany's past and future and in her cultural contribution. Although aware of Germany's need of further democratization, Cohen hailed his country as a progressive state, which had introduced universal suffrage in national elections and initiated the most advanced social legislation of the time. The German spirit expressed itself in Kant's philosophy and Germany's history in the nineteenth century represented the realization of Kantian ethics to a high degree. The Prussian military and bureaucratic traditions were not in opposition to this spirit, but integral parts of it. The "nation of thinkers and poets" was one and indivisible with the nation of "fighters and creators of states."[83] "Luther's universal compulsory education and Scharnhorst's universal military service," Cohen noted in 1914, are "the two institutions which provide the discipline for Kant's idealism."[84]

This was undoubtedly an overstatement produced in the elated atmosphere of the moment. Nevertheless, what made this identification easy for Cohen was the conception of the ethical character of the state,[85] of which he never freed himself; it distinguished him from most Anglo-American liberals or socialists. More strongly than almost any other German liberal thinker, Cohen emphasizes the integrity of the individual as a demand of the categorical imperative. At the same time, he recognizes the central role of the state, for not only the individual has rights. He stresses: "the state too is a person." *(Auch der Staat ist Person.)*[86] The state, however, is not identical with the nation, Cohen warns. The state is an ethical entity, the nation is not. The nation is subordinate to the state. Nationality has been instrumental in creating states. Nationalism, absolutized and separated from the ethical principles of the state, becomes a form of barbarism.[87]

4.

The new note which Wilhelm Windelband introduces into the Neo-Kantian discussion is the reformulation of the distinction between the methods of the natural and the historical sciences. As a practising historian of ideas, certainly more famous today for his standard *History of Modern Philosophy* than for his philosophical speculations, Windelband is particularly conscious of the peculiar logic of historical studies. Yet Windelband by no means repudiates the basic assumptions of Cohen and Natorp of the world as the construct of rational consciousness. Nevertheless, on a very important point, Windelband modifies this concept of the Marburg School, when he holds that axiological laws, not logical ones, form the basis of objective reality. Logic, too, analogous to ethics and aesthetics, is a normative science, the science of how one should think, and as such it is not descriptive of reality. Norms are "valid" *(gelten),* not "real" *(wirklich),* Windelband observes. In this sense, the laws of Nature are not identical with those of logic.[88] This distinction between logic and Being implies, to be sure, a greater recognition of the existence of irrational elements in reality, but by no means leaves room for subjectivism in values. For the norms have their basis not in the individual psyche, but in consciousness as such. Whether in science, logic, ethics, or aesthetics, these values are absolutely valid and timeless, and they alone make life and reality meaningful. They confronted Windelband, Rickert observes, "as that which should be in eternity without really having to be. By transforming the valid into the real, our existence receives a living meaning which makes it truly worth living."[89] Concerned more centrally with questions of values than Cohen and Natorp had been, Windelband and Rickert turn their main attention from methodological and epistemological questions of the natural sciences to those of the social sciences.

The importance of Windelband's famous inaugural address, as rector of the University of Strassburg in 1894, on "History and Natural Science" lay in its programmatic call for a special logic of the historical sciences. The observation that the methods of the natural sciences are not applicable to the study of history, but that history requires a methodology and epistemology of its own, is not new and had been the common property of the Historical School. Nor did Windelband actually work out such a methodology in the lecture. He distinguished between "rational" sciences, such as philosophy and mathematics, and "experiential" sciences (Erfahrungswissenschaften). The latter were not classified by subject matter, as had been the custom, but in terms of methodologies. Windelband, as Cohen before him, considered the distinction between the natural sciences and the Geisteswissenschaften an unfortunate one. Psychology, for example, could be approached as a natural science. The difference in the two types of science lay in the kind of knowledge at which they aim; whether they wish to reduce events to abstract relationships or to "describe fully and exhaustively a unique event limited in time." The one set of sciences sought laws, the other facts.

For the natural sciences Windelband uses the Greek term "nomothetic" (lawgiving), and for the historical disciplines "idiographic" (describing the separate, distinct, individual).[90] The same content often can be approached by either method, as holds true in the case of languages, physiology, geology, psychology, and even astronomy. The great weakness of traditional logic is that it overstresses the nomothetic approach of the natural sciences, and neglects the logical reflexion involved in the study of historical reality.[91] Although both types of science are empirical, neither deals with experience in a naive sense. Both approach experience with scientific criteria and highly refined methods; they use precise quantitative measurements or stylistic analyses.[92] Neither deals with mere phenomena. A naked event is of no more significance for the historical sciences than it is for the natural sciences. Both types of science are concerned with establishing relationships, although different types of relationships. The natural scientist seeks laws and tends toward abstractions. He wishes to reduce colorful reality into a conceptual system, "a world of atoms, without color or sound, without the earthy smell of qualities perceived through the senses—the triumph of thought over perception." The historian, unable to free himself from concepts entirely, turns to contemplation *(Anschauung)*. The ultimate aim of history is to regain "from the mass of material the true shape of the past in its life-filled clarity," to present "pictures of human beings and human lives in the full richness of their unique development, preserved in their living individuality."[93] Although individual historical events can and must be subsumed under general scientific laws in order to be understood, there is always an element in each event and in each individual which escapes analysis, "an incomprehensible residue, something which cannot be expressed or defined."[94]

Windelband left untouched in his lecture the question how the historian can distinguish the historical event from the mere event. Obviously, a principle of selection is required. If the principle is to be found in the subjective interest of the historian, then history is necessarily subjectivistic. If the subject matter of history purely consists of autonomous, unique events, it is impossible for the historian to discover objective criteria by which he can determine what is historically significant.

The answer which Windelband gave in his uncompleted lectures of *The History of Philosophy*, published posthumously in 1916, is surprisingly realistic. History is not mere chronology. It deals with actions which are held together by purposes. In this sense, one can speak of progress, regression, or standstill in history and presuppose certain values.[95] These values enable the historian to decide what is of historical interest and what is not. Historical is that which has a place in this development; unhistorical is that which has not. "The particular is of significance if it possesses significance for a superior *(übergeordnetes)* whole in the human community. This value relatedness to a human community is the decisive fact which gives the individual event the character of being historical."[96] The historian singles out the man for study who is historically significant. He singles out as historical those nations "who not only come and go on the stage of universal history but who stamp their character on the development of the whole."[97] The task of the historian resembles that of the natural scientist insofar as both seek to establish regular patterns *(Regelmässigkeiten)* in history. A fundamental difference between the historian and the natural scientist is that the former deals with that which can only be narrated, not reduced to laws. But narration requires general concepts.[98] While the historian deals with "the particular," he selects the "particular" not for its own sake, but because it has a place in a chain of development of a meaningful whole, of a great social unity, or of mankind as a whole.[99]

The principle of selection is found, therefore, in the objective subject matter of history itself. Windelband emphatically rejects the notion that truth in history is relative to the historian. Historical truth exists independently of the historian in the same manner that mathematical truth is valid, even if no mathematician has discovered it. "Historical truth as an object *(Gegenstand)* remains intact, even when memory or reconstructive phantasy are lacking or wrong; and it is equally true that what has happened cannot be made undone by forgetting. . . . Therefore the validity of historical truth is independent of our knowing."[100] What complicates the quest for objective historical knowledge, Windelband recognizes, is the condition that the historian of human history, in contrast to the student of other aspects of the past, is never confronted by the events of the past themselves but largely deals with traditions. Tradition tends to distort our picture of the past in two ways: not only have the victors of the past written or remembered history from their viewpoint, but the historian himself is part of a living tradition. In this sense "the total memory of the species, which we possess in historical science, is itself a product of history, a work of tradition, a collective achievement of the human race, and thereby one of the most valuable parts of our culture."[101] The task implicit in the theory of knowledge is therefore to determine the extent to which cultural and traditional factors color historical knowledge.

Nevertheless, what makes history possible for Windelband is the reality of human development in an objective sense. The historian proceeds on the assumption that "historical life is no meaningless accident *(Ungefähr),* no mechanism of a biological sort devoid of reason, but that a rational purpose *(Sinn)* governs it, a *logos* which makes the historical world, too, into a cosmos." This belief cannot be proved, but it has become increasingly apparent in the course of millenia of intellectual work.[102] The unity of this process lies in the "idea of humanity" itself. This idea signifies that mankind is not merely a "zoological species," but a "real entity of value" *(eine werthafte Realität)*.[103] This entity, "mankind as a universal unit of life," does not yet exist, but is a task given to man to realize, an idea which can never be fully attained.

> Mankind as a unit of life in which a rational total purpose develops is never given *(gegeben)* as something completed, as, for example, mankind is as a biological species, but is always given as a task *(aufgegeben),* but an absolutely necessary task from which there is no escape. History is therefore the process by which mankind fulfills this task.[104]

Thus, by definition, all is historical which contributes to this development. There remained for Windelband, as for Cohen, a universal, rational standard which transcends historical institutions and positive law and serves as a possible criterion by which historical institutions could be judged. Windelband did not wish to return to eighteenth-century conceptions of natural law. He rejects the idea that the jurist could create new laws on the basis of a static, abstract rational law, but maintains that philosophy of law permits us "to inquire to what extent higher necessities of reason actualized themselves in the human artifice of law." For above "the individual nations which always create their states and laws in imperfect fashions that are bound to what is naturally and historically given . . . there stands the ideal of the rational collective consciousness of mankind which would represent the highest form of conscience."[105]

This concept of a rational ideal directing human efforts involves an optimism toward the future, akin to that of Hermann Cohen, although Windelband was much more perceptive of signs of danger in the Europe of his time. With Burckhardt, he feared that modern technological mass society threatened the traditional values of our civilization. In "Friedrich Hölderlin and his Fate," he voices the concern that the same madness which befell the poet would befall modern society as the complexity of modern civilization, with its demands for specialization and intellectualization, strip man of the

harmony and the integration of personality which had been the heritage of the Classical civilization.[106] As a good European, deeply
aware of the spiritual unity which this heritage had given to Western
Civilization, Windelband regretted in a lecture on Fichte, delivered
in 1890, the decline of the cosmopolitan spirit of the eighteenth
century and the hardening of national division.[107] But the same lecture, held on the occasion of the emperor's birthday, ended with a
panegyric on the political and social accomplishments of the Prussian
state in the course of the nineteenth century. The confidence regarding the future, which well overshadowed Windelband's isolated dim
observations,[108] had not yet been shattered by the outbreak of World
War I.

5.

An important step toward ethical relativism was taken by
Windelband's younger colleague at Freiburg, Heinrich Rickert, although Rickert certainly would have strongly resented the label
"father of historical relativism" which later scholars attached to
him.[109] For Rickert shared with Windelband the basic Neo-Kantian
assumptions regarding the timeless and universally valid character of
the judgments of logic and ethics. Similar to Cohen and Windelband,
Rickert was convinced that objective scientific knowledge of the
physical and the historical world was possible. Nevertheless, he not
only rejected the notion that history was a real process of development which provided the historian with a principle of selection, but
also denied that the philosopher could judge the concrete institutions,
ideas, and values of a culture by the abstract principles of a timeless
ethics. The task of the historian, he agreed with the Historical
School, was not to evaluate *(werten)* historical events or constellations in terms of his own values, but to ascertain what these values
were and to relate the manifestations of a culture to its basic values
(Wertbezogenheit).

This approach implies a thoroughgoing ethical relativism in historical practice which seems to contradict Rickert's ethical absolutism as a philosopher. Aware of this contradiction, Rickert attempted
to solve it through a doctrine of immanent values which proposed
that the values expressed by a culture were manifestations of timeless, absolutely valid norms. This position would have been much

easier to defend had Rickert been able to maintain his belief in history as a meaningful process, as conceived by Hegel, Humboldt, or Ranke. Nor did his Neo-Kantian ethical assumptions permit him to accept the Neo-Platonic conception of a pluralism of absolutely valid, timeless ideas. As a result, Rickert's attempt to see in the manifold and clashing values of historical cultures the expression of an eternal ethics appears as another unfortunate effort to reconcile irreconcilables. Rickert was unwilling to follow the more plausible solution of his colleague at Freiburg, Max Weber, who restricted the task of the social scientist and historian strictly to the study of value relationships in historical cultures, and denied the possibility of any objective study of universally valid values.

Rickert agrees with Windelband that the primary difference between history and natural science is not one of content but of method. There is only one reality which includes all that exists, body as well as spirit. This reality must be viewed "monistically" as an integrated whole. Spirit *(Geist)*, too, can be studied by the methods of the natural sciences; not spirit *(Geist)* but history is therefore the counterpart to Nature. Nature conceives all of existence in terms of general law; history approaches it from the standpoint of the unique one-time event *(einmaliges Geschehen).*[110]

But Rickert did not believe that Windelband had exhausted the difference between history and Nature by his distinction between a nomothetic and an idiographic method.[111] History describes reality no more than does natural science. In reality, all is in flux and all is different. Understanding in history, no less than in natural science, requires the reduction of this flux and diversity into concepts.[112] The historian along with the scientist does not paint a picture of reality *(abbilden),* but transforms *(umbilden)* and simplifies the picture. Only in this way does irrational reality become rational.[113] Ranke and Windelband both misunderstood this by stressing that the historian approaches the past with intuitive contemplation *(Anschaulichkeit)* rather than with rational concepts.[114] For historical research, too, requires an a priori, a prejudgment *(Vor-Urteil),* with whose help it can reduce the "heterogeneous continuum of real happening" to concepts.[115] The historian must be able to distinguish between the essential and the nonessential in the past, between "historically significant individualities affected with meaning" and those who are "merely different."[116] This requires a principle of selection.

This principle of selection is not found by relating an event, individual, or constellation to an objective process of history, but by establishing its relationship to cultural values *(Wertbezogenheit)*. For in an important way the difference between Nature and cultural history is one of content as well as of values. In Nature all grows freely without human direction; in a culture all requires human labor. "Every cultural event *(Kulturvorgänge)* embodies some value recognized by men, for the sake of which it was either brought about or, if it had already come about, is cultivated." Values cling to all cultural objects *(Kulturobjekte)*. Natural processes, on the other hand, are devoid of such values. In this way, we can distinguish between "value-related *(wertbezogene)* cultural goods" *(Kulturgüter)* and "value-devoid" objects of nature. The science which studies "value-related objects of culture," Rickert continues, might thus be preferably named the "science of culture" *(Kulturwissenschaft)* rather than history.[117] The historian or cultural scientist selects those "individual objects" which "in their individual peculiarity as expressions of complexes of meaning, actually embody cultural values or stand in some relation to them." Only by relating these objects to the values attached to a culture can he conceive of a historical individuality that can be depicted meaningfully.[118]

The historian, Rickert holds, is therefore interested in values only insofar as persons have held these values and attached them to objects. He is not interested in the validity of these values. Hence his approach is not one of valuing *(werten)*, but of relating objects to values *(wertbeziehen)*. He may, of course, have opinions regarding history based upon his own values, but he does not hold these opinions as a historian. Rather, he studies the values of a culture as facts, free from his own value positions.[119] Thus he cannot decide whether the French Revolution was beneficial or detrimental to France, but merely whether it was significant within French or European historical development and should be included in a history of Europe.[120] In the multiplicity of values held by subjects in the course of history, he must be able to distinguish between "arbitrary" and "objective" ones. The question remains what are the values around which he should organize history. Are there any objective criteria for his choice? Rickert's reply is in the affirmative. There are certain values in a culture, generally accepted, which can be known empirically and hence objectively.

> The fact that *cultural values are universal* is what keeps concept-formation in the historical sciences from being arbitrary individual decisions *(individuelle Willkür)* and provides a basis for the objectivity of these concepts. What is historically essential must be *significant* not for this or that person but *for everyone*.[121]

Rickert, of course, makes two highly questionable assumptions here. First, he believes that there are certain values in every culture which are universally accepted within that culture as valid; and, second, that historians who proceed objectively and free of bias, must agree on what these values are. From this it follows that if historians differ in their interpretation of a historical situation, it is because of a lack of objectivity on their part. Rickert leaves aside the very real possibility that cultures may not be integrated systems, but rather contain a great diversity of values. He also does not admit the extent to which the social, psychological, or historical position of the historian may determine his interests or cause him to see perspectives of the historical problem he is studying, rather than its entire character. If Dilthey assumes that historical knowledge is always conditioned by the personality of the observer and hence highly subjective, Rickert discounts psychological or sociological factors in knowledge and considers cognition as primarily a rational and objective act.[122]

Of course, if the historian has to organize history around leading values of a culture, then universal history is impossible. All the historian could write would be the history of the separate cultures. To go beyond this would require the existence of objective values shared by all men.[123] Within a culture, the historian can speak of a development unique to the culture and measured in terms of its values. But to speak of progress of mankind in empirical history would not be possible, for progress is a value-charged term which is meaningful only if there are objectively and universally valid values. For Rickert, therefore, the question of progress belongs to the philosophy of history and not to historical science.[124]

Nevertheless, Rickert recognizes that it is difficult to speak of the objectivity of the cultural sciences or of cultural history if the whole of history is dissolved into a large number of isolated processes, each centering around a different set of values. In the natural sciences, too, theories are modified, but we still may assume that "natural laws are absolutely valid, even if no single law is yet known to us." The values held by the various cultures come and go, so that it appears that "apart from mere facts, there are then as many different historical truths as there are culture circles."[125] Here, Rickert's understanding of truth is different from that of the Historical School. The description of the ephemeral event is not truth. "A scientific truth must have a definite relationship, i.e., must more or less approximate what is theoretically *valid,* even if this is *not known.* Without this presupposition, there is no longer any sense in speaking of truth. . . . All historical *concepts* are then valid only for a definite *time.* But this means that they do not have the value of truths, for they have no definite relationship to that which has *absolute* and timeless validity."[126] But if this is true, the whole cultural and intellectual enterprise of man is meaningless; as in Nietzsche's fable, it is a presumptuous self-deception in a remote corner of the universe by an intelligent animal lasting only an instant in the eternity of time, "the most arrogant and mendacious minute in the history of the universe, but nevertheless only a minute."[127]

But Rickert is unwilling to accept this. "This point of view is, if one will, indeed consistent," he comments. "But its very consistency destroys the objectivity of *every* science, that of the natural sciences as well as the cultural sciences . . . The *scientist* is the very one who must assume the *absolute* validity of theoretical values if he does not wish to cease being a scientist."[128] In sharp contrast to Max Weber,[129] Rickert insists that a strictly value-free approach to science is impossible, even in the natural sciences. Just as empirical study in the natural sciences must assume "unconditionally and universally valid laws of nature," so the cultural sciences must assume that there are "unconditionally and universally valid values" which the objects and institutions of cultural life approximate to a greater or lesser extent. Without this assumption, no meaningful principle of selection can exist. But this assumption, Rickert recognizes, lacks empirical foundation. It is a philosophic rather than a scientific assumption. We therefore must conclude that for Rickert there is "no historical science without a philosophy of history."[130]

But how can empirical history and transempirical philosophy be reconciled? Rickert tries to solve this dilemma by a theory of values which sees in the diverse cultural values manifestations of universally valid values adjusted to specific and unique historical situations. For is not natural science itself a product of culture, he asks, and yet does it not possess real validity? May not the same be true of other products of culture?[131] To be sure, no philosophy is capable of constructing a comprehensive system of cultural values "from mere concepts. A system of cultural values that lays claim to validity can be found only in meaningful historical life and can only gradually be elaborated *from* it by our asking what general and *formal* values underlie the substantive and constantly changing multiplicity of cultural life and its individual complexes of meaning as it manifests itself in history."[132] With this theory Rickert has essentially returned to the German Idealistic faith in the meaningfulness of history and the validity of the diverse values to be found in history.

Rickert defends this belief in the validity of individual historical values in more detail in his *Limits to the Formation of Concepts in the Natural Sciences*. The norms of ethics are universally valid and timeless, Rickert agrees with Kant. But these norms, central to which is the categorical imperative, are purely formal. Norms are always valid *(gelten)*, never real *(wirklich)*, but values are linked with reality in two ways: they occur either in the actions of a subject as value judgments *(Wertung)*, or they are attached to cultural objects.[133] It is an error, therefore, to think of ethical norms as class or generic concepts *(Gattungsbegriffe)* applicable to every instance in the same way that laws of nature are, since "man never lives as an example of a generic concept among examples of the genus but only individually as an individual." Every individual is different and the situations in which he finds himself vary, so that "ethical tasks must be also individual. The highest ethical duty of man must therefore consist of cultivating his individuality in such a way that he is suited to fulfill the individual ethical tasks which are put to him." The categorical imperative must thus be reformulated to take into account the individual character of ethical norms:

> You shall, if you wish to act well, carry out through your individuality at the individual point of reality which you occupy that which only you can carry out, since no other person in this completely individual world has exactly the same task as you; and you shall fashion your life in such a way so that your life forms a development which in its individual totality can be viewed as the fulfillment of a task in life which will never be repeated.

The norms of ethics can be absolute and universal, and at the same time apply to very different individual situations because they are purely formal in character.[134] The question may be asked, of course, what meaning such a definition of the categorical imperative still possesses. Kant, too, defined the categorical imperative as purely formal, without specific content. Nevertheless, it formally called on the individual to "act only on that maxim through which you can at the same time will that it should become a universal law." For Rickert, in fact, the categorical imperative, as the timeless, universal norm of ethics, stated that there are as many norms as there are individuals, and that all these norms are of equal validity. Indeed, it is impossible to find any universally human ethical ideal with a specific content. The content of the ethical imperatives is always derived from the historical developments of cultures and, above all, of nations.[135] For this reason, it is the individual's "ethical duty to be above all a member of a nation since we can fulfill most of our duties only as members of a nation." The nation provides him with "positive, definite culture aims" which humanity does not. In turn, each nation has "always an individual task, which no other nation can have. Only by elaborating the unique character of the nation can anything be accomplished."[136] Similarly, the law of Nature must be viewed in purely formal terms. In the world of concrete reality, however, "only historical law as the product of historical cultural development is real law. Natural law exists as little as there exists a quantitative world of atoms or some other hypostatized metaphysical universal concept."[137] There is no standpoint above history other than a purely formal one.[138]

Nevertheless, Rickert vigorously defends his position against the charge of historicism or relativism. As a method of studying cultural values, the historical approach alone is correct. But as a *Weltanschauung* "historicism is a monstrous thing *(Unding),* a form of relativism and skepticism," which "carried to its logical conclusion can lead only to complete nihilism."[139]

Similarly, any attempt to explain life from life itself, without reference to transcendantal rational norms, is absurd.[140] The very rational nature of our consciousness requires that values are real and not merely arbitrary. The Ought *(Sollen)* of the categorical imperative requires that we not only Want what is good but Do it. This, in turn, Rickert argues, requires that our ethical actions, those which correspond to our diverse, individual tasks, also produce ethical results. In the case of our own individual actions, we can will that which is absolutely right but we cannot produce absolutely good results. We are led, therefore, to assume the presence of a "holy power which brings about what we are incapable of bringing about, i.e., which through actions realizes unconditionally universal values. The awareness of our impotence in regard to what should be, thus requires an objective, good or holy reality." This reality cannot be fully grasped by scientific concepts, Rickert admits.

> Only through our conscience, which orders us to act, and through our awareness that we want only the good but cannot act in accordance with the good, something is required which can never be the object of our cognition. But at the same time it is required unconditionally because otherwise all actions would lose their meaning.

Nor would logical thought be possible, for logical thought requires that the judgments of logic are true. Logical thinking itself is a form of normative action.

> In a reality which is fully indifferent to all Ought to be *(Sollen)*, or in a world unsuitable for the realization of truth value, all judgments would lose their meaning. Thus the assumption that through our judgments we can realize unconditional truth value already presupposes belief in a reality which makes this value real through our judgments. And thus the meaningfulness of all cognition becomes dependent on the conviction, which transcends not only all logic but also all ethics, that the world is organized in such a manner that cognition is possible in it."

This, Rickert admits, is a "metaphysical conviction," but one which we cannot avoid. And so he closes his heavy tome on *The Limits to the Formation of Concepts in the Natural Sciences* by pointing to the philosophic necessity of having "faith in an objective cosmic power of good which can never be the object of our cognition."[141]

6.

Max Weber, Rickert's good friend and one-time colleague at Freiburg, could not share this faith. Weber was deeply influenced by

Rickert's *The Limits to the Formation of Concepts in the Natural Sciences*. Indeed, two central concerns of Rickert run through all of Weber's major essays on the methodology of the social sciences, written between 1903 and 1920[142]: the question of values and value judgments in the social and cultural sciences, and the problem of formulating a rational methodology for the study of cultural phenomena. With Rickert he defines culture in terms of "value ideas . . . Empirical reality becomes 'culture' for us because and insofar as we relate it to value ideas."[143] Weber agrees with Rickert that the social scientist must study cultural phenomena in terms of their value-relatedness, free from his own value judgments. He, too, realizes that the cultural sciences, in dealing with unique and qualitative events, require methods of inquiry different from those of the natural sciences. However, he recognizes the need of concepts, theory, and generalizations in historical sciences, and goes considerably further than Rickert in exploring and defining the character of such general concepts.

Thus the thin link between ethics and reason, which still existed for Rickert is abruptly cut by Weber. Two radically different worlds confront each other in Weber's essays: the irrational world of values, and the rational world of cognition. Values, Weber agrees with Dilthey, are "never the product of progress in empirical knowledge,"[144] but are *Weltanschauungen* with nonrational, noncognitive foundations. Unlike Dilthey, he no longer sees a unified cosmic reality, Life, manifest itself in these conflicting philosophies of life. The "irreconcilable conflict" of the various system of values is something given.[145] The cultural scientist cannot discern any deeper meaning behind them. When values become the object of empirical investigation, they lose for him the character of norms; they no longer are valid *(gültig),* they are merely *seiend.*[146] No one can seriously believe any more that the world has a meaning *(Sinn).*[147] We are confronted by the "ethical irrationality of the world."[148] On the other hand, in best Neo-Kantian tradition, Weber is convinced that rational and objective cognition is possible. He devotes the major part of his writing to the formulation of methods for the scientific study of social phenomena. His great contribution to the social and historical sciences was doubtless not his insistence upon a value-free approach to social and historical phenomena but, as H. Stuart Hughes observes, his attempt to "introduce conceptual rigor into a tradition where either intuition or a naive concern for the 'facts' had hitherto ruled unchallenged."[149]

Weber's insistence upon the value neutrality of the investigator of cultural phenomena is closely linked with his faith in the possibility of a scientific approach to society and history. Values vary with cultures and individuals, but scientific method is one and universal. "For it is and will remain true that methodologically correct proof in the social sciences, if it is to achieve its purpose, must be acknowledged as correct even by a Chinese, who, on the other hand, may be deaf to our conception of the ethical imperative."[150] This, of course, assumes that correct human thought is governed by categories which are uneffected by social or psychological factors. Despite his extensive reading of Freud and Dilthey, Weber maintains his firm belief in the possibility of rational thought and cognition uneffected by emotional forces. Thought for him is not a function of the subconscious; where it became one, it deviated from attainable norms of correct reason.[151] In this sense, Weber thoroughly remains a Neo-Kantian. For him, as for Hermann Cohen, correct method of thought is identical with the method of sciences, only that he similar to Windelband and Rickert is much more aware of the special methods required by the cultural sciences than the Marburg philosophers had been. "When we distinguished in principle between 'value-judgments' and 'empirical knowledge,' we presupposed that there actually exists an unconditionally valid type of knowledge" in the social sciences.[152] Ideally, there was nothing subjective about the findings of the social investigator, provided he used methods in conformity with the "norms of our thought *(Normen unseres Denkens)*." Only his choice of a topic of inquiry is subjective. "For scientific truth is precisely what is *valid* for all who *seek* the truth."[153]

Along with the writers in the tradition of the Historical School, Weber recognizes that the cultural sciences require a method different from those of the natural sciences. The task of the social sciences is not exhausted by the formulation of quantitative laws or causal explanations because these sciences deal with cultural and intellectual processes *(geistige Vorgänge)*, "the empathic understanding of which *(welche nacherlebend zu 'verstehen')* is naturally a problem of a specifically different type from those which the schemes of the exact natural sciences in general can or seek to solve."[154] Weber agrees with Rickert that the social scientist who studies cultural phenomena is dealing with their relation to ideas of values, and that these can never be reduced to quantitative laws or causal relationships although such relationships may be an important means of furthering understanding.[155] This concept does not exclude the possibility that social and cultural phenomena cannot be explained causally. It does mean that such an explanation, if possible, would not reach the heart of the problem, for culture is filled with meaning. It represents an excerpt from the meaningless infinity of world events which man has filled with meaning *(Sinn und Bedeutung)*. The generalized laws of science empty reality of its content while the cultural sciences must always deal with a specific and individualized content. "Knowledge of cultural processes *(Kulturvorgängen)* is inconceivable except on the basis of the *meaning* which the reality of life, which always takes on individualized forms, has for us in specific, individual relationships."[156] But this does not mean, as the Historical School had maintained, that generalizations and theory have no place in the social sciences. The failure to understand this was, in Weber's opinion, one of the great weaknesses of the German Historical School of Economics which attempted to replace the laws of classical economics by a descriptive approach to national economies, and insisted that these could be understood only as expressions of a national spirit *(Volksgeist)* that defied conceptual definition.[157] In history or social science, no less than in the natural sciences, Weber agrees with Rickert, understanding is possible only with the use of concepts. However, these concepts must be adapted to the peculiar task of the historian or the cultural scientist.

What distinguishes the social from the natural sciences for Weber is less exclusively their subject matter than the type of knowledge they wish to obtain. The natural sciences seek general explanations in quantitative terms. Such an explanation may be possible of certain types of human and social behavior, too. Indeed, without the application of general, scientific laws to concrete cultural phenomena, understanding of them would be impossible. The subordination of these phenomena under general categories *(Gattungsbegriffe)* does not suffice, for these categories are only the means. The cultural sciences are not concerned with generalizations, but with grasping the significance *(Bedeutung)* of the unique.[158] The cultural phenomena, too, can be understood only within **a** context, although they require not a general concept *(oberster Begriff)* under which all can be subordinated, but a total view which takes into account their individual character.[159] Nor is the world of human behavior devoid of all regularity and law, for men generally act rationally. German Idealism and history had been wrong in identifying human freedom with unpredictability. Rational action follows rules. To assume that "freedom of will is identical with irrationality of action" is a mistake, Weber comments. Unpredictable behavior is the mark of insanity. *(Unberechenbarkeit . . . ist das Privileg des Verrückten.)* "On the other hand, we associate the highest measure of an empirical feeling of freedom with those actions which we are conscious of performing *rationally,* i.e., in the absence of physical and psychic 'coercion,' emotional 'affects' and 'accidental' disturbances on the clarity of judgment, in which we pursue a clearly perceived end by means which are the most adequate in accordance with the extent of our knowledge, i.e., in accordance with empirical rules."[160]

It is this element of rational behavior in human actions which makes social science possible for Weber. Social science primarily studies the operative effect of cultural values. It can never discover valid norms or ethical imperatives. "An empirical science cannot tell anyone what he *should* do, but only what he *can* do, and—under certain circumstances—what he *wants* to do."[161] But since men generally act rationally, to an extent an empirical science can predict, explain, and understand their behavior. As an empirical discipline, ethics can investigate the practical consequences that result from value positions which actually have been chosen by individuals or groups. This examination can proceed on three levels. One is a logical analysis of the value positions. What are these chosen values reduced to their ultimate axioms? Are these value positions logically consistent or do they contain contradictory elements? A second is an examination of the practical consequences which would follow from these "ultimate values or axioms"; if they could effect practical events, without the interference of other factors. Finally, an empirical ethics can investigate the concrete consequences *(faktischen Folgen)* which would result from the application of these values in a concrete situation. This would particularly involve the questions of means and of undesirable side effects resulting from such an action.[162] Since we live in an ethically irrational world, "no ethics in the world can dodge the fact that in numerous instances the attainment of 'good' ends is bound to the fact that one must be willing to pay the price of using morally dubious means or at least dangerous ones—and face the possibility or even the probability of evil side effects."[163]

But beyond the logical and empirical analysis of values, a science of social behavior is possible if it works with general concepts and uses methods as rigorous as those of the natural sciences. The social scientist obviously can not work with the concept of necessary general laws which Comte or Buckle considered to be operative in the social as well as in the natural world. Nevertheless, on the basis of the value positions held by members of a social group, the social scientist can work out how men would ideally behave in accordance with these values. This, of course, assumes a great deal of rationality in human behavior, yet permits space for deviation.

Max Weber, on the basis of certain chosen values, calls these schemes of ideally rational behavior ideal types. A language in' a sense may be defined as such an ideal type. When studying a language, the linguist is confronted with a tremendous empirical diversity of usage. Nevertheless, he attempts to bring order into the chaos by defining an ideal grammar, syntax, and vocabulary in terms of the ideas of correct usage held and practised by the men speaking the language. This ideal, although derived from actual practice, never fully corresponds to actual usage. However, to a great extent, practice is guided and can be understood in this context. The laws of grammar are neither an attempt to prescribe how people should speak in any ethical sense nor a description of how they do speak, but an attempt to define the rules and regularities which their usage appears to follow. Similarly, an institution such as the Christian religion, with its set of historical and social phenomena, can be approached only as an ideal type. As an objective reality, Christianity exists no more than do such abstract concepts as capitalism, the nation, bureaucracy, a historical fact, and the like. Such complex constructs exist "empirically" only "in the consciousness of an undetermined and changing plurality of individuals and in their minds assume multifarious nuances as to form, content, clarity and meaning."[164] For this reason, they can be grasped only as ideal types. Only with the use of such ideal types is the comprehension of social processes, such as the operation of the economy or of political power or of historical transformations, possible. However, the ideal type is never a description of empirical reality, but merely a heuristic means to understand such a reality. Although it attempts to find the common and typical elements in the diversity of social phenomena, it does so not in order to subordinate reality to abstract class concepts, as the natural sciences do, but to bring out clearly "the uniquely individual character *(Eigenart)* of cultural phenomena."[165] Such ideal types are always tentative. With the advance of scientific knowledge and understanding, the cultural theorist constantly needs to revise and replace those concepts by which he attempts to understand empirical reality. Nevertheless, these concepts and ideal types permit the social scientist to observe a high degree of rationality and regularity in human and social behavior.[166] For German Idealism or the Historical School the spontaneity and individuality of human behavior excluded the possibility of a methodical, scientific approach to history and cultural activity. Weber, on the other hand, as H. Stuart Hughes observes, seeks "to combine the Germanic sense for history and philosophy with the Anglo-French and positivist notion of scientific rigor."[167]

But did Weber really save social science from subjectivist relativism, as he thought? Weber distinguished the totally irrational realm of ultimate values from the absolutely rational character of method and logic. By the conscious exclusion of value judgments from his procedures of inquiry, the investigator would obtain objective knowledge of the social world. Weber, of course, assumed here, as the Neo-Kantians had before him, that man can reason logically and independently of psychological factors. But even if Weber is right in believing that a purely logical method of inquiry is possible, the problem remains that this method is purely formal in nature. It has to be applied to a content. In the natural sciences, this content is the world of Nature which can be conceptually reduced into general and universally valid relationships. In the social sciences, the investigator is confronted by a diversity, and with the use of ideal types he can reduce this into a large number of individualized complexes of relationships. Truth, in the sense of universal validity, no longer exists. The social investigator is concerned neither with the search for universal human values nor with universal human nature, but with specific values and forms of human nature in specific situations. He attempts to bring order into the immense diversity by introducing classifications and typologies. Through a comparison of aspects of one culture with another, such as Weber attempted in his comparative studies of bureaucratization and economic rationalization in China, India, and the Modern West, he may be able to define more clearly the unique characteristics of a particular civilization or certain ideals or institutions. One may argue, as Carlo Antoni has, that such an approach does not offer truth in any scientific sense nor does it present us with historical reality; rather, it dissolves history into some other abstract form of thought.[168] The only truth which remains in the social sciences is that of the correct method.

But assuming, as we well may, that the conceptual presentation of concrete social reality in its full diversity is the closest form in which we can approach "objective" knowledge of human reality, we may ask whether Weber's methodological premises permit objective cognition. In Weber's opinion they did. The social scientist faces the problem of selecting from the tremendous variety of social reality the objects of his investigation. Once he has made this choice, he can apply rational methods to the study of his subject matter. This selection, Weber concedes, is made upon the basis of the subjective interests and values of the observer. Indeed "without the investigator's evaluative ideas *(Wertideen),* there would be no principle of selection of the subject matter and no meaningful knowledge of concrete, individual reality." All "knowledge of cultural reality, as may be seen, is always knowledge from a specifically particular point of view."[169] Thus, although Weber considers social science "a science of reality" *(Wirklichkeitswissenschaft),* he admits that there is no " 'objective' scientific analysis of cultural life . . . independent of special and 'onesided' points of views."[170]

This does not mean, however, that "scientific *research* in the area of the cultural sciences can only have *results* which are 'subjective' in the sense that they are valid for one person but not for another. Only the degree to which they interest one person and not another changes."[171] The investigator obtains only one very limited perspective of reality. This is true in the natural sciences, too, but with a difference. From his limited position in space and time, the natural scientist nevertheless is able to discover relationships of general value. Because his view is only perspectivistic, the concepts which he formulates to explain natural phenomena are subject to revision. But because nature has common characteristics, we can speak of progress in the theories of natural sciences. This is possible to a much smaller degree in the social sciences, as they are understood by Weber. There are no common links for Weber in human society, such as a constant human nature or a constant and objective system of ethics. Every culture is so complex and diversified that the investigator always picks out only a very limited aspect which is not necessarily in any logical or organic relationship with the rest. The result may be that the history of social science will not reflect progress in the development of more extensive and consistent explanatory theories, but merely an anarchy of interpretations. Each of these interpretations may be methodologically correct; yet, because there are objective criteria of selection, the explored aspects of social reality are relatively insignificant to the core of the area of investigation or in little or no relationship with other interpretations of the same group of social phenomena. What saves Weber in practice from such a dilemma is his firm faith in the presence of a high degree of rationality among men in all culture groups.

From Weber's concept of the relationship of science and ethics, certain obvious implications follow in regard to the nature of politics. Weber developed these most eloquently in his classic lecture on "Politics as a Vocation,"[172] held toward the end of his life, but they are contained in much of Weber's political writing. On the one hand, science could discover no political norms; on the other, men never could escape holding value positions and acting in accordance with them. The result, as we already saw, is the perpetual struggle of *Weltanschauungen* and ideals.[173] What ultimately decides the issues of politics is force *(Gewaltsamkeit)*[174]; yet the politician can never act effectively without a belief.

> He may serve national or generally human, social, ethical, cultural, worldly or religious ends. . . . However, some kind of faith must always be *present*. . . . The mere 'power politician' may achieve strong effects, but his achievements will be empty and senseless.[175]

The mere pursuance of ethical beliefs in politics leads nowhere. We must distinguish between an ethics of sentiment *(Gesinnungsethik)* and one of responsibility *(Verantwortungsethik)*.[176] The responsible politician is concerned with the consequences of his action, not merely with abstract ethical principles.

Here, Weber's deep faith in the potential rationality of men is linked with his recognition of the ethical irrationality of the world.

Politics, as the science of the technique of power, can investigate the consequences of political actions. An ethics, which is unwilling to compromise with the evil in the world and use the necessary means, even if at times these are in conflict with its ultimate principle, remains ineffective or destroys its own goals. An example of an ineffective ethics is the Sermon on the Mount, with its refusal to oppose evil, its commandment to turn the other cheek, which Weber calls "an ethics of undignified conduct" *(Ethik der Würdelosigkeit)*. Another example is offered by the absolute demands of revolutionary movements, whose unwillingness to take into account the compromises required by social realities, inevitably lead, to the corruption of these movements.[177]

> Whoever wants to engage in politics at all and especially in politics as a vocation, has to realize these ethical paradoxes. He must know that he is responsible for what may become of *himself* under the impact of these paradoxes. I repeat, he lets himself in for the diabolic forces lurking in all violence.[178]

What distinguishes the legitimate use of power *(legitime Gewaltsamkeit)* from bare force *(Macht)* is the responsible and rational employment of power toward the desired end.

Weber's own political principles, defined long before he began to deal with the epistemological problems of the social sciences, remained relatively unchanged during his life. Weber belonged to that large group of liberal-thinking intellectuals in Wilhelminian Germany who ardently advocated democratization and social reform, but lacked a theory of democracy. For them democracy and reform were what constitutionalism had been for an earlier generation of German liberals, a means for the attainment of the highest political value, national unity and power.

In 1895, as professor at Freiburg, Weber's inaugural address on "The Nation State and Economics"[179] was perhaps the clearest exposition of the political principles of the nationalistic and democratic imperialism of the group around Friedrich Naumann. Two years previously, in a study for the *Verein für Sozialpolitik,* he had held that the agrarian problems of the Eastern provinces of Prussia could not be approached in purely economic terms, but must be evaluated from the standpoint of national interest. From the viewpoint of economic rationalization the policy of East Elbian aristocrats *(Junker)* to hire cheap Polish labor, and the resulting migration of small German farmers away from the land to industrial towns, made sense. From a national standpoint, however, it was catastrophic. The predominantly German character of the German East must be saved by closing the frontier against Polish immigration and subsidizing agriculture. In his inaugural address, Weber attempted to provide a theoretical foundation for this position. The economic developments in East Elbia and the replacement of the German peasant by the Polish farm laborer were part of the age-old struggle between races and nationalities for existence and elbow room. In this case, a nationality, which had competed with another over centuries and had demonstrated its cultural superiority, was being threatened with displacement by an "inferior race" *(tieferstehende Rasse)*.[180] Economics was merely an extension, "another form of the struggle of the nations with each other."[181]

What mattered in this struggle, Weber holds, is not "peace and human happiness," but the *"eternal struggle* for the preservation and upward selective breeding *(Emporzüchtung)* of our national kind *(Art)."*[182] In the tradition of German Idealism, Weber condemns a utilitarian *(eudämonistisch)* ethics which places welfare over the fulfillment of a higher idea by man. "We want to improve by breeding *(emporzüchten)* not man's well being but those characteristics with which we associate the feeling that they constitute human greatness and the nobility of our nature." In this cold world of struggle the "words *'lasciate ogni speranza'* over the gate of the unknown history of mankind greet the dream of peace and human happiness."[183]

But it is Germany's very struggle for existence in the modern industrial age which required democratization of German society. Bismarck's heritage had had its unfortunate aspects for Germany. Bismarck himself had been able to provide effective leadership in an age of diplomatic and military conflict. He had left a system which gave undue strength to two institutions, one the aristocracy, out of tune with the changing economic and social realities; the other, the bureaucracy, incapable of inspired leadership. Germany needed leaders which could break the inertia of bureaucratic government, and this leadership could emerge under modern conditions only within the framework of a national, parliamentary democracy. None of the existing classes possessed the instincts of power needed in a world of conflict; neither the proletariat nor the bourgeoisie, least of all the aristocracy. As an "economically declining class," it was no longer in touch with the realities of a modern, highly industrialized world. For Germany the British Parliament, with its real powers of decision and its constant internal struggles for political success, was a worthy example of the way in which effective political leadership could be found and trained. The trend toward increasing bureaucratization could be countered only by politicians whose life was "struggle" and "passion."[184]

This remained the core of Weber's political beliefs throughout his life. The final criteria of political and economic policy remained for him the "economic and political power interests of our nation and of its agent *(Träger),* the German national state."[185] He supported Naumann's attempt to integrate the laboring classes into the monarchy on the grounds that "the purpose of our work in the area of social policy is not to make the world happy but to *unify* our nation *socially . . .* for the hard struggles of the future."[186] He agreed with Naumann that the social position of the laboring class depended upon the success or failure of the imperial expansion of the German Empire. Weber closely linked the unemployment problem to the problem of an expanding population. It could be solved only by expanding the geographic boundaries of the German economy which, in turn, required the extension of German political power.[187] He strongly favored Tirpitz's naval policy, but followed with concern the development of German foreign policy under Wilhelm II. What was needed was a sober pursuit of national power interests rather than a search for prestige.

In contrast to his friend Naumann, Weber watched with deep concern the growing alienation of England. Wilhelm the Second's dangerous "political dilettantism" seemed to him a proof of the leadership vacuum which Bismarck's system had brought about, and of the need for an extension of parliamentary control over foreign and military affairs. But Weber was swept along by the general enthusiasm of 1914. Germany's aim in the war must be to secure firmly her position as a world power. However, he warned against an unrealistic estimate of German strength, kept aloof from the extremist position on annexations, and correctly saw the decision to resume unrestricted submarine warfare as an invitation to defeat.[188] Although a monarchist, Weber was able to welcome the Weimar Constitution, which basically corresponded to his conception of a national democracy more completely than it did to those of many other German liberals. He participated in the advisory committee of experts that prepared the initial draft of the constitution, and apparently was largely responsible for the provision of a president elected directly by universal suffrage, although without the extensive, almost monarchical powers which he wished to give the charismatic leader of a plebiscitarian democracy.[189] Nevertheless, defeat and revolution did not lead him to question the rightness of his belief in national power. The aims remained the same, even if their fulfillment had to be postponed.[190]

Max Weber thus came to be hailed both as a founding father of the Weimar Republic and as a Machiavellian figure, more extreme than Treitschke and Droysen in reducing all politics to the power interests of the state.[191] Both labels, democrat and Machiavelli, contain an element of truth. Weber had consistently called for the extension of political democracy. But, as a recent critic observes, democracy for him "ceased being a form of government possessing a special dignity. Its advantage rested purely on its greater efficiency in foreign policy."[192] In Weber's eyes, the prime cause of the failure of German policy was the vacuum of capable leaders which the Bismarckian system had left. By depriving the Reichstag of real political power, Bismarck had made possible the growth of bureaucratization of German political life, with its resultant stagnation. Parliament, as an arena of political struggles, in his opinion was the ideal training place for charismatic leaders, and the best check against the claims of administrative bureaucrats incapable of providing leadership. Unable to recognize objective values, Weber possessed no criteria for distinguishing between "genuine democratic charisma aiming at the realization of positive values in the service of the total community, and that false type of charisma which through its appeal to the lower instincts and emotions of masses corrupts the will of the people and uses the people as a lever to erect its reign of force."[193]

Nor does it seem that Weber viewed power as dispassionately as his conception of politics required: as a value-neutral technique, used by the politician to attain the ends he has chosen in awareness of its consequences. For Weber never seemed to distinguish very clearly between power, state, and nation as empirical facts and as values. There remained for him a good deal of the faith of nineteenth century German liberals in the positive value of the powerful nation state. With Burckhardt he recognized the diabolic character of power, but nevertheless he always regarded power as something positive, as the prerequisite for the cultural creativity of a people.[194]

In Weber's view of the future, notes of moderate optimism and extreme pessimism existed side by side. He never despaired of Germany's mission or future. On the other hand, in a world in which science could not discover objective norms, progress in any objective value sense was impossible.[195] Nevertheless, Weber was as firmly convinced as the best of the Enlightenment thinkers in the constant and irresistible march of reason in human events. "Scientific progress is a fraction, to be sure the most important fraction, of that process of intellectualization which we have been undergoing for thousand of years."[196] It has resulted not merely in increasing technical perfection in the control of nature, but in the growing application of reason to the organization of society as well. However, for Weber reason had ceased to be a reflection of the divine in any way and had become a spectre. Far from being the key to wisdom and social justice, reason had become a purely value-free instrument for the attainment of irrationally chosen ends in a rational manner. In only one important sense it preserved a possible ethical element: it enabled ethical man to act responsibly, once he had chosen his value positions. But the illusion that there is meaning *(Sinn)* in the world had been steadily destroyed in the course of the intellectualization and rationalization of life and society. The progress of science had also been the progress of the disenchantment of man. As civilization progressed along the lines of intellectualization, progress itself became increasingly problematic and life grew empty. Abraham could die satiated with life, Weber agrees with Tolstoy, "because he stood in the organic cycle of life; because life in terms of the meaning he gave it had given him at the end of his days what it could have offered, because no riddles remained which he wanted to solve and he thus had been able to have enough of life." For modern civilized man *(Kulturmensch)*, never able to grasp finality, always confronted by the provisional and the imperfect, death became meaningless. "And because death is meaningless, civilized life as such is meaningless. By its meaningless 'progressiveness' it has given the imprint of meaninglessness to death."[197] But "rationalization and intellectualization" and, above all, the "disenchantment of the world," Weber concludes, constitute "the fate of our age." Whoever could not bear this lot manfully would find refuge in the ever-waiting arms of the church, but in doing so he would sacrifice his intellectual integrity.[198]

The picture for the future was not pretty. Weber saw the steady progress of bureaucratization of all aspects of social life as an aspect of the steady rationalization of life, the threat of an image of something uncomfortably resembling Orwell's 1984. A system of bureaucratic rule was inevitable. Weber's comparative study of Western and non-Western civilizations convinced him that there was no known example of a bureaucracy being destroyed, except in the course of a general cultural decline. He left open the possibility that bureaucratization might be prevented from totally destroying spontaneity in social and cultural life by the charisma of great leaders who could concretely symbolize values lost in the modern mass society and that the bureaucracy might be kept in check by legal restraints, as they existed in the Western European democracies and in the United States.[199]

Max Weber was certainly far from being a nihilist. Few men have been as deeply and passionately committed to values, scholarly and political. In many ways he represented what was best in the German liberal scholarly tradition of the nineteenth century—the commitment to truth, the belief in the social and political responsibilities of the scholar, the defense of intellectual liberty. Weber was, perhaps, the last great humanist in this tradition. More than any German scholar of the nineteenth century, he was willing to scrutinize all beliefs in the light of reason.

Nevertheless, by the road of reason, Weber reached a point which was not that different from that reached by another humanist, Nietzsche, who pursued the road of unreason.[200] God, even Rickert's God, was dead now. History ceased to be a meaningful process and became the scene of insoluble value conflicts. Man, confronted by the ethical meaninglessness of the universe, found nothing left but the will to power. The idealistic historicism of Herder, Humboldt, and Ranke, which still lived on in Dilthey. Troeltsch, and even Rickert, had been finally refuted. Weber left a dangerous heritage, for his willingness to examine all values had shied away from the one idol which the entire tradition had worshipped: the idol of the nation.

CHAPTER VII

The "Crisis of Historicism" II

ERNST TROELTSCH AND FRIEDRICH MEINECKE

PERHAPS no intellectual biographies illustrate the crisis of German historical thought better than do those of Friedrich Meinecke and Ernst Troeltsch. Similar to Heinrich Rickert and Max Weber, both men were born in the fateful 1860's—Meinecke in 1865, Troeltsch in 1862—but, unlike their Neo-Kantian contemporaries and friends, their thought was still deeply rooted in the heritage of the German Historical School. Otto Hintze, the colleague and friend of Troeltsch and Meinecke at Berlin, later in retrospect called Troeltsch "the epigone" of the German Idealism of Leibniz, Hegel, and Ranke. In Hintze's words he was still "full of faith and truth that world history had rational meaning and (was) motivated by an invincible ethical driving force."[1]

Meinecke, too, possessed this "faith and trust" in history, even if for him contemplation played a somewhat greater part and ethical concern a lesser role than they did for Troeltsch. For neither of the two men history had become a construct of the mind, as it had to an extent for the Neo-Kantian philosophers or for Max Weber. History remained for both men a real and meaningful flow of events which could be grasped only in its full, living reality. The distinction which Rickert and Weber had made between a Realm of Values and a Realm of Being did not exist for them. Values had no existence apart from history. Only history revealed value. They never lost Ranke's faith that, behind the manifold and seemingly irrational manifestations of individuality in history and the apparent anarchy of

174

values, there lay a "common divine primal cause" *(Urgrund)*,[2] the "substantive and individual identity of finite spirits with the infinite Spirit."[3]

This faith was shaken, but never destroyed by intellectual and political upheavals. However, these upheavals did leave their deep impact upon both thinkers, and what had been an almost naive faith in history in their younger years became a highly problematic one in the course of time. If the historical approach to human reality seemed at first to open a way for genuine understanding of real life, it now threatened to unveil the relativity of all knowledge and of all value. All norms that once had appeared firm seemed now to be swept away by historical and social scientific inquiry, and history began to reveal itself as a flux devoid of meaning or ethical value. Troeltsch's concern with ethical and epistemological relativism was initiated by the methodological discussions of the Neo-Kantians, and by the currents of irrationalist thought at the end of the century. His doubts were intensified by war, collapse, and revolution, which Meinecke considered the decisive factors in forsaking his optimism regarding the harmony between power and ethics. Troeltsch's entire intellectual career was a pathetic attempt to find norms through the study of history by which the "endless restlessness of the historical lifestream" might be dammed in, and his own belief in meaning in human history be justified. To a lesser extent, the same holds for Meinecke, who never traveled as far on the road to pessimism as Troeltsch did.

The *Historismus* discussion of the 1920's has made us link the names of Ernst Troeltsch and Friedrich Meinecke more closely, perhaps, than they deserve. Actually, both men were very different in personality, background, and orientation. They shared in the concern to keep the historical orientation from leading "into the bottomless pit of relativism" *(haltlosen Abgrund des Relativismus)*.[4] Both participated in common circles of philosophic discussion, and were influenced to varying degrees by Windelband, Rickert, and Weber without succumbing to them. Windelband and Rickert had been Meinecke's colleagues and personal friends at Freiburg; Weber had been Troeltsch's colleague at Heidelberg. Both Troeltsch and Meinecke belonged to the circle of professors around Friedrich Naumann who, in the years before World War I, worked for parliamentary reform, social legislation, and colonial expansion.[5] Meinecke came to Berlin as professor of history in the fall of 1914; Troeltsch as professor of philosophy in the spring of 1915, after the conservative forces in the church had opposed his appointment to a chair of theology. From then until Troeltsch's death in early 1923, a close exchange of views took place, particularly in the informal setting of regular Sunday morning walks in Berlin's *Grünewald*, where they were joined by other liberal intellectuals such as Otto Hintze or, occasionally, by Hans Delbrück and Walther Rathenau.[6] Their main point of contact lay, however, on the borderline between politics and philosophy. In their scholarly contributions to the war effort, both attempted to define and defend the "German spirit" against Western war propaganda. Both belonged to that group of nationalistic liberals who, analogous to Max Weber or Friedrich Naumann, patriotically supported the war effort, but strongly urged the need for democratic reforms and warned against the unrealistic chauvinism of the Pan-Germans. With the collapse of the monarchy they—along with Max Weber—offered their services and especially their pens to the defense of the new republic against its enemies from the extreme Left and Right. This was less because they were liberal democrats in principle than because the democratic republic best suited the interests of the nation.[7]

Nevertheless, both men had very different points of departure and of direction. Ernst Troeltsch never freed himself from his theological past, Friedrich Meinecke from being an historian of the Prussian School. As the son of a Bavarian Protestant physician, who early introduced him to the thinking of the natural sciences, Troeltsch was confronted by the problem of harmonizing his Christian faith with modern scientific and historical knowledge. Coming from the conservative Lutheran home of a small-town Prussian official, Friedrich Meinecke, the student of Sybel and Treitschke, was forced to reconcile his faith in the Prussian state and the Bismarckian solution with the social and, above all, the international realities of the twentieth century. Troeltsch never lost his Christian belief, but it became increasingly problematic for him. What had begun as a search for religious certainty in the never-ceasing stream of history became increasingly a search for any sort of firm ethical values.

As Carlo Antoni observed, Troeltsch was perhaps "the last of the German intellectuals to remain faithful to the old gods, to the Christian order of life, to culture, to liberal progress, to history, to civilization. He was the last to believe in them, in the theological faculties of the Protestant church itself."[8] But even for him "all was tottering" *(alles wackelt),* as he told a group of theologians as early as 1896,[9] and with the years the "tottering" appeared to increase. Friedrich Meinecke never entirely lost his faith in the positive nature of power, in the ethical worth of the German past, and in the meaningfulness of history. Nevertheless, he was increasingly forced to recognize the dichotomy of power and ethics, the element of meaninglessness in history, and the demonic and diabolic aspects of the German political tradition.

1.

Troeltsch's theological work began with an effort to emancipate himself from the Christian dogmatism of his teacher, Albrecht Ritschl. The latter had attempted to protect Christian theology against naturalism and historicism with the help of the Kantian argument that upon the basis of perceptions of phenomena, human reason is unable to attain knowledge of the things-in-themselves. Natural as well as rational theology are thus impossible. God can never be known as a thing-in-himself, but only as He reveals Himself in concrete manifestations in the phenomenal world. The only basis of Christian theology therefore remains His revelation in the historical figure of Jesus Christ. For Troeltsch such isolation of religious thought from reason was impossible. As he pointed out in his doctoral dissertation on "Revelation and Reason in Melanchthon," even orthodox Protestant theology in the days of the Reformation had assumed that Christian faith was in harmony with Nature and history. It did not unilaterally derive Christian doctrine from the teachings of Jesus, but from reason and natural law.[10]

The grave crisis which Christianity faced in his time had its origin, Troeltsch believed, less in a decline of religious sentiment than in the growing gulf between Christian tradition and modern conditions of life. Much more dangerous than the this-worldliness of modern concepts of happiness was the challenge of modern scientific knowledge. But Troeltsch held that, contrary to popular belief, natural science does not constitute the principal threat to Christianity among the sciences. Natural science had indeed destroyed old anthropomorphic concepts of God's working, but these tenets are not vital to religious belief and often had been questioned on religious grounds by those who were seeking a more profound concept of God. It had not been possible as yet to reduce the world of spirit to physical causality.[11] Religiosity remains a universal human need springing from the nature of the human consciousness. And the common structure of consciousness, which Troeltsch optimistically assumed in Neo-Kantian fashion, appears to indicate the existence of a transcendent religious apriority amidst the variety of religious experiences corresponding to the apriority that governs aesthetic, ethical, and logical judgment.[12]

Much more serious was the threat to the Christian religion posed by modern history. Comparative studies had steadily destroyed the special position of Christianity as the sole true religion. It had shown itself to be merely one of the historical great religions of the world with deep historical roots in earlier primitive religious traditions.[13] "Christianity," Troeltsch observes, "has been a purely historical phenomenon at every point of its development with all the limitations of an individual, historical phenomenon, like any other religion." Whatever was historical was also relative, for "historical and relative are identical." Hence Christianity had lost its claim to be the "absolute religion."[14]

Had Troeltsch been willing to draw the full consequences of his position, he might have concluded that all theology is meaningless, and that the study of religion should restrict itself to the history of religion. This he refused to admit.[15] In his *The Absolute Character of Christianity and the History of Religion* in 1902, he stresses that "history is no longer merely one way of looking at things . . . but the basis of all thought about values and norms."[16] But he nevertheless assumes that real values manifest themselves in history. The theologian turns to the history of religions not because he wishes to observe the variety of religious experiences, but because only from this variety can he win an understanding of religious norms.[17] For history is not chaos. The great religions all show points of similarity and each appear to reflect a nucleus of truth. There is no reason to assume that values and norms which appear in history do not contain a large element of truth. The task of history is not merely to explain the genetic origin of norms, but "its most important work is exactly the clear presentation *(Hervorstellung)* of norms." Troeltsch essentially agrees with Rickert that "absolute, immutable values, unconditioned by any temporal factors," exist outside of history, but they manifest themselves and can be known only within history. In the historical world, these norms always assume an individual and limited form, and our knowledge of them is always subjective and relative to a degree.[18]

But the history of religion by no means reflects an anarchy of values. Actually, only a very limited number of value-complexes, represented by the higher religions, have emerged. These religions all seem to point to a common transcendent aim. Comparative study helps us to approach this ideal, although all judgments which we form, all criteria which we establish upon the basis of the most impartial study, remain tinged with our subjectivity. The direction toward which the history of religion and of values points enables us to form the concept of universally valid norms, although these norms themselves can never be perceived or achieved perfectly in history.[19] Yet Troeltsch saw a meaningful trend in history, but not a pre-imposed logical pattern. Every great value system or religion represents a new breakthrough *(Durchbruch)* toward the ideal, and "these few great breakthroughs of religious thought" give us reasons to expect confidently "the victory of the purest and most profound idea of purpose rather than the aimless play of variety."[20] The meaningfulness of religious thought and religious norms had been saved. Christianity could not claim to be the absolute religion. But all seemed to point to the Christian religion as the "climax *(Höhepunkt)*" and "point of convergence" of all historical religions of the past, and as the point of actual departure *(Voraussetzung)* of the religiosity of the future.[21]

In all this Troeltsch still seems very close to German Idealist conceptions of development. He is firmly convinced that behind the phenomena of history there are absolute values guaranteeing meaningful growth. Hegel's imposition of a logical pattern upon history seemed to him to be a violation of historical individuality, the sacrifice of history on the altar of an abstract concept.[22] But neither was he able to accept Ranke's conception of the equal worth of all epochs before God. Rather, the many diverse values, ideas, and individualities within history seemed to be links in a chain of development toward an absolute, timeless value lying beyond history. We could approach this absolute through intuition and faith *(Ahnung und Glauben),* but never really know it.[23]

The central problem of Hegel's philosophy, the question of the relation of "history to norms, of development to the criteria by which this development can be measured" *(Geschichte und Normen, Entwicklung und Entwicklungsmasstab),* remains vital in Troeltsch's opinion. Hegel was forced to deal with this problem as the result of the progressive collapse of the "rationalistic-metaphysical dogmatism" upon which, not only traditional theological beliefs, but all of our ethical and spiritual conceptions and values had been based. But the Hegelian synthesis of history and reason could not hold, and with its decline modern man was faced with naturalistic explanations, skepticism, and a resultant anarchy of values.[24] Troeltsch therefore greeeted Rickert's *Cultural Science and Natural Science* as the first serious attempt to solve the question of finding objective norms in history without doing violence to it.

Troeltsch reviewed Rickert's book in a long article in the *Theologische Rundschau* in 1904. Much more interesting than the extensive praise which Troeltsch bestows on Rickert for his formulation of the problem and his development of a logic suited to the historical sciences is the relatively brief criticism of Rickert's philosophy of history; for here Troeltsch's strong commitment to objective idealism becomes apparent. Rickert had not really solved the problem of finding objective norms in history, he argues. Rickert had thought that he had done so by seeing the source of all values, as well as of all cognition, in the transcendent logical consciousness of man. But, Troeltsch continues, Rickert had actually contributed little to the problem which is relevant for us: the relation between complexes of values held in history *(historische Wertbildungen)* and objectively valid norms *(dem gelten sollenden Ideal).* Rickert had considered valid norms *(gelten sollende Ideale)* to be purely formal without specific content. Troeltsch, on the other hand, holds that the valuations which we find in history are always real, limited, and subjective. The result is a vicious circle which Rickert could not break. Needing objective norms, we turn to history with its factual and subjective valuations as the only place where we can find real values. Here we search for the "empty, formal normative" implied in these values, a normative which tells us nothing about the concrete values that may guide our actions in specific situations. In brief, absolute validity, with no relation to reality, confronts historical values which possess no absolute validity.[25]

This circle can be broken only, Troeltsch reasons, if we assume that history is a real process, not merely a construct of the mind, and that a real relationship exists between the concrete values which appear in history and historical development. Individual value judgments must not be considered as arbitrary, subjective, and mutually contradictory, but as parts of a broad historical context. Within this context successions of values appear as part of a process of development. Each complex of values is meaningful in itself. But from the perspective of universal history, it occupies a role in an ascending process which contains its own inner laws *(einem innerlich zusammenhängenden Stufengang).*[26] Hence the subjective and the objective, which Rickert had separated so sharply, are reunited; the World of Facts *(Tatsache)* is synthesized anew with that of Ideas *(Idee).* Indeed, the solution of the circle involves an "element of religious faith." Without this faith in its solubility, all reasoning about values and history becomes meaningless. This circle between logical consciousness and psychological consciousness contains the "original riddle of all reality and all things human" wherein all other riddles— the antinomies of fact and value, of change and perennial constancy, of freedom and necessity, pluralism and monism—have their basis.[27] But with this solution of the circle, we return from Rickert's approach to the problems of history and values, in terms of the logical structure of human consciousness, to metaphysics. Troeltsch gladly admits this. Without metaphysics and the assumption that a real context and real development exist, history is not possible.[28]

Once we recognize history as a real process, the problems of causality, values, and objective knowledge in history can be answered, Troeltsch believes. For Rickert history had no reality, but was essentially a way of looking at events. Rickert had declined to recognize the distinction between spirit *(Geist)* and Nature, except on methodological grounds. However, this distinction is fundamental, Troeltsch now argues. History is not merely a method of forming concepts regarding the individual and the unique, but an attempt to understand a real subject matter. In this way, it sharply differs from the natural sciences. In the physical sciences, we are restricted to the mere observation of relations which are determined by the structure of our consciousness. In the world of mind, however, the establishment of such relationships does not suffice. The phenomena we perceive of a mental event are merely the outward reflections of its inner being. Understanding therefore requires not merely the perception of the outward expressions of the event, but the grasping of its essence. In admitting that historical subjects possess such an essence, we recognize that we are dealing with "a reality which is not merely empirical but metaphysical."[29]

The fact that the objects of history really exist and are significant makes it possible for us to discover meaningful development. History is no longer a "subjective arrangement,"[30] as Rickert proposed, and the work of the historian, but rather the portrayal of an objective context which we begin to grasp as we immerse ourselves in the actual subject matter of history. The cultural values are no longer subjective, but possess objective value. Our own understanding of history, of course, as well as our selection of values, remains subjective, colored by our individuality and the historical moment. We can never attain "the absolute, pure, immutable idea of the world . . . for despite its relationship to absolute values, everything historical remains irrational and individual." Our judgment is never fully subjective, but is itself a part of the objective process of history.[31] The aim of historical study, however, is not restricted to the understanding of the unique and the particular; it also involves the discovery of common characteristics. These characteristics may be formulated, as Max Weber, Georg Jellinek, or Jacob Burckhardt tried to do, either in terms of ideal types which do not reduce historical situations to causal laws or relate them to abstract ideas, or in an attempt to define their characteristic elements. Again, they may be depicted as the tendencies and ideas operative in history in the Rankean sense. According to Troeltsch, history is not governed by laws of nature in the sense of the natural sciences or by a rigid Hegelian dialectics. Nevertheless, it shows a certain coherence and unified development from common points of origin to common goals.[32]

Thus, in a sense, Troeltsch's early theological work represents a reassertion of the German Idealistic faith that history is not chaos, but the source of truth and value and that all the apparent relativity and subjectivity found within history merely reflected the many sides of an objective and living truth. Troeltsch defends this faith against Christian dogmatism and scientistic naturalism as well as against Neo-Kantianism to which he owed so much.

Troeltsch did not repudiate his faith in history in the essays written on the church and society in the following decade. They appeared in 1912 as the *Social Teachings of the Christian*

Churches.[33] Nevertheless, the problems with which he dealt now were different, no longer questions of religious truth and the objectivity of religious knowledge or of ethical values, but the study of religion as an historical and social phenomenon. There was, of course, a connecting link to his earlier writings. His insistence that knowledge and values must be sought in history requires an historical approach to religion. Troeltsch never accepted Weber's conception that values are totally culture-bound and have no significance as values beyond the social settings within which they operate. Nevertheless, he now treated religious doctrines not from the standpoint of truth, but as cultural facts.

The book, written in Heidelberg, strongly reflects the influence of his colleague, Max Weber, in the formulation of the problem which Troeltsch had set for himself: the interrelation of religious ideas and institutions and social and economic movements, particularly the role of Calvinism in the rise of capitalism, the attempt to develop a typology of religious institutions and ideas, the pessimism over the role of religion in modern society, and the recognition of a sharp contradiction between an ethics of principle *(Gesinnungsethik)* and the harsh realities of life. Like Weber, Troeltsch is interested in the applicability and the limits of a Marxian theory of ideology to religious ideas and religious institutions.[34] Religion in its pure form cannot be explained in economic terms, he concludes. Jesus's teaching and his formation of a religious community are neither the products of economic forces nor of the class struggle. Jesus's message is purely otherworldly, relating to the salvation of man's soul and paying no heed to the political or economic realities of this world.[35] But as soon as Jesus became the object of worship and a lasting community of faithful gathered, the Christian religion became part of the social order. Its dogma received a different meaning in each type of religious organization—whether church, sect, or mystic fellowship—and these, in turn, were influenced by, and to an extent themselves influenced, the social and economic conditions of the time.[36]

Troeltsch did not intend to present a systematic philosophy in the *Social Teachings* nor did he define his position on theoretical questions of history, as he had in his earlier writings. But there is a clear shift apparent in his basic assumptions, a shift to a much more pessimistic picture of man and of history than was found in his theological writings. Christianity is no longer viewed as the point of convergence of man's religious development and the point of departure for further progress. Instead, it is merely one historical religion, belonging to the West, always a part of the total culture of the age.[37] Nor is there a Christian religion, in his opinion. Since Christianity ceased to be the purely spiritual and otherworldly message of Jesus and became a religious community, Christian doctrines of belief, as well as Christian teachings on ethical, economic, and political questions, differ with the forms of organization which these religious groups have assumed and the social forces that act upon them.

Troeltsch did not portray history as a process or a development. He does indeed follow the changes of Christian social ethics from their origins to the eighteenth century. A central concern of Troeltsch is the role of religion in the formation of modern capitalistic, industrial society, but essentially he analyzes various types of religious societies as isolated static facts rather than trace their dynamic relationship. History appears as the recurrence of change, among different types of institutions and ideas, instead of development. Troeltsch no longer speaks of growth, but now refers to Ranke's concept of the immediacy of all epochs to God.[38]

Troeltsch is skeptical of the ability of religions to carry out their social ethics. He insists that the ethics of the gospels was not made for this world. It can be carried out, only if the sinful character of the world is recognized and compromises are made.[39] Thus the Catholic Church, and later in an even more radical form the Lutherans, recognized the need to transform the absolute conception of natural law (which had been a central part of Christian ethics) into a relative one that would leave room for repression, authority, and inequality.[40] But Christian social ethics, Troeltsch argues, cannot teach us anything lasting about ethical truths. For Christian ethics has never possessed an "immutable and absolute point," but has always been concerned with "mastering" a given, socially conditioned situation.[41] A science of values in any ultimate sense is impossible, Troeltsch holds, but he does not follow Weber all the way. Perceptions or values are not purely subjective without a content of truth. They are taken out of history in the conviction that "here we perceive absolute Reason in the revelation which is addressed to us in a form given it in the present context."[42] The contribution which Catholic or Protestant social ethics can make to the present social situation is pitifully small, however. Not only has the role of the church declined in the modern world, but no Christian ethics has been formulated which can answer meaningfully the social problems of the modern capitalistic world at this stage of its development.[43]

A more confident note, particularly in regard to the worth of German culture, appears not surprisingly in the many lectures that Troeltsch gave, between 1914 and 1916, as his contribution to the war effort.[44] Already before the war, in *Social Teachings,* Troeltsch had explored fundamental differences between German and Western civilization. He found that these differences in spirit between Germany and the West were profoundly influenced by the different religious traditions, by the impact of Lutheranism in Germany and of Calvinism in the West. Lutheranism, with its greater recognition of the sinfulness of human nature, had seen political power as part of the divine order. Man is born into his vocation *(Beruf)* in society or is called to it by the political authorities *(Obrigkeit).* For Calvinism, man has to find his calling. The Calvinist believes that the actions of the state are always judged by the criteria of Christian morality and natural law. For Luther, on the other hand, force and violence are the basis of law and justice in a sinful world.[45] The state is governed by an ethics of its own.

These different conceptions of power, Troeltsch warns, by no means led to a total estrangement between Germany and the West, for modern ethical and political systems can never be entirely explained as secularized forms of Lutheran and Calvinist teachings. But Troeltsch believes that Luther's political ethics and the Lutheran church kept alive a political system in Germany which was already dying in the West in Luther's time. The gulf became much sharper, once the common Christian religious bonds were loosened by the Enlightenment. This gulf made possible the radical reaction of German Idealism against the Enlightenment concepts of natural law. The early nineteenth century thus saw Germany in the midst of its romantic nationalistic revival, cut loose from the moorings of a Western, Christian tradition of natural law which continued to play a central role in French, British, and American life. But other forces of the modern world were already bringing the two cultures together again, Troeltsch confidently observed in 1913. Capitalistic conditions were carrying a bit of the Calvinist ethic into Germany, and with it the promise of an extension of democratic rights. These same conditions were also leading to a modification of Western liberalism in the direction of social responsibility and the assertion of public interest. The contrast between Germany and the West thus did not constitute an unbridgeable problem or a barrier to understanding. Indeed, Germany had a good deal to learn again or anew from the West, particularly from the American and British democracies which still embodied a good deal of the Calvinist ethics.[46]

These sober observations lost a good deal of their sobriety with the outbreak of the war. The Western concept of natural law was now sharply distinguished from the German idea of history. The "Ideas of 1789," still guiding the Western democracies, sharply contrasted to the German "Ideas of 1914." Troeltsch was setting up a straw man in a West committed to classical ideas of natural law, an atomistic concept of society, and a lack of understanding of historical and social forces. He was willing to overlook what he had recognized in his *Social Teachings:* the extent to which Western liberalism had undergone profound changes in the course of the nineteenth century under the impact of modern conditions. Germany's "idea of freedom," its Lutheran heritage now were affirmed with little qualification. The West was no longer unqualifiedly committed to the cult of reason and the idea of progress, as Troeltsch claimed, but had been also deeply affected by the currents of historical thought and of irrationalism which, since the Romantic Revolt, had become increasingly common European property. The "German idea of freedom," Germany's Lutheran heritage, her break with natural law ideas, which in *Social Teachings* had appeared to Troeltsch as very mingled blessings, were now affirmed with little qualification. The German tradition of historical thought, represented by Hegel, Ranke, Sybel, and Treitschke, had been proven to be right. They had destroyed the "democratic illusions that the state is an institution of individuals serving the purpose of their security and their happiness."[47] They had recognized that the state is an ethical end in itself, "an ethical unit of will," which transcends the interest of the individual and must be guided by an ethics of reason of state. States "like all living things must grow and progress."[48]

In espousing this ethics, Troeltsch asserts that the German historians and philosophers had not championed a mere struggle for national power or biological survival. Rather they understood that the growth of national power is part of God's overall intent; that mankind *(Humanität)* is not "a rational league of nations, a rigid expression of universally identical Reason, but a living, moving abundance of great national spirits which each in their way reflect the divine world." In this sense, the states in following their interests were indeed acting on principles different from those of private morality. But they were principles on a higher level that were in harmony with the aims of private morality, as well as in the interest of mankind.[49]

The idea of freedom, Troeltsch holds, differs with every people. The German historians and philosophers had understood the central role of the state in culture. The modern German state and its idea of freedom had arisen from this recognition. The roots of the German state were found in "Prussian power *(Machtwesen),* Kantian duty consciousness and the German-Idealistic, cosmopolitan content of our culture," a synthesis which must be maintained "not because we want to remain Germans in the sense of our history but because it constitutes the essence of every genuine political ethics."[50] Freedom, in the German sense, Troeltsch argues, is not "equality but service by the individual at his proper place" within the social organization.[51] Analogous to the French and English ideas of freedom, the German idea recognizes a sphere of individual liberty, particularly in matters of spirit.[52] It stresses the participation of the individual in the state, and hence has room for equality before the law and parliamentary institutions.[53] However, it recognizes the link and subordination of the individual to the community. Summed up in a few words, it synthesizes "political socialism and cultural individualism" *(Staatssozialismus und Bildungsindividualismus).*[54]

While Troeltsch considers the German "Idea of Freedom" superior to Western concepts of freedom, because it rests upon a truer conception of the state, Troeltsch agrees with Friedrich Naumann that it has not yet been fully attained. In one important way Germany has lagged behind the West: in the democratization of her political life. A "plutocratic electoral law," he agrees with Max Weber and Friedrich Naumann, has retarded the broad popular participation in government which marks the modern democracies. Germany remains an authoritarian state *(Obrigkeitsstaat);* it must become a people's state *(Volksstaat).* The important thing is not parliamentary responsibility. Germany, because of her exposed geographic position, needs a strong central power, but the remainders of "class-and-caste rule" *(Klassen-und Standesregiment)*[55] must go.

As the war proceeded, the "spirit of 1914," uniting Germans of all classes and parties, withered, and Troeltsch's lectures became less frequent. The military leadership increasingly dominated policy, opposed political reforms, and unleashed the unrestricted U-boat war. In 1922, reviewing the contrast between German thought on politics, history, and ethics, and Western European and American thought, Troeltsch recognized that the German idea of individuality, which had been so fruitful for historical study, had also had "some very doubtful *(bedenkliche)* consequences."[56]

> The conception of the abundance of national spirits was transformed into a feeling of contempt for the idea of Universal Humanity. The pantheistic idolization of the state turned into blind respect, devoid of all ideas, for success and power. The Romantic Revolution sank into a complacent contentment with things as they are. From the idea of a particular law and right for a given time and place, men proceeded to a purely positivistic acceptance of the state. The conception of a morality of a higher spiritual order which transcends bourgeois conventions passed into moral scepticism. From the urge of the German spirit to find embodiment in a state there arose the same kind of imperialism as anywhere else in the world.[57]

In his essay "On Standards for Judging Matters Historical"[58] in 1916, Troeltsch returned to the problem of historical relativity with which he had dealt in his earlier theological work, and this occupied him until his death in 1923. Since his *The Absolute Character of Christianity,* Troeltsch had increasingly viewed religion as an expression and a part of the total culture. The problem which now concerned him, providing the connecting thread to the many essays to be written during the next six years, was somewhat inchoately thrown together in *Historicism and Its Problems,*[59] published in 1922. It was less a question of finding absolute theological knowledge[60] within the flux of history than of observing an objectivity of the values to be discovered in a culture.

Significantly, very little had changed in Troeltsch's philosophy since his early writings. Troeltsch was still convinced that knowledge and values could be won only from history. He still believed that history is meaningful and that the truths and norms won from history, although relative to specific historical situations, reflected an absolute truth hidden behind history. Indeed, since this absolute manifested itself only in individual, historical forms, history became the only way to gain true knowledge and the historical approach constituted the most significant achievement of the modern spirit. But what had once seemed self-evident to Ranke, Sybel, or even Troeltsch in his younger years, namely, the central role which history plays in the intellectual, moral, and aesthetic formation of man, now became problematic for Troeltsch.

The nineteenth century had approached all cultural and intellectual life genetically. But instead of giving us understanding, historical study had undermined "all firm norms and ideals of human existence."[61] "Politics, law, morality, religion and art were all dissolved in the stream of history and became comprehensible only as parts of specific historical developments." Intellectual life lost its autonomy, no longer reflecting "transcendental, stable, immutable truths." It became part of a "continuous but always changing stream of life in which only transient vortices formed which gave the illusion of having duration and existence of their own."[62] History, or rather *Historismus,* the belief that all reality is historical, had thus "worked itself into an internal contradiction."[63] For the historical spirit not only had "shattered our ethical systems," the belief in humanitarian progress and in the autonomy of reason which had replaced the older Christian and dynastic concepts,[64] but it had undermined its own scholarly method. How was objective knowledge still possible if all human cognition was historically and socially conditioned?[65]

There is no logical solution to the "problems of historicism." For if man can never see beyond the flux and change of history, he obviously cannot find a firm resting place on intellectual grounds. His ideas and ideals always remain bound to his culture. The only solution is to find within the history of Western Civilization the reflection of transcendent truth and value. Thus Carlo Antoni observes that just as Troeltsch had once "hoped to derive from history itself the proof of the extrahistorical, absolute character of Christianity, so now he proposed to derive from the study of history the antidotes for unlimited historicism, that is, the proof of the absolute character of the values of Western Civilization in their historical formations."[66] Troeltsch wished to have his cake and eat it, too; to see in history the only key to knowledge and to value, and yet be assured of absolute, transcendent values. This could only be done on the basis of faith. And so a very deep contradiction appears in Troeltsch's essays and in his book on historicism. On the one hand, he presents the logical and ethical problems of historicism, the inescapability of the historical approach, and the collapse of modern ethical and logical values not primarily as the result of the political and social catastrophes, but as the logical consequence of the historical approach.[67] On the other hand, he refuses to accept the "unlimited relativism"[68] which logically results from this approach; nor is he willing to consider alternatives to a purely historical method. His answer to the insoluble problem of finding truth and validity in a world of change remains a religious one. His belief in God[69] in many ways is still the God of Ranke: "an ultimate unity,[70] a vague trust in the rationality of the world as a whole."[71]

This is the solution Troeltsch offers in his lecture "On Standards for Judging Matters Historical"; with minor modifications, it remains his answer to the *Problems of Historicism*. There is no question in his mind that the "liberal, humanitarian, rationalistic philosophy of history" of the nineteenth century is in a state of crisis; nor is there any question that this crisis has not merely been the result of the catastrophes of our time, but the outcome of the "development of Western thought itself" in refuting abstract rationalism.[72] The same historical approach to human ideas and human ideals which has brought about this crisis seems to rule out the possibility of a solution. For by its very nature the "genetic-historical way of thinking" is relativistic and "hopelessly" in contradiction with any attempt to find "universally valid and absolute goals" in history.[73] There is thus no strictly logical solution to the problems of historicism. The "absolute, timeless values" required for its solution cannot be found on the basis of historical study. The dilemma is increased by the reality that neither our "will to live" *(energischer Lebenswille)* nor our "ethical convictions" will permit us to renounce the search for meaningful values.

But the dilemma is only apparent, Troeltsch confidently concludes. It arises from the mistaken identification of reason with abstract norms, and the failure to realize that the concrete values held by historical societies also reflect reason; that the apparently irrational and spontaneous, too, can be an expression of rationality. Values and standards are indispensable to man, Troeltsch recognizes, but they need not be universally valid, timeless, absolute, and abstract values irreconcilable with the always specific and unique character of history.[74]

The pressing problem for our age is, of course, that of finding a new synthesis of values which are valid to us in the face of the destruction of traditional values. But how can we discover such norms? Troeltsch's reply remains that this is possible only through the study of history. More specifically, we find valid norms through a "critical selection of the cultural possession of a great system of interaction, such as in our case the whole of Western Civilization."[75] Yet since our judgment is always conditioned by historical and subjective factors, it would seem that our selectivity would be purely subjective. This fear, Troeltsch believes, can be banished if we have faith that at every moment in history reason manifests itself. We are safest from subjectivism in the choice of values and standards when we immerse ourselves into the historical context within which these standards have arisen. For both the subject matter of history and the historian are part of a great divine process. The great value systems of history are "revelations" of divine truth, won intuitively in contact with historical movements. The great syntheses of values can be neither constructed along a priori lines, nor can they be reduced to rational formulas. They "break forth with a feeling of pressing necessity and clarity" on the great creative individuals, the prophets, the political leaders, philosophers, artists, and historians or even in the consciousness of the masses.[76]

However, Troeltsch hastens to avoid the impression that the intuitive perception of values proceeds without scientific or rational controls. The formation of meaningful values presupposes an understanding of the great contexts of development in history. Such an understanding in turn involves comparative study, necessary to define the essential character of a specific culture; for it is within these cultures that the values, valid for its members, are embodied. Nevertheless, the formation of standards is a matter of religious faith. It involves considering "a content taken out of life as the expression and revelation of the divine foundation of life *(göttlichen Lebengrundes)*" and accepting "the ideal which grew out of a time-bound situation as representing the unknowable Absolute."[77] Although an element of artistic creativity is involved in the recognition of these ideals, their isolation requires the careful scientific analysis of the culture from which they spring. This, of course, assumes that cultures are integrated systems, and that a study of them will reveal their essential character. Further, among the manifold value ideas expressed by the members of a culture, there are certain values which are proper to the culture and reflect its basic ideals; yet there is little empirical evidence that cultures in fact embody such central ideals. Indeed, every culture seems to be a conglomeration of contradictory forces, beliefs, and ideals which in no way can be reconciled logically. Troeltsch admits this, but he refuses to concede that this rules out the possibility of understanding the essence of a given culture through scientific means and from the actual content of the culture "working out" *(herausarbeiten)* its ideal. It is possible to do this despite the apparent contradictory forces in a culture because "the tensions among religion, art, science, politics, law and the economy are not logical contradictions and their unification does not constitute the logical but rather the trans-logical unity of an individual, time-bound synthesis."[78]

Thus all the apparent contradictions and dilemmas, created by the application of the natural sciences and of historical analysis to human reality, seem overcome. Although "timeless, eternal, universally valid and absolute values" are unattainable, we can discover objective norms. "Individuality is not identical with subjectivity."[79] Mankind is manifold and yet there is one purpose behind it. All we can ascertain are separate cultures which seem to exclude a progress of mankind; yet "we are in steady movement toward the Absolute which in the unity of the fullness of its life exists only for itself and cannot be rationally comprehended because it is not at all a rational concept."[80] No science can ever master the "stream of life in its entirety." Nevertheless, this stream of life must possess "unity, connectedness, and meaning; otherwise scientific thought would be incapable of grasping *(erfassen)* and defining *(fixieren)* its individual constellations empirically or in terms of their norms."[81] Thus God stands behind all as the *sine qua non* of all thought and understanding. Without the concept of God or an analogous idea, the formulation of objective standards or values is impossible.[82]

The 777 pages of *The Problems of Historicism* add little to this faith in the meaning of history.[83] Again the apparent dilemmas of the historical approach are presented, and again an idealistic philosophy of history provides the solutions to the apparent conflicts between subjectivity and objectivity, the relativity of all values and their validity, the variety in history, and the basic unity of the world. If history at every point reflects the "unknowable absolute," then history is also the key to truth and values. And history for Troeltsch, as for Ranke, is a real process which cannot be reduced to the concepts that Rickert proposes.

Troeltsch attempts to protect history against the efforts of the Neo-Kantians to reduce it to concepts. For him history is more than merely the way in which the historian "arranges" the facts, as it is for Rickert. History is "a movement within the subject matter itself, into which one can immerse oneself intuitively," and from which we can gather the unique values valid at our point in the historical stream.[84] Since history is real, the approach to it involves a much simpler logic than dreamed of by the Neo-Kantians. It consists of the "concrete, immediate, visual presentation *(konkrete, anschauliche Darstellung)* of the timebound, individual and unique structures in history," from which we can alone win values. Ideal types or socio-logical analysis, no matter how useful, are never able to reflect the full richness of life. The methods of history need no logical formulation. The historian practises them.[85] They involve rational analysis less than empathetic understanding *(nachfühlend verstehen),*[86] "see-ing, rather than thinking" *(Schauen, nicht Erdenken).*[87] The basic elements of history are "individual totalities," an individual, a class, a people, or a culture. What makes them into individualities is the fact that each of them is centered around a meaning or a value characteristic only of it. This meaning is original and unique *(ursprünglich, einmalig).*[88] Each can be grasped not through causal explanation, but can only be "understood." Nevertheless, such un-derstanding is by no means arbitrary or subjective. It is guided by the objective fact that the subject matter remains the same, even if the formulations of our questions may differ. These objectively existing and individual totalities in history each possess a center of meaning around which their manifold manifestations can be organized. Con-fronted by an historical reality, and thoroughly imbued by it, our minds grasp it spontaneously.[89]

What makes intuitive understanding possible is the unity of all spiritual reality through the mediation of God. Yet this unity does not mean the pantheistic identity of God and Nature, for this would imply a basic conformity of all existence and a denial of real, absolute individuality. The Leibniz theory of monads, of which each is a closed self-contained individuality that nevertheless reflects the divine order, seems to Troeltsch to come closer to the truth. "For not Spinoza's identity of thought and being or of nature and spirit, but the substantive and individual identity of finite spirits with the infinite spirit and therefore the intuitive participation in its concrete content and its motion-filled unity of life provides the key to the solution of our problem."[90]

From this concept of individuality, Troeltsch arrives at two conclusions, one negative, the other positive. On the one hand, there can be no history of mankind for "mankind as a whole has no cultural and intellectual *(geistige)* unity and hence no unified development."[91] Since the most comprehensive unity of meaning we know is a culture, there can only be the histories of individual cultures such as that of Western Civilization. But because each civilization is a unity of meaning, we can find the values proper to it. At this point, Troeltsch sees the solution of the crisis of values in the modern Western world. History has destroyed the traditional values of the West by showing their genetic character. Historical study of the West can now uncover the real essence of "Europeanism," study its course of development, and establish the values which are proper to it. Values cannot be invented; they have to be organic parts of a cultural tradition. But out of the rich tradition of the West, the historian can create a cultural synthesis *(Kultursynthese)* of that which is best in Western development and remains worthy of aspiration and capable of realization. This "cultural synthesis" can then serve as a guide for action toward the future of the European world.[92]

Carlo Antoni sees in Troeltsch's "history of Europeanism . . . only a revision of that chapter in (Spengler's) *The Decline of the West* which deals with our own civilization."[93] This is true in a sense. For Troeltsch, generally, human values, world history, and human progress all cease to exist.[94] Even reason loses its universal character, and has meaning for us only in the form in which it developed within the Western community of peoples with its roots in Antiquity and Christendom.[95] Nevertheless, Troeltsch's spirit is not one of despair. Western Civilization becomes identical with the highest achievement of the human mind. In a sense it merges with civilization and mankind as such. Within it are embodied the traditions of rationality, humanity, and liberality through which the modern world can gain new strength and new harmony. Spengler's book therefore seems to him an invitation to return to barbarism by sacrificing the rational and scholarly ideals of the West and to be itself an "active contribution to the decline of the West."[96] Troeltsch remained a man emotionally and unshakably committed to the values of the West, even when his intellect revealed to him the problematic character of his beliefs. The doubts, the dread suspicion that all is meaningless flux, breaks through again and again in Troeltsch's thought from his early theological writings to the lectures on *"Der Historismus und seine Überwindung."*[97] Committed to the historical approach, Troeltsch could never effectively refute these doubts on rational grounds. The tragedy of his lifework lay in the persistent contradiction between his desire for intellectual honesty and his inability to accept the full consequences of his thought.

2.

Friedrich Meinecke's intellectual biography reflects the crisis and dissolution of German historical faith perhaps even more sharply than does Ernst Troeltsch's lifework. Troeltsch began his scholarly career profoundly conscious of the inner contradictions of the historical approach to truths and values, and ended his life in this awareness without ever being able to face heroically the logical consequences of his thought. Friedrich Meinecke grew up in an atmosphere in which the heritage of Ranke and the political historians had not yet become problematic. He died amidst the spiritual ruins of post-World War II Germany in the bitter realization that Germany had traveled a wrong road not only politically, but philosophically and in its historical scholarship. And yet Meinecke, similar to Troeltsch, remained incapable of freeing himself of many of the vestiges of a past faith.

Friedrich Meinecke's roots were planted deeply in Prussian traditions. His formative years were spent in much greater isolation from the main currents of late nineteenth-century discussion than were those of Ernst Troeltsch, the son of a liberal Protestant Bavarian physician. In his biography, Meinecke describes the Christian, conservative atmosphere of his youth in small-town Salzwedel, where for decades his father and grandfather had been postmasters, devoutly Lutheran, and devoted to the Prussian dynasty. At the University of Berlin, Meinecke was deeply influenced by Droysen's lectures on the methodology and philosophy of history[98] (Droysen was then in his seventies) and was guided in his studies by Sybel and Treitschke. Meinecke then worked under Sybel in the Prussian state archives, and later assisted him in editing the *Historische Zeitschrift*. In later years, Meinecke emphasized that he had never been "overwhelmed" by Treitschke, and that he had been aware of the agitator role which Treitschke had played to some extent in the lecture hall.[99] Nevertheless, it was Meinecke's initiative that led to the appointment of Treitschke as chief editor of the *Historische Zeitschrift* upon Sybel's death in 1895. Treitschke had just broken with Hans Delbrück and the more liberal collaborators of the *Preussische Jahrbücher*.[100]

For Meinecke, as for his teachers, belief in the central role of the state in human culture and in the spiritual character of political power was not merely a question of scholarly approach, but a matter of profound religious conviction. Meinecke was fully aware of the epistemological discussion which Dilthey had stimulated. The thesis he wrote for his state examination in philosophy, comparing the methods of the natural sciences and the *Geisteswissenschaften,* reflected the influence of Dilthey as well as of Droysen.[101] Surprisingly, Meinecke's own position was little influenced by these discussions. His disillusion with the objective idealism which underlay the outlook of the Prussian-German political historians was less the result of intellectual developments, as it had been with Ernst Troeltsch or Max Weber, than of the traumatic experience of World War I. His first break with the optimism of his teachers in the Bismarckian solution came on political grounds. His realization of the "misfortune that the monarchy was ruined by such an emperor (Wilhelm II)," and his disappointment in the failure of the Conservative party to adopt a program of social reforms, gradually brought him into the camp of Friedrich Naumann between 1895 and 1898.[102] Yet this swing was much less radical than it might appear; for Meinecke's Christian conservatism had always been socially oriented,[103] and Naumann's liberalism stressed the central role of state, nation, and community over the individual. In a sense, Meinecke's new position was much more in harmony with the spirit of "the Era of Reform," which the political historians had idealized in the days before 1870, than with the reactionary conservatism of the old Treitschke. It was this spirit of reform which Meinecke depicted in his biography of Field Marshal Boyen, the advocate of popular conscription who championed liberal reforms and enlightened social legislation "in sharp contrast to the reactionary policies of an 'ossified nobility.' "[104]

In 1896, the year the first volume of the Boyen biography appeared, Meinecke assumed the editorship of the *Historische Zeitschrift,* which he held until 1935 when he was forced to resign under Nazi pressure. His elevation to the editorship coincided with the first serious (and rather spectacular) attack on the Rankean and Prussian traditions of historiography made within the German historical profession.

In his monumental *German History,* and in a subsequent flood of articles and brochures, Karl Lamprecht declared war against the individualizing, descriptive method of German historians. "The natural sciences have long overcome the age in which a descriptive method distinguished phenomena merely in terms of distinctive, individual characteristics," Lamprecht observed. Historical science similarly must replace a descriptive method by a genetic one which tries to formulate general laws of development. Such an approach must necessarily not concern itself with political history exclusively, but must assign a central role to cultural, economic, legal, and intellectual history.[105] Ranke's theory of ideas was untenable. It had its time, Lamprecht continued, and will remain as a lasting monument to a great period in German historiography and to a great historian. "But the history of science will leave it behind, as it has already moved beyond the metaphysical, mystical systems of philosophic idealism."[106] German historians must turn from the mystical conception that a personal God manifests Himself behind the "ideas," a standpoint of personal faith rather than of scientific conviction,[107] to the empirical study of historical development.

The historians rallied to the defense of the sacred tradition thus profaned. Although Meinecke remained relatively in the background, the *Historische Zeitschrift* became the main organ of the counterattack against Lamprecht. For Friedrich Meinecke, Georg von Below, and Max Lenz, Karl Lamprecht represented the attack of Western Positivism against the tradition of German Idealism. In retrospect, the differences between the two positions seem much less pronounced than they did at the time when they were obscured behind the vehement language and the peculiar phraseology of both sides.[108] The historians quoted Windelband and Rickert against Lamprecht. They failed to realize that the Neo-Kantian critique of historical knowledge constituted a much more serious challenge to the basic theoretical assumptions of the German historiographical tradition than did Lamprecht's search for laws. For despite the passages quoted above, the basic issue between Lamprecht and the "older direction of history" did not center around the question of objective idealism nor really deal with the methods applicable to history. Karl Lamprecht was as fully convinced that history was a real process as were his critics, who sought Lamprecht's intellectual roots in Comte and Mill, although they really were much more firmly bedded in Hegel, Schelling, and Romantic organicist conceptions of society.

Once deprived of the positivistic connotations of his terminology, Lamprecht's "stages of development," as Below correctly remarked, seemed suspiciously similar to Ranke's "ideas" and "tendencies" in history. Lamprecht had labeled these as mysticism.[109] The basic difference between Lamprecht and the traditional historian's approach was whether the historian should concentrate on social or on political history. This decision, as Otto Hintze recognized in the one brilliant essay which came out of the controversy, was a matter of emphasis.[110] The state continued to occupy a central, directing role in Lamprecht's conception of society. A strong foreign policy remained for him a prerequisite for economic progress. For that matter, ideas and social and economic forces occupied an important role in Treitschke's and Sybel's historiography. Lamprecht continued to insist that *"individuum est ineffabile,"* that a residue of individuality eludes all causal analysis of social relations and "can only be divined" *(lässt sich nur ahnen).*[111] However, he insisted that history as a science, like any other science, is concerned with generalizations[112] and with the reduction of empirical perceptions to concepts.[113] This position was not radically different from that of Rickert. Lamprecht recognized that the purely individual could never be understood scientifically; one could only begin to define it by scientific and conceptual means.[114] Nevertheless, a very large area, indeed a major area of social activity, he insisted, could be approached by a "collective" method, for in society there is "uninterrupted continuity of development" which does not arise from the free actions of individuals.[115]

But Lamprecht maintained that although all science is "basically one" *(alle Wissenschaft ist im tiefsten Grunde eine),*[116] the historian could not establish social laws similar in rigidity to those of the natural sciences. "Herr von Below . . . knows basically only one form of 'typical,' namely the one he calls 'law,' " Lamprecht defended himself.[117] Causality, after all, is not something which has objective reality, but a category of our thought. The historian is necessarily obliged to see regularities within historical subject matter, although he can not establish rigid laws of development.[118] The role of individual freedom, no matter how limited, forbids a monistic, deterministic picture of history. "The presentation of an unbroken causal chain is (therefore) almost impossible," Lamprecht observed, and an artistic approach, he believed, can at times yield more "scientific" understanding of historical processes than science itself.[119] Lamprecht foreshadowed Troeltsch and Spengler, when he sought to limit the search for regularities to cycles of development within limited units of mankind. "All present-day historians are convinced that a history of mankind is not possible," he observed.[120] The units of history, he held, are not civilizations, as Troeltsch and Spengler later thought, but nations which for the most part were organized into states.[121] Each nation has its individuality, its own cycle of development, so that "every study which henceforth will seek to establish regularities within the historical process will have to restrict itself to typical national developments." But comparative, morphological studies between cycles of national development—for example, a comparison of Renaissances, Middle Ages, or receptivity to elements of other cultures—are possible.[122]

Meinecke's own brief crossing of swords with Lamprecht added little that was new. Meinecke challenged Lamprecht's extreme statement regarding the applicability of the principle of causation to individual actions,[123] modified by Lamprecht in subsequent writings. Most significant, perhaps, was Meinecke's observation that scientific methodology and *Weltanschauung* could not be strictly separated, as Lamprecht had maintained.[124] Although Meinecke found Lamprecht's "strongly positivistic thinking" a shallow approach to social problems, he also regretted those neo-Rankian trends in German historiography which looked upon history as an "aesthetic spectacle," and avoided ethical or political commitments. "Those of us who believe the idealistic world view and the intensive feeling for the state of the older generation are by no means dead," Meinecke wrote in his obituary for Sybel, "will preserve his (Sybel's) heritage faithfully without permitting it to rigidify into an immovable dogma."[125]

Lamprecht's attack against the Idealistic heritage of German historiography remained ineffective. Nevertheless, the issues of the *Historische Zeitschrift* began to reflect an increasing shift from a predominant occupation with political, and particularly Prussian, history to a consideration of cultural factors, although less in the form of social and economic history than of intellectual, cultural or even art history. In 1900 the art historian Carl Neumann could thus remark in the pages of the *Historische Zeitschrift* in an analysis of Burckhardt's *History of Greek Civilization* that Burckhardt would have regarded the issues between Lamprecht and the traditional historians as insignificant, for they basically involved only questions of style.[126]

Meinecke began to recognize Lamprecht's contribution to German historiography. Lamprecht, he wrote in the Preface to the one hundredth volume of the *Historische Zeitschrift* in 1908, had at least warned against the narrowness and lack of ideas of historians who had become one-sided craftsmen. Lamprecht had attempted to reintroduce ideas and theories into historical thought, even if the relationship which he proposed was an unfortunately "hybrid" one. Sybel's optimism that the "true method of historical research" would lead without great difficulties to an "objective" history of significance to the nation had proved to be wrong. His expectation that history for the broad public would occupy the place which philosophy had held also turned out to be false. Philosophy and the cultural sciences had absorbed the sense for history which a good deal of professional historical research had lost. Moreover, Sybel's faith that the historian, through the application of scholarly methods, could largely exclude the element of subjectivity in his judgments of political history had been lost. Meinecke admitted. History must not give up its central concern with the concrete realities of state and nation, he counseled. Without these, it would become "vague dilettantism." But for its own regeneration it must renew the lost contact with philosophy or at least with the philosophic spirit.[127]

In *Cosmopolitanism and the Nation State,* Meinecke undertook to write a history that would combine politics with the history of ideas. "My book," he wrote in the Introduction, "rests on the opinion that German historical research, without renouncing its methodological heritage, must raise itself to establishing free contact with the great forces of political and cultural life, that without incurring harm, it may immerse itself courageously in philosophy as well as in politics, that only through this contact can it develop its own essence and be at once universal and national."[128] The theme of the book is the transformation of Germany from a *Kulturnation,* a national culture, to a *Staatsnation,* a national state. The basic assumption upon which the book rests is the faith of Ranke and the Prussian School in the *"real-geistige"* character of states and nations, the belief that each nation or state is an individuality whose external form reflects an individualized, but nevertheless real and timeless idea.

For Meinecke, the history of German unification could thus best be portrayed as a history of ideas; as the story of the steady realization by German thinkers and statesmen of the truth that universal ideas could be expressed meaningfully only in concrete, historical individualities and institutions; and of the subsequent organization of Germany into a political body which would reflect cosmopolitan ideals in a specific, national form. The Prussian-German national state in the form in which it emerged represented not merely a political attainment, but also the concrete manifestation of philosophic truth. The victory of this idea was the work of great individuals, not of blind social forces.

All of this reminds us of Droysen and Sybel. Ideas, not political and military motives, seem to be almost the exclusive motivating forces of political change. The sensitivity which Sybel and Treitschke had possessed for social and economic factors, in a time less affected by the industrial revolution, is missing entirely in Meinecke. For him the men who created the German national idea were foremost poets and thinkers: men such as Möser, Herder, Novalis, Wilhelm von Humboldt, Friedrich Schlegel, Fichte, Adam Müller, Haller, Hegel, and Ranke. Although the statesmen played a more important role after 1848, when the German national idea was given its political form by the Prussian state, the Gagern brothers and Bismarck were noteworthy for Meinecke primarily in their role as thinkers. Meinecke's sense of history demanded that this process of national transformation be presented in concrete, individualized terms. In the transformation which took place, cosmopolitan ideas were not, of course, simply replaced by national ones. Rather, out of the tension of the two, a new and truer relationship between universal and national ideals arose. Meinecke believed that this transformation could not be portrayed as a dialectical process occurring on the level of abstract thought. Instead, it had to be placed within a concrete context, but this context required less an analysis of the changes in public opinion than an understanding of the great personalities who created these ideas. The way to approach the history of the transformation of German politics was therefore not in terms of the social history of the broad masses, but through the biographies of the great "creative thinkers" who participated in this dialogue.[129]

Nevertheless, one cannot help feeling that in his individual biographies Meinecke seriously violated the "historical sense" *(historischen Sinn)* which he demanded. Perhaps not fully conscious of doing so, Meinecke infused a strong dose of Hegelian dialectics into a Rankean conception of individuality. Meinecke had criticized Droysen for reading direction into history. Droysen had violated the concept of individuality when he read a German mission into Prussian history, and thus failed to study the Prussian state as an autonomous, political individual *(autonome Staatspersönlichkeit)* which followed its own interests and developed its own unique character.[130] But the thinkers and statesmen whom Meinecke presented seemed to appear less for their own sake than as the concrete expression of certain ideas. All of them seemed to be less ends in themselves than stages in the development of an objective process. Since Meinecke saw in German history not a mere transformation of political forms and ideas, but the steady approximation of the true state, he found an abstract standard by which he proceeded to judge the actors in the drama. Despite all his warnings against applying external principles to the evaluation of an individual,[131] Meinecke did not cease to moralize, and to judge each of the characters in his drama by the extent to which he had freed himself from the illusions of cosmopolitanism.

Basic to Meinecke's conception of history was his firm belief that in this best of all possible worlds no basic conflict exists between the power interests of the state and the principles of ethics, between the development of nationalism and that of individual liberty. For the state is not merely a complex of power or of individuals, but the concrete manifestation of a universal idea. Analogous to all universal ideas, it could take on reality only in an individualized, living form. What had real existence, such as the state, was therefore of necessity also good because it was the expression of an ideal. Fichte's great contribution had been to overcome the apparent contradiction between Machiavelli's view of power and that of his critics by "recognizing the power drive of the state as a natural and beneficient life drive and placing it within the context of an ethical world view."[132] The state could do no wrong in any fundamental sense, as long as it followed its own judgment. "For nothing can be immoral which derives from the most profoundly individual nature of a being."[133] Admittedly, the interests of the healthy state appeared to be in contradiction with the principle of ethics and law, for "not peace and tranquillity, but struggle, care, and friction are the fate of the genuine nation state." But this conflict existed only when we confused ethics with abstract principles, and failed to realize that "the unwritten law of the great forces moving in history stands above the formal written law."[134]

The development of these forces in German history had not only brought about the German national state, but also the attainment of liberal institutions. Here, as in the case of national unification, leadership had to come from a Prussian state which received its spiritual basis from the culture of the German nation. In retrospect, Meinecke did not regret the failure of the liberals in 1848. The course of events had shown that Friedrich Wilhelm IV and Bismarck had been right, and the Gagerns, Droysen, and Dahlmann had been wrong, as had been those liberals who, in 1848, wished to achieve German unification at the expense of Prussia or who, in the Prussian constitutional conflict of 1862, placed parliamentary rights over the military and power-political needs of the Prussian state.[135] The road which Germany had traveled had been the only one which could have led to a strong and free national state. Bismarck had succeeded in giving Germany a constitutional form of government which skillfully harmonized Prussian leadership with the continued, autonomous existence of the smaller German states, and balanced parliamentary institutions with a strong monarchical executive. In the baptism of fire of 1866 and 1870, Bismarck had then redeemed constitutional government which had been so thoroughly discredited in the German public mind.[136]

This satisfaction with the recent past on Meinecke's part reflected a conception of liberty basically different from that of classical Western liberals. For Meinecke, as for the Prussian moderate liberals of the nineteenth century, liberty was meaningful only within the framework of a strong and united nation. Meinecke could accept Bismarck's German solution because he still rejected parliamentary supremacy; even the limited degree of parliamentary government which existed was viewed with a high degree of skepticism. He suggested that "the introduction of parliamentary institutions in Prussia had in the final analysis probably divided the Prussian people more than it had united them."[137] What was wanted was constitutional, not parliamentary government.[138] Meinecke could thus speak of the conservative constitution, decreed by the Prussian king in 1848 after the collapse of the revolutionary forces, as "highly liberal in content" because it introduced constitutional forms.[139] Meinecke agreed with Friedrich Naumann that the predominance of Prussia within the German Reich and the old Prussian conservative forces within Prussia marked an unfortunate aspect of the Germany of his day. The political power of the aristocratic and agrarian forces in the Germany of 1908 was hardly in harmony with modern economic and social conditions. It showed that the transition from the "modernized old Prussian national state" to the "German national state" had not yet been completed.[140] Nevertheless, Bismarck's solution, although "hardly ideal",[141] had been absolutely necessary in the interest of national power and cohesion. The predominance of the "old Prussian conservative tendencies in the Reich," although clearly in disharmony with economic and social conditions, was necessary for the existence of a strong state in Europe until the "new German, liberal, bourgeois, industrial forces were sufficiently strong to pursue the "power politics and power needs" of the German Empire.[142] This required not only that middle-class liberals become more aware of the role of power in politics, but that they be able to close the gap which existed between them and the social-democratic working class movement. What Meinecke apparently had in mind but did not spell out, as the final form of a German national state, was a plebiscitarian dictatorship (*temporäre Vertrauensdiktatur*) based upon a broad, democratic suffrage which he advocated a few years later. Parliaments, he agreed with Max Weber, must be a prime instrument in the selection and rise of leaders in whom they deposit their confidence.[143]

This optimism regarding the nature of power explains Meinecke's confidence in Germany's future at the outbreak of World War I. Since 1910, through contributions to newspapers, Meinecke had actively supported the cause of Friedrich Naumann. He had hoped for a conciliation of Left and Right in Germany, for a recognition by the conservatives of the need for social reforms and an understanding on the part of the Social Democrats for the national requirements of power. In the August days of 1914, the nation seemed united for the first time in any real sense. The war had brought the spirit of unity of the entire nation above lines of parties and class, and made possible the renovation of the nation. Meinecke, with Troeltsch, Lamprecht, and Cohen, and almost all the intellectuals of the Reform movement, was swept along by the wave of enthusiasm. Thirty years later, amidst the bombs of World War II, he wrote:

> On August 3, (1914), I experienced . . . one of the most beautiful moments of my life which suddenly renewed my deep confidence in our people. . . . We were standing in the crowd at St. Martin's Gate on the Kaiserstrasse in front of the bulletin box of the *Freiburger Zeitung* and read the telegram that the Reichstag had unanimously approved the war credits. . . . Then the German Social Democrats will not abandon the fatherland. What I had cared, longed, and hoped for for two decades had thus been fulfilled. . . . It also justified what we had sought to attain in our heated Freiburg election campaign two years earlier to the dismay of many of those closely connected with us. Still today (1944) in my old age, after the bitter experiences of three decades and after the further disintegration, division, and finally the violence done to our national life, I still affirm the sentiment which moved me at that moment in front of the bulletin box of the *Freiburger Zeitung*.[144]

Meinecke, as he soon admitted, had not yet seen the demonic aspects of national power. He still believed firmly in "the good meaning and content of power politics and of the martial collisions of nations. . . . In this state of mind," he wrote, "I had in *Cosmopolitanism and the Nation State* depicted the emancipation of purely political thought and action from universalistic and cosmopolitan considerations as one of the greatest achievements of the middle of the nineteenth century."[145] What Meinecke expected from the war was not German world hegemony, but a cleansing of the nation's inner life. In the collection of war essays, *Die deutsche Erhebung von 1914 (The German Uprising of 1914)*, he compared the spirit of 1914 with that of the Wars of Liberation in 1813 as a reaffirmation of faith in nation and freedom.[146] Regarding Germany's territorial expansion after the war, Meinecke was perhaps one of the more moderate of the liberals. Nevertheless, in 1915 Meinecke advocated the annexation of parts of Poland and Kurland with expulsion of the non-German population and return of the Volga Germans. He favored continued controls over Belgium after the war and a harsh peace with France and hoped for naval parity with Great Britain. But he soon thought that this was out of the question and began to call for a peace of conciliation.[146]

As did Weber and Troeltsch, Meinecke fought against the chauvinism and lack of a sense of reality of the Pan-Germans. His main journalistic activity, during the later war years, served the growing demand for constitutional reforms, although his chief concern remained the reform of the Prussian suffrage laws rather than an extension of the powers of parliament over foreign and military affairs.[147] The very nature of the German idea of the nation, Meinecke confidently replied to Western critics of German culture, made impossible any ruthless imperialistic policy on Germany's part. The worlds of Weimar and of Potsdam, of Kant and Bismarck, were not two fully divorced traditions in Germany. Rather, the German national idea, born in the Age of Reforms and the Wars of Liberation, reflected the constant interaction of both these poles. Power and spirit, state and culture, were interwoven. This distinguished the "national idea" from its degenerate offspring, "nationalism," which especially in its neo-Darwinian and racist forms had become a European disease.[148] Unfortunately, the much needed synthesis between culture and state, spirit and power, was not yet complete. But the history of man, Meinecke confidently observed, shows "a slowly ascending development. The crude means and aims of power politics were giving way to nobler and more humanitarian ones." This greater "humaneness in power politics" would not mean that the state would pursue its interests any less vigorously, but rather that it would defend cultural aims to an ever greater extent. Thus, "while our culture in these tremendous days is being mobilized entirely in the service of the state, our state, our power politics, and our war," Meinecke maintained, "are imperceptibly serving the highest values of our national culture."[149]

In 1915, Meinecke still confidently argued against Otto Hintze and Eduard Meyer's fears that World War I marked the beginning of the decline of European culture.[150] In 1916, he first admitted in

Friedrich Naumann's weekly, *Die Hilfe,* that German "national culture" contained perhaps even greater tendencies of degenerating into
"ruthless nationalism" and the misuse of spiritual values in the service of naked power than did Western utilitarianism.[151] By 1917, he
was aware of the terrible dilemma that war in its modern form could
no longer be regarded as "a suitable means for continuing politics
and for attaining by force certain requirements of life," but that "the
struggle for power among states and nations" remained nevertheless
an inescapable condition of human political life and of man's inherent instinct for power.[152]

The course of the war had thus disproven the objective idealism
reflected in *Weltbürgertum und Nationalstaat,* with its optimistic assumption in the basic harmony of spirit and power, irrationality and
reason. Meinecke's first major work after the war, and his most
significant one, *Die Idee der Staatsräson,* reflects this disillusionment.
In 1915, Meinecke announced his intention to write a book which
would attempt to "understand the changes in the character and spirit
of power politics since the days of the Renaissance and to trace the
emergence of our modern conception of history."[153] Meinecke still
assumed optimistically that a study of the development of the modern theory of the state could be united with the history of modern
historical thought. Both led in the same direction, "in the feeling
radiating from Machiavelli for the most individual and concrete interests of the particular states." This sprung from the belief that the
important achievement of both modern power politics and of modern
historiography was the emancipation from universal, ethical notions.
But in the midst of the tragedy of the war, such a conception of
modern political practice soon seemed "much too simple" to
Meinecke. It failed to take into account the "demonic character of
power." And although Meinecke refused "to declare power as such
as evil, as Burckhardt had done," he nevertheless became deeply
aware of the problematic character of power.[154] The result was a
reformulation of the problems. Chapters written during the earlier
part of the war remained mostly unpublished. If *Weltbürgertum und
Nationalstaat* had pointed to a progressive solution of the problems
of power and historical understanding in the modern nation state,
*Die Idee der Staatsräson (Machiavellism. The Doctrine of Raison
d'Etat)* saw the recurrent problem, posed by the tensions between
power and spirit, never capable of a satisfactory solution. Political

power and the state proved to be not only the creators of cultural values, but also their destroyer. Power and ethics, nature and spirit, now appeared to Meinecke as opposing and constantly struggling forces in perennial conflict. The elemental drive for power as such lacked spiritual content. It was neither part of the economy of the world in Hegel's sense nor a material expression of spiritual forces in Ranke's view. The objective idealism of Meinecke's prewar writings were now replaced by a dualistic conception of reality.

What kept Meinecke from accepting a radically pessimistic theory of the state and of political power was his new definition of "the reason of state." He still believed that this reason must constitute "the fundamental principle of political conduct." It represents the "ideal course of conduct" which a state must follow at each given moment in order to preserve itself and expand.[155] The idea of "reason of state," he maintains, is sharply different from an abstract theory of the state. It defines the interests of the state not in terms of an ideal "best state," but only in terms of the concrete, existing state.[156] Nevertheless, "reason of state" is not identical with "power politics;" for the maintenance and attainment of spiritual and moral values might be an important factor in the consolidation or expansion of the power of the state. It is the task of the statesman to establish the balance between ethics and powers demanded by the situation. A certain harmony between spirit and power thus continued to exist for Meinecke. "A bridge," he writes

> exists on the highest plane of political life between *kratos* and *ethos,* between action motivated by power and ethically responsible action. This bridge is the reason of state, the consideration of what is expedient, useful, and beneficial, of what the state has to do to reach its optimal existence at any given time.[157]

But this harmony is not an automatic one. Meinecke still remained confident that the state, because it required ethical forces for its existence, directly contributes to the creation of higher values. Civilization would not have been born had it not been for the elemental drive for power of the ancient despots. This power can never rest on mere force; always, at least in a primitive way, it has to respond to man's inherent need to spiritualize Nature.[158] To maintain itself, power must create law and morality. Thus the very requirements of power help to transform the state from the expression of arbitrary personal force to an "ethical institution for promoting life's highest values."[159] But because the state rests on this delicate interplay of elementary instincts of power and spirit, it is constantly threatened by relapses into barbarism. These relapses are not the result of the personal weaknesses of the men who control the state, but are in the very nature of the state itself. All other social organizations could be organized and could act in strict adherence to ideal norms. These norms might be violated in practice, but in theory they remain intact. However, the state cannot even have a "clean theory of action," especially in the realm of international affairs where it must be willing to unleash the elemental and culture-destroying forces of war in the defense of its rights. The state has to sin and sully itself by violations of law and morality.

"This," Meinecke observes sadly, "is the most terrible and deeply disturbing fact of world history, that it is impossible radically to transform into an ethical institution that human community which exists to protect and further all other communities."[160] A solution to the problem is not possible. The drive for power is perennial, as is the attempt of statesmen to channel it. What changes are the unique situations of states, their concrete interests at each moment, and the conceptions of the reason of state which arise out of the interaction of these interests with the dominant *Weltanschauungen*. With no progress in the doctrine of the reason of state, the book could thus merely relate the "tragic" story of the recurrent conflicts of the idea of the reason of state, and the dominant philosophic notions and *Weltanschauungen* of modern political thought.[161] The most the historian can do is to view the processes of life within the framework of the great forces operating in history. He can never define the character of spirit or determine the ideal relationship of spirit or ethics to the concrete situations of historical reality.[162]

Meinecke saw the central theme in the history of political thought since the Renaissance as the tension between the doctrine of natural law and the hard "unavoidable" facts of historical and political life.[163] In a complicated interrelationship the idea of the state as power, a reality with vital interests and a will of its own, or as an instrument of welfare subject to ethical law, confronted and transformed each other. The needs of the absolute state stimulated the concern with the reason of state in the early modern period. The idea of the reason of state, by questioning all traditional ethical and political standards, then prepared the way for the Enlightenment.[164] The latter, in turn, fought the reason of state, and helped to destroy the same absolutism which had given birth to the idea but which had also restrained it in its narrow confines. Yet the very realities and experiences of life forced the Enlightenment statesman, whether he was Frederick the Great or a French revolutionary politician, to realize that the state was a "life force" *(Lebensmacht)*.[165] Out of this interaction, so complex that it could not be reduced to a simple line of development,[166] there grew a fuller sense of history, and with it a more complete understanding of the state as a concrete, historical individuality. Machiavelli had still lacked such understanding for the highly individual character of the state when he prescribed general precepts of political conduct. However, comprehension of the nature of the state by no means solved the conflict between the interests of the state and the demands of ethics.

In the philosophy of identity, German nineteenth-century thought had attempted to construct a grandiose synthesis of individual will and universal order which had seemed plausible until World War I. Hegel, perceiving the source of reason in history rather than in individual consciousness, had been able to show that the state, too, is rational and that, in fulfilling its power-political needs, it serves a higher ethical purpose. But by subordinating the state to a grand pattern of world development,[167] Hegel had done violence to the individuality of the state. Even more seriously, he had laid the basis for a new and more radical Machiavellism by regarding the power interests of sovereign states as the instruments by which the absolute spirit develops to perfection. Machiavelli had recognized that the reason of state requires it to act counter to moral principles at times, but he had never claimed moral sanction for these actions. For him the reason of state remained outside the moral realm; for Hegel, however, it became the cornerstone of the ethical world. War, the violation of treaties, and treachery could all be parts of the cunning *(List der Vernunft)* by which reason achieves the ultimate good.

"What happened now," Meinecke observed, "was almost like the legitimization of a bastard."[168] But Ranke had not solved the problem, either, by stressing the individuality of the state, Meinecke now recognized. Perhaps his insistence upon absolute individuality should have led to the "anarchy of values," to the radical relativism which threatened German historicism. It did not, however, because Ranke's *Historismus* still contained strong elements of the philosophy of identity, as well as of natural law and of Christian doctrine.[169] Yet, in his writings, there was a deep and irreconcilable conflict between Ranke, the historian, and Ranke, the Christian. Ranke's historical feeling told him that every epoch must be judged in terms of its own inherent values; his moral consciousness called for transcendent values. Thus he was never able to accept or even excuse Machiavelli's principles, although he recognized the reason of state as a legitimate life function of states as personalities in a higher sense.[170] Hegel's "doctrine whereby the world-spirit produces events as it were by deception, and makes use of human passions to achieve its aims," Meinecke quoted Ranke, "is founded on a supremely unworthy conception of God and of humanity."[171]

Nevertheless, Ranke came close to Hegel's position in his own optimistic view that the struggles for power in history have almost always helped to create higher values and that there have been "few significant wars for which it could not be proved that genuine moral energy achieved the final victory." Political power for him always remained something spiritual.[172] What prevented Ranke from drawing Hegel's final conclusions in regard to the sanctity of the reason of state and power politics was his religiosity. "Reverence for what was unfathomable, and the moral law in his breast, prevented him from taking the last step which would deify world history and its supreme protagonist, the State, and place them absolutely above morality."[173] But even more extreme than Hegel's affirmation of political power was that of his own teacher, Treitschke, Meinecke now recognized. For Treitschke saw the state not merely as an ethical institution, but at one point of his career identified the state with sheer power. The purely natural and animal-like in the drive for power now became an ethical absolute, which took its concrete form in history in the perennial struggle for biological existence.[174]

The "philosophy of identity," which the German historians once hopefully had thought would settle the problem of the conflict of power and ethics, instead had led to the glorification of power and the destruction of the last barriers restricting it, Meinecke now sadly admitted. Only World War I had made this apparent to "those of us who think historically" *(wir historisch Denkenden)*. To be sure, an analysis of the intellectual and social trends of the nineteenth century should have revealed the dangers of this optimistic conception of power, and the extent to which modern technical civilization had been in revolt against Western culture. Reason of state had directly contributed to this conflict. The "will to power and life" of modern states had built the efficient, rationally organized modern governmental machinery as an instrument of power, and had called forth the intellectual forces which made this transition possible: free thought, utilitarianism, and that trend of thinking which seeks to explain and organize all of life along rational lines. The result had been the destruction of the traditional ethical and spiritual restraints on power. First the church, then the humanitarian ideal of the Enlightenment, and finally the ethical individualism of the nineteenth century had each collapsed as effective spiritual forces. The very humanity of man was rendered doubtful by the progressive rationalization and technicalization of life. The three new forces of militarism, nationalism, and capitalism had radicalized the reason of state and revolutionized the character of war. The rise of modern democracy, dominated by mass emotions, had progressively limited the ability of statesmen to act rationally in terms of state interests. The idea of the reason of state called forth demonic forces which it could no longer control and which threatened to destroy our Western civilization. It was those forces which German idealistic philosophy helped to unleash in its optimistic interpretation of power as an ethical concept.[175] We have come to realize, Meinecke concludes,

> that what is rational certainly ought to exist, but cannot, simply be said to do so. The chasm between what is and what ought to be seems to us greater and the tragic guilt of power struggles therefore heavier than in the older German Idealism, which was not able to represent to itself the revelation of God in history as great enough, mighty enough, or comprehensive enough, and saw even the abysses of life resplendent with it.[176]

Although our Western culture is threatened, it is not necessarily doomed, Meinecke consoles his readers. We can no longer accept Ranke's optimism regarding the reason of state. "The historical world seems to us more obscure and, with respect to its future course, more uncertain and dangerous than it did to him and to the generations who believed in the triumph of reason in history." In the face of these terrible realizations, we must seek to build new dams

against power and re-establish the relation of politics to morality
which had been broken in the course of the nineteenth century.[177]

There was no simple solution. The relation of German thought to
the West and to the Christian and natural law traditions, which had
been broken by German historicism and idealistic philosophy, had to
be re-established. But a simple return to natural law theory was not
possible. For neither natural law theory in its Western form nor
German historicism had provided an effective check against the
"modern hypertrophy of the reason of state." Western thought had
failed because it could not conceive of any organic tie between political ethics, abstractly conceived, and the concrete realities of political
life. German historical thought, on the other hand, by idealizing
power politics as part of a higher ethical order, had paved the way
for a crude, naturalistic and biologistic ethics of force.[178] The one
had recognized the dualism of spirit and nature, of what ought to be
and what is, but had failed to bring the two into an organic relationship. The other had viewed life organically, but erased the dividing
line between these realms that was necessary for any meaningful
political ethics.

The answer to this dilemma, Meinecke believes, is to be found in
the idea of individuality. To be sure, in the course of nineteenth-
century German thought, the idea had been badly compromised by
its unfortunate marriage with the idea of identity. The philosophy of
identity had proven to be a dangerous mistake. But Meinecke maintains that "the idea of historical individuality continued to hold good
as an indispensable key to the understanding of intellectual and natural phenomena." Within the idea of individuality there is room for a
conception which views the individual or the state as an organic
whole, but recognizes a tension between what it is and what it ought
to be.[179]

It is difficult to follow Meinecke here. On the one hand, he sees
the need of a "general, pure, and strict ideal of morality," of "moral
commandments" of universal validity. On the other hand, he rejects
the rational ethics implied by this position. Ethics must be general
but not abstract. On these grounds he rejects Kant's formulation of
the categorical imperative. In Kant's "general type of ethics," he
observes,

> in the universally binding moral law, the divine element in man
> speaks to him in a pure and unadulterate manner. In the individual

ethic, he can hear it together with the dark undertones of nature.
. . . For life is nothing else but the inexplicable conjunction of
mind and nature, which are causally linked together and yet essentially gape apart.[180]

But here we again come dangerously close to the philosophy of
identity which Meinecke rejects. Every individual must be understood from within, in terms of his values which he understands immediately and subjectively. But these values, Meinecke holds, however different among individuals, are part of a higher ethical order
and a universal moral law which expresses itself in different individual forms.

Thus Meinecke is able to save a good deal of what was dear to
German historical and idealistic thought. He now agrees that a political morality, separate from morality as such, is untenable. But he
argues that the statesman may still act ethically in terms of an individualized ethics when he places the interests of the state above all
other moral considerations. "In the conflict between politics and morality, the statesman who thinks to save the individuality of the state
at the expense of morality, is not acting according to a special state
morality, but according to that wider type of individual ethics."[181] If
this is true, then there must still exist some sort of identity between
the power interests of states and a higher order of things, Meinecke
partly admits. The main threat to the modern international order, he
believes, has not come from the doctrine of the interests of state, but
from the introduction of emotional demagogic elements into the foreign policies of modern governments. Not power politics and compet-
itive armament have led to the brink of the abyss, but modern
nationalism and democracy. "If everywhere in the world, strength
dwelled side by side with strength, and there were no weak and
decadent spots left between, this would in fact constitute a significant
guarantee for world peace."[182] Bismarck, in Meinecke's opinion, was
the last statesman to understand this fully, and the last one who tried
to defend the reason of state in its pure form against aberrations by
nationalisms and ideologies.[183]

Accordingly, Meinecke, in a sense, returns to his starting point,
possibly an older and wiser man who experienced and understood
the terrible dangers inherent in the doctrine of the reason of state.
Although he has freed himself from certain illusions, he reaffirms the

interests of the state as something positive. He admits that any meaningful political ethics require a dualistic concept of man, a tension
between what man wants and what he ought to do. Actually, however, he has returned to the philosophy of identity which he had
refuted. The doctrine of individuality conceived by Meinecke is
hopelessly interwoven with the idea of identity. In the sphere of
individual ethics, the prime ethical responsibility of the individual
consists of the preservation and the full development of his personality. In the realm of international relations, this is complicated by the
assumption with which Meinecke opens his book that "the state is
also an individual structure with its own characteristic idea of
life,"[184] and that the state in its relations with others could not be
guided by an external norm such as international law.[185] For
Meinecke the state's primary responsibility remains the development
of its potentialities. In the tradition of nineteenth-century German
thought, he continued to view these potentialities in political and
military terms rather than by economic, cultural, or social standards.
The classical liberal idea of the state as an instrument for the welfare
of those individuals who composed it remained distasteful to him.
The state for him was an end in itself. Although he had become
aware of shadowy aspects of the state and had warned against its
glorification, he nevertheless continued to regard it as something almost holy.

From his pessimistic insights regarding the character of political
power, Meinecke might reasonably have been led to a clear-cut dualism between history and ethics; between the world of historical realities, with its conflicting interests, and a realm of ethical values. This
was the position of natural law theorists, as well as of ethical rela-
tivists such as Max Weber. Each, from very different points of departure, realistically recognized the ethical irrationality of the historical
world. Meinecke, however, refused to do this. He continued to
believe firmly that real values manifest themselves in history. The
dualism which he saw was not one between Being and Value or
positive and natural law, but one between power and spirit. If the
state had come into conflict with ethical norms, it was not because of
any disharmony between historical individuality and such norms.
Rather, it was because the state was "bound more closely than almost any other type of historical individuality to natural, biological
necessities which kept it from becoming thoroughly spiritual and

ethical."[186] Meinecke continued to be confident that spirit in its manifold developments reflects the Will of God and cannot go astray.

Meinecke could thus dedicate the next decade and a half to his announced study of the modern historical spirit *(modernen Historismus)*. He solved the problem of the demonic character of power by cutting the close link between the historicist approach and the studies of the interests of the state which had marked his prewar writings. He now sought the roots of modern historicism "in the wholly unpolitical realm" of changes in thought and values *(in dem ganz unpolitischen Gebiete seelischer und weltanschaulicher Wandlungen)*.[187] Not politics but religion and art were the highest cultural values because they were most divorced from the natural, biological world; after them came philosophy and science.[188] Although he recognized that cultural values must act on practical life and political reality, pure contemplation now represented for him one of the highest values.[189] He believed, therefore, that the history of the modern historical attitude must be written as a history of ideas.

In his 1923 review of Ernst Troeltsch's *Der Historismus und seine Probleme,* Meinecke presents in a few pages all the basic ideas of his ambitious work on the origins of modern historicism, *Die Entstehung des Historismus*. He hails the turning away of German intellectual life from the main currents of Western culture in the late eighteenth century as one of the "greatest revolutions in human thought."[190] This revolution, he rejoices, had broken the hold which the narrow and rigid philosophy of natural law had held over Western thought from the time of the Stoics to the modern positivists. A line of thinkers from Leibniz through Herder, Goethe, Humboldt, and the Romantics to Ranke had steadily gained increasing insight into the dynamic, living character of human reality via the idea of individuality. Troeltsch describes it as

> . . . the idea of inimitable, unique individuality developing according to its own, organic laws of life, incapable of being comprehended by the means of logical thought, not to speak of the laws of mechanical causation, but demanding to be grasped, contemplated, experienced, and empathetically re-experienced by the totality of one's spiritual energies.[191]

Meinecke admits that this idea carries within it the danger of relativism because it stresses that all individualities, whether "single individuals" or "collective structures found in history such as states, nations, religions, and indeed all cultural phenomena, even whole cultures,"[192] evolve according to their own laws of development rather than according to general laws. But only apparently so, for we escape the "anarchy of values," Meinecke continues, when we realize that every individuality contains within it its own ideal. Thus we return to Ranke. The realization that all values are relative to an individual *(Wertrelativität)* is not identical with ethical relativism *(Relativismus)*, particularly if we can maintain our belief "in a common, divine, original cause from which all individualities emerge." Within every individuality, fact *(Faktische)* and value *(Seinsollende)* are intertwined. It is our ethical task to discover this individual ideal and raise the particular individuality above the purely natural and biological level to an approximation of its ideal.[193] The stream of history threatens to relativize all. Neither a romantic adherence to the past nor an optimistic philosophy of progress can escape the stream because they both fix goals within the stream itself. The only escape is a vertical one, to find the eternal within the historical moment. This, Meinecke concludes, was the intent of Goethe, Ranke, and Troeltsch, and this, he holds, is the only answer to the problems of historical relativism.[194]

Meinecke made his peace with the political institutions of the West. He became a sincere defender of the Weimar Republic against its enemies from the Right as well as the Left, although his political position of the 1920's lacked the ideological foundation in his theoretical writings which his early endorsement of the Bismarckian empire had possessed.[195] Politics and scholarship to a degree now appeared as two separate compartments in his life.[196] Philosophically, he remained a determined opponent of the West, particularly of the Enlightenment, and a champion of the German past. Politically, Germany might have erred; in the realm of values and insights, its traditions were essentially sound. Behind Meinecke's concept of individuality, there was a deep distrust of the Enlightenment concept of rationality and utility which he saw continued in nineteenth-century positivism. Although he sharply rejected Spengler's "crude naturalism" and the political consequences that Spengler drew,[197] he nevertheless shared Spengler's belief that modern rationality is primarily responsible for the threat to culture by technical civilization. Intellectuality is an obstacle to culture; culture is not identical with human welfare, peace, or democracy.

> We can begin to speak of culture *(Kultur)* as against civilization *(Zivilisation)* only at the point when man first assumes the struggle with nature not merely with his reason and will but with his whole inner self; when he acts value oriented *(wertend)* in a higher sense, i.e., when he does something good and beautiful for its own sake or pursues truth for the sake of truth.[198]

Thus, despite his emphasis upon individuality, Meinecke did not consider the individual person as he concretely exists, as an end in himself. The purpose for which the individual exists is determined only by the ideal which manifests itself in him. For these ideal suprapersonal values, the individual must be willing to sacrifice his own welfare and happiness. In this sense, Meinecke's concept of individuality did much more violence to the individual personality than did natural law theories which recognize a common element of rationality in all men.

Die Entstehung des Historismus, published in 1936, traces the revolt against the Enlightenment concept of man within the broad framework of European intellectual history. Confronted by and deeply concerned with the Nazi rise to power, Meinecke proceeded to trace the triumph of German spirit in at least the nonpolitical sphere. If *Weltbürgertum und Nationalstaat* remind us of Hegel, so does *Die Entstehung des Historismus* to some extent. Both works basically violate the historicist principle that every individuality should be judged in terms of the values immanent within it. Historicism appears in both works less as a unique historical phenomenon than as an almost absolute norm, "the highest stage reached until now in the understanding of things human,"[199] Meinecke uses this norm to judge the various thinkers whom he discusses in the book. The chapters on the emergence of historicism as a view of life read like those in which Meinecke, thirty years earlier, had traced the development of the German national state. They are less the biographies of actual individuals than stages in the development of spirit to self-fulfillment.[200] We are shown how, in an almost progressive manner, successive thinkers replaced the rigid natural law concept of a common human nature, and how a rational ethics with a conception of man and a philosophy of value recognized the elements of individuality, diversity, and change in historical reality.

This movement was European in scope. Almost every major strain of seventeenth and eighteenth-century thought in England, France, Italy, and Germany (pietism, Enlightenment, traditionalism, associationist psychology, Neo-Platonism, the Pre-Romantics, the new concern with universal history), contributed to some aspect of the new historical outlook. Shaftesbury, Leibniz, Gottfried Arnold, and Vico, each in very different ways, struggled against the narrow Cartesian intellectualism and recognized the role of nonrational components in cognition. Leibniz was able to conceive of the harmony between unique individualities and the divine will, and to understand that "rational life" can take on many individual forms. Voltaire, despite his narrow rationalistic moralism, portrayed a kaleidoscope of times, men, and peoples in which he preserved a sense for the total meaning of history. Similarly, Montesquieu and Gibbon, despite their universalistic moral concepts and their search for the typical and lawful, were able to portray Roman history in its uniqueness. The Pre-Romantics and Burke contributed a fuller realization of the role of the irrational and a new appreciation for the Middle Ages.

But only in Germany were these various new insights woven into a coherent world view which overcame the dichotomy of reason and unreason. It understood the historical world in terms of the dynamic interaction of autonomous individualities, each governed by inner laws of growth and yet in harmony with the whole. In three progressive stages,[201] the German development reached its high point in Möser, Herder, and Goethe. Meinecke admires Möser's understanding of the interrelationship between rational and irrational in each life process; his interest not in man as such, but in the concrete, historically determined man; his search for reason in local traditions; his awareness of the inner structure of periods, institutions, and peoples; his recognition of the reason of state; and, not least important, his rejection of the Enlightenment "ideal of a better life for man and a better state."[202] But Möser's conservatism reintroduced a static element which prevented him from historically understanding his own time. Herder, in his early years, before his concern with the idea of humanity led him to question the power strivings of the state,[203] was able to view the world as a living process composed of unique, individual cultures, each ends in themselves, yet parts of the total stream of history. All values were relative to a given culture and no culture, not even that of the Greeks, could be recreated. But the high point of the historical conception was reached by Goethe who combined Herder's understanding for individuality and vitality with a firm faith in "ultimate, absolute values" and a "final, absolute source of all life."[204] This affirmation made possible the synthesis of relativity and absolute, of individuality and ideal. In the last analysis, this synthesis could not be defined or defended on rational terms. Not the intellect but the soul determined our fundamental philosophic positions. Only as this faith became increasingly doubtful in the course of the nineteenth century, and the bond between history and philosophy loosened, did the historical attitude lead to the excesses of relativism.

Critics are puzzled why Meinecke assigned Goethe such an important role in the emergence of historicism.[205] Meinecke was well aware of Goethe's negative attitude toward history. Had Goethe not spoken of history as the "garbage can" of the past and referred to world history as "the most absurd thing there was?"[206] Only in Nature and in art, as an outgrowth and reflection of the dynamic lawfulness of Nature, did Goethe expect to find objective truth. Meinecke tells us how Goethe complained about the subjectivity involved in historical study; how he was annoyed by the element of chance in history which cannot be reduced to the lawfulness of Nature; how he refused to seek morphological structure and lines of development in history, as he did in Nature and in other aspects of human life.[207] His contribution to history was in part a negative one. He rejected the mechanistic psychology of the pragmatic Enlightenment historiography, and sought the relatedness of all human activities and thoughts to the stream of life. In the place of Newtonian concepts of abstract, transcendent laws of Nature, Goethe sought immanent laws of growth and viewed Nature in vitalistic, dynamic terms. He understood the extent to which understanding of Nature or of the past requires less the empirical perception of facts and details than the intuitive apperception of their significance and content. Goethe thus contributed to freeing historical thought "from the rigidity into which the natural law, pragmatism, and intellectualism of the Enlightenment"[208] had brought it. But his greatest "philosophic" *(weltanschauliche)* contribution lay in an opposite direction, in his recognition of elements of permanence within change. Goethe's deep faith in an element within historical change, which transcends history, preserved him from the "abyss of relativism."[209] Goethe recognized the relatedness of all truth, value, and beauty to life and Nature, but his relativism was of an affirmative, positive sort. He was still able to see "the antinomies of life and history not as anarchy but as necessary dissonances within the total harmony of universe."[210]

Goethe thus represents in Meinecke's view the highest point historicism had reached,[211] and yet Goethe by Meinecke's own admission was no historicist at all. He was "only the greatest of the men who paved the way for emergent historicism," Meinecke tells us, "and did not himself represent it fully."[212] But what came after Goethe, the true historization of life and thought, marked a decline in the quality of historical thought. When faith in the total meaning of history was lost in the course of the nineteenth century, historicism led to antiquarianism, soulless specialization, or that kind of relativism which "understands all *Weltanschauungen,* but no longer has one of its own."[213] In his ability to see "historical life in its temporal, individual form as well as *sub specie aeterni,"* as only few German historians of the nineteenth century were able to do, Goethe occupied the "most elevated position on history which is perhaps possible. . . .[214] As an historical thinker," Goethe, in Meinecke's opinion, thus stood "not only between the Enlightenment and later historicism, but to a certain extent above both at the same time."[215]

But who were the true representatives of historicism to whom Meinecke alludes, the few great representatives in the nineteenth century who transcended the shallow relativism of later historicism? Meinecke discusses only Ranke whose greatness consists of his ability to transcend the empirical and purely historical, to divine *(ahnen)* the eternal ideas hidden within transient, individual reality.[216] And so the book ends in a contradiction. At the outset Meinecke proclaims historicism as "the highest stage yet reached in the understanding of things human";[217] but the high point of historical thought is reached in Goethe whose greatness was his ability to understand temporal individuality, yet see it *sub specie aeterni.* Historical thought, when it frees itself from reference to the eternal, is doomed to shallowness. Thus, unwittingly perhaps, Meinecke ends by demonstrating the untenability of historicism as a philosophic doctrine, destructive of all truth and value. He portrays the decline of German historical thought as it turned toward historicism. In a sense, of course, historicism (as it appears in the book as an outlook on life) has little to do with history any more. Meinecke finds "the core of historicism in the replacement of generalizing ways of viewing *(Betrachtung)* historical-human forces by an individualizing one."[218] He stresses the element of individuality rather than that of development. Thus Meinecke is able to reach a position which he recognizes as Neo-Platonian in its doctrine of eternal, but individualized ideas.[219] This is very far removed from Herder's or Ranke's faith in history as a concrete, meaningful process.

But in another sense, too, the book had to end with Goethe. For Meinecke, disturbed by the irreconcilability of power and spirit, now views historicism as a purely spiritual movement with no applications to the political realm.[220] Therefore, if *Weltbürgertum und National-staat* had to begin with the cosmopolitanism of Weimar, the *Entstehung des Historismus* had to close at this point. What followed, the *Späthistorismus* (Late Historicism) by necessity and by its involvement with political power, is a perversion of the highest cultural ideal.[221]

The problem of the relation of political power to ethics which Meinecke raises in the *Idee der Staatsräson* remains unsolved in the *Entstehung des Historismus*. Meinecke simply omits from the book the question of the interests of the state. But it is doubtful that this could really be done that simply. After all, Meinecke defines the state as an individuality. And since every individuality is governed by its own immanent laws, there can be no judge above states or any external ethical principles by which the actions of states can be judged. Meinecke still views the state as he had done in his early writings: the state must develop according to the idea inherent in it. A dualism exists only in the sense that within the state there is a tension between this idea of its better self, and the elemental forces which drive the state. The state must be spiritualized and brought to follow its true interests. But in assuming that these interests are in harmony with ethics, Meinecke is essentially returning to the philosophy of identity, which he had condemned, to the position that the state in following its interests and developing its personality is fulfilling a role in a greater pattern. This meant a reaffirmation of the idea of the reason of state. As he concludes in the *Idee der Staatsräson,* the demonic forces of political power were unleashed not because states followed their political-power interests to the fullest, but because in the age of mass democracy and nationalism they were diverted from following their true interests by the impact of mass emotions.[222]

Nevertheless, it is surprising to what extent Meinecke was able to sympathize with German foreign policy during the Hitler period, despite his abhorrence of the Nazis. The domestic policies of the Nazis, the destruction of a state based upon law, the stifling of intellectual liberty, represented to him a serious threat to Western culture. He never endorsed the regime. In 1935, he was relieved of his editorial responsibilities on the *Historische Zeitschrift,* and several of his more prominent students were forced to emigrate. Notwithstanding all this, he faced the policy of expansion with an almost naive optimism. "Winning Austria," Meinecke wrote to Hajo Holborn in exile a few weeks after the annexation, "has advanced all of German history with one jump and fulfilled old desires and ideals."[223] In the summer of 1938, he saw the main threat to peace in the Czech "military party."[224] The rapid defeat of France filled him with patriotic enthusiasm. "You now have tremendous things to accomplish," he wrote to his son-in-law, "as a part of the great collective force which is now punishing France for the Treaty of Versailles. I, too, am full of admiration for what our army is accomplishing, which far transcends all expectations. To have made it possible to build such an army in a few years is the greatest positive achievement of the Third Reich. I recognize this unreservedly but never once forget the negative which has happened."[225] Writing Heinrich von Srbik of the "profound emotion, pride, and joy" which he experienced at the events, Meinecke compared his position to that of the liberal opposition of 1866. "We would indeed like to (join in),—but we cannot yet. . . . It almost seems as if the propelling force of great and necessary revolutions had its source more in the bad than in the good sides of human nature."[226]

The changes in the European political order had to come, he continued, and there was hope that Hitler would guide them into a direction which would bring about European reconciliation, stimulate economic activity, and establish Germany as a power equal to America.[227] Never during the war did there seem any question of his loyalty to the German cause. As the tide turned, he thought that the war had to be continued at all cost in order to stop the Bolsheviks.[228] Despite his awareness of the deportation of Jews, he denied that the Anglo-Americans in their conduct of the war reflected any moral

superiority over the Germans.[229] Occasionally, a pessimistic note occurred in his letters in regard to the future of modern culture, but
then again he confidently saw German culture reborn out of the
ashes of war, provided Germany would not fall prey to the
Bolsheviks.[230]

Die deutsche Katastrophe, written in the aftermath of defeat, was
a re-examination of the German intellectual past to a much lesser
extent than the *Idee der Staatsräson* had been. A terrible catastrophe
had broken over Germany, spiritually as well as politically. However,
the seeds of this disaster were to be found not in the classical German spirit, but in the "optimistic illusions of the Age of Enlightenment and the French Revolution."[231] What had happened in
Germany had to be viewed as a European rather than as a peculiarly
German phenomenon. Hitler's actual rise to power had no deep organic ties with the German past. The transfer of power on January
30, 1933, had been an "accident" in German history *(Zufall),* in
large part the result of Hindenburg's weakness and poor judgment.[232]
What made possible the rise of "Hitlerism" as a political force was
the steady destruction of the synthesis of spirit and power, of culture
and state, of *Weltbürgertum und Nationalstaat* in the course of the
nineteenth century.[233] The destruction of old social bonds in the
revolution, the new search for material well-being and power, the
radicalization of democracy and liberalism in modern imperialism
and socialism paved the way for Caesarism and the "Machiavellism
of the masses."[234] Power replaced culture as the middle classes lost
their spiritual substance, a process which Meinecke admitted had
taken on an especially acute form in Germany.[235]

In Germany, nationalist and socialist movements had found their
most extreme expressions and had been further radicalized by one
tradition of Prussian militarism.[236] However, the idea of the national
power state arose not from the classical German spirit but in revolt
against it. Germany had inherited from Goethe's age perhaps the
most unique and purest insight into the interrelationship between
spirit and nature and individuality and society. The tragedy of the
nineteenth century was the corrosion of this heritage, but the great
line of national thinkers were unaffected by this corrosion. They
included the reformers of the early nineteenth century, the classical
liberals around the *Preussische Jahrbücher* (of whom Meinecke still
considered Heinrich von Treitschke "perhaps the greatest" represent-

ative), Friedrich Naumann, and to an extent even Bismarck.[237] Interestingly enough, Meinecke found the last great demonstration of the "humane" idea of the age of Goethe in the national enthusiasm of the early days of World War I.[238] Another observer might easily have viewed this as a product of the very forces of the mass civilization which Meinecke condemned. Yet this very identification underlines the gulf between Meinecke's political thought and the classical liberalism of the West.

Even after the catastrophes of Nazism and world war, Meinecke remained convinced that on the whole the nationalism of the German classical liberals, with their emphasis upon national power and the subordination of individual welfare to the higher needs of the nation, was right. Nazism had to be destroyed; but militarism, he still believed, had its very positive as well as its demonic side. Despite all that happened, the introduction of compulsory military training in Prussia in 1814 still appeared to Meinecke as one of the epoch-making achievements not only of "national but of world history."[239] Burckhardt had been wrong when he had seen behind Germany's striving for unity and might "a blind striving of the masses to whom culture meant nothing. Rather it was borne along, as Burckhardt was not quite fully able to understand, by that great idea of an inner union of spirit and power, of humanity and nationality," a union "which was disrupted through our own fault."[240] For power in itself is not evil if it serves the creation of great cultural values, as the German nationalist movement of the last century did. It becomes evil, in Meinecke's opinion, only when it loses its bond with the spirit and is an end in itself.[241]

The classical German spirit remained sound. Germany merely had to cleanse itself from the aberration of modern times. Meinecke thus concludes:

> We do not need any radical re-education in order to function effectively again in the Western cultural community. Only Nazi megalomania with its unculture and false culture (*Afterkultur*) must disappear completely. But its place must not be taken by a pale, abstract cosmopolitanism void of content, but by a cosmopolitanism which in the past was formed by the cooperation of the most individually German spiritual achievements and which is to be further formed in the future. The German spirit, we hope and believe,

after it has found itself again, has still to fulfill its special and irreplaceable mission within the Western community.[242]

A more pessimistic note enters into the final brief writings and lectures of Meinecke. In his famous lecture to the German Academy of Sciences, in East Berlin in 1948, he wondered whether Burckhardt, with his deep pessimism regarding man, material civilization, power, and the masses, had not understood the modern world more correctly than Ranke.[243] In two articles, one on the 1848 Revolution written in 1948, the other on "Erroneous Paths in Our History?" published in 1949, Meinecke traces the tragic roots of Prussian history. Few of the political values of the German past, "except the highest ideas of 1813," have remained intact. Only the tradition of classical culture goes unchallenged. At three decisive points, 1819, 1848, and 1866, Prussian politics failed to take the turn which might have transformed Germany from an authoritarian *(Obrigkeitsstaat)* into a popular state *(Gemeinschaftsstaat)*.[244] But were power politics and militarism really at fault for the tragic course of German history, Meinecke asks. Was the "path of misfortune" also a "path of error?"[245]

In words which remind us of the affirmation of power in *Weltbürgertum und Nationalstaat* more than four decades earlier, Meinecke once more asserts that "what can, yes, must once awaken in a great and strong nation cannot be condemned as an inclination to pursue an erroneous path." Germany's "natural striving for autonomy" and Prussia's endeavor "to become an independent power" cannot be viewed as errors. They must be seen as Germany's "fate," the result of Germany's geopolitical position in Europe which forced her to become a power vacuum or a power state.[246] Prussian history is filled with tragedy, but a good deal less with error. And the errors, Meinecke still believes, lie less in Prussia's attempt to build a strong state than in her failure to create a popular state.[247] "From the viewpoint of eternity *(sub specie aeterni)* in the immediate relationship of historical epochs and configurations to God," questions of success, failure or errors, become irrelevant. What matters are the eternal "cultural values of truth, goodness, beauty, and sanctity." Seen from this perspective, Prussia, despite her imperfections and excesses of power, will always remain a storehouse that is rich in heroic individualities and full of individualized and permanent cultural values.[248]

Meinecke's work thus ends on a disconcerting note, for he is aware of the problematic character of philosophic and political beliefs but emotionally incapacitated to face fully the consequences of his own insights.

Unlike Troeltsch, Meinecke never faced the problem of the inner contradictions of the German Idealistic tradition. For Troeltsch the world of the classical values of Christian, Western, or German thought were "tottering" from the beginning of his intellectual career. Although Meinecke had become conscious of certain shortcomings in the political and social structure of Wilhelminian Germany, his faith in the central values of the German national tradition of historical thought and in German political institutions remained unshaken until well into World War I.

Die Idee der Staatsräson doubtlessly marks the highpoint and the turning point in Meinecke's thought. Here, he clearly recognizes the inadequacy of the optimistic conception of history of the German Idealistic tradition, which had failed to see the tragic conflict between *kratos* and *ethos*. Analogous to Max Weber, he realizes the extent to which the state is doomed to ethically irrational behavior. Meinecke thus sacrifices the philosophy of history of the German Idealistic tradition. However, he is unwilling to repudiate the philosophy of value which is inextricably interwoven with this conception of history. He continues to cling to what he calls the "idea of individuality," the belief that individualities, persons, and institutions, are manifestations in the phenomenal realm of transcendent metaphysical ideas. In his political philosophy he is thus forced into a highly ambiguous position. On the one hand, he maintains a sharp dualism between spirit and power (only spirit could be ideal); on the other hand, he continues to view the state as an individuality, as an end in itself, to be guided by its innate values and interests rather than by external standards of ethics or human welfare.

Troeltsch had tried to find a way back from German Idealism to a common Western heritage while Meinecke continued to affirm, as essentially beneficial, the separate way the German spirit had gone since the Enlightenment. Nevertheless, Meinecke's defense of the German Idealistic position, cut loose from its philosophy of history, led him to insoluble contradictions. In the *Entstehung des Historismus,* he views positively the ability of German historical thinkers to recognize the interrelation of spirit and life, but attempts to isolate culture from society and politics. His revised concept of individuality permits him, in the face of the rise of Nazi barbarism, at one and the same time to hail the triumph of the German spirit in the nonpolitical sphere and be disturbed by Nazi domestic politics, but to see in Hitler's foreign policy an expression of the healthy demands of German *raison d'état*. In *Die deutsche Katastrophe* Meinecke once more pronounces the German tradition of classical culture as sound. He could witness the massacre of European Jewry whom he sees as victims of a fanaticism partly nourished by a perversion of German Idealistic notions, and yet place the guilt for the catastrophe almost exclusively on Western rationalism and democracy. In creating modern conditions, of life, these forces had disturbed the harmony between spirit and power. Beyond this, he ascribes a significant share of the responsibility for this process to the "negative and disintegrating influence" of the Jews.[249] The deep seriousness which attends Ernst Troeltsch's and Max Weber's search for meaningful and intellectually tenable values in a world in crisis, and also permeates *Die Idee der Staatsräson,* is missing in Meinecke's later writings.

CHAPTER VIII

The Decline of the German "Idea" of History

THE IMPACT OF TWO WORLD WARS AND TOTALITARIANISM ON GERMAN HISTORICAL THOUGHT

1.

WORLD WAR I and the German collapse, at first, had remarkably little impact upon the working assumptions of German historians. To be sure, Walter Goetz called for a thorough re-examination of the political presuppositions of German historiography and castigated a national tradition of historical writing which "since the Wars of Liberation had been so attached to the monarchy and the cult of the Hohenzollern House" that it had lost the ability to approach objectively the political realities of the post-1918 period.[1] However, a majority, including such well-established scholars as Georg von Below, Erich Brandenburg, Dietrich Schäfer, Max Lenz, Erich Marcks, and Johannes Haller remained loyal to traditional philosophic and historiographic assumptions. Defeat and war-guilt theses seemed to give them new incentives in their defense of the Bismarckian solution and the rightness of German intellectual and political traditions. Friedrich Meinecke, deeply committed to these traditions, remained relatively isolated among his colleagues when in 1924, in his study on *The Idea of Reason of State in Modern History,* he suggested that the interests of the state were often in conflict with morality.[2] There were divergent tendencies: Otto Hintze's concern with institutional history, Friedrich Meinecke's stress on the role of ideas (both of which antedated the war), and Franz Schnabel's broad social and intellectual approach in his study of early nineteenth-century Germany. Schnabel even argued that the idea of a German nation-state,

229

under Prussian leadership, had no deep roots in the German past.[3] Nevertheless, these reorientations represented a minority.

Hans Herzfeld has suggested,[4] that the year 1917 should have seen a "Copernican Revolution" in German historiography. The entry of the United States into the war and the Bolshevik Revolution in Russia might conceivably have led to a revision of the European-centered approach to history and to a more modest conception of the role of Germany in the world. For most historians, however, they did not. Temporarily, Meinecke, Hintze, and others feared a Europe dominated by an Anglo-American hegemony. Troeltsch foresaw the end of great power status for Germany, and expressed the hope that Germany might become another Switzerland.[5] But with the withdrawal of the United States and Great Britain from an active role in continental affairs, German historians returned to the traditional themes of national history and continued to stress the primacy of foreign policy. In the face of the Treaty of Versailles and French pressure, they relied more than ever on the state as "the firm scaffold of the nation."[6] Even the writings of an historian who accepted the Weimar Republic, such as Hermann Oncken, were essentially a re-affirmation of national traditions and panegyric of Bismarck.[7]

In a sense, we may distinguish two strains of thought which continued from the Wilhelminian period into the Weimar Republic. The first, and probably more strongly represented at the German universities, numerically speaking, included men such as Georg von Below, Dietrich Schäfer, Ernst Marcks, and Max Lenz. Almost unqualifiedly they had supported the established order before 1914; now, equally staunchly, they opposed the Republic. Ludwig Dehio and Hans-Heinz Krill have spoken of a Neo-Rankean School which, after 1890, attempted to apply Ranke's concept of the great European powers to the world scene in an age of imperialist expansion.[8] More important, these historians turned from the liberal political conceptions of the great historians of the Prussian School, whom they still admired, to the conservatism of Ranke[9] who was neither an imperialist nor a nationalist. In their admiration of power and national expansion, the Neo-Rankeans undoubtedly stood closer to the Treitschke of the 1880's. They ardently supported navalism before the war, opposed constitutional reforms, and during the war urged annexations.

A second group, which included men such as Meinecke,

Troeltsch, Delbrück, and Hintze, all of whom were deeply aware of the social transformations prevailing in the 1890's, turned to Friedrich Naumann. They shared the conception of the central role of the state, and the need of the German state to pursue its power-political interests on a world scene. For the most part, they also supported navalism and imperialism. In the early days of the war, as long as they were confident of victory, they wished to see a redress of the world balance of power on the high seas and in the overseas colonies, and they justified the war as a struggle against British world control.[10] They joined their more conservative colleagues in identifying themselves with the traditional methodological conceptions of German historiography which they had once jointly defended against Karl Lamprecht in the pages of the *Historische Zeitschrift,* who, incidentally, had shared their conceptions of navalism and an expansive foreign policy. They were monarchists and distrusted parliamentary government. Nevertheless, with their liberal forefathers in the Prussian School, they envisaged the transformation of the monarchy from an authoritarian *Obrigkeitsstaat* to a popular *Volksstaat,* and strove for both social reforms and democratization. They dreamed of bridging the gap between state and nation, between monarchy and people. They were much more sensitive to the realities of the time than were their more conservative colleagues, and hence much more aware of the limitations of German power. Relatively early in the war, they called for a peace of understanding, resisted the demands of the annexationists, and sought to prevent unrestricted submarine warfare. In 1917, they organized themselves into the *Volksbund für Freiheit und Vaterland* (People's Association for Freedom and Fatherland) to counter the influence of the Pan-German Association. After November 1918, they supported the Weimar Republic, not on ideological grounds, but because in the given situation they regarded the Republic as a matter of "iron political necessity."[11] Similar to Meinecke, they continued to be "monarchists at heart," but "republicans by reason" *(Vernunftrepublikaner).*[12] They viewed the Republic as "that form of government which divides us least"[13] and to which there was no alternative.

The acceptance of the Republic therefore did not necessarily mean a break with traditional historical conceptions. These supporters of the Republic, who had been among the critics of the Wilhelminian regime, recognized errors in German policy since 1890, and even in Bismarck's domestic policies after 1871. They were less willing to call into question Bismarck's conduct of foreign policy or the "Bismarckian solution." Walter Goetz was relatively isolated among academic historians when he questioned the view of German development which had seen "1849 as a derailment, but the Bismarckian time as the only justified continuation of our history."[14] The publication of the diplomatic documents, published in the forty-volume *Grosse Politik der Europäischen Kabinette* between 1922 and 1927, released new sources for the study of Bismarck's politics. The resultant host of monographs for the most part only reaffirmed the traditional Bismarck picture. However, a number of studies, including those by Johannes Ziekursch and by men more marginal to or outside of German academic life, such as Veit Valentin, Arthur Rosenberg, and Erich Eyck, undertook a revision.[15]

The two most important new notes introduced into German historical thought doubtlessly were contained in Meinecke's *Idee der Staatsräson,* and in Otto Hintze's scattered essays and book reviews of the 1920's and the early 1930's. Meinecke's work, combining old and new, reaffirmed the German Idealistic concept of individuality and continued to view the state as an individuality. At the same time, it broke with the optimistic Idealistic view of the state as an ethical institution and recognized the tragic dichotomy of power and spirit. Meinecke continued to understand political power in terms relatively isolated from social forces. Hintze's challenge to traditional historiographical concepts was much more radical. His influence was diminished by the fact that he wrote no book during this period nor even an article that would present his thoughts on methodological questions in a systematic form. His collected essays were published only after his death, during World War II, by an editor who either failed to understand or chose to misunderstand the significance of Hintze's methodological writings, and omitted several of the most important essays from the collection.[16] The climate of opinion was not as receptive to Hintze's approach then, as would be the case after 1945.

Along with Meinecke, Hintze was deeply steeped in Prussian traditions. Born in Pomerania,[17] he came to Berlin as a student in 1880, where he was deeply influenced by Droysen and even more so by Schmoller. For years he worked on the history of the Prussian silk industry for Schmoller's *Acta Borussica*. In 1902, he was appointed to a chair for Constitutional, Administrative, and Economic History and Politics at Berlin. Until 1919, his research very largely centered upon Prussian economic and administrative history, and the major work coming out of this period was *Die Hohenzollern und ihr Werk*.[18] These studies combined classical German historiographical notions with a deep understanding of social and economic forces. Hintze avoided Schmoller's idealization of Prussian social policy. He joined Schmoller in emphasizing the central role of the state and of political forces in economic history. Particularly conscious of the role of international relations in economic development, in a sense he carried into economic history the Rankean "primacy of foreign policy." Nevertheless, he did not like to think of himself as a Prussian historian. His aim, as he explained to the Prussian Academy of Sciences in his inaugural address, was to write a comparative constitutional and administrative history of the modern political world, and thus fill the gaps which Ranke had left in his lifework. Prussia was to serve only as a model by which the emergence of the modern state could be studied.[19] Hintze, sufficiently aware of the limits of traditional historical method in Germany, with its dislike for generalizations and its one-sided concern for political events, occupied an intermediate role in the *Methodenstreit*. This was somewhere between Lamprecht's typological approach and the prevailing individualizing method.[20]

The events from 1917 to 1919 marked no radical break in Hintze's thought, but they brought about a reorientation toward a greater concern with methodological questions. In a series of brilliant critical reviews, Hintze examines the basic theoretical assumptions of a number of important social theorists of the 1920's: Ernst Troeltsch, Werner Sombart, Hans Kelsen, Franz Oppenheimer, Rudolf Smend, and Carl Schmitt. These articles do not contain a systematic presentation of Hintze's theoretical views. Nevertheless, they constitute a searching analysis of basic German Idealistic notions. Strongly influenced by Max Weber, Hintze questions the Idealistic attempt to link institutions to objective values, whether they are eternal values in Rickert's sense or the historically unique values of Troeltsch. Such an identification introduces an unnecessary metaphysical element, he holds.[21]

Hintze also questions the *Ideengeschichte* approach to understanding social and political processes in purely intellectual terms.[22]

Social institutions and processes must be approached nominalisti-
cally. Viewed in this way, they would not turn out to be individualities at all. The state has a basis in reality, but it can not be compared
to a person. Rather, it is the condition by which a community is able
to bring about a common will and common action. In the final
analysis, the state consists of individuals in interaction, and there is
no state as such. The concept "state" is rather an "ideal type," an
"abstraction derived from perception" *(anschauliche Abstraktion)*
through a selection of characteristic elements not entirely free of a
degree of arbitrary choice.[23] There is nothing holy about the state
which warrants the "worship" *(Andacht)* it has received in German
thought since Hegel.

The misuse of power in the age of imperialism and world war
(and by the victor powers since the war) destroyed the illusion that
the "civilized world lived in a secure state of law," and showed that
"all power, at least all preponderant power *(Übermacht),* is generally misused, and misused even more to the extent that it drapes
itself in moral and legal consideration."[24] The state is no "end in
itself" but, as Max Weber suggests, an *Anstalt* (institution) or
Betrieb (an enterprise, e.g., an industrial plant).[25] Similarly, Hintze
denies that one can speak of "modern capitalism" as an "historical
individual." Economic processes can be understood only in terms of
the interaction of all cultural and civilizational factors, of which political factors are the most significant. Capitalism is no more the result
of the spirit of Protestantism than the modern state and modern
imperialism are the products of capitalistic conditions. Rather, all are
aspects of a common cultural and civilizational situation. The individualizing approach to institutions is therefore inadequate, unless we
are permitted to speak of the total Western culture as an individuality.[26]

Interwoven with the idea of individuality, is the theory that every
individuality represents an idea. History, Troeltsch insists, is a spiritual process. Hintze denies this, claiming that spirit and body are
interwoven. They are separated only in the mind of the historians.[27]
Similarly, Hintze rejects Troeltsch's assumption, shared by the Historical School since Humboldt and Schleiermacher, that individuals
understand the spiritual life of other individuals, collective bodies,
and cultures through an intuitive act of *Verstehen,* incapable of psychological analysis. This, Hintze observes, involves the untenable

metaphysical assumption of a "common relationship" of all human spirit with the "Divine Spirit" which contains them all. There are few closed processes operating in history. The idealistic attempt to explain change and development in terms of an inner logic within the social body forgets that in all great social transformations purposive and accidental factors interact.[28] Every attempt to reduce historical life to lines of development constitutes merely a "scheme" or "ideal-type" for the "preliminary intuitive understanding of a historical context."[29] Hintze essentially calls for a demythologization of German political and historiographical thought; a nominalistic approach to the study of social institutions; a broad comparative approach to history, taking into account the interrelationship of political, economic, and social factors which Troeltsch and Meinecke were still unable to accept, for they were much more closely attached to Idealistic traditions.

Hintze's political views are far less clearly defined than those of Meinecke or Troeltsch. Hintze, too, had changed from a monarchist to a supporter of the Weimar Republic. Deeply skeptical of democracy, yet aware of the need of placing the state on a broad, popular basis, he was more qualified in his support of the Republic than Meinecke who preferred a plebiscitarian presidential regime to a parliamentary state. By the late 1920's, Hintze lost a good deal of his faith in the viability of the Republic and was deeply disturbed by the German political climate which he largely blamed on the Treaty of Versailles.[30] He viewed totalitarianism in Russia and Italy as a characteristic political form of the postwar world rather than as a transient phenomenon, but was still confident in 1929 that Germany would escape Fascism.[31]

Two further aspects of Hintze's political thought, which went counter to prevailing views, should be mentioned. Hintze, far more deeply than his colleagues, sensed the impact which World War I had exerted upon social, economic, and political conditions, and the transformation of politics from a European to a world scene wherein regional federations and blocks would become increasingly important. Moreover, the type of nation-state, which his colleagues had idolized, would become increasingly inadequate.[32] Hintze also questioned the emphasis which German thought had placed upon the search for power, as a determining factor in international relations. The development of modern national states could not be explained primarily in terms of the power-political striving of the great states; nor could imperialism be understood primarily as a search for economic wealth or political power. Both were rather attempts to create more rational conditions and achieve greater efficiency. What distinguished Western Civilization from all other cultures, Hintze agreed with Max Weber, was not the "Faustian" striving for the infinite, of which Oswald Spengler and Werner Sombart had spoken, but the irresistible drive for the "intensification and rationalization" of life and thought.[33]

Nevertheless, the extent of Hintze's influence upon historical writing was very limited during his lifetime. Hintze retired from university teaching in 1920 due to illness. He wrote no book after *Die Hohenzollern und ihr Werk,* which had appeared in 1916, but merely journal articles that were collected only after his death. Nor did he leave a school behind him; only after 1945, historians became seriously interested in him.

Indeed, the 1920's saw the decline of the struggling tradition of social history which had existed in Germany. Eckart Kehr was not entirely unjustified when he wrote in 1933 that the last traces of social history had disappeared with Schmoller's death, and that no historian was left in Germany who had even the slightest understanding of economic history.[34] The *Vierteljahrschrift für Sozial-und Wirtschaftsgeschichte,* founded in the early century by a strange combination of socialists and reactionaries,[35] survived the war. The medievalists continued to have a deeper awareness of economic forces and social structure than did the modern political historians. Kurt Breysig wrote universal history from a broad comparative social standpoint, although it was steeped in metaphysical and German Idealistic jargon.[36] Certainly, the political atmosphere at the German universities had shifted to the Right. The rejection of Versailles and Weimar carried with it not only an intensified emotional rejection of socialism and democracy, but of social history as well. Eckart Kehr was not far from wrong when he wrote of "a grotesque identification of social history with socialist history. Whoever writes social history," he observed, "is held to be a socialist historian even if he is really an imperialist and a conservative."[37] Historiography became more narrow in its political and nationalistic orientation than it had been before the war. Even the historical writings of a man such as Hermann Oncken who, as we have mentioned, was distinctly favorable to the Weimar Republic, was marked by ultranationalism and an exaggerated hatred of the French.

Eckart Kehr's *The Building of the Battle Navy and Party Politics, 1894-1901. An Attempt at a Cross Cut Through the Domestic Political, Social, and Ideological Presuppositions of German Imperialism*[38] published in 1930, perhaps marked the boldest challenge to the Idealistic assumption of traditional German historiography. Kehr rejected the assumption that politics is determined by the requirements of foreign policy. He sought to establish the close relationship between German navalism and imperialism, at the turn of the century, and economic interest groups. German foreign policy, around 1900, was dominated by domestic political considerations. In place of the *Primat der Aussenpolitik* (Primacy of Foreign Policy), of which German historians had traditionally spoken since Ranke, Kehr put the *Primat der Innenpolitik* (Primacy of Domestic Policy). German politics was marked by the peculiar circumstance that here, in contrast to the West, capitalist industry and finance were unable to break the hold of a precapitalistic bureaucratic and military state. Having attained its economic aims within the framework of the bureaucratic and aristocratic political structure, the German *bourgeoisie* surrendered its political ambitions. But Kehr's influence was negligible. He died at the age of thirty in the United States in 1933, only to be rediscovered by a new generation of German historians in the 1960's.[39]

The reception of Eckart Kehr's work reflects the shadow-and-light aspects of the academic climate in Germany during the Weimar Republic. Fritz Hartung and Hermann Oncken unsuccessfully sought to prevent Kehr from receiving a Rockefeller grant for a comparative study of the interaction of economics and politics in Prussia and Western nations in the period of the French Revolution and Napoleon. The professional journals also bitterly criticized his work. Meinecke, on the other hand, guided Kehr's dissertation which constituted a direct refutation of his own concept of the primacy of reason of state in international affairs and challenged the whole concept of *Ideengeschichte*.[40] In Kehr's view, Meinecke's *Ideengeschichte* was a peculiarly German phenomenon which arose from specific German social conditions. It was an attempt to escape the unpleasant alternatives of "recognizing and supporting power politics or opposing it as a Social Democrat." Unwilling to face the unpleasant facts of political and social life, *Ideengeschichte* tried to view the world from a distance and transform history from a science into an art.[41]

It is difficult to tell along what lines professional German historiography would have developed, had there been no Nazi dictatorship. The historical profession of the Weimar Republic never experienced a change of generations. The university chairs were still largely held by men who held them during the Wilhelminian period. The Weimar Republic had seen a younger group of historians appear, such as Hans Rothfels, Hans Herzfeld, and Gerhard Ritter, who were still deep committed to national traditions. Others, notably Otto Westphal, turned to an emotional hypernationalism, in response to the war experience. But there was also a group of promising young historians, especially students of Friedrich Meinecke. They included Hajo Holborn, Hans Rosenberg, Ernst Simon, and others, who were committed to democratic and republican values. None of the younger men of this last category occupied a university chair; a handful had been admitted to university teaching *(habilitiert)*. All of them left Germany as a result of the political events after 1933; none returned to Germany on a full-time permanent basis after 1945. Unlike the sociologists and political scientists, the men who returned from emigration, such as Hans Rothfels and Hans-Joachim Schoeps, were of a conservative, national orientation. Golo Mann has since left Germany again, and is a relatively isolated example of a democratically oriented historian who returned from exile.[42] Whether the Weimar Republic, had it survived, would have found room in its universities for its democratically oriented historians is an open question. The fact is that the field was left open for those historians who were willing to live in peace with the Nazi regime, whether they endorsed its ideology or not.

2.

Among cultural scientists and philosophers, as well as among broad segments of educated German opinion, the war marked a greater break; war and defeat introduced a strongly relativistic and pessimistic note, and led to a radical critique of older political values.

German historical thought had been relatively free of pessimism in the years prior to World War I, despite the warning voices of a

Burckhardt or a Nietzsche. German Idealism had been basically an optimistic philosophy, and German cultural thought remained committed to it until the war. The increasing orientation toward the natural sciences, in the course of the nineteenth century, was not essentially in contradiction to this; for basic to German Idealism was not the concept that reality is idea, but that the world is a meaningful process. Feuerbach and Marx did not refute this theory; in a sense, rather, they translated basic concepts of German Idealistic philosophy into the language of a more scientifically oriented age. Thinkers, such as Feuerbach, Marx, and Karl Büchner, merely represented extremes of German thought. Positivism as a philosophic conception of history, in the sense of Auguste Comte or Henry Buckle, had no significant representatives among German professional historians, even if certain positivistic concepts and terms were integrated into essentially idealistic frameworks of thought, as in the writings of H. von Sybel or Wilhelm Dilthey. Karl Lamprecht came closest to positivism in his search for laws of historical development through the use of comparative studies, but his approach was more reminiscent of Herder or Hegel or even Burckhardt than of French or English thinkers.

The hold of German Idealism on German thought had not been essentially shaken by the methodological debates at the turn of the century. In their essential aspects, the methodological writings of Dilthey, Windelband, and Troeltsch preserved the Idealistic faith in history as a meaningful process and in the possibility of objective cognition. Max Weber had recognized the "ethical irrationality" of the world and the impossibility of solving ethical questions on scientific grounds. But even he remained convinced of the possibility of rigorously objective inquiry in the social sciences and history. In practice, he continued to be deeply committed to traditional scholarly and political values.

Historicism became a problem for German scholars only in the course of World War I. The basic elements of the intellectual climate of the 1920's were already present before the war, but their full impact was to be felt only when the original hopes and the enthusiasm of the war were dissipated. Before 1914 there existed increasing doubts regarding the possibility of rational or objective knowledge and growing awareness of the relativity and historicity of values. Men as different as Max Weber and Friedrich Nietzsche had insisted that values have no objective basis in reality, but are life functions, matters of subjective decision. The vitalistic glorification of will and power, the hypertrophy of integral nationalism, the rejection not only of "bourgeois" morality, but of democracy and social welfare as positive values all existed before 1914.[43] Oswald Spengler began to work on his *Decline of the West* before the war,[44] to be sure; however, not only the broad masses, but also the academic world remained relatively immune from the underlying currents of cultural pessimism.[45]

Three notes gained importance in postwar philosophic thought about history. The first was that history does not exist as an objective process. Rickert had already viewed history as a construct. Theodor Lessing now questioned whether history existed at all as a process.[46] All reconstruction of historical developments was pure myth-building. History is not science *(Wissenschaft)*, but volition *(Willenschaft)*.

Lessing's book *Geschichte als Sinngebung des Sinnlosen* was widely criticized, partly because of the author's democratic convictions and Jewish background. The radical assumption that history has no basis in reality found little acceptance.[47] Nevertheless, Lessing's position was in a sense a logical continuation from the *Verstehen* epistemology, once the metaphysical basis upon which this epistemology rested had collapsed. German historical thought from Schleiermacher and Humboldt to Dilthey and Troeltsch, in insisting that cognition in the human sciences requires an act of subjective understanding, assumed that there is a basic identity between the subjective act of cognition of the historian (himself part of a real, objective process) and historical reality. Once this identity was no longer tenable, Lessing's "epistemological" nihilism appeared as an inescapable conclusion.

More important, however, was a second note: the belief that there is no one human history, but only the history of separate, closed cultures; that all values are culturally related, and that the understanding of other cultures is therefore always limited or impossible. To an extent, this position was already implicit in Romantic organismic concepts of society, as well as in the anthropological literature later in the century. It developed from Rickert's definition that cultures are oriented around unique values. In 1916, Troeltsch expressed the view that there is no human history and that understanding of other cultures is always perspectivistic.[48] In its extreme form, this position was formulated by Spengler in his *Decline of the West* when he held that scientific thought, even mathematics, can never transcend its cultural limitations.

The third and most important note, however, undoubtedly was the re-evaluation of all political and social norms which took place in broad segments of opinion and found its most radical expressions in Spengler's book. In a sense, the path from the classical idea of progress to Spengler's conception of doom is not as great as it might appear. There is a degree of continuity in the very different analyses of the dominant trends of history and of the character of the age by thinkers as diverse as Condorcet, J. S. Mill, Weber, and Spengler. All saw the irresistible scientification and technicalization of life and thought. Only rationality and Enlightenment, which for Condorcet had been absolutely positive factors in the liberation of man, now increasingly appeared as a threat to human values. For Spengler they became the very antithesis to life and spirit: the "heroic" qualities of the knight and the priest replaced the humanistic and humanitarian values of the West. To Troeltsch the *Decline of the West* seemed an invitation to barbarism and itself an "active contribution to the decline of the West."[49] Nevertheless, Troeltsch's cumbersome essays were read by few. Spengler's book, however, became a Bible, and a source of inspiration for tens of thousands of educated middle-class Germans during a period of bewilderment.

In a less extreme way, these rational and scholarly ideals of the West were now being sacrificed by a broad current of irrationalist literature. As Karl Heussi noted in 1932 in *The Crisis of Historism*,[50] the great change which had taken place in German historical thought after World War I had been the loss of faith in the possibility of an objective study of history. Even a man as deeply influenced by Marx as Karl Mannheim denied the possibility of an objective method for the social sciences. Weber had recognized the irrationality of values, but was convinced that logic and scientific method were one and universal.[51] Mannheim now denied the universality of method. Thought itself does not proceed deductively, but rather expresses "unreflected life," he agreed with the vitalists. The categories of reason themselves are not eternal, but subject to change. What prevented Mannheim from despairing about the scientific enterprise was his firm belief, inherited from German Idealism, in the "mysterious *(geheime)* relationship of thought and reality and the essential *(wesenhafte)* identity of subject and object." Rejecting the reduction of living historical reality to logical relationships, Mannheim nevertheless also condemned the irrationalist insistence that nothing exists except isolated human epochs. Mannheim, like Troeltsch, remained convinced that history is a meaningful process; hence the subjective cognition of the historian or social scientist contains objective, even if one-sided or perspectivistic, views of truth, because he himself is part of the great process.[52]

Mannheim, with his interest in the role played by social and economic factors in history, stood outside the main tradition of German historical thought. Much more decisive in forming scholarly opinion in the 1920's were Eduard Spranger,[53] and especially Erich Rothacker, who applied to the social sciences the concepts of *Lebensphilosophie.* Rothacker, in his *Introduction to the Geisteswissenschaften* (1920) and his *Logic and Systematics in the Geisteswissenschaften* (1927)[54] set out to "re-approach the problems" raised by Wilhelm Dilthey. Every methodological controversy, Rothacker asserted, is a philosophical one. Every methodological position is determined by a *weltanschauliche* position. Hence opponents in a scientific controversy, at least in the social sciences, can no more convince each other than opponents in a philosophic quarrel. Social science has to restrict itself to classifying theories of sociological or of historical explanation in terms of the three basic types of *Weltanschauungen,* suggested by Dilthey. At one point or another, Dilthey also implied that the choice of methods is determined by prior philosophic orientation; yet his primary concern was with the methods of philosophical speculation, not of scientific inquiry. In a sense, Dilthey stood much closer to Auguste Comte and the positivists than Rothacker wished to admit. For Dilthey thought that, once it would be accepted that the answers to all metaphysical questions reflect the philosophy of life *(Weltanschauung)* of the speculative thinker rather than the demands of logic, the methods of the individual cultural sciences could be formulated. Then these fields of study would be raised to a scientific level.

Dilthey still assumed, as Ranke had earlier and Troeltsch would later, that the subject matter of history has real existence and structure. This faith now was shattered, and with it the belief in real continuous development central to classical German historical thought. For Rothacker, in contrast to Dilthey, the philosophy of life, which colors and shapes man's methodological position, has little to do with cognition. Every philosophy of life, and hence every so-called scientific picture of human and social reality, is an act of will and of creation. History, Rothacker stressed in arguing against Spengler's fatalism, involves constant creativity by individuals. These acts of creativity are not governed by a general logic, but are concrete, specific, and individual.[55] The individual is obliged to choose whenever he acts, and every choice is subjective and one-sided. However, Rothacker and Mannheim were saved from despair about man's intellectual enterprise by their continuing Idealistic faith in the ultimate identity of subjectivity and world.

But the idea of freedom developed by Rothacker could be carried further, if one assumes that every individual, constantly confronted by choices in concrete historical situations, has neither abstract reason nor tradition to guide him. It is not surprising that a generation which never had faith in the ultimate rationality of man or the universe should also lose its faith in history and tradition after the catastrophes of the age. This loss of faith occurred among the writers of the 1920's, including the political scientist, Carl Schmitt; the writer, Ernst Jünger, and the philosopher, Martin Heidegger who in current German writings are labeled "political Decisionists."[56] For Jünger and Schmitt nothing was left but life, and life knows nothing but movement and action. Morality and civilization for Jünger are merely ways for the spirit to commit treason against life. The only value that remains is struggle. On the political scene, those healthy forces which still accept struggle—the soldier and the revolutionary worker—need to merge to preserve the vitality of life. Indeed, Prussianism and Bolshevism are kindred movements. Jünger holds, and they alone might still regenerate life.

Historicism as a theory had now arrived at its logical conclusion. If all truths and value judgments are individual and historical, then no place is left for any fixed point in history; neither for forces of history in Rothacker's sense nor for life in Dilthey's. All that remains is the subjective individual.

The concept of *Geschichtlichkeit* (historicity), which began to dominate German philosophic discussion after the appearance of Martin Heidegger's *Being and Time*[57], marked the negation of classical historicism. As a doctrine, *Geschichtlichkeit* assumes—as did historicism—that man has no nature, only a history. But it rejects the idea that history has objective existence of its own; rather it sees history as an inseparable aspect of man. It would be difficult to recapitulate the basic arguments of this fundamental work of German *Existenzphilosophie,* which at many points are open to conflicting interpretations. Nevertheless, the hard world of real, objective Being seemed to dissolve. Man has no essence for Heidegger, only an existence. This existence places him in a Being-Here *(Dasein),* in which he is constantly confronted by decisions. A characteristic of human existence is the reality of death. Conscious of the finitude of his existence that leads to death, man is filled by care *(Sorge)* and anguish *(Angst),* which constantly force him to define himself. Yet there are no objective values to which man can orient himself. Man is radically free, and in his freedom must make decisions. These decisions always involve choice and creativity, a choice within the framework of the concrete possibilities of the situation *(Lage).* In this circumstance, man is confronted by a heritage which contains not one history, but the "possibility of various histories." The individual creates his history not upon the basis of the objective happenings of the past, but by the decisions he directs toward the future.

Historicism now reached the end of its road: the last eternal values and meanings had dissolved. All that was left was historical, temporal, and relative. Even God had died, and History had yielded to Historicity *(Geschichtlichkeit)* and Temporality *(Zeitlichkeit),* the basic human condition of never being able to transcend time. Constant in the flow of time are only the conditions of human existence, and these no longer possess any content *(Gehalt),* but were merely a structure or form *(Gestalt).*

A process that had begun with the philosophic discussion of the neo-Kantians was now completed. Dilthey, Windelband, Rickert, Weber, and Troeltsch had all recognized the relativistic implications of German historicism for ethics and epistemology. All, except Weber, had attempted to avoid the logical conclusions involved in their positions by clinging to the optimistic view of history implicit in the German Idealistic doctrine of Identity. Even Weber, who courageously faced the ethical meaninglessness of the world, remained committed to the Bismarckian state and its power-political interests. The impact of World War I had shattered these illusions. Men such as Troeltsch and Meinecke attempted to salvage whatever they possibly could from the ruins of the historicist faith. Among more radical thinkers, i.e., Spengler, Heidegger, Jünger, and Schmitt, the historicity of man spelled the anarchy of values. For them the break with the humanistic values of Western civilization, from which the classical tradition of German Idealism had never completely divorced itself, was now complete.

3.

The break with political and historiographical traditions was much deeper and more real after 1945 than it had been after 1918. Expressive of this reorientation is the concern over the "break" to be found in the writings of contemporary German historians. The Roman historian Alfred Heuss entitled a recent paperback book *The Loss of History*. History has remained a scholarly discipline, he observes sadly; as a living memory, however, it has been lost.[58] As conservative a historian as Reinhard Wittram admits that "historiography *(Historie)* has taken the place of tradition."[59] All philosophers, sociologists, and historians who have attempted to assess the German present since 1945, Wittram notes, have become convinced "that a turn has taken place which can be compared only to the greatest upheavals known in history."[60] Hermann Heimpel, the well-known medievalist and director of the Max Planck Institute for History in Göttingen, confesses that Germans have become thoroughly alienated from their past. This alienation has had its good sides, he believes, in putting an end to naive historicism.[61] Theodor Schieder, the present editor of the *Historische Zeitschrift,* also speaks for other social historians, such as Fritz Wagner at München or Werner Conze at Heidelberg, when he stresses the role of discontinuity as a major aspect of all history.

The nature of the break was complex. To an extent, Germany shared its loss of traditions and historical consciousness with the rest of Europe. Particularly the new school of social historians stressed the radical rupture which had taken place in the Western world with the emergence of a technological mass society. The abyss separating the present from the past, Schieder notes, has widened since Burckhardt and Tocqueville first observed it. The very structure of history has changed. In the contemporary world, the "present has run away from the past." The historical consciousness of modern industrial society "builds on discontinuity."[62] But for Schieder, as for almost all historians who critically observed postwar German realities, the gulf is even deeper in Germany than in the West. This is partly because of the terrible aberrations of the period of 1933 to 1945, and partly due to the failure of German historiography and historical thought until 1945 to take into account the great socio-economic transformations of the nineteenth and twentieth centuries as broad currents of French, American, and British historiography and social philosophy had done.

This consciousness of a rupture introduced a reexamination of German intellectual, political, and historiographical traditions which had not been possible after 1918. The German national orientation, the emphasis upon political history, and the German Idealistic tradition all became questionable now to such an extent that Gerhard Ritter, in a review of Fritz Fischer's recent book on German war aims in World War I, bitterly complained that an "increasingly one-sided self-deprecation has replaced the former self-deification in German historical consciousness."[63]

Nevertheless, the break with the older patterns of thought was by no means complete. Theodor Litt, who had consistently opposed the Nazis, and Erich Rothacker, who had not, continued to defend the German Idealistic conception of history. The events of the Nazi years and World War II seemed to have had little effect upon their historical thought. Eduard Spranger's piece in the *Historische Zeitschrift* on "The Task of the Historian" consciously borrowed the title of Humboldt's classical essay. Once more Spranger defined the tasks of the historians in terms reminiscent of Humboldt and Ranke.[64] More aggressively, the aged Litt in a series of writings engaged the "opponents of historicism" and called in the *Historische Zeitschrift* for the "reawakening of historical awareness." He once more defended the historicity of all values. History is not devoid of meaning. Within every "concrete situation" there are to be found the values which fit the specific individual. The "Ought" was never universal but always unique. Historicism had been accused of ignoring the search for the essence of human nature. But man has no stable nature; his nature is in constant growth and consists in his historicity *(Geschichtlichkeit)*. "it is indeed exactly this, the fact that man's character is not shaped by nature, that distinguishes him from all subhuman nature."[65]

Erich Rothacker, once more in 1954, presented in systematic

form his contention that all thought is related to *Weltanschauungen,* and that all *Weltanschauungen* are functions of life. Thought always requires dogmatic expressions, and since all truths and values outside the realms of strict logic or pure facts always involve a creative response to a life situation, there are as many truths and values as there are great styles of life. "The problems of historicism are the simple result of the simple fact that there are distinct cultural systems with distinct dogmas explaining these systems."[66] What prevented Spranger or Litt, or probably even Rothacker, from assuming that all values and cognition are purely arbitrary and subjective, was their belief that a radical distinction between the subject and the object of history does not exist—a point re-emphasized in the recent important work by Hans-Georg Gadamer on hermeneutics *(Truth and Method).*[67] The historian himself is a part of the historical process. This gives his observations, no matter how subjectivistic, an element of objectivity. There are no universal values. The only truth is that of the "absolute historicity of existence." Even more radical, of course, is Martin Heidegger's position. Although many intellectuals believe that Heidegger rendered valuable services to the Nazis, before 1933 by his subjectivistic approach to ethics and history and after the advent of Hitler in his capacity as rector of the University of Freiburg, Heidegger's concept of *Geschichtlichkeit* continues to play an important role in German philosophic thought on history.[68]

The stress on the relativity of all values and the role of *Weltanschauungen* in historiography is still strongly reflected in the writings of Walther Hofer, a Swiss historian who taught at the Free University of Berlin until his return to a chair in Switzerland in 1960. Hofer, too, is convinced of the "historicity of all human cognition." Nevertheless, Hofer no longer believes that values are found within history. Man always approaches history with his subjective values. In a sense, this is Heidegger's position, with the exception that Hofer's values are those of the democratic, humanistic West. Objectivity in approach is possible, according to Hofer, but in order to attain it historians must take into account the role played by their biases. Bias or subjective interest must never determine the results of the historian's inquiries; it always determines the formulation of the problems of inquiry. Despite his admiration for Meinecke, to whom he devoted his first important work, Hofer insists that the historian never gains meaning from the study of the subject matter of history, but must always approach history with a previously formulated conception of history. And this is, indeed, what the great historians in the *Historismus* tradition did. Ranke and the historians who followed in his tradition were never opposed to philosophy, Hofer argues. They applied philosophic categories and political values to history. Without such concepts their historical writings would have remained chronicles. No longer does "the man who thinks want to know merely what really happened *(wie es eigentlich gewesen),*" Hofer decides, "but what is to become of him and of his history."[69] History always has sought "to throw light on our existence" *(Existenzerhellung),* and thus reflects the concerns of the present. Human knowledge is always limited and perspectivistic. However, this very limitation, Hofer believes, could be overcome to some extent if man did not restrict himself to national history, but attempted to attain a degree of objectivity through broad studies of universal scope.[70] Hofer still believed in the historicity of all values. However, historicism became untenable for him, because it assumes that values can be discovered through historical study. The concept of *Geschichtlichkeit,* as understood by Martin Heidegger and in a modified form by Walther Hofer, implies that man carries his values to history, but that these subjective values are themselves won in historical situations.

For the first time since the Enlightenment, important German thinkers began to challenge the historicist position and attempted to go back to something resembling natural law; namely, to the belief that there are certain perennial human values to be derived from the nature of man. The philosopher Gerhard Krüger opened the attack on the historicists, as well as on Heidegger, in two highly controversial essays written shortly after the collapse of the Third Reich. History, as the sphere of human freedom and creativity, reflects the anarchy of values and opinions, Krüger argues. But there have been perennial human traditions which have not been broken by the catastrophes or social transformations of our time; the appeal to "reason and common sense, patriotism and concern for the common good, loyalty, humaneness, freedom and truth." More important than the question of what was, is the question of "what ought to be and what always is, the old Platonic question about goodness and justice and about the constant ideal form of things. . . . Lasting truth is more important than our changing fate." This for Krüger assumes an objective order of things, an objective physical as well as moral world.

"This is to say that things are not as we view and judge them but as they are themselves *(an sich selbst).*"[71]

Karl Löwith argues along similar lines. He, too, stresses that history is an objective, "dynamic process, independent of all written history."[72] But within history we can discover no meaning. "History, too, is meaningful only by indicating some transcendent purpose beyond the actual facts," he writes in *Meaning in History,*[73] a book first published in English before his return from exile which later became a paperback best-seller in Germany. With Krüger, Löwith believes that modern man can learn from the Greek conception of history. The Greeks viewed history as a sphere of the irrational, devoid of ultimate meaning; for meaning, one had to turn to Nature. Jews and Christians basically misunderstand the character of history when they see it primarily as the history of salvation. In a secularized form, this faith in the meaningfulness of history survived in the idea of progress and in historicism. Today, man must free his "conception of world history from its theological origins and regain a natural concept of the world. This concept must be based not on the nature of the natural sciences, but directly on nature herself as the measure of all that is natural."[74]

In a similar vein, Leo Strauss, a refugee from Nazism who did not return to Germany from exile in the United States but whose writings have attracted more attention in their German translations than in English, defends natural law against historicism. "To the unbiased historian," he argues in *Natural Right and History,* " 'the historical process' revealed itself as the meaningless web spun by what men did, produced and thought by nothing more than unmitigated chance—a tale told by an idiot."[75] What remains constant is nature and human nature, truth and justice. Far from legitimizing the historicist inference that all values are bound by an historical situation, he holds that history "seems rather to prove that all human thought, and certainly all philosophic thought, is concerned with the same fundamental themes or the same fundamental problems, and therefore that there exists an unchanged framework which persists in all changes of human knowledge of both facts and principles. . . . If the fundamental problems persist in all historical change, human thought is capable of transcending its historical limitations or of grasping something transhistorical."[76]

The desire of Krüger, Löwith, and Strauss to return to the Greek models of natural law represents a somewhat extreme form of anti-historicism, and interest in natural law has apparently decreased in recent years.[77] Nevertheless, a broad group of historians and social thinkers now appear to share in the belief that there are basic characteristics common to all men, and that from this common human nature there derives a common morality by which historical institutions may be judged. In a recent article, Karl Ludwig Rintelen sees the great contribution of historicism in its recognition of individuality and development, its great error in the identification of historical individuality with value. Since the appearance of the great prophets in East and West, more than two thousand years ago, he agrees with Karl Jaspers, mankind has been in accord on certain norms such as "moderation, the desire for peace, willingness to help one's neighbors, readiness to compromise, freedom, and humaneness." These norms have formed the core of natural law as well as of Christian ethics. The historian must keep his sense of individuality, but combine it with judgment in terms of this common human morality. In their treatment of contemporary history *(Zeitgeschichte),* German historians have increasingly come to such a position, Rintelen thinks. Friedrich Meinecke, Hans Herzfeld, K. D. Bracher, Walther Hofer, Hans Rothfels, Theodor Eschenburg, and Ludwig Dehio are among the historians who, in Rintelen's opinion, have effected this synthesis between historicism and natural law.[78]

Most of these historians contributed to the publications of the Institute for Contemporary History *(Zeitgeschichte)* and its quarterly, the *Vierteljahrshefte für Zeitgeschichte,* the most important journal on the study of the Nazi past. Robert Koehl, an American historian of contemporary Germany, in a recent article on the Institute, arrives at an assessment of those men which resembles Rintelen's viewpoint. "Relativism and positivism, history as myth and history as propaganda, have all become so identified for Institute writers with the totalitarian *Weltanschauung,*" Koehl writes, "that they have sought in the roots of their traditions the basis for a sounder scholarship. They seem to have found a threefold foundation in (1) the Christian ethic of responsibility, (2) the classical universality of the *Aufklärung,* and (3) the critical empiricism of scientific history."[79]

Closely bound with the rediscovery of the universally human element in history is the re-emergence of the belief in one human history, a highly unpopular theory in the period after World War I. "We proceed upon the assumption that there is a history of man or of mankind," Golo Mann writes in the *Propyläen Weltgeschichte,* and this history is not merely "the history of individual cultures which are completely separate from each other."[80] Not that Mann can accept the grandiose conception of human history as a unified process, as portrayed by Karl Jaspers in his postwar *The Origin and Goal of History.*[81] The idea of progress is dead, Mann emphasizes. History does not contain a simple, easily definable direction, but the fact that it is human history gives it meaning. Nevertheless, there have been advances toward the attainment of "slightly more" individual liberty and prosperity. However, these gains have always been threatened by the destructive aspects of unchangeable human nature. Mann quotes Kant when he declares that man has become civilized much more rapidly than he has become moralized. He must find a transcendent belief that will give logical urgency to his "belief in mankind and human decency." Otherwise, his civilizational and technical progress may well end in disaster.[82] That history has now become world history, few historians will still doubt, although Theodor Schieder asks the pertinent question whether this world history can really be projected into the past,[83] and Reinhold Wittram wonders "whether apart from pale generalities, there really can be found anything that Neanderthal man had in common with Goethe."[84]

The concern with world history has led historians away from the concern with the individual culture or state to comparative studies and the search for the typical. Max Weber and Otto Hintze previously had pointed in this direction. Once historians had emphasized the distinction between the "generalizing" methods of the natural scientist and the "individualizing" approach of the historian; now, with few exceptions, they were convinced that generalizations play an essential role in historiography. Even Gerhard Ritter, himself a part of the classical German tradition, in 1949 told the German historians, at their first national convention since the war, that "after all, both the typical and the unique can be found in historical reality."[85] History is concerned not always with the individual, but also with the typical, Hermann Heimpel writes. In studying what man *was,* the historian grapples with the problem of what man *is.*[86] No matter how we comprehend historical individuality, Theodor Schieder observes, we cannot dispense with generalizations. "Con-

sciously or unconsciously the way we look at individualities is determined in part by our images of types."[87] Max Weber's concept of the
"ideal type" is taken seriously by social historians as a means of
bridging the gulf between the individualizing method of the historian
and the generalizing approach of the scientist which Rickert had
considered to be unbridgeable.[88]

The new concern with the typical and with social history served
to strengthen the revival of interest in Jakob Burckhardt whose
words of warning increased this appeal. Meinecke, in his now famous
1948 address before the German Academy of Sciences, wondered
"whether, in the end, Burckhardt will not have greater importance
than Ranke for us as well as for later historians."[89] But for many
social historians, Burckhardt's conception of cultural history already
seems too narrow in the mass technological age of the mid-twentieth
century."If we confront Ranke and Burckhardt as Meinecke last
attempted to do," Fritz Wagner writes in 1962, "we shall not get
beyond a narrow—we might call it an aristocratic—conception of
culture. . . . Men who like Ranke and Burckhardt moved in the
higher spheres of creative individual achievements and belonged to
the small groups of Europeans engaged in exemplary action could
hardly be expected to join in the realm of the anonymous millions of
the remaining population of the earth who, so to speak, formed the
dregs of hierarchically arrayed world history."[90] For Wagner and others, German historians too long had neglected social and economic
history at the expense of political and intellectual history.

4.

Turning to their own past, German historians began to reassess
their national history. They were in virtually unanimous agreement
that something had gone wrong, although they widely differed on
what it was, and the extent to which traditional interpretations of
German history needed to be revised. Interestingly enough, those
least critical of German traditions were a group of eminent historians
of the older generation: Gerhard Ritter, Hans Rothfels, Hans Herzfeld, and the venerable Friedrich Meinecke (d. 1954), who to a
degree all had suffered from Nazi persecution on political or racial
grounds or both. These men were to become the most important
guild masters of the German historical profession in the years follow-

ing 1945. All of them had deep roots in the national traditions of historical and political thought. Perhaps because they themselves had not succumbed to the ideology of Nazism, they did not recognize the responsibility of the German Idealistic tradition for preparing the intellectual road to Nazism. Few of the *émigrés* of 1933 returned (Hans Rothfels was the major exception); or if they did, they retained their academic homes abroad and exercised a marginal influence upon the German academic scene as temporary visitors or lecturers.[91] There were few radical reinterpretations of the German past, at least outside East Germany. The few attempts to discover an "erroneous path"[92] (Meinecke) in Germany's peculiar political development were written by men marginal to the German academic scene, i.e., Heinrich Heffter's *German Self-Administration in the 19th Century*,[93] or F. C. Sell's *The Tragedy of German Liberalism*.[94] Important interpretations were written abroad; for example, Erich Eyck's studies of Bismarck, the Wilhelminian period, and the Weimar Republic; Hans Kohn's writings on German nationalism and historiography and Hans Rosenberg's *Bureaucracy, Aristocracy, and Autocracy. The Prussian Experience 1660-1815,* which has not yet been translated into German. These were received critically or remained relatively ignored, as were the Heffter and Sell books.

The tone of the revision was set by two brief writings which have received wide attention in Germany: Friedrich Meinecke's *The German Catastrophe,* already discussed, and Gerhard Ritter's *Europe and the German Question, Reflections on the Historical Peculiarity of German Political Thought*.[95] Both works recognize the hypertrophy of power and militarism in German history. However, Meinecke sees Prussian militarism, in contrast to the modern civilian militarism, in a less problematic way than he did in the *Idee der Staatsräson,* and he still greets the introduction of universal military service in Prussia during the Wars of Liberation as one of the great achievements of German culture.[96] Something had nevertheless gone wrong in Germany's political and cultural development since the mid-nineteenth century. Ritter thus dedicates his monumental work, *Statecraft and the Art of War: The Problem of "Militarism" in Germany,* to the problem of why it was that the "German people, for centuries one of the western nations most disposed to peace, should have become the terror of Europe and the world, hailing as their leader an adventurer who will go down in history as the destroyer of the old European order." In no European country, Ritter admits, was the supremacy of the civilian government as undermined by the military as in Germany, a development which had some roots in the past but matured only after 1890.[97] Meinecke witnessed the emergence of a "Machiavellism of the masses" with roots in Prussian militarism, a development which he considers by no means peculiar to Germany. Both came to recognize the fallacy of Ranke's optimism regarding the ethical character of power.[98]

Nevertheless, in a sense both *The German Catastrophe* and *Europe and the German Question* are apologias, attempts to rehabilitate German Idealism and the national political tradition. Basically, Meinecke and Ritter agree, Nazism was not a German but a European phenomenon. The roots of Nazism were to be found less in Prussian traditions than in modern European civilization, for Meinecke in the materialistic outlook of the modern West in the breakthrough of a naturalistic, utilitarian world view; for Ritter in the collapse of traditional religious and moral standards in an age of general cultural decay and mass democracy. Ritter, in the 1936 Preface to his biography of Frederick the Great, had shown the line of development which led from Frederick via 1813 to Bismarck and Hitler.[99] But later he saw in the old Prussian spirit the main bulwark against the victory of Nazi barbarism.[100] The historical precursors of Adolf Hitler were "neither Frederick the Great, Bismarck nor Wilhelm II (but) the demagogues and Caesars of modern history from Danton to Lenin and Mussolini."[101] The events of January 30, 1933 were by no means inevitable. Meinecke views Hindenburg's appointment of Hitler as Reich Chancellor as an accident. Indeed, this accident was made possible by the general barbarization of the German and European spirit since the nineteenth century. There "existed no pressing political or historical necessity" in Hitler's appointment, Meinecke comments, "such as had led to the downfall of William II in the autumn of 1918. Here it was no general tendency, but something like chance, specifically Hindenburg's weakness, that had turned the scales."[102]

Gerhard Ritter denies that there was a militaristic streak in German traditions. He regrets the extent to which the "demonic character of power" has been underestimated in Germany and like Meinecke, he regards as a tragedy the gulf that developed between German intellectual life and culture and German politics after 1848.

Neither Frederick the Great nor Bismarck had been militarists, certainly not if by militarism is meant the domination of military over political factors. Frederick the Great had been a power politician *(Machtpolitiker)*; Bismarck the last great cabinet politician *(Kabinettspolitiker)*[103] and European. Both were guided by the sober demands of *raison d'état.* Only in the Wilhelminian period had popular opinion made it possible for military considerations to outweigh political ones. But even during this period German nationalism and imperialism must be seen within a European scope. Furthermore, the defensive character of German policy, including the Schlieffen Plan, must be recognized. Germany had no expansionist aims before 1914, Ritter insists; nor did her government, least of all Bethmann-Hollweg, want war. The Pan-Germans were not taken seriously by any "educated Germans." Only in the course of World War I, with the explosion of popular nationalism, did a policy of expansionism develop which, in Ritter's opinion, represented a radical rupture with German traditions. Without the experience of the front line, fascism would have been impossible, but the war and the front were European experiences. Without Versailles and the depression, Hitler's "proletarian nationalism" would have been unthinkable. Even so, Ritter remarks in a later edition of *Europe and the German Problem,* the one party state appeared in Germany in the post-World War I period later than in other European states, a consequence of the generally European phenomenon of the failure of mass democracy.[104]

Ritter's definition makes impossible any identification of Prussian society or government with militarism. For Ritter militarism has little to do with the domestic social structure of a state or the role it assigns to the military or to military values in the society. In fact, it has little to do with the military *(Soldatische).* Militarism always involves expansionism in foreign policy. *(Militarismus hängt immer mit aussenpolitischem Tatendrang zusammen.)*[105] It consists in the "onesided determination of political decisions on the basis of technical military considerations"; in other words, the failure to take into account the demands of "reason of state." It further involves emphasis upon aggressive, militant policies.

Gerhard Ritter's essay on the "Problem of Militarism in Germany" was delivered at the German Historical Convention in 1953, only eight years after the war. It was a bold reaffirmation of the classical doctrine of reason of state, and thus a reassertion of the superiority of the classical German national or Prussian heritage of the state over Western democratic traditions. Frederick the Great, in contrast to Charles XII, Peter the Great, or Louis XIV, did not act as a militarist even when he seized Silesia. Instead, he sought to pursue the task of true politics, which for Ritter meant "to create a lasting order of laws and peace, to further general welfare, and to moderate the conflict of interests." Frederick knew "nothing yet of the ruthless sacrifice of all life to the purposes of war." War for him was still an instrument of politics.[106] Reason of state and the pursuit of well-understood national interest thus appears as the very negation of militarism. Although Ritter speaks of the "demonic character of power," he lacks the understanding for the conflict between power and ethics which permeates Meinecke's *Idee der Staatsräson*. Ritter is quite willing to admit the militarization of German politics after 1890, a militarization which, in the course of World War I, became more extreme in Germany than elsewhere. However, the roots of this militarism were to be found not in Prussia, but in the West. Modern militarism, Ritter insists, is a product of the French Revolution which swept aside the distinction between civilian and military.[107] In the place of wars, which sought to re-establish a lasting political order, the revolutionary governments (and later Napoleon) sought "the total destruction of the enemy."

The process of democratization and militarization of the political mentality proceeded more slowly in Germany than elsewhere, Ritter observes. Indeed, "the German people is by nature not militaristic,"[108] he comments. Bismarck appears to Ritter as the last "cabinet statesman" who, in contrast to his generals (Moltke, for example), subordinated military to political considerations. Cabinet government is understood in the German sense, not the British, as decisions made in the monarch's cabinet, free of the pressures of public opinion or party politics. But even Bismarck did not succeed in subordinating military rule to civilian government. The result was the fateful turn of German foreign policy, after Bismarck's dismissal in 1890, and the steady loss of the "principle that the military should only be an instrument of the leading statesmen."[109] Ludendorff appears as a chief villain in the German tragedy, as a prototype of the military mind *(Urtyp des Militaristen reinsten Wassers)*.[110] But Gerhard Ritter exonerates the army from major responsibility for the rise of Hitler. The Weimar Republic was not destroyed "by the militarists of the army but by the militarism of a National Socialist popular mass movement."[111] The army was a bulwark against civilian militarism in the dark days from 1933 to 1945, but never was it as subordinated to the state as it was under Hitler. Yet it was the army, Ritter replies to Gordon Craig, which sought to prevent Hitler from acting in a way calculated to destroy national interests. The army was helpless, Ritter concludes, for in the days of Hitler's brilliant triumphs up to 1941, how could it really have done something against the will of 80% of the German people?[112]

A similar exoneration of the German national tradition takes place in the literature on the German resistance to Hitler. Indeed, two very different aspects on the resistance movement emerge, one in East Germany, the other in West Germany. Each tells a different story, the one developing the myth of the widespread and well organized opposition to the Nazi regime by a class-conscious German proletariat under the heroic leadership of the Communist party; the other stressing the broad opposition to Hitler by generals, high bureaucrats, and churchmen, all of whom fought and labored for Hitler until after Stalingrad. Forgotten were the thousands of neither category who suffered in concentration camps and prisons or were forced into exile. The tone of the immense West German literature on the resistance is set by Hans Rothfels's book, *The German Opposition to Hitler*. Based upon a public lecture first delivered by Rothfels at the University of Chicago in 1947, it was published in Germany in 1949. Rothfels rightly reminds the world that there was an active German opposition to Hitler. He reconstructs the developments leading to the unsuccessful attempt to overthrow Hitler on July 20, 1944. Similar to Meinecke and Ritter, Rothfels seeks to dissociate the German national tradition from the rise of Nazism. The Rothfels book is both an indictment of the racially, ultranationalistic Right and of liberal democracy. Along with Ritter, Rothfels interprets Nazism not as essentially German, but as a European phenomenon. "In many respects," Rothfels observes, "National Socialism can be considered as the final summit of an extreme consequence of the secularization movement of the nineteenth century."[113] "Modern mass civilization generates a reservoir of evil forces whose release spells naked barbarism . . . What triumphed after the pseudo-legal revolution of 1933 was in fact and to a great extent the dark forces forming the sediment of every modern society."[114]

Rothfels recognizes the existence of a socialist opposition, but barely devotes four pages to it.[115] Effective resistance to the Nazi totalitarian state was possible only by men who themselves were part of the state machinery. The resistance movement had its main basis of support in the conservative institutions, in the Prussian officer corps, among high officials such as Carl Friedrich Goerdeler, and in the Confessional Church. To be sure, Rothfels recognizes the broad political basis of the resistance movement and its inclusion of men of democratic or socialist persuasion; for example, the Social Democratic and labor leader Julius Leber. But it was "the traditions of a genuine 'Prussian militarism' " which formed a chief "bulwark against nationalistic and demagogic excesses."[116] The Germany which men like Goerdeler wished to construct had little in common with Western patterns of democracy. It represented the best in German and Prussian conservative traditions, and sought to restore what could be saved of Christian values and corporative institutions. "Goerdeler," Rothfels writes, "intended to return to German traditions of a period when politics had not yet been collectivised, in other words, he proposed a 'de-massing of the mass.' "[117]

Gerhard Ritter in 1955 interpreted the story of the German opposition very similarly in his *Carl Goerdeler and the German Resistance Movement*.[118] Ritter again emphasized that it is erroneous to see National Socialism as the final consequence of a German development. "At its core," writes Ritter, "National Socialism is not an originally German growth, but the German form of a European phenomenon: the one-party or *Führer* state."[119] The latter cannot be explained in terms of older traditions, but must be understood as the result of a specifically modern crisis: the crisis of liberal society and politics. Nazism, he agrees with Rothfels, is the product of "modern industrial society with its uniform mass humanity."[120] Ritter now reaffirms national values much more openly and calls for a rebirth of national consciousness. A healthy state requires a positive attitude toward its past, but the new national consciousness must not again be seduced by "false concepts of honor and national power."[121] Nevertheless, duty to the nation appears as a higher norm than adherence to transnational, political, or ethical principles. Ritter now sharply distinguishes between those opposition movements which co-operated with the Allied powers to defeat the Hitler regime, and the circle around Goerdeler which sought to remove Hitler but fought for the national cause. The men of the *Rote Kapelle,* who supplied the Red Army with military information, were traitors. They had no part in the "German Resistance (but) stood in the service of the enemy abroad." In Ritter's opinion, their execution by the Nazis was both legally and morally justified.[122]

Much less charitable about the German past than Ritter or Rothfels is Ludwig Dehio, the first postwar editor of the *Historische Zeitschrift.* Along with Ritter and Rothfels, he grew up in the old historiographical tradition. Dehio recognizes a strong line of continuity in German policies from World War I to World War II.[123] Germany's fate in the late nineteenth and twentieth centuries was "typical" of all hegemonic powers driven to expansion and catastrophe by the demoniac character of power. But aside from this "typical" condition inherent in the nature of power, rather than in the German character, there was also a "uniquely" German or Prussian element which contributed to the terror of the German threat. Dehio does not believe that Frederick the Great and Bismarck were the direct ancestors of Hitler, but he thinks that there was a line of continuity; that "old Prussian" ways of thinking about power dominated German political thought in the twentieth century, and merged with new German ambitions in a particularly explosive mixture.[124]

Outright attempts at an uncritical rehabilitation of the German past are few in the scholarly literature. They are more frequent in the popular historiography and memoirs dealing with the World War II period. Ritter, Meinecke, Rothfels, and Hans Herzfeld all recognize that German history has traveled along unfortunate paths, at least since Bismarck's dismissal, although they stress that Germany's errors had their roots in a general crisis of European civilization. After 1890, Germany traveled the road to ruin partly because she forsook her Idealistic heritage and permitted her diplomacy to succumb to the pressures of mass opinion. All agreed, however, that the German national tradition had underemphasized the demonic character of power. Burckhardt, as Meinecke admitted in 1948, had seen more deeply the dynamism and the dangers of power than had Ranke.

Walther Hubatsch is relatively isolated in his attempt to justify the path of German history from the Great Elector to the invasion of Norway in 1940. His defense of Hindenburg is, in a sense, also a defense of Hitler's early years in power. In the Introduction to the re-edition of Erich Marcks's Hindenburg biography, which Marcks wrote in 1932 (undoubtedly with the German presidential election in mind), Hubatsch seeks to revive the myth of Hindenburg as a man comparable to Bismarck in status, one of the "immortal" personalities of history.[125] Hubatsch defends Hindenburg's appointment of Hitler as chancellor. The aged president acted only in terms of the necessities of the time in appointing the leader of the strongest German party. And until 1938, Hitler's foreign policy seemed largely justified. Germany's *Drang nach Osten* over the centuries, and especially in the twentieth century, is a myth. Only in 1938 did Germany, in Hubatsch's opinion, turn from a justified policy of national consolidation to an unjustifiable one of imperialist expansion.[126] Although Hubatsch is relatively isolated academically, it is nevertheless disturbing that the *Bundeswehr* has commissioned him to write a German history for the army.

Yet even Hubatsch does not seek to free Germany from major responsibility for unleashing World War II. Two non-German historians have tried to do this: A. J. P. Taylor in *The Origins of the Second World War*[127] and David Hoggan in *Der erzwungene Krieg*.[128] Both books were received critically in Germany when they appeared in 1961. The basic theses, however, were popularized in nonacademic works, such as Hellmuth Rössler's *German History, the Fate of the People in Europe's Center*,[129] circulated by the Bertelsmann Book Club and in the ultranationalistic right-wing weekly press. Rössler places major blame on England and Poland for the outbreak of the war, and assures his readers that no people resisted Hitler as strongly as the Germans. He justifies German bombing attacks against civilian centers as compatible with international law in contrast to the terror attacks of the Allies.

Most of German historiography—and this is true of school texts as well—accepts neither Dehio's critical re-examination of the past nor Hubatsch's blind apologia. The crimes of the Third Reich are clearly recognized, but the relationship between the Third Reich and the German past are explored only superficially. The basic assumption of this historiography is called by Immanuel Geiss "the thesis of the discontinuity of German history in the twentieth century."[130] Hitler does not fit into the framework of German history, and must be understood as a European phenomenon essentially alien to German traditions. German conservatism could then be rehabilitated. Any attempt to glorify the Prussian-German *Machtstaat* or to denigrate political democracy, as German historians had widely done until 1945, is now out of the question. Racial *(völkisch)* concepts of history have become unthinkable. Indeed, the historiographical tradition of the ultranationalistic right, represented in the Weimar Republic by such men as Otto Westphal, Johannes Haller, or Dietrich Schäfer, is dead once and for all; with it died the stab-in-the-back legend. The heroes of yesterday, including Ludendorff, are the villains of today while Bethmann-Hollweg, who sought to moderate the annexationist war aims in World War I, has been rehabilitated. In brief, what had been the minority position in the Weimar Republic, defended by moderates loyal to the Republic (Friedrich Meinecke, Otto Hintze, Hermann Oncken, and Walter Götz), has now become the major stream of historical thought.[131]

But this newly predominant orientation is nonetheless conservative and nationalistic, and continues the tradition of German historicism. A great deal of effort went into studies which sought to rehabilitate the image of Prussia. There was little of a serious attempt to examine the image of Bismarck or the adequacy of the state Bismarck created in 1871. Erich Eyck sought to do this, but his monumental biography,[132] which Gerhard Ritter calls "the first great biography of Bismarck based on critical research in the sources,"[133] was received critically and had surprisingly little influence upon subsequent literature on Bismarck which appeared in Germany. Historians such as Walter Bussmann, Hans Rothfels, Werner Conze, and others, still believe that Bismarck's solution of the German problem was the only one which had been possible within the concrete settings of the time,[134] and that the German state he created was essentially a sound one.[135] Bismarck must not be made responsible for the mistakes of his successors.[136] To be sure, the image of Bismarck has been modified, and he appears less as a German here than as a European, the last great "cabinet statesman." Indeed, for Rothfels Bismarck represents the rare statesman who, in the face of the pressure of public opinion in his time, was able to see the limitations of nationalism. For Bismarck the state remained of higher value than the nation. It is important to Rothfels that Prussia was never a purely German state, but a multinational one which encompassed Germans, Slavs, and Balts alike in the East. In this sense, Bismarck's

Second Reich, viewed as a member of a European community of states, opposed everything for which the Third Reich stood.[137]

The German national tradition of historiography thus survived in the historical writings of the post-World War period. But at the same time, there were also marked reorientations in the subject matter that historians chose as well as in their methodological assumptions and political values.

A sharp break with traditional historiographical practices was represented by the new school of *Strukturgeschichte*. Karl Lamprecht finally appeared to have triumphed. An important group of German historians, including Fritz Wagner in Munich, Werner Conze in Heidelberg, Otto Brunner at Hamburg, and Theodor Schieder at Cologne, increasingly turned to the methods of the social sciences. Social history had not been new in Germany. Schmoller and Hintze had represented important predecessors. But until World War II the economic and institutional historians more or less had shared in the national historiographical tradition. They had emphasized the central role of the state and of great individuals as well as the unique element in national institutions. The new social historians recognized the power of impersonal social forces. As Theodor Schieder points out, the "quest for typical processes *(Abläufe)* of historical change has begun to take the place occupied a hundred years ago by the principle of individuality."[138]

These historians reject Rickert's distinction between the methods of the two sciences. Weber's concept of the ideal type, which attempts to find regularity among individual social phenomena, seems indispensable to the historian.[139] German social historians increasingly turn to Western models and to American social science. Above all, they look to the French historians around the journal *Annales: Economies, Sociétés, Civilisations,* who in the tradition of Lucien Febvre, Marc Bloch, and Fernand Braudel paid great attention to the material life of the common man and sought structural continuities in history.[140] To them classical German historiography belongs to a pre-industrial, pre-technological age.

In a 1962 article on Ranke's image of history, Fritz Wagner recites its faults, its blindness to the impact of social forces upon politics, and to the effect of science and technology on the transformation of warfare.[141] Radically new social conditions require radically new historiographical methods. Nevertheless, the new social historians recognize that the role of political factors in changes of the social structure must not be ignored, and that individuals like Lenin may play a decisive role in creating new structures and giving them their personal imprint or, in the case of Hitler, in destroying them.[142] But political history and individual initiative must never be isolated from a social context.

So far, however, *Strukturgeschichte* has remained largely a program which only slowly is being translated into practice. In contrast to the older generation of politically oriented historians whom we have just discussed—Dehio, Meinecke, Herzfeld, Ritter, Rothfels— the advocates of *Strukturgeschichte*—Conze, Brunner, Schieder, and Wagner—were able to pursue their careers relatively unhindered during the Hitler years. For them 1945 marked a much sharper break with the German past than for their elders. Basic to their conception of history and historical writing is the idea of discontinuity, introduced into the historical world by the emergence of a technological mass society. The idea of the radical rupture of the modern industrial age from the past is not novel to the post-1945 period. It was already well developed in German social thought in the 1930's,[143] although not yet considered seriously by historians. The concept of discontinuity makes it possible to see in Nazism a modern European phenomenon with few German roots. Terrorism and revolution have belonged together since the French Revolution, Schieder observes. In Germany, however, there was no revolutionary tradition until 1918, he maintains, and terrorism was unknown. The roots of Auschwitz, Schieder continues, are to be found not in "German servility," but in depersonalization which is a phenomenon of a technological, bureaucratic age.[144] Even more than the older historians we have discussed, Schieder, Conze, and Wagner live in a dual world. They are far more able to see the German nation-state and its past in a broad, historical perspective. At the same time, they themselves are still deeply committed to the nation and to the Idealistic tradition. In their programmatic formulation they look beyond this; however, their historical writings for the most part still follow traditional lines, both in methodological approach and in political valuations.[145]

Nevertheless, the emphasis upon *Strukturgeschichte* has undoubtedly contributed to the increasing interest in social history in Germany. From seminars conducted by Schieder and Conze a new generation of scholars has emerged. They are democratically oriented, well informed on trends in historiography abroad, especially in France and the United States, and at last freed of the German Idealistic tradition, both in methodology and political values. Institutes have sprung up for the study of social history, such as Werner Conze's *Institut für Sozial-und Wirtschaftsgeschichte* in Heidelberg. Particular interest has been given to the history of the German labor movement. For the first time, a great deal of attention is being given to the comparative study of social institutions. Conze, Schieder, Brunner, Hans Mommsen, and others, again and again stress that the past separation between social and political history must be overcome and a methodology be developed which will integrate the structurally oriented and generalizing approach of sociology with the individualizing and event-oriented perspective of the political historian. An ambitious program of research, which has not yet resulted in major publications, has been initiated at the Max Planck Institute for History in Göttingen. Under the direction of Dietrich Gerhard, a student of Friedrich Meinecke who emigrated to the United States during the Nazi period and continues to maintain his affiliations with Washington University, the modern history section of the institute is undertaking a broad comparative study of the interrelation of corporative institutions and absolute monarchy in Germany and elsewhere in the eighteenth century.[146]

If the concern with social history reveals a sharp break with the traditional methodologies of classical German historiography, the new intense interest in the history of the recent past *(Zeitgeschichte)* marks an even more pronounced rupture with traditional political values. For German historiography, whether conservative or liberal, the years from 1933 to 1945 mark the ineradicable, disturbing experience, the *unbewältigte Vergangenheit*.[147] As a young German historian, Manfred Schlenke, recently remarked:

> Probably no modern European nation has until now been confronted in its history by as radical a military, political, and spiritual bankruptcy as the Germans have been after the end of the Hitler Regime. For here it was not merely a question of a state falling apart *(Staatszerbrechen)* such as France experienced several times since the French Revolution, but of a state falling apart *(Staatszerbrechen)* burdened by crimes of state *(Staatsverbrechen)* of an unimaginable dimension.[148]

A great deal of recent German history has dealt with the Nazi period, the Weimar Republic, and to a lesser extent the Wilhelmninian epoch. A major center of research on the Nazi period has been the *Institut für Zeitgeschichte* in Munich, subsidized by the federal government and the *Länder* (states). Since 1953, the institute has issued the *Viertelsjahrhefte für Zeitgeschichte,* originally edited by Theodor Eschenburg and Hans Rothfels, as well as an important series of monographs. From its beginning the institute prepared expert opinions for the government in war crime and de-Nazification cases. The institute and the journal saw their task more broadly, however, as a study generally of political forces in the modern world since the end of the dominant role of Europe in world affairs in the critical years 1917-1918.[149] The institute has concerned itself not only with the phenomenon of Nazism, but with totalitarian movements generally, including communism, and has unrelentingly studied the aberrations of the Nazi period. In this effort, it has enjoyed the broad support of German historians who on the whole still view German traditions positively; for example, Hans Rothfels, Hans Herzfeld, Theodor Schieder, and Werner Conze, along with younger historians who are much more critical of their antecedents.

Perhaps this support is possible because the *Vierteljahrshefte für Zeitgeschichte* has not generally attempted to seek the roots of Nazi totalitarianism in the German past. As Hans Rothfels wrote in the introductory article to the first issue of the *Vierteljahrshefte,* the journal seeks to avoid self-humiliation as well as apologia.[150] Even Kurt Sontheimer's study of antidemocratic thought in the Weimar Republic does little to seek the sources of right-wing German political thought of the 1920's in prewar traditions.[151] The question of the continuity of German political traditions is seldom raised. Basically, the picture of the resistance which emerges is similar to that portrayed by Ritter and Rothfels. The authors saw a large segment of the army as belonging to the "other Germany" which opposed Hitler and sought to protect the resistance movement from charges of treason from within.[152]

The concern with *Zeitgeschichte* has led to a basic re-evaluation of the relationship between history and political science. Political science died in Germany as an academic discipline, early in the nineteenth century. Its place was taken by the historicist conception of the historical state as an end in itself. The study of politics or political ethics in the abstract gave way to the study of the concrete historical state. The conception of the state which emerged in German historiography is a rather narrow one which absolutizes the Prussian-German monarchy as the normative state. Such a conception of the state leaves little room for an understanding of the social and political forces released by modern industrial conditions. Serious concern with politics as a scholarly discipline emerged only in the Weimar Republic. But the *Hochschule für Politik,* founded in the 1920's in Berlin as an adult education center, received academic recognition only in the 1950's, when it was integrated into the Free University of Berlin as the Otto Suhr Institute. The first chairs of political science were established in 1950. By 1962, political science was taught as a separate discipline at 12 of the 18 universities in the Federal Republic. The initiative for the establishment of these chairs came more frequently from the *Länder* (states) eager to develop a democratic consciousness in the public than from the still relatively conservative universities.[153] The dividing line between history and political science became a very tenuous one as historians, especially those men whose aloofness from conservative national traditions made it difficult for them to be called to traditional chairs of history, were appointed to new chairs in political science and political scientists came to fill chairs in *Zeitgeschichte.* If history, with its stress on the particular, had once determined the concept of the state, now political science, with its concern for generalizations, models, and ideal types, influences historical writing. The most significant attempts at such history are the two monumental studies by Karl D. Bracher, *The Disintegration of the Weimar Republic*[154] and the *National Socialist Seizure of Power.*[155] Bracher frankly asks whether the individualizing method of traditional historiography suffices for an understanding of the rise of National Socialism to power unless supplemented by the analytical tools of "the science of politics in the age of mass democracy." Bracher's study proceeds on the assumption that "politics is the struggle for the power of the state," and tries to analyze the Nazi rise of power in terms of a model of the decay of political power in a democracy.[156]

Although *Strukturgeschichte, Zeitgeschichte,* and political science called for a new concept of the state, they did not in themselves require a radical re-evaluation of traditional political values; for many historians, however, they did. A far more direct challenge to the German political heritage is contained in Fritz Fischer's *Germany's Aims in the First World War,*[157] a work more traditional in its methodology. Fischer worked almost entirely with official state papers, and even rejected memoirs as primary sources. Drawing upon the microfilmed papers of the Foreign Office and, for the first time, also utilizing extensively the central archives of the Prussian and German Imperial Governments, now located in Potsdam and Merseburg in East Germany, Fischer analyzes German war aims in World War I. From the first formulation of an official program in September 1914 to the eve of the collapse, the war aims of the German government were consistently expansionist. Not only Pan-German generals but supposedly moderate civilian leaders, such as Bethmann-Hollweg, wanted to establish Germany as a world power and to assure German hegemony in Europe. Government war-aim plans called for the annexation of all or part of Belgium as well as industrially valuable portions of France, German territorial expansion to the East, the creation of a Central European common market dominated by Germany, the establishment of German political spheres of influence in areas of Eastern Europe or the Arab World freed from Russian or British control, respectively, and the formation of a consolidated German colonial empire in Central Africa. Fischer attacks the "legend of the opposition" to these imperialist war aims.[158] These goals received broad support from all segments of political opinion, including the Majority Social Democrats, the Center, and the liberal professors. Basically, the war aims in World War I resembled those of the Nazis in World War II, and the book is seen by Fischer as "a contribution to the problem of continuity of German history from the First to the Second World War."[159]

Gerhard Ritter condemns Fritz Fischer's work as lacking a feeling of scholarly and political responsibility, and writes that he "put the book down with sadness and worry for the coming generation."[162] Nevertheless, Fischer's study has been seriously received in Germany, even if for the most part very critically.[163] The *Historische Zeitschrift* lent its pages to the controversy on Fischer's theses.[164] Sessions were devoted to the controversy both at the 1964 meeting of the German Historical Association in Berlin and at the 1965 meeting of the International Congress of Historical Sciences in Vienna. The issue is still very much alive, and has caused a re-examination of the problems of continuity in German history even among Fischer's critics. In a major study, a student of Fritz Fischer has now sought to analyze the interaction of economic interests, social structure, and politics during the period of German unification.[165] It is not surprising that Eckart Kehr's essays are being republished at this time.[166]

Now in the late 1960's we can no longer speak of one main tradition of German historiography. The scholarly presuppositions and political values of German historicism remain very much alive in current German historiography, but they no longer dominate historical thought or writing to the extent they once did. The gulf between historiography in Germany and elsewhere has narrowed as a younger generation of German historians, generally freer from German Idealistic traditions, increasingly views history as an international science. As in Western countries, we are confronted by a multiplicity of historical philosophies and orientations, for historians in Germany, too, have become increasingly aware of the relevance of the social and behavioral sciences for historical study. Alongside the remnants of a conservative national political tradition, there have arisen an increasing number of historians committed to democratic values.

The change of guard that will bring the historians trained after 1945 to university chairs has just begun. An older generation of "grand old men"—Ritter, Rothels, Dehio, Herzfeld—educated in the Wilhelminian period, for whom the First World War remained a central experience, has now retired or died. The chairs of history are now largely held by a generation of scholars trained in the Weimar Republic, of whom many began their careers in the Third Reich. The changed realities after 1945 have forced these men to reexamine their methodological views and their political values. Still emotionally attached to idealistic conceptions and traditional national values, some historians of this generation, such as Schieder, Conze, and Wagner, have, nevertheless, been profoundly aware of the inadequacies of traditional German historiography. With Fritz Fischer and Hans Herzfeld they have trained a new generation of scholars much more skeptical of German political and historiographic traditions, scholars who are now in the process of *Habilitation* or in a few cases have actually been called to university chairs. The coming years will tell whether these younger scholars with democratic commitments and a broader social perspective of history will gain a dominant position in German historiography.

Conclusion

1.

THE tradition of classical historicism will continue to form an important part of the heritage of German historical scholarship, and rightly so. Classical historicism introduced into the study of history a respect for the uniqueness of the historical subject and an understanding for the peculiar methodological problems of the cultural sciences, which first made possible the development of history into a scholarly discipline. Nevertheless, the concept of individuality needed revision, not only because German social realities changed, but also because the concept itself limited historical cognition from the beginning.

The fatal weakness of classical German historicism rested in its aristocratic bias, its methodological onesidedness, and its philosophy of value. We shall speak more about the methodological onesidedness of German historicism in the second part of this conclusion. The aristocratic bias linked to a dislike for generalizations restricted German historicism in its understanding of the richness and variety of historical reality in an age when new forces appeared on the political and social scene. It also led to an overly narrow focus on the great political personalities and on foreign policy. Historicism carried into a technological and scientific age a conception of society and a methodology better suited to the study of certain aspects of the politics and the intellectual life of a predemocratic age. For reasons which we sought to explain in the introduction, especially the belated political development of Germany, German historical scholarship remained a captive of its classical tradition of historiography to a much greater extent than did the historiographies of other countries, France and the United States, for example, and responded much less clearly to the profound changes in technology, society, and politics, which have marked the past century and a half. Only the impact of the defeat of 1945 began to make an increasing number of German historians aware of the cultural gap between the twentieth-century realities of a technological mass society and an historical outlook that reflected the peculiar remnants of the aristocratic cultural and political bias of a nineteenth-century Prussian *Bildungsbürgertum*.

The third basic weakness of German historicist doctrine was contained in its philosophy of value. This weakness was the most serious, because it involved the core of historicist theory, the ideas that objective truths and values exist, that they are manifested in certain persons and in institutions that have developed historically, and that history is the sole guide to the understanding of things human. But in the course of the nineteenth century the theological and metaphysical assumptions upon which this philosophy rested increasingly lost their credibility. Historicism thus came to be confronted by ethical nihilism as the logical consequence of its position that all values and cognitions are bound in their validity to the historical situation in which they arise. The course of German history, moreover, showed the insufficiency of the historicist attempt to base an affirmative ethics containing many of the traditional libertarian political values of the West on a doctrine of historical relativism and an undue optimism regarding historical development.

Despite its disdain for the idea of progress, German historicism represented until the First World War the most radical expression of historical optimism in Western thought. Confident in the meaningfulness of the historical process, German historians and political theorists from Wilhelm von Humboldt's political writings in the 1810's to Friedrich Meinecke's *Weltbürgertum und Nationalstaat* in 1907, almost a century later, were willing to view the state as an ethical institution whose interests were in the long run in harmony with freedom and morality. This confidence had a basis in the Lutheran religiosity of its adherents. Ernst Troeltsch has sought to explain the significance of Luther's reinterpretation of natural law for German political thought. Without repudiating the existence of an objective world of value, Luther removed the Stoic and the rationalistic elements of natural-law doctrine and saw natural law embodied in the established authorities existing in history.[1] He agreed with Paul that "there is no authority except from God, and those [authorities] that exist have been instituted by God (*Romans*, 13:1)." The existing institutions were thus themselves the concrete expressions of rationality and of God's will. Ranke in a similar spirit could thus observe later that all states are "individualities . . . spiritual substances . . . thoughts of God" and thus stand above the judgment of the historian. "All states that count in the world and make themselves felt are motivated by special tendencies of their own", which derive their origin from God.[2] In a similar vein, Meinecke could still note at the beginning of this century in defense of the doctrine of the reason of state that "nothing can be immoral which comes from the innermost individual character of a being."[3]

Once the theological foundation upon which this philosophy rested was destroyed by the growing secularization and scientism of the nineteenth century, the door was opened to the biologistic ethics of sheer national power of the old Treitschke. For Ernst Jünger, Oswald Spengler, Carl Schmitt, not to mention a host of other political and social thinkers and prophets, this ethics found an even more radical expression after the national humiliation of 1918. For these men nationalism remained a meaningful value, but the German Idealistic philosophy had become meaningless, and the admiration of state and power, now freed from ethical restraints, merged into a nationalistic philosophy of violence. To be sure, the historians, more closely committed to the national state in its traditional form, remained for the most part relatively loyal to the idealistic heritage until the collapse of the national state in 1945, though the intellectual and social foundations of this faith hardly corresponded any longer to modern realities.

But if the course of events demonstrated the intellectual inadequacy of the philosophy of value of German historicism, it showed equally the inadequacy of this philosophy of value for a liberal theory of politics. Closely related to the crisis of German historicism was the crisis of German liberal thought. Undoubtedly historicism contained strongly conservative implications. But many of the German liberal and democratic thinkers in Germany from the Wars of

Liberation to the Weimar Republic—Humboldt, the "classical liberal historians" of the *Vormärz,* the men around Friedrich Naumann such as Max Weber, Hugo Preuss, Ernst Troeltsch, and Friedrich Meinecke, who formed an important part of the non-socialist liberal opposition of the Wilhelminian period and were among the intellectual godparents of the Weimar Republic—stood in this tradition.

Admittedly liberalism and conservatism are ambiguous terms, and especially in the German setting the dividing line between the two is difficult to draw. Nevertheless, the rejection of natural-law doctrine was not accompanied in Germany by an equally radical rejection of the ethical and political values associated with the natural-law tradition. If by liberalism is meant the affirmation of the notion of the absolute value of the human personality, of human dignity and worth, and the affirmation of the rights of individual persons to develop fully their potentialities, than many thinkers of the historicist orientation stood in the liberal tradition, as they did in their demands for constitutional government, due process, individual liberties, and representative institutions. German liberal thought saw in historicism a better theoretical foundation for a theory of liberty than in natural law. Its basic position, as in Humboldt's expression of the *Humanitätsideal,* was that the natural-law conception restricted the true freedom and spontaneity of individuals to develop their unique individuality. The dignity of the individual rested not in the common human nature he shared with all men, but in his uniqueness.

Nevertheless, historicism was not a very suitable theoretical foundation for political liberalism, even for the conservative liberalism of the German classical liberals. Despite its stress on individuality, historicism was essentially a theory of collectivism. Its individual was not the empirical private individual of natural-law theory with his concrete needs and desires, but most often a collective entity, an institution. The basic assumption of historicism was that these institutions, particularly the state, possessed a metaphysical reality. The classical German historians assumed rightly that freedom is meaningful only within an institutional framework. They prided themselves on possessing a much more realistic understanding of the role of power in society than did their Western colleagues closer to natural-law traditions. Nevertheless, they showed themselves relatively incapable of the empirical, value-free analysis of power and political behavior that Max Weber demanded. Their metaphysical conception of the state as a group person prevented them from developing a truly political concept of the state. Their state stood above party politics. Their conception of the doctrine of the reason of state left little room for a realistic, empirical approach to the complex interactions of domestic and foreign policy or the interplay of forces that constitute political behavior. With all their concern for power the German liberal historians showed little understanding of the political conditions that make possible the functioning of liberal institutions. Classical liberalism in the West understood the demonic character of power much better than did German historicism. Out of its skepticism regarding power arose its insistence on limitations and checks upon the state. Its optimism consisted largely in too great a confidence in human rationality and goodness, qualified, however, by its recognition that this rationality and goodness were only potentials in men. On the other hand, German historicism assumed that the existing institutions and positive laws themselves represented rationality and morality. In the conflict between state interest and individual liberty at the crucial points in their history, German liberal historians were thus repeatedly willing to acquiesce to the political interests of the state.

Germany's own traditions of liberal thought, insofar as they rest on historicist assumptions, thus require serious re-examination. In this connection the question may, of course, be raised whether ideas play any significant role in the formation and preservation of political institutions. If ideas are merely epiphenomena of underlying social conditions, the question of the ideologiclal foundations of German liberalism becomes largely irrelevant. The ideology of historicism developed in a specific historical situation, as did natural-law doctrine. Nevertheless, it is difficult to escape the conclusion that historicism, once formulated in its classical form, became part of an intellectual heritage that attained a degree of independence from the social and political conditions of its origin. Undoubtedly the survival of historicist attitudes was an important contributory factor in the unwillingness of Germans in the Weimar Republic to accept liberal democratic institutions. To an extent, the survival of historicist traditions into the present is an index of the survival of older premodern and predemocratic attitudes. Insofar as post-1945 Germans will come to accept liberal democratic institutions not as a mere expedient but as a desirable form of government, it would appear that they will also have to assimilate certain of the ideological traditions of liberal democracy.

The question remains, however, what relevance the heritage of natural law still has for twentieth-century political thought? As a matter of fact, the doctrine of natural law never played the role in Western liberal thought that German writers attributed to it. In the seventeenth and eighteenth centuries a good deal of liberal thought had its source in the Non-Conformist religious tradition, which saw in the individual a responsible agent possessing a conscience and containing a spark of the divine. In the nineteenth century French and British liberal thinkers largely repudiated the theory. It has often been said that the basic element of liberalism is an openness of mind and that the very nature of liberalism excludes any doctrine or clearly defined theory, including the doctrine of natural law. The liberal attitude is said to be a pragmatic and experimental one. Here the difference between the liberal attitude and totalitarian political orientations bound to a social philosophy is seen. Moreover, forms of rationalism and natural-law theory have been used to provide theoretical foundations for such different forms of government as royal absolutism (Hobbes and Frederick the Great), collectivistic democracy (Rousseau), and the Catholic, monarcho-feudal society of the Middle Ages (Thomas Aquinas).

Nevertheless, there is an element of truth in the identification of liberalism with natural law. Few nineteenth-century thinkers were willing to accept the theory in its more doctrinaire form, which held that on the basis of abstract reasoning man could construct a rational system of universally valid and binding political rights and institutions, such as the authors of the French Declaration of the Rights of Man had undertaken. Most nineteenth-century liberal writers recognized the role of historical forces in shaping society and ideas. Nevertheless, liberal writers generally accepted the basic ethics of natural-right theory even if they rejected its metaphysics. They accepted as an ethical axiom the assumptions that man is a morally responsible agent and that historical institutions should be judged by a transhistorical criterion, namely the extent to which they respected the integrity of the individual. This was true of the British Utilitarians, who explicitly rejected the theory of natural rights. In this sense liberal thinkers continued the basic ethical assumption of natural-law theory that positive laws and historical institutions must be measured by a higher law. In another way, too, men like John Stuart Mill continued the faith of the natural-law tradition that a rational approach to the problems of value was possible. Mill, indeed, denied that man could have certain moral knowledge. Nevertheless, his very justification of the principal of utility reflected a rational approach to ethics, as did his insistence on freedom of inquiry, on an openness of mind and an experimental attitude.

In their recognition of the social character of freedom, German liberals saw a proof of the superiority of their conception of freedom over the Enlightenment conception, particularly when in the period of rapid industrialization it became apparent that the real restrictions on individual freedom and self-development often came from non-governmental concentrations of economic power and that intervention of the state was required to protect this freedom. But in the West, too, a fundamental revision took place in liberal thought under the impact of industrial conditions. If the older liberalism had identified freedom with the absence of governmental restraint, the new liberal theorists of the late nineteenth century increasingly realized to what extent, in L. T. Hobhouse's words, the state needed to "secure the conditions upon which mind and character may develop themselves."[4] Liberal theorists in Great Britain and France like Theodore Greene, Bernard Bosanquet, and Charles Renouvier looked to German philosophy for guidance in the revision of their libertarian theories. The break with the atomistic sociology and with laissez-faire economic principles was almost complete. Nevertheless, in their basic conceptions of society, the main currents of democratic thought in the Western countries remained fundamentally different from the tradition of German liberalism. Although they recognized the increasing role of the state in society, most Western democratic thinkers continued to believe that the state was not a group person, an ethical institution in its own right, but an instrument in the service of the interests and welfare of the individuals that composed it.[5]

The theory of natural law in its Lockean formulation had long been dead, it is true. Jeremy Bentham and James Mill had already rejected the conception of an original social contract and viewed man as inseparable from society. But in one important way all major liberal thinkers in late nineteenth-century and early twentieth-century Britain and France remained loyal to the core of natural-law tradition, namely in their insistence that the state was not an end in itself but served ethical ends. Even a thinker as close to an organicist conception of society as T. H. Greene argued that "there is a system of rights and obligations which *should be* maintained by law, whether it is so or not, and which may properly be called 'natural.' "[6] This ethical end was never conceived, not even by utilitarian thinkers, primarily in terms of the attainment of economic goals. Wherever social reform movements and socialism stood within the liberal tradition, as they did in most of the countries of northwestern Europe and of the English-speaking world, they continued to view individual liberty and self-development as central elements of this ethical end.

We have suggested that a consistent theory of libertarian politics requires certain assumptions regarding the nature of man that are similar to those presupposed by classical natural-law theory. Libertarian theory requires faith that man possesses moral worth and dignity (a faith shared by the German liberals) as well as the belief that despite all human diversity there is a common human nature and that from this common human nature there derives at least a minimal ethics applicable to all men. This minimal ethics consists in the precept that man always be respected as an end, free "to develop himself by his own energies in his perfect individuality,"[7] and that all institutions must be judged as means towards this end. This ethics is in conflict both with a type of laissez-faire liberalism, like that of Herbert Spencer, which permits the state to stand idly by while the autonomy of the individual is challenged or destroyed by stronger individuals or associations of individuals, and with the German historicist type of liberalism, which subordinates the interests of the individuals to those of the social institutions. This ethics assumes that there exists a moral order, which if it has no basis in the cosmic structure of the universe at least rests on our common humanity and reveals itself in the individual man *qua* man through his reason or his conscience. But against this ethics the question may be raised whether the conception of natural law or of the nature of man upon which it rests is not an illusion. For not only historicism, but the social and psychological sciences as well have in the course of the past century and a half steadily undermined the natural-law image of man as a rational creature and emphasized the relativity of all social and ethical theories. May one not ask whether the historicity, and therefore relativity, of all values and cognitions is an inescapable part of the human condition? If this is so, was not German historicism in a sense a last grandiose attempt to save traditional political philosophy in the face of the hard fact of man's total historicity by maintaining a faith that although universal, timeless norms did not exist, the unique values and insights embodied in human ideas and institutions reflected an ethical order?

There is no question that historicism contributed to our understanding of man by showing how various ethical, philosophical, religious, and social systems emerged in the course of history and were related to specific human cultures. Historical study unearthed the diversity and the richness of human creativity, but it also pointed out the historicity and relativity of all human values and ideas, including those central to the civilization of the West. Once secularization, intellectual insights, and the disillusionment that followed the great political and social calamities of more recent times had destroyed the Christian and Idealistic faith of German thinkers in the historicist tradition, the German educated public was going to be confronted by an anarchy of values. This is not to suggest that historicism paved the way for German fascism, nor to deny that the intellectual situation in traditionally Western democratic countries in many ways resembled that in Germany. But it is difficult to escape the thought that the political ethics of historicism in its recognition of the rights of the state and its denial of minimal universal norms of political behavior contributed in a significant way to breaking down the barriers against political nihilism and totalitarianism in German.

The question remains, however, whether there is an alternative to the historicist position. There is no longer a return possible to a static rationalistic ethics. Not only has historical study shown the time-boundness of classical liberal political philosophy and its link to social and intellectual conditions that have long since disappeared, but, as we have already mentioned, psychology and anthropology have destroyed much of the Enlightenment conception of rational man. Nor is the optimistic historicism of Herder or Ranke any longer tenable after the terrible calamities of our age. Yet does ethical or epistemological nihilism necessarily follow as the logical consequence of this disillusionment? May there not be amidst the incessant flux of ideas and ideals in history a constant element in human nature that may provide the basis of objectivity both in matters of knowledge and in matters of ethical judgment? This is a question that we can only pose and do not presume to answer within the scope of this book. Nevertheless, on the reality or non-reality of such an objective factor in the human situation rests the question whether liberalism possesses rational ethical foundations and thus reflects perennial human needs, or whether it merely represented the operative ideals of a historic society that has now largely moved into the past.

Many of the social and economic conditions as well as the intellectual setting in which liberal democratic theory emerged are now irrevocably gone. In the technological mass society of our age the state and large-scale organizations will play an ever larger role. Mass organization may not of necessity be incompatible with the central liberal idea of the free autonomous individuality. Nevertheless, the viability of the libertarian idea under the changed conditions of modern society and modern thought will doubtless involve the continued affirmation of the dignity and autonomy of the individual as a constant norm by which political and social institutions, policies, and actions may be judged. Such a norm will have to find renewed theoretical foundations, either in a reasoned conception of a constant element in human nature or in an affirmation in the meaningfulness and dignity of individuality as an act of faith.

2.

In the preceding pages we have sought to examine critically the ethical and political presuppositions of German historicist thought. In conclusion we wish to consider once more the adequacy of historicism as a theory of historical knowledge.

As we have already suggested, there is a core of historicist theory that remains invaluable for all scholarly historiography—the ideal of objectivity, the critical apparatus of historical scholarship, the concern of the historian to understand a historical situation within its own terms and at the same time his recognition that historical reality, involving life, spontaneity, and meaning, requires an empathetic approach different from that suited to the study of nature. But historicism was always more than a methodology. It involved metaphysical as well as political assumptions, which had a limiting influence on historical writing. As Fritz Wagner observed in his recent book *The Historian and World History*[8], Ranke and the German historical school fundamentally altered the function of the historian. Western historiography from the Greeks to the Enlightenment had sought answers in history to the fundamental questions of human existence. For Herder and Ranke, history still fulfilled this task, because they optimistically assumed that there existed an automatic harmony between empirical fact and metaphysical truth. For a later generation of historians who had lost this idealistic faith, history became a professional, scholarly enterprise no longer concerned with broader philosophical questions. Indeed history and philosophy became antithetical terms. The subject matter of history, the uniqueness of all human activity, excluded the possibility of any historical contribution to a scientific approach to the questions of the nature of man or of the overall direction of human history.

History must not give itself over to the fancies of speculation. It must maintain a rigorously experiential base. Nevertheless, we may wonder whether history deals only with unique phenomena and whether all aspects of human existence are subject to constant change. Human existence certainly takes place within a framework shared by all humans. We live in a physical world that has common characteristics for all of us. Although cosmological conceptions may differ in every age and in every culture, the objective structure of the world remains stable. Likewise, although theories of knowledge may vary, the inherent structure of the reality within which we exist requires a logic and a mathematics that remain constant throughout the ages. Similarly, there is not only a biological, but also a psychological structure to human life, which is constant through the ages and common to all men. It seems a paradox that the historical school that emphasized the historicity of all human phenomena based its critical method on the assumption that there were constant factors that served as criteria for the authenticity of documents and the plausibility of events. For what was the critical method in history of which the nineteenth-century historians were so proud but the insistence on the recognition of the coherence of physical nature in the case of the criteria of external criticism and of human nature in relation to the principles of internal criticism. As W. H. Walsh suggested:

> It was generalizations about human nature which ultimately lay behind historical explanations . . . we could not even begin to under-

stand [the past], unless we presupposed some propositions about human nature, unless we applied some notion of what is reasonable or normal in human behavior.[6]

But if there are elements of constancy in human nature, the historian must be concerned with typical as well as unique phenomena, and with their interplay. History is then concerned not merely with narrating a set of events, but with the comparative study of institutions and with the attempt to isolate constants in political, economic, or other behavior in diverse historical settings. The task of the historian thus moves much closer to that of the sociologist, the psychologist, the economist, or the anthropologist. Like them, the historian is forced to pose questions that relate to the problem of the nature of man. A century ago Jakob Burckhardt stressed the important role that concern with the typical should occupy in historical scholarship, but the idea remained marginal to German historical scholarship into the twentieth century, and not only in Germany but in much of the world where the German historical profession had provided the model for scholarly history. Only in recent decades have comparative studies attained a degree of respectability.

The influence of objective historicist notions regarding the nature of history not only presented barriers to broad comparative studies of human behavior, but also limited the scope of the historian in approaching the problems of the dynamics of historical development. Judaeo-Christian as well as secularized Enlightenment thought assumed a unity of human history. This assumption was challenged by historicism, which held that human history took place within the framework of separate human cultures and that each culture was a self-contained unit of study. This conception negated the idea of linear development in history. Linear development and progress were incompatible with the spontaneity and individuality found in human societies. All historical phenomena were to be viewed for their own sakes and not subordinated to impersonal processes.

It is this insistence on the unique value of every idea, institution, or personality in history that made Ranke proclaim that all epochs were equally immediate unto God and that led later subjective historicism, which was emancipated from belief in a divine basis of history, to observe that history confronts us with facts but that "facts as such have no meaning."[10] Nevertheless, fully recognizing the uniqueness of every historical situation, it is difficult to escape the notion that in certain areas of man's historical existence there appears to be directional development. Thus the historian of science, it will readily be admitted, is not at all confronted by a multiplicity of facts of equal significance. Rather the history of science appears as a process in which not only knowledge is progressively accumulated, but in which scientific theories confronting each other in a continuous dialogue are refuted, modified, or reformulated. The history of science thus presents us with a very different picture from that which Dilthey offered in his treatment of the history of philosophy. We are confronted not by a variety of *Weltanschauungen,* "mere reflections of our own agitated inner life,"[11] but by continuing attempts to approximate interpersonal and intercultural truths. Every scientific undertaking takes place within a given set of historical and social conditions. In this sense science is culture-bound. Nevertheless, logic and scientific method possess a degree of validity independent of the historical setting in which they originate. Each scientific theory is an attempt to define aspects of the underlying structure of reality common to all human existence. The structure of reality thus seems to determine the history of science. No matter how uncoördinated the efforts of individual scientists may be, the very character of science appears to force scientific conceptions in a general direction. In this sense the freedom and creativity of the individual scientist is not necessarily in conflict with the overall direction of the history of science. What is true of the history of science is also true of the history of technology. Like science, all technology is culturally and historically bound. And yet the history of technology points forward toward man's increasing control over nature.

Few historians would dispute that there is a degree of direction in the history of science and technology. More difficult is the problem of establishing direction in those areas dealing with the interaction of men with men rather than with external nature. The core of the dispute between positivism and the German historical school in nineteenth-century social thought revolved around this question. Comte, Buckle, Spencer, and Lamprecht provided formulae for historical development that were certainly inadequate to deal with the complexities of historical change and were patterned too closely on the nineteenth-century models of the natural sciences. The historical school, however, not only rejected the positivist position, but refused to consider the problem of regularities or of direction in social change as one at all capable of scientific study. Nevertheless, not only the positivists, but also twentieth-century social theorists such as Max Weber, Ferdinand Tönnies, Oskar Hintze, and Werner Sombart, themselves products of the German historicist tradition, have spoken of certain continuing trends in Western civilization or in the history of man.in general, among which are the increasing role of science, the mechanization of life, the organization of society along increasingly rational lines, bureaucratization, and urbanization. Condorcet, Auguste Comte, and Max Weber, each from very different points of view, saw the steadily increasing growth of the role of reason in human existence. There is indeed a remarkable similarity between the analyses of the forces operating in modern society by the adherents of the idea of progress like Condorcet, Saint-Simon, Comte, and Mill and the starkest cultural pessimists like Kierkegaard, Burckhardt, and Spengler. Both groups see similar trends toward a highly organized, industrial, commercial mass society dominated by rational organization and planning, but they evaluate these forces from very different points of view. For Condorcet, reason is still a guide to positive value. A rational society is synonymous for him with a just society, in which man can develop his potentialities to the fullest. The progress of reason is thus also the progress of freedom and justice. For Weber, reason has become a cold tool of analysis. The irresistible march of reason brought with it the demythologization of all world views and the destruction of all illusions, and it threatened the spontaneity of cultural creativity. These observations must be regarded as grandiose hypotheses but they do raise questions that deserve serious historical study. They raise problems of developing a methodological apparatus for determining and measuring social trends in history. They raise the question whether such trends have operated only in Western civilization or in other cultures as well and lead to broad comparative studies of civilization. They raise again the hypothesis of a world history, disreputable since the eighteenth century. And while the answers are far away if at all obtainable—for the nature of history may indeed, as the historicists have maintained, speak against linear development in history—it is nonetheless regrettable that historical scholarship has left these questions to the speculative philosophers of history.

The question also arises whether values and *Weltanschauungen* are indeed as irrational as historians have maintained. Historicism, both of the objective and the subjective varieties, has stressed the uniqueness of all expressions of values, ethical, aesthetic, religious, political, or other, and dismissed the question of the relation of values to the structure of human nature as irrelevant to historical study. Nevertheless, it would be a legitimate concern of historical study to investigate whether the comparative study of ethics, religion, law, art, and social philosophies or institutions reflects the total diversity of cultures and civilizations or reveals elements of uniformity or similarity amidst these differences, and whether these similarities are purely structural and formal or substantive as well.

To take an example: Is the Decalogue solely the expression of a unique Hebraic civilization at one point of historical development, or does it touch on generally human needs and aspirations that express themselves in analogous forms in other cultures at similar stages of development?

Related to the question of the comparative historical study of norms is the idea of progress. The history of science, we have argued, reflects a development of ideas toward greater objectivity and truth. The diversity of scientific views in different cultures and ages does not in itself refute the ideal of scientific truth. The history of science resembles in many ways a dialectical process in which sets of theoretical conceptions are progressively replaced by more convincing ones. This dialectical process takes place with reference to the structure of reality, which is the object of scientific study. Important achievements of Hellenistic science, such as the heliocentric theory or the circulation of the blood, were forgotten in the Middle Ages and had to be "rediscovered." Nevertheless, the inherent structure of reality gives a point of reference to the history of scientific thought. Thus while progress in science is by no means inevitable, it does in a sense seem to lie in the nature of things. Not that the truth will always prevail—indeed it will often be trampled down, because men do not think only rationally and will often refuse to accept the consequences of their rational insights— but error will sooner or later appear to rationally thinking men to be in conflict with the structure of reality. What men like Condorcet, Kant, Hegel, Marx, or Comte, or more recently in a less dogmatic form Karl Jaspers[12] and E. H. Carr,[13] have suggested is that a similar dialectical process occurs in the social and cultural realms, that social ideals and institutions relate to the structure of human nature in a sense not entirely unlike the relation of scientific ideas to the structure of natural reality, and that social institutions undergo changes partly because of their inadequacy to meet human needs. In this sense, these thinkers believe, a process takes place toward more rational forms of social organization, rational in the sense that they correspond more closely to the structure of human nature. Karl Jaspers has pointed to parallels in the development of religious and moral conceptions among the major European and Asian civilizations and distinguished between primitive and higher religions in terms of progress, not merely change, in religious and moral conceptions. Eastern European Marxist critics of Toynbee have sought to point at the similarities in the structural development of diverse civilizations.[14]

The process of history undoubtedly seems much more complex than it appeared to the theorists of progress of the eighteenth and nineteenth centuries. Thinkers like Condorcet, Comte, or Marx assumed that there was a normal state of human behavior to which man would progress. It was normal for man to develop his full potentialities in freedom; it was abnormal for man to be restricted from such development by forces external to him. Exploitation, ignorance, disease, deprivation, although present in all past history, were such abnormal states. The estrangement of man from his true nature provided the moving force of historical change. This was the core of Condorcet's, as well as of Marx's, dialectic. The emancipation of man from the great irrationalities of history, from violence, oppression, and inequality, was assured no matter how tortuous and painful the process toward this end might be. Today we view this optimism with justified skepticism. The theorists of progress operated with an overly naïve psychology that emphasized man's actions in terms of his enlightened self-interest, but overlooked the role of destructive and self-destructive inclinations in man. There was no place for the great demonic outbursts of irrationality in Condorcet's vision of the future, for the gas chambers of Auschwitz or the hell of Hiroshima or even Stalin's institutionalization of terror did not fit into Marx's scheme. Nevertheless, the forces that the theorists of progress saw operating in history have dominated the nineteenth and twentieth centuries. We are much closer in 1968 to the world that Condorcet projected in 1794 in his *Sketch on the Progress of the Human Mind* than to the nightmare of 1984 that George Orwell depicted in the late 1940's. The onward march of science, technology, health, literacy and general welfare, the disappearance of slavery, the emancipation of women, the increase in economic and educational opportunities, which Condorcet foresaw almost two centuries ago, have all come about. The great social revolutions of the twentieth century in Mexico, China, Russia, and Cuba, no matter how filled with new abuses of power, and the awakening of the colonial world can be viewed as part of a continuing struggle of the masses for emancipation from the irrationalities of the past. But violence has certainly not disappeared from the scene. The onward march of civilization in the form of a technological mass society not only produced the conditions for the possible physical annihilation of mankind, but created a widespread feeling of cultural malaise and a heightened awareness of what many regarded as man's alienation from his true self. Not only the spectacular advances in the struggle against poverty, disease, and ignorance, but also totalitarianism and modern total war were symptoms of the age. Progress has turned out to be a two-edged sword.

These remarks are not intended in defense or criticism of the idea of progress. Even less should they be understood as an espousal of a theory of historical determinism. Rather they seek to suggest that history is concerned with more than the reconstruction of a given situation, that the dynamics of history itself is a subject of legitimate historical study, and that methods must be developed to assess the role of personalities as well as of the great collective forces in historical change, of continuity as well as of discontinuity, of the uniquely individual elements in the stream of history as well as the recurring typically human.

Historicism undoubtedly greatly impoverished historical scholarship when it dismissed the great theoretical questions facing man as legitimate problems of scholarly study. Perhaps a certain dialectic operated in the history of historical thought itself. The German historical school rightly pointed to the shortcomings of the philosophical history of the Enlightenment—its oversimplified conception of human nature and of society and its blissful neglect of empirical data. It developed methods for the critical evaluation of evidence, but in insisting that history dealt exclusively with the particular historicism in fact broke the link not only with philosophy but also with science, insofar as science is never concerned with the particular in isolation but seeks to establish relationships. The German historical school maintained that in its concern with the particular, it fulfilled a philosophical as well as a scientific function, because it saw in the historical fact a phenomenal reflection of transhistorical truth and regarded the concrete mores, values, and policies of existing institutions as expressions of a higher morality. With the collapse of this metaphysics of identity, German historicism was forced to draw nihilistic conclusions for both knowledge and ethics and to see a world exclusively of volition, struggle, and chaos. Too deeply bound to its origin in the eighteenth century conservative revolt against the forces of modernity represented by the Enlightenment and the French Revolution, historicism was unable to come to grips with the great social transformations that have occurred in the modern world. It showed understanding for the role of the irrational, the spontaneous, and the unique in history, but it underestimated the elements of rationality and regularity. In posing again questions of a theoretical character regarding the nature of man, society, and historical change, historiography must escape the abstract speculations of the classical philosophers of history and seek to integrate the critical apparatus of the historical school and its respect for fact and diversity with methods suited to the empirical, comparative study of human institutions.

Notes

[1]The term "historicism" is of such recent usage in America that it was not yet included in any of the standard dictionaries of the 1950's. Only in the 1930's, when American historians, social scientists, and theologians, shaken in their confidence in the past, increasingly looked to European thought, did the term become widely known in this country. Since then, it has been so rapidly adopted and has acquired so many often contradictory meanings that it defies definition. Widely varying uses of the term, as they appeared in German, Italian, and English writings, have been appropriated by the American literature. Definitions of the term have generally agreed that historicism, to quote the 1961 edition of *Webster's Third New International Dictionary,* is a "theory that all socio-cultural phenomena are historically determined." But beyond this, there has been little consensus on the meaning of the word as it relates to the objectivity of knowledge, the rationality of values, or the lawfulness of historical development. Most, if not all, writers have agreed that historicism involves the position that historical cognition, too, is an historical, time-bound act. Some have drawn from this relativistic implications for the theory of historical knowledge.

Thus, Karl Mannheim, in the *Encyclopedia of the Social Sciences,* interpreted Ernst Troeltsch's historicism as meaning that ideas are only "reflex functions of the sociological conditions under which they arose." Others have stressed the emphasis which historicism places upon the irrational and the intuitional. While this may be true of the use Friedrich Meinecke made of the term, it hardly holds for Benedetto Croce. History for Croce is thought, but such thought is by no means irrational. "Historicism is a logical principle," he writes in *History as the Story of Liberty* (New York, 1955), which was widely read in paperback form in this country. "It is, in fact, the very category of logic; it is logicality in its full acceptation, the logicality of the concrete universal" (p. 74). He concludes in almost Hegelian fashion: "Our history is the history of our Soul and the history of the human Soul is the history of the world" (p. 117).

For the most part, historicism has been identified with ethical relativism, with the recognition "that there are no absolute values,

287

categories, or standards" (*Webster's Third New International Dictionary*, p. 1075). In Ortega y Gasset's words; ". . . Man has no nature, what he has is . . . history." ["History as a System" in Raymond Klibansky and H. J. Paton, eds., *Philosophy and History* (Oxford, 1936), p. 313]. But Morris Cohen still spoke of historicism as an exaggerated "faith that history is the main road to human wisdom" in *The Meaning of History* (LaSalle, Ill., 1947), p. 11. In general, historicism has been identified with the recognition that the subject matter of history is life in its unique, many-sided reality, and that the spontaneity of life makes impossible the reduction of history to general laws, as found in the natural sciences; cf. Hans Meyerhoff, Introduction to *The Philosophy of History in our Time: An Anthology*, pp. 10-11 (New York, 1954). Karl Popper, in *The Poverty of Historicism* (Boston, 1957), defines historicism as "an approach to the social sciences which assumes that *historical prediction* is their principal aim, and which further assumes that this aim is attainable by discovering the 'rhythms' or the 'patterns,' the 'laws' or the 'trends' that underlie the evolution of history" (p. 3).

The term "historicism" was preceded in English by the term "historism," but even "historism" was rarely used. It appears in the *Dictionary of Philosophy and Psychology*. J. M. Baldwin, ed. (New York, 1901-1905), refers to "historism" as a term "used mainly in the German *Historismus*." Charles Beard and Alfred Vagts discussed German "historism" in "Currents of Thought in Historiography," *American Historical Review*, 42 (1936-1937), pp. 460-483, which contained an extensive discussion of Meinecke's *Entstehung des Historismus* (München, 1936). Meinecke in a letter to the American historian Koppel Pinson (Berlin, May 7, 1937) in *Ausgewählter Briefwechsel* in *Werke*, VI (Stuttgart, 1962), pp. 171-173, labels their discussion a caricature of his own thought. The term "historicism," which largely replaced "historism" in the late 1930's, seems to have come into English from Italian rather than German. Benedetto Croce extensively uses the term "historicism" in *History as the Story of Liberty*, first published in English in 1941. The translator had rendered the title of Droysen's *Historik* as *Elements of Historicism* in Croce's earlier *History, Its Theory and Practice*, translated by Douglas Ainslie (New York, 1921), but Croce had not yet used the term in the Italian original. *Historik* was translated as *Elementi d'Istorica*. Guido de Ruggiero referred to "historicism" in the *Encyclopedia of the Social Sciences*, VII (New York, 1932), p. 570. The Italian term *"storicismo,"* as used by Croce and others—e.g., Carlo Antoni—had a much more Hegelian connotation than the German term *"Historismus."*

Karl Popper was therefore not as unjustified in applying the term to Hegel and Marx as his critics, e.g., Meyerhoff, have maintained. Popper sharply distinguishes between "historicism," which "insists upon historical prediction," and "historism," which "analys(es) and explain(s) the differences between the various sociological doctrines and schools, by referring either to their connection with the predilections and interests prevailing in a particular historical period . . . or to their connection with political or economic or class interests," in his *The Poverty of Historicism* (p. 17), first written in the 1930's. It is, however, the latter meaning of historical relativism and diversity which has been attached most commonly to the term "historicism" in America, since Beard and Vagts discussed Meinecke's *Entstehung des Historismus*. Hans Meyerhoff, in the Introduction to his *The Philosophy of History in Our Time, An Anthology* (p. 10), describes historicism as the view that "the special quality of history does not consist in the statement of general laws or principles, but in the grasp so far as possible, of the infinite variety of particular historical forms immersed in the passage of time." More recently, Erich Kahler, in *The Meaning of History* (New York, 1964, pp. 171, 175, 176, and 186), distinguishes between an earlier "historism," by "which we may understand the tendency to see and explain everything historically," and its "degeneration" toward the end of the nineteenth century into a relativistic "historicism."

Erich Rothacker in "Das Wort 'Historismus,' " *Zeitschrift für deutsche Wortforschung,* 16 (1960), pp. 3-6, traces the use of the term in German back to the late eighteenth century. It was widely used, however, only after 1880 and acquired different and often contradictory meanings. Karl Werner used the term in 1879 in his book on Giambattista Vico to refer to Vico's view that the human spirit knows no other reality than history because man makes history. Carl Menger and Adolf Wagner polemicized against the historism (*Historismus*) of the historical approach to economics of Gustav Schmoller. Rudolf Eisler in the *Wörterbuch der philosophischen Begriffe,* I (Berlin, 1910, p. 490), identifies *Historismus* with Hegelianism. Nevertheless, the term acquires an anti-Hegelian connotation in the German literature.

The German Historical School, with its emphasis upon diversity and individuality, is interpreted as an expression of historism in contrast to the attempts by the Hegelians to see in historical development a unified, logical process. Ernst Troeltsch's and Friedrich Meinecke's uses of the term have strongly influenced German usage. (See Chaps. II and VII.) Briefly, the term has denoted two different but not entirely opposed ideas: (a) a philosophic doctrine of relatively recent origin, which holds that all existence is historical, that history is flux, that man, too, is in this flux; and that the growing recognition of the historical character of all human ideas, ideals, and institutions threatens to destroy the whole world of values; and (b) an older, more optimistic tradition of historical thought that recognizes the historical character of all cognitions and values but sees in history the expression of real value and divine will.

For a discussion of the meaning of the term, see Dwight E. Lee and Robert N. Beck, "The Meaning of 'Historicism' " in *American Historical Review,* 59 (1953-1954), pp. 568-577; Karl Heussi, *Die Krisis des Historismus* (Tübingen, 1932), especially pp. 1-21; Pietro Rossi's attempt to distinguish between German and Italian historicism in *Storia e Storicismo nella Filosofia Contemporanea* (Milano, 1960); Friedrich Engel-Janosi, *The Growth of German Historicism* (Baltimore, 1944); Leo Strauss, *Natural Right and History* (Chicago, 1953), especially pp. 9-34; Waldemar Besson, "Historismus," in *Geschichte* (Frankfurt, 1961), pp. 102-116 of *Das Fischer-Lexikon;* Calvin G. Rand, "Two Meanings of Historicism in the Writings of Dilthey, Troeltsch, and Meinecke" in *Journal of the History of Ideas,* 25 (1964), pp. 503-518. See also Alan Donagan, "Popper's Examination of Historicism," in *The Philosophy of Karl Popper,* P. A. Schilpp, ed. (to be published as a volume in *The Library of Living Philosophers).*

²See Carlo Antoni, *L'Historisme* (Génève, 1963).

³Friedrich Meinecke, *Die Entstehung des Historismus,* Vol. III of *Werke* (München, 1959), p. 4.

⁴Ernst Troeltsch, "Naturrecht und Humanität in der Weltpolitik (1920)" in *Deutscher Geist und Westeuropa,* Hans Baron, ed. (Tübingen, 1925), p. 4. Translated as "The Ideas of Natural Law and Humanity in World Politics" in Otto Gierke, *Natural Law and the Theory of Society, 1500-1800,* Ernest Barker, trans. (Cambridge, 1934), I, p. 202.

⁵See Klaus Dockhorn, *Die Staatsphilosophie des englischen Idealismus* (Bochum, 1937); *Der deutsche Historismus in England. Ein Beitrag zur englischen Geistesgeschichte des 19. Jahrhunderts* (Göttingen, 1950); *Deutscher Geist und angelsächsische Geistesgeschichte. Ein Versuch der Deutung ihres Verhältnisses* (Göttingen, 1954); also Jurgen Herbst, *The German Historical School in American Scholarship* (Ithaca, 1965).

⁶Cf. Carlo Antoni, *L'Historisme.*

⁷*Strassburg, Freiburg, Berlin, 1901-1919. Erinnerungen* (Stuttgart, 1949), p. 192.

⁸Cf. M. C. Brands, *Historisme als Ideologie. Het "Onpolitieke"*

en "Anti-Normatieve" Element in de duitse Geschiedswetenschap (Assen, 1965).

⁹Cf. Carlo Antoni, *Der Kampf wider die Vernunft* (Stuttgart, 1951).

¹⁰Carlo Antoni, *L'Historisme,* p. 9.

¹¹Cf. M. C. Brands, *Historisme als Ideologie.*

¹²Leopold von Ranke, "Das politische Gespräch" in *Sämtliche Werke* (Leipzig, 1873-1890), IL/L, p. 318. English translation of essay in Theodore H. Von Laue, *Leopold Ranke. The Formative Years* (Princeton, 1950).

¹³Leopold Ranke, "Das politische Gespräch in *Werke,* IL/L, p. 328.

¹⁴*Ibid.*

¹⁵*Weltbürgertum und Nationalstaat* in *Werke* (München, 1962), V. p. 83

¹⁶Leopold Ranke, "Das politische Gespräch" in *Werke,* p. 327.

¹⁷Cf. Carlo Antoni, *L'Historisme,* p. 4; Hans Kohn, *The Mind of Germany* (New York, 1950), p. 11.

¹⁸See p. 112.

¹⁹Cf. Helmuth Plessner, *Die verspätete Nation. Über die politische Verführbarkeit bürgerlichen Geistes (*Stuttgart, 1959).

²⁰Carlo Antoni, *L'Historisme,* p. 55.

²¹Cf. Joachim Wach, *Das Verstehen* (Tübingen, 1926-33), 3 vols.; Erich Rothacker, *Einleitung in die Geisteswissenschaften* (Tübingen: 1920).

²²See Chap. VI.

²³"Die Ideen von 1914" in *Deutscher Geist und Westeuropa,* p. 49.

²⁴John Hallowell, *The Decline of Liberalism as an Ideology with Particular Reference to German Politico-Legal Thought* (Berkeley, 1943), p. 19.

²⁵Georg Lukacs, *Die Zerstörung der Vernunft* (Berlin, 1954), p. 49.

²⁶Hajo Holborn, "Der deutsche Idealismus in sozialgeschichtlicher Bedeutung" in *Historische Zeitschrift,* 174 (1952), p. 364, hereafter to be cited as *HZ.* Regarding other studies of the divergent German development, see Helmuth Plessner, *Die verspätete Nation;* Ernst Troeltsch, "Naturrecht und Humanität" in *Deutscher Geist und Westeuropa;* Georg Lukacs, *Zerstörung der Vernunft;* Hans Rosenberg, *Bureaucracy, Aristocracy and Autocracy. The Prussian Experience, 1660-1815* (Harvard, 1958); Heinrich Heffter, *Die deutsche Selbstverwaltung im 19. Jahrhundert* (Stuttgart, 1950);

Leonard Krieger, *The German Idea of Freedom* (Boston, 1957); Gerhard Ritter, *Das Deutsche Problem* (München, 1962).

[27]Leonard Krieger, *German Idea of Freedom,* p. 13.

[28]Hajo Holborn, "Der deutsche Idealismus in sozialgeschichtlicher Bedeutung" in *HZ,* 174 (1952), p. 365.

[29]Regarding the positive attitude of German Enlightenment toward the state, see Wilhelm Dilthey, "Friedrich der Grosse und die deutsche Aufklärung" in *Gesammelte Schriften,* III (Berlin, 1927), pp. 81-205.

[30]"Ideen zu einem Versuch, die Gränzen der Wirksamkeit des Staats zu bestimmen" in *Gesammelte Schriften,* I (Berlin, 1903-1936), p. 106.

[31]Rosenberg, *Bureaucracy, Aristocracy and Autocracy,* p. 204.

[32]*Ibid.,* pp. 232-233.

[33]Eckart Kehr, "Neuere deutsche Geschichtsschreibung" in *Der Primat der Aussenpolitik.* Hans-Ulrich Wehler, ed. (Berlin, 1965), pp. 254-255.

[34]*Ibid.;* Walter Bussman, "Zur Geschichte des deutschen Liberalismus im 19. Jahrhundert" in *HZ,* 186 (1958), pp. 527-557.

[35]The *Habilitationsschrift* is a second thesis, after the doctoral dissertation. Generally more ambitious than the former, it is required for admission to university teaching.

[36]Attempts have been made to introduce something which corresponds to a departmental structure in new universities such as Bochum; dual or even multiple chairs in a field are no longer uncommon, and the *Habilitation* has been waived in some recent appointments to university chairs.

[37]Cf. Chap. VIII.

CHAPTER II: THE ORIGINS OF GERMAN HISTORICISM

[1]*Poetics,* Chap. 9. Cf. *The Basic Works of Aristotle,* p. 1,464. Richard McKeon, ed. (New York, 1941): "Hence poetry is something more philosophic and of graver import than history, since its statements are of the nature rather of universals, whereas those of history are singulars."

[2]Cf. Andreas Kraus, *Vernunft und Geschichte. Die Bedeutung der deutschen Akademien für die Entwicklung der Geschichtwissenschaft im späten 18. Jahrhundert* (Freiburg i.B., 1963); Herbert Butterfield, *Man on his Past. The Study of Historical Scholarship* (Boston, 1960).

[3]For an English translation of the third ed. (1744), see *The New*

Science of Giambattista Vico trans. by Thomas Goddard Bergin and Max Harold Fisch (Garden City, New York, 1961).

[4]*Auch eine Philosophie der Geschichte zur Bildung der Menschheit. Beytrag zu vielen Beyträgen des Jahrhunderts* (1774) in *Sämmtliche Werke* V, Bernhard Suphan, ed. (Berlin, 1877-1913), pp. 475-594.

[5]*Entstehung des Historismus,* p. 49.

[6]Cf. *ibid.,* pp. 504-525 on Goethe's "negative relation to history."

[7]*Weltbürgertum und Nationalstaat,* Vol. V of *Werke* (München, 1962).

[8]Carlo Antoni, *Der Kampf wider die Vernunft* and *L'Historisme.*

[9]Antoni, *L'Historisme,* p. 9.

[10]*Ibid.,* p. 10.

[11]For a study of early expressions of historicist thought in Switzerland as well as Germany, see Carlo Antoni, *Der Kampf wider die Vernunft.*

[12]For a study of the general impact of historicism and historical thought upon the development of the social and cultural sciences, see Bruce Mazlish, *The Riddle of History. The Great Speculators from Vico to Freud* (New York, 1966).

[13]Romans 13:1. Cf. Ernst Troeltsch, *Soziallehren* in *Gesammelte Schriften,* I (Tübingen, 1919), especially pp. 560-571. Translated by Olive Wyon as *The Social Doctrines of the Christian Churches,* (London, 1931), 2 vols.

[14]Meinecke, *Entstehung des Historismus,* p. 33.

[15]Hajo Holborn, *A History of Modern Germany, 1648-1840* (New York, 1964), II, p. 155.

[16]Quoted in Roy Pascal, *The German Sturm und Drang* (Manchester, 1953), p. 90.

[17]Both Meinecke in *Entstehung des Historismus* (cf. pp. 408, 425) and Rudolf Stadelmann in *Der Historische Sinn bei Herder* (Halle, 1928) regard *Auch eine Philosophie der Geschichte* as the high point of Herder's historical thought and his later concern with the *Humanitätsidee* as "a step backward" (Meinecke, p. 425). See also G. A. Wells, "Herder's Two Philosophies of History" in *Journal of the History of Ideas,* 21 (1960), pp. 527-537; F. M. Barnard criticizes Stadelmann in "Herder's Treatment of Causation and Continuity in History" in *Journal of the History of Ideas,* 24 (1963), p. 197; Wells criticizes Meinecke's interpretation of Herder's supposed nondeterminism in "Herder's Determinism," *Journal of the History of Ideas,* 19 (1958), pp. 105-118.

[18]"Auch eine Philosophie . . .," V, p. 509; on J. G. Herder's con-

cept of individuality, see also Leo Spitz, "Natural Law and the Theory of History in Herder" in *Journal of the History of Ideas,* 16 (1955), pp. 453-478, particularly pp. 458-459.

[19]Cf. "Auch eine Philosophie . . .," V, p. 509; cf. "Ideen zur Philosophie der Geschichte der Menschheit," XIV, p. 8; cf. Stadelmann, p. 47; Robert Reinhold Ergang, *Herder and the Foundations of German Nationalism* (New York, 1931); Royal J. Schmidt, "Cultural Nationalism in Herder" in *Journal of the History of Ideas,* 17 (1956), pp. 407-417.

[20]"Auch eine Philosophie . . .," *passim,* cf. V, 484ff., especially pp. 489-491.

[21]Cf. *ibid.,* pp. 535, 537.

[22]Cf. *ibid.,* pp. 501, 502, 537, 542.

[23]*Ibid.,* p. 510.

[24]Cf. Reinhold Aris, *History of Political Thought in Germany from 1789 to 1815* (London, 1936); G. P. Gooch, *Germany and the French Revolution* (London, 1920); Wilhelm Dobbek, *Johann Gottfried Herder* (Weimar, 1950), p. 129; Jacques Droz, *L'Allemagne et la Revolution Française* (Paris, 1949), and F. M. Barnard, *Herder's Social and Political Thought. From Enlightenment to Nationalism* (Oxford, 1965).

[25]Despite Herder's later endorsement of the French Revolution, see his repeated condemnation of Enlightenment political ideals in "Auch eine Philosophie . . . "; e.g., his attack on "Freiheit, Geselligkeit und Gleichheit," p. 576; on "Freigeisterei," p. 579; on Enlightenment philosophy, p. 538, especially p. 555.

[26]*Ibid.,* p. 509.

[27]*Entstehung des Historismus, Werke,* III, p. 579.

[28]"Auch eine Philosophie . . .," V, p. 487.

[29]*Ibid.,* p. 513; cf. pp. 558-559.

[30]Cf. H. A. Korff, *Humanismus und Romantik* (Leipzig, 1924) and *Geist der Goethezeit,* 4 vols. (Lepizig, 1923-1958), especially Vols. I, II. Paul Kluckhohn, *Die Idee des Menschen in der Goethezeit* (Stuttgart, 1946); Franz Schultz, *Klassik und Romantik der Deutschen,* 2nd ed. (Stuttgart, 1952), I, pp. 159-244.

[31]*Ideen zur Philosophie der Geschichte der Menschheit* in *Sämtliche Werke,* XIII, p. 189.

[32]Cf. H. A. Korff, *Humanismus und Romantik,* pp. 35-36.

[33]Cf. "Betrachtungen über die Weltgeschichte," in *Gesammelte Schriften,* III, Albert Leitzmann, ed. (Berlin, 1903-1936), p. 357. This essay was written at a somewhat later period, probably around 1814.

[34]Cf. "Ideen zu einem Versuch die Grenzen der Wirksamkeit des Staats zu bestimmen," *ibid.*, I, p. 126.

[35]"Idee zu einer allgemeinen Geschichte in weltbürgerlicher Absicht," *Werke,* IV (Leipzig, 1912-1922), p. 154.

[36]Cf. Johann Albrecht von Rantzau, "Deutschland und die hedonistische Glückseligkeit," *Die Welt als Geschichte,* 22 (1963), pp. 107-123.

[37]Kant, "Idee . . .," (see above, n. 35), IV, p. 152.

[38]Cf. e.g., *Vorlesungen über die Philosophie der Geschichte,* vol. XI, *Sämtliche Werke.* Hermann Glockner, ed. (Stuttgart, 1928), pp. 34-35.

[39]*Ibid.,* p. 40.

[40]Cf. "Denkschrift über die deutsche Verfassung" (December, 1813), *ibid.,* XI, pp. 97-98.

[41]"Über die Aufgabe des Geschichtschreibers," *ibid.,* IV, p. 50.

[42]Das politische Gespräch," *Sämtliche Werke* (Leipzig, 1873-1890), L, p. 327.

[43]This is admittedly a very abbreviated discussion of a complex process. For two very different approaches to the emergence of German political nationalism, see Meinecke, *Weltbürgertum und Nationalstaat* and Eugene N. Anderson, *Nationalism and the Cultural Crisis in Prussia, 1806-1815* (New York, 1939). Meinecke stresses that cosmopolitanism and nationalism are not two mutually exclusive sets of values and that cosmopolitan elements never fully disappeared from German nationalism, although he considers the attitude that "German national feeling at its best always includes an idea of a supranational humanity" to be an oversimplification of a very complex relationship.

[44]*Briefe zur Beförderung der Humanität in Sämtliche Werke,* XVII, p. 319.

[45]Cited in Siegfried A. Kaehler, *Wilhelm von Humboldt and der Staat,* 2nd ed. (Göttingen, 1963), p. 270; cf. *Wilhelm und Caroline Humboldt in ihren Briefen,* IV, Anna V. Sydow, ed. (Berlin, 1906-1916), 308ff.

[46]Ernst Moritz Arndt, "Des deutschen Vaterland," *Fremdherrschaft und Befreiung.* Robert F. Arnold, ed. (Leipzig, 1932) in *Deutsche Literatur, Reihe Politische Dichtung,* II, p. 136.

[47]*Ideen zur Philosophie der Geschichte* . . . in *Sämtliche Werke,* XIII, p. 340. Cf. Stadelmann (above, n. 36), p. 113; Schultz, *Klassik und Romantik der Deutschen,* I, pp. 179-181; Ergang, *Herder and German Nationalism,* pp. 242-244.

[48]Cf. "Denkschrift . . .," (above, n. 40), *Gesammelte Schriften,* XI, p. 98; in contract, see "Ideen zu einem Versuch die Grenzen der

Wirksamkeit des Staats zu bestimmen." *Ibid.,* I, pp. 97-254, written in 1791-1792.

⁴⁹*Einige Vorlesungen über die Bestimmung des Gelehrten* in *Werke,* I, Fritz Medicus, ed. (Leipzig, n.d.), p. 234.

⁵⁰*Der geschlossne (sic!) Handelsstaat* in *Werke,* III, pp. 417-543.

⁵¹*Reden an die deutsche Nation* in *Werke,* V, pp. 356-610; translated by R. F. Jones and G. H. Trumball as *Addresses to the German Nation.* (Chicago, 1922).

⁵²*Machiavell,* 2nd ed., Vol. 163 of *Philosophische Bibliothek.* Hans Schulz, ed. (Leipzig, n.d.), p. 28.

⁵³Cf. *Grundlinien der Philosophie des Rechts,* Vol. VII, *Sämtliche Werke.* Hermann Glockner, ed. (Stuttgart, 1928), p. 446; cited here from "The Philosophy of Law" in *Hegel Selections,* Jacob Loewenberg, ed. (New York, 1929), p. 468.

CHAPTER III: THE THEORETICAL FOUNDATIONS OF GERMAN HISTORICISM I

¹See the studies by Siegfried Kaehler, *Wilhelm von Humboldt und der Staat* (München, 1927), reprinted (Göttingen, 1963); Eduard Spranger, *Wilhelm von Humboldt und die Humanitätsidee* (Berlin, 1909); Bruno Gebhardt, *Wilhelm von Humboldt als Staatsmann,* 2 vols. (Stuttgart, 1896-99); Friedrich Schaffstein, *Wilhelm von Humboldt. Ein Lebensbild* (Frankfurt, 1952); Wach, *Das Verstehen* (Tübingen, 1926-1933), especially "Die hermeneutischen Lehren Wilhelm von Humboldts," vol. I, chap. IV, pp. 227-266.

²Cf. *Briefwechsel zwischen Schiller und Wilhelm von Humboldt.* A. Leitzmann, ed. (Berlin, 1900).

³Cf. S. A. Kaehler, *Wilhelm von Humboldt und der Staat* (see above, n. 1).

⁴For a description of Humboldt's trip to Paris, see "Tagebuch der Reise nach Paris und der Schweiz" in *Tagebücher* in *Gesammelte Schriften* (Berlin, 1903-1936), hereafter to be cited as *GS,* XIV, pp. 76-236; cf. G. P. Gooch, *Germany and the French Revolution* (London, 1920), pp. 91-118.

⁵*Ideen zu einem Versuch die Grenzen der Wirksamkeit des Staats zu bestimmen* in *GS,* I, p. 180, cf. I, p. 143.

⁶*Ibid.,* I, p. 126.

⁷*Ibid.* See Chaps. III, VI, VII, VIII.

⁸*Ibid.,* I, p. 236.

⁹*Ibid.,* I, p. 106.

¹⁰Cf. *ibid.,* I, pp. 126-127. It is interesting that Humboldt views the state as something mechanical. Organismic concepts of the state generally erased the division between state and society, permitted the

state an active role in society, and considered the liberal state to be mechanical. For Humboldt at this time all states were artificial, not organic parts of society threatened through their intervention in society to turn men into machines.

[11]*Ibid.,* I, p. 106.

[12]*Ibid.,* I, p. 109.

[13]*Ibid.,* I, p. 131. Humboldt ascribes "absolute power" (*Gewalt)* to the state and sees the essential element of the concept of the state in "uncontradicted power (*widerspruchslose Macht);*" cf. discussion in S.A. Kaehler, *op.cit.,* pp. 141-144.

[14]*GS,* I, pp. 131-132.

[15]S. A. Kaehler, *op.cit.,* p. 132.

[16]Lausanne, November 1, 1789; *GS,* XIV, p. 221.

[17]Cf. "Idea for a Universal History from a Cosmopolitan Point of View," in Immanuel Kant, *On History,* ed. Lewis White Beck Indianapolis, (1963), pp. 15-16, 19; also "Perpetual Peace," *ibid.,* pp. 110-111.

[18]*GS,* I, p. 137.

[19]*Ibid.*

[20]*Ibid.,* I, p. 126; cf. "Über den Geist der Menschheit (1797)." *Ibid.,* II, p. 325; Rantzau, "Deutschland und die hedonistische Glückseligkeit," *op.cit.*

[21]*Ibid.,* I, p. 239.

[22]*Ibid.,* I, p. 243.

[23]*Ibid.*

[24]*Ibid.,* I, p. 244.

[25]*Ibid.,* I, p. 245.

[26]*Ibid.,* I, pp. 239-240.

[27]*Ibid.,* I, p. 240.

[28]*Ibid.,* I, p. 127.

[29]*Briefwechsel zwischen Schiller und Wilhelm von Humboldt.* A. Leitzmann, ed. (Berlin, 1900), p. 50.

[30]The book was first published in Breslau in 1851. Some excerpts, including the chapter about war, were published at the time of writing in the *Berliner Monatschrift* and in Schiller's *Neuer Thalia.* For a discussion of Humboldt's reasons for not publishing the book, see Kaehler, *op. cit.,* pp. 146-150.

[31]"Ideen über Staatsverfassung, durch die neue französische Constitution veranlasst. Aus einem Briefe an einen Freund vom August 1791," in *GS,* I, pp. 77-85. The friend was Friedrich Gentz.

[32]*Ibid.,* I, pp. 79-80.

[33]*Ibid.,* I, pp. 82.

[34]"Über die Gesetze der Entwicklung der menschlichen Kräfte," apparently written in 1791 in *GS*, I, pp. 86-96.

[35]*Ibid.*, I, pp. 88-92.

[36]Cf. "Theorie der Bildung des Menschen," a fragment probably written in late 1793 in *ibid.*, I, pp. 282-287.

[37]"Über den Geist der Menschheit" in *ibid.*, II, pp. 324-334.

[38]*Ibid.*, II, p. 324; cf. p. 325.

[39]*Ibid.*, II, p. 325.

[40]S. A. Kaehler in the Introduction to Wilhelm von Humboldt, *Eine Auswahl aus seinen politischen Schriften* (Berlin, 1922), p. 22.

[41]There exists an extensive literature on Humboldt's views on education and his role as a reformer. For a discussion of his ideal of education, see especially E. Spranger, *Wilhelm von Humboldt und das Humanitätsideal* (Berlin, 1909) and "Philosophie und Pädagogik der Reformszeit" in *HZ*, CIV: (1910), pp. 278-321, See also discussions of his role as minister of education in S. A. Kaehler, *Wilhelm von Humboldt und der Staat, op.cit.*; Friedrich Schaffstein, *op.cit.*, and particularly the extensive treatment in Bruno Gebhardt, *op.cit.*, I, pp. 95-368.

[42]*Wilhelm von Humboldt und der Staat, op.cit.*, p. 379. Kaehler is quoting Friedrich Meinecke's remarks about Adam Müller, considering them applicable to Humboldt as well.

[43]"Denkschrift über die deutsche Verfassung (December, 1813)" in *GS*, XI, pp. 95-112.

[44]*Ibid.*, XI, pp. 97-98.

[45]*Ibid.*, XI, pp. 97.

[46]*Ibid.*

[47]From "Beilage zum Bericht des in der zur Bestimmung des Staatsbedarfs niedergesetzen Commission angeordneten Ausschusses," June 15, 1817 in *GS*, XII, p. 170.

[48]Quoted in S. A. Kaehler, *Wilhelm von Humboldt und der Staat*, pp. 276-277.

[49]Quoted *ibid.*, p. 270. For a discussion of Humboldt's orientation toward the French, see the treatment of his diplomatic activity in Bruno Gebhardt, *op.cit.*, Vol. II.

[50]"Denkschrift über Preussens ständische Verfassung (4. Februar 1819). An den Staatsminister von Stein" in *GS*, XII, pp. 225-296.

[51]*Ibid.*, XII, p. 252.

[52]Among the extensive literature on Humboldt's theory of ideas, see the works of E. Spranger (mentioned above, n. 41); also Richard Fester, "Humboldts und Rankes Ideenlehre" in *Deutsche Zeitschrift für Geschichtswissenschaft*, VI (1891), pp. 235-256; L. Ehlen, "Die

Entwicklung der Geschichtsphilosophie Wilhelm von Humboldts," in *Archiv der Geschichte der Philosophie* (1911), XXIV, pp. 22-60; and Eberhard Kessel, "Wilhelm von Humboldts Abhandlung über die Aufgabe des Geschichtschreibers" in *Studium Generale*, II (1949), pp. 285-295.

[53]The most careful study of Humboldt's theory of *Verstehen* is contained in Joachim Wach's *Das Verstehen* (see above, n. 1).

[54]*GS*, III, pp. 350-359. This essay was written some time between 1814 and 1818. See also the essay, "Betrachtungen über die Weltgeschichte," *ibid.*, III.

[55]*GS*, III, p. 353.

[56]*GS*, III, pp. 353-354.

[57]*GS*, III, p. 357.

[58]*Ibid.*

[59]*Ibid.*, III, p. 364.

[60]*Ibid.*, III, p. 354.

[61]*Ibid.*, III, p. 357.

[62]"Über die Aufgabe des Geschichtsschreibers" in *GS*, IV, pp. 35-36. A translation of this essay "On the Historian's Task" appears in *History and Theory*, 6, (1967), pp. 57-71.

[63]*GS*, IV, p. 50.

[64]*GS*, IV, p. 55.

[65]"Das achtzehnte Jahrhundert," written between 1796 and 1797 in *GS*, II, p. 98.

[66]In the Introduction to the above essay (see n. 65) in *GS*, II, p. 2.

[67]Humboldt describes the subject matter of history as the "sum of existence (*Summe des Daseyns)*" in *GS*, IV, p. 37.

[68]*GS*, IV, pp. 35-36.

[69]Although the task which Humboldt assigns the historian approximates that of the philosopher, he carefully distinguishes between history and philosophy in *GS*, IV, p. 46.

[70]*GS* IV, pp. 39-40.

[71]*Ibid.*, IV, p. 41.

[72]*Ibid.*, IV, p. 37.

[73]*Ibid.*

CHAPTER IV: THE THEORETICAL FOUNDATIONS OF GERMAN HISTORICISM II

[1]For a discussion of American interpretations of Ranke, as well as of the extensive German literature on Ranke, see Georg G. Iggers, "The Image of Ranke in American and German Historical Thought" in *History and Theory*, II (1962), pp. 17-40.

[2]Herbert B. Adams used this expression in "New Methods of Study in History," in *Johns Hopkins University Studies in History and Political Science,* II (1884), p. 65, and in "Special Methods of Historical Studies as Pursued at the Johns Hopkins University and formerly at Smith College," in A. D. White, W. F. Allen *et al., Methods of Teaching History* (Boston, 1885), p. 143.

[3]"Leopold von Ranke" in *American Historical Association Papers,* III (1888), pp. 104-105.

[4]"The Practice Method in Higher Historical Instruction" in *Methods of Teaching History* (Boston, 1885), p. 42.

[5]"History and the Philosophy of History" in *American Historical Review,* XIV (1908-1909), pp. 223-236.

[6]Walter P. Webb, "The Historical Seminar: Its Outer Shell and Its Inner Spirit" in *Mississippi Valley Historical Review,* XLII (1955-56), p. 11.

[7]Cf. discussion of the new positivism in German juridical and historical studies in Alfred Heuss's discussion of the question why Mommsen did not write the missing fourth volume of his *Roman History* in *Theodor Mommsen und das neunzehnte Jahrhundert* (Kiel, 1956).

[8]*Man on His Past* (Cambridge, 1954); cf. Andreas Kraus, *Vernunft und Geschichte, op.cit.*

[9]"Über den Zweck dieser Zeitschrift," *Zeitschrift für geschichtliche Rechtswissenschaft* (1815), I, pp. 1-17.

[10]Cf. "Der Bildungswert des römischen Rechts" in *Quellenbuch zur Geschichte der deutschen Rechtswissenschaft,* Erik Wolf, ed. (Frankfurt, 1949); also Friedrich Carl von Savigny, *Vom Beruf unserer Zeit für Gesetzgebung und Rechtswissenschaft,* 2nd ed. (Heidelberg, 1828).

[11]*Geschichten der romanischen und germanischen Völker* (the title significantly in the plural), and *Zur Kritik neuerer Geschichtschreiber,* published separately. Both appear in Ranke's *Sämmtliche Werke,* to be henceforth cited as *SW* (Leipzig, 1873-1890, vols., 33-34); *Zur Kritik,* was considerably revised, so that we shall cite the Leipzig and Berlin 1824 ed. In the appendix of *Zur Kritik,* pp. 182-202 are devoted to "Machiavelli, Especially His Political Writings." Heinrich Leo in the introduction of his translation of Machiavelli's letter, *Die Briefe des Florentinischen Kanzlers und Geschichtschreibers Niccolò di Bernardo dei Machiavelli an seine Freunde* (Berlin, 1826). Ranke replied to Leo privately at first, in a letter acknowledging receipt of a copy of the translation, answering some of Leo's charges, and expressing the hope that their disagreements may not lead to a public dispute (April 21, 1826; *SW,* 53/54), pp. 155-157.

But Leo nevertheless wrote a biting review of Ranke's *Geschichten* . . . and *Zur Kritik* in the *Jenaer Allgemeine Literatur-Zeitung;* Ranke replied in the *Hallische Literaturzeitung (SW* 53/54), pp. 659-666.

[12]*Ergänzungsblätter zur Jenaischen Allgemeinen Literatur-Zeitung* (1828), cols. 129-136.

[13]*Ibid.* See also Meinecke's discussion of Ranke's treatment of Machiavelli in terms of Ranke's views of the relation of ethics and power in *Die Idee der Staatsräson in der neueren Geschichte* (München, 1957), pp. 445-447.

[14]*SW* 33/34, vii.

[15]*Zur Kritik,* pp. 202, 206.

[16]*Die Briefe,* p. xxiii.

[17]*Ibid.,* p. xv.

[18]*Ibid.,* pp. v-viii.

[19]*Ergänzungsblätter,* pp. 138-139.

[20]*SW,* 53/54, p. 663.

[21]*Ibid.,* p. 665.

[22]*Ibid.,* pp. 665-666.

[23]Theodore H. Von Laue, *Leopold Ranke. The Formative Years.* (Princeton, 1950), p. 109.

[24]*Über die Epochen der neueren Geschichte in der Weltgeschichte* IX, ii (Leipzig, 1888). See also Theodor Schieder, "Die Entstehung von Rankes 'Epochen der neueren Geschichte' " in *HZ,* 199 (1964), pp. 1-30.

[25]Particularly in the lectures on the idea of universal history, among the *Nachlass* at the *Westdeutsche Bibliothek* in Marburg, and published in part in Eberhard Kessel, "Rankes Idee der Universalhistorie" in *HZ* 178 (1954), pp. 290-308 and in Erich Mülbe, *Selbstzeugnisse über seine historische Theorie und Methode im Zusammenhang der zeitgenössischen Geistesrichtungen* (Berlin dissertation, 1930), pp. 124-132. These lectures probably were held in 1831. Also significant are Georg Waitz's handwritten notes of a *"Kolleg"* given by Ranke in the Winter Semester, 1935-1936. These notes belong to the *Historisches Seminar* of the University of Göttingen.

[26]Über die Verwandtschaft und den Unterschied der Historie und der Politik," Ranke's inaugural lecture as a full professor (*Ordinarius)* at the University of Berlin in 1836, trans. from the Latin (*SW* 24), pp. 280-293.

[27]The story of the foundation of the two journals is treated in C. Varrentrapp, "Rankes Historisch-Politische Zeitschrift und das Berliner Politische Wochenblatt" in *HZ* 99 (1907), pp. 35-119. Ranke

reflects on the foundation of the *Historisch-Politische Zeitschrift* in his autobiographic "Diktat vom December 1875" (*SW* 53/54), pp. 49-51.

[28]Johann Albrecht Eichhorn, a high official in various positions in the Prussian government, should not be confused with the historian of law, Karl Friedrich Eichhorn, whom we have cited as one of the founders of the Historical School of Law.

[29]For a discussion of Ranke's contacts with the liberal circle around Varnhagen von Ense, see Wilhelm Mommsen, *Stein, Ranke, Bismarck. Ein Beitrag zur politischen und sozialen Bewegung des 19. Jahrhunderts* (München, 1954); also Von Laue, pp. 31-32, and Ranke's "Diktat" *(SW* 53/54), p. 50.

[30]*SW* 53/54, p. 50.

[31]This was partly because Ranke's ponderous, scholarly approach to the political questions of the time failed to attract a broad reading public; see Von Laue, p. 81.

[32]Cf. "Diktat" (*SW,* 53/54), pp. 50-51.

[33]*Historisch-politische Zeitschrift,* I (1832), p. 1; also in *SW* 53-54, p. 3.

[34]*SW*, p. 3-4.

[35]*Ibid.,* p. 3.

[36]*Ibid.,* p. 4.

[37]Essay on "Frankreich und Deutschland," p. 72.

[38]*Ibid.,* p. 71.

[39]*Ibid.,* p. 72.

[40]Cf., essay "Über die Restauration in Frankreich," p. 9.

[41]*Ibid.,* p. 73.

[42]See particularly the essay "Über die Trennung und die Einheit Deutschlands."

[43]*Ibid.,* p. 172.

[44]*Ibid.,* p. 152.

[45]Cf. essay "Frankreich und Deutschland," pp. 66-67.

[46]Cf., "Über die Trennung . . .," p. 150.

[47]*Ibid.,* pp. 148-149.

[48]*Ibid.,* p. 162.

[49]Cf. "Einleitung," pp. 4-5.

[50]Cf. essay "Über die Restauration in Frankreich," pp. 8-60.

[51]There is an extensive literature on Ranke's epistemology and supposed empiricism, including Joachim Wach's treatment in *Das Verstehen,* III, pp. 89-133. Wach sees in Ranke's steady return to life, his dislike for a priorisms, and his search for understanding out of the things themselves the beginning of a tradition which led to Dilthey. Almost all of the German discussions of Ranke have

stressed his philosophic intent (see Georg G. Iggers, "The Image of Ranke"). Recent studies have seen a strong Neo-Platonic element in Ranke's thought, i.e. Carl Hinrichs, *Ranke und die Geschichtstheologie der Goethezeit* (Göttingen, 1954); also Meinecke, *Entstehung des Historismus,* and cf. Moriz Ritter, *Die Entwicklung der Geschichtswissenschaft* (München, 1919), pp. 413-414.

[52]1831 lecture "Über die Idee der Universalhistorie" published in Eberhard Kessel, "Rankes Idee der Universalhistorie" in *HZ* 178 (1954), p. 284.

[53]"Vorwort" to *Die deutschen Mächte und der Fürstenbund* in *SW* 31/32, viii.

[54]Almost all studies of Ranke have attempted to point out similarities and differences between him and Hegel (see Georg G. Iggers, "The Image of Ranke"). The most extensive study of this question is to be found in Ernst Simon, *Ranke und Hegel* (München, 1928).

[55]Cf. comments, "Aus dem Briefwechsel Friedrich Wilhelms IV mit Bunsen," *SW* 49/50, pp. 392-3. See also Gerhard Masur, *Rankes Begriff der Weltgeschichte* (München, 1926), p. 58.

[56]Eberhard Kessel, *op.cit.*, pp. 290-292.

[57]*Ibid.*, p. 294.

[58]*Ibid.*, p. 295.

[59]*Ibid.*

[60]*Ibid.*, p. 296.

[61]*Ibid.*

[62]*Ibid.*, pp. 296-297.

[63]*Ibid.*, p. 301.

[64]*Ibid.*

[65]*Ibid.*, p. 302.

[66]*Weltgeschichte,* 9. Teil, 2. Abt., p. 5.

[67]Generally this has not been fully understood by the many scholars who have stressed the impact of Christian or Lutheran theology on Ranke's thought.

[68]"Die grossen Mächte" in *SW* 24, p. 10. An English translation of this essay is found in Von Laue, pp. 181-218.

[69]*Ibid.*, pp. 39-40.

[70]"Das politische Gespräch" in *SW* 49/50, p. 321; English translation in Von Laue, pp. 152-180.

[71]*Ibid.*, p. 323.

[72]*Ibid.*, p. 325.

[73]*Ibid.*, p. 329.

[74]*Ibid.*, p. 327.

[75]*Ibid.*, p. 328.

[76]*Ibid.*, p. 332.

[77]*Ibid.*, p. 328.
[78]*Ibid.*, p. 333.
[79]*Ibid.*, p. 334.
[80]*Ibid.*, p. 338.
[81]*Ibid.*, p. 334.
[82]*Ibid.*, p. 335.
[83]*Ibid.*, p. 336.
[84]*Ibid.*
[85]*Ibid.*
[86]*Ibid.*, p. 333.
[87]*Ibid.*, p. 337.
[88]*Ibid.*, p. 95.

[89]*Die weltgeschichtliche Erfassung des Orients bei Hegel und Ranke* (Göttingen, 1958), p. 271; cf. Sybel's somewhat similar observation about Ranke in his "Gedächtnisrede" in *Vorträge und Abhandlungen* (München, 1897), p. 305.

[90]"Politische Denkschriften aus den Jahren 1848-1851. Bestimmt für König Friedrich Wilhelm IV, gerichtet an dessen Flügeladjutanten Edwin Freiherrn von Manteuffel" in *SW, 49/50,* pp. 583-623.

[91]For a good discussion of the evolution of Ranke's political ideas, see Mommsen, *Stein, Ranke, Bismarck;* also Otto Diether, *Ludwig von Ranke als Politiker* (Leipzig, 1911), criticized by Friedrich Meinecke, "Zur Beurteilung Rankes (1913)," in *Schaffender Spiegel, Studien zur deutschen Geschichtsschreibung und Geschichtsauffassung* (Stuttgart, 1948). Meinecke defends Ranke against Diether's charge that Ranke had been intellectualistic in his approach to politics and, unaware of the new social forces represented an eighteenth-century outlook. "Ranke," Meinecke asserts, "broke through the confines of the quiet time before the storm in restoring the idea of the unconditional self-determination of the state and that of realistic power politics to a position of honor in his historical writing against all the ideological dogmas of right and left." For an analysis of Ranke's concept of society, see especially Rudolf Vierhaus, *Ranke und die soziale Welt* (Münster, 1957) which rejects the notion that Ranke neglected social forces in his historical writings, but recognizes that he was little aware or little interested in the economic and technical transformation of European society in the nineteenth century.

[92]*SW,* 49/50, p. 605.

[93]*Ibid.*, p. 588; cf. the expression of a very similar sentiment already during the 1830 Revolution in Ranke's letter to Heinrich Ritter from Venice, October 4, 1830: "Can we endure journeymen and street urchins wanting to govern us?" (*SW,* 53/54), p. 242.

[94]*SW,* 49/50, p. 603.

[95]*Ibid.,* pp. 597-598.

[96]Cf. Mommsen, *Stein, Ranke, Bismarck,* pp. 170-171.

[97]*Geschichte der neueren Historiographie* (München, 1936), p. 481.

[98]*Ranke und die soziale Welt* (Münster, 1957), cf. pp. 1-2.

[99]*Ibid.,* p. 116.

[100]*Tagebücher,* Walther Peter Fuchs, ed. (München, 1964), p. 239.

[101]"Die Ranke-Renaissance" in Joachim Streisand (ed.), *Studien über die deutsche Geschichtswissenschaft* (Berlin, 1963-1965), II, p. 130.

[102]*Ranke und die soziale Welt,* p. 125.

[103]*Ibid.*

[104]Cf. *Ibid.,* p. 78.

[105]*Kleinere historische Schriften I* (Stuttgart, 1880-1897), p. 358.

[106]*Deutsche Geschichte des neunzehnten Jahrhunderts* IV (Leipzig, 1889), p. 467; see also 4th ed. (Leipzig, 1899), pp. 413-414.

[107]See pp. 130, 199, 230.

CHAPTER V: THE HIGH POINT OF HISTORICAL OPTIMISM

[1]Leopold V. Ranke, "Über die Verwandtschaft und den Unterschied der Historie und der Politik" in *SW,* 24, pp. 288-289.

[2]Cf. Heinrich von Sybel, "Über den Stand der neueren deutschen Geschichtsschreibung" in *Kleine historische Schriften,* 3rd ed., I (Stuttgart, 1880), p. 358; also Heinz-Otto Sieburg, *Deutschland und Frankreich in der Geschichtsschreibung des 19. Jahrhunderts, 1848-1871* (Wiesbaden, 1958), p. 202.

[3]Cf. Wolfgang Hock, *Liberales Denken im Zeitalter der Paulskirche, Droysen und die Frankfurter Mitte.* (Münster, 1957), and Walter Bussmann, "Zur Geschichte des deutschen Liberalismus im 19. Jahrhundert," *HZ,* 186 (1958), pp. 527-557. Of these men, Rudolf Haym was not a historian in the strict sense, but a philosopher and literary historian.

[4]For a study of the early years of the *Preussische Jahrbücher,* see Otto Westphal, *Welt- und Staatsauffassung des deutschen Liberalismus. Eine Untersuchung über die Preussischen Jahrbücher und den konstitutionellen Liberalismus in Deutschland von 1848 bis 1863* (München, 1919).

[5]E.g., Friedrich C. Sell, *Die Tragödie des deutschen Liberalismus* (Stuttgart, 1953).

[6]Cf. Walter Bussmann "Zur Geschichte des deutschen Liberalismus" (above, n. 3).

[7]Cf. Leonard Krieger, *The German Idea of Freedom, op.cit.*, pp. 4-5, suggests that "the Germans shared so much of and so internally in western norms and practical arrangements that they named their own values and actions in western terms and saw in their divergence only their positive cultural creation within the common western pattern," and that their peculiar idea of liberty founded upon older national assumptions saw princely authority and state power not as the polar antithesis, but as the historical associate of political freedom.

[8]Sometimes more fittingly called "liberal conservatism" (see below n. 106); cf. Hans Rosenberg, *Rudolf Haym und die Anfänge des klassischen Liberalismus* (n. 106). (München, 1933); also Wolfgang Hock, *Liberales Denken im Zeitalter der Paulskirche. Droysen und die Frankfurter Mitte, op.cit.*

[9]Later, however, after his break with liberalism, Heinrich Treitschke became anti-Semitic. Similarly, Max Duncker, although the son of a Jewish mother, expressed his sympathy with the anti-Semitic movements of the 1880's. Cf. *Allgemeine Deutsche Biographie*, 1817-1844 (Frankfurt, 1959). See also below, n. 145.

[10]Cf. Alfred Heuss, *Theodor Mommsen und das 19. Jahrhundert* (Kiel, 1956), and Albert Wucher, *Theodor Mommsen. Geschichtsschreibung und Politik* (Göttingen, 1956). The first two volumes of the projected three-volume biography of Mommsen's life by Lothar Wickert have already appeared. See also *Theodor Mommsen. Eine Biographie* (Frankfurt, 1959-), Albert Wucher, *Theodor Mommsen, Geschichtsschreibung und Politik* (Göttingen, 1956).

[11]Cf. Walter Bussmann, (above n. 3), p. 542.

[12]Quoted in Bussmann, *ibid.,* p. 543. The Bussmann reference to the *Preussische Jahrbücher,* 1866, II, p. 46, is incorrect.

[13]For a discussion of these historians' position on Hegel, see especially Wolfgang Hock (above, n. 3).

[14]Heinrich v. Treitschke, "Frankreichs Staatsleben und der Bonapartismus (1865)" in *Historische und politische Aufsätze III* (Leipzig, 1871), p. 48.

[15]F. Gunter Eyck warns against the overly sharp distinction traditionally made in "English and French Influences in German Liberalism before 1848" in *Journal of the History of Ideas,* 18 (1957), pp. 313-341.

[16]Cf. Heinz-Otto Sieburg, *Deutschland und Frankreich in der Geschichtsschreibung des neunzehnten Jahrhunderts* (Wiesbaden, 1954), p. 94. See also Heinrich Heffter, *Die deutsche Selbstverwaltung im 19. Jahrhundert* (Stuttgart, 1950).

[17]Sieburg (above, n. 16), p. 262.

[18]*Allgemeine Geschichte vom Anfang der historischen Kenntnis bis auf unsere Zeiten,* translated into English as *General History of the World* (Philadelphia, 1840-1841 and 1851).

[19]See the articles in the *Staatslexikon* on "Bewegungspartei und Widerstands- oder Stillstandspartei" and "Konstitution," largely reproduced in Federico Federici, *Der deutsche Liberalismus* (Zurich, 1946). Cf. Eyck (above, n. 15), pp. 325-328.

[20]*Gesammelte und nachgelassene Schriften,* IV (Pforzheim, 1843), p. 400.

[21]*Gedanken über das Ziel und die Aufgabe des deutschen Liberalismus,* reprinted as an Appendix to P. A. Pfizer's *Briefwechsel zweier Deutschen* (Berlin, 1911), pp. 331-366.

[22]*Ibid.,* p. 336.

[23]*Ibid.,* pp. 337-338.

[24]*Ibid.,* p. 341.

[25]*Ibid.,* p. 346.

[26]*Ibid.,* pp. 347-349

[27]*Ibid.,* p. 349.

[28]Dahlmann acted as secretary to the perpetual deputation of the estates of Schleswig-Holstein and defended their interests before the German Diet. After his appointment to the University of Göttingen in 1829, he collaborated on the formulation of the Hanover Constitution of 1832, later revoked by King Ernst August in 1837. On F. C. Dahlmann, see also Hermann Heimpel, *Zwei Historiker. Friedrich Christoph Dahlmann; Jacob Burckhardt* (Göttingen, 1962).

[29]*Die Politik auf den Grund und das Mass der gegebenen Zustände zurückgeführt,* ed. with an Introduction by Otto Westphal (Berlin, 1924), p. 54.

[30]*Ibid.,* p. 55.

[31]*Ibid.*

[32]*Ibid.,* pp. 54-55.

[33]*Ibid.,* p. 55.

[34]*Ibid.,* p. 57.

[35]*Ibid.,* p. 55.

[36]*Ibid.,* p. 56.

[37]*Ibid.,* p. 197. Dahlmann also rejects the theory of civil disobedience.

[38]*Ibid.,* pp. 55-56.

[39]*Geschichte der englischen Revolution,* 1844, and *Geschichte der französischen Revolution,* 1845.

[40]Eduard Fueter, *Geschichte der neueren Historiographie,* 3rd ed. (München, 1936), p. 539.

[41]Quoted in Walter Bussmann (above, n. 3), p. 532. See also Klaus Lutze, *Georg Gottfried Gervinus, seine politische Ideenwelt bis zur "Einleitung in die Geschichte des 19. Jahrhunderts"* (1853). Unpublished dissertation (Freie University Berlin, 1956).

[42]Quoted in Wolfgang Hock (above, n. 3), p. 103.

[43]*Grundzüge der Historik* (Leipzig, 1837).

[44]*Ibid.*, p. 63.

[45]*Ibid.*, p. 20.

[46]*Ibid.*, p. 65.

[47]*Ibid.*

[48]*Ibid.*, p. 67.

[49]Hock, p. 60.

[50]Cf. *Ibid.*, p. 57. Hock considers this to be particularly true in Droysen's case, less in the case of Gervinus.

[51]Gustav Rumelin (1815-1888), political and social theorist and a member of the moderately liberal faction at the Frankfurt Parliament, quoted by Hock, p. 101.

[52]*Grundriss der Historik* (Leipzig, 1868); henceforth to be cited as *Grundriss;* translated into English as *Outline of the Principles of History* with a biographical sketch. E. Benjamin Andrews, trans. (Boston, 1893). On J. G. Droysen, see Günter Birtsch, *Die Nation als sittliche Idee* (Köln, 1964).

[53]*Historik. Vorlesungen über Enzyklopädie und Methodologie der Geschichte.* Rudolf Hübner, ed. (München, 1937), henceforth to be cited as *Vorlesungen.* This edition also contains the *Grundriss der Historik.*

[54]J. G. Droysen to Friedrich Perthes, Berlin, February 8, 1837 in *Briefwechsel,* I. Rudolf Hübner, ed. (Berlin, 1929), p. 118. Hock lists three grounds upon which Droysen criticizes Hegel: Hegel's political position as the "philosopher of restoration," his supposed lack of a truly Christian position, and his failure to understand historical method (See pp. 12-13).

[55]To Friedrich Perthes, Berlin, October 30, 1836 in *Briefwechsel,* I, pp. 103-104.

[56]*Vorlesungen über die Freiheitskriege,* I (Kiel, 1846), p. 5.

[57]Cf. Hock, pp. 14, 17.

[58]*Freiheitskriege,* I, p. 6.

[59]*Geschichte Alexanders des Grossen,* 1833, continued as *Geschichte des Hellenismus,* pp. 1836-43.

[60]For example, in the following essays in Droysen's *Politische Schriften.* Felix Gilbert, ed. (München, 1933): "Preussen und Deutschland (1847)," p. 105 and "Zur Charakteristik der europäischen Krisis (1854)," pp. 338-339.

[61]"Preussen und Deutschland," *ibid.*, pp. 107-110.

[62]"Die politische Stellung Preussens (1844)," *ibid.*, p. 40; cf. Wolfgang Hock, p. 122.

[63]Cf. Hock, p. 123.

[64]*Freiheitskriege,* I, *Vorwort* and p. 284. Cf. Wolfgang Hock, pp. 124-125; also Felix Gilbert, *Johann Gustav Droysen und die preussisch-deutsche Frage* (München, 1931) as Beiheft 20 of the *HZ,* particularly pp. 50-77.

[65]"Die preussische Verfassung (1847)," *Politische Schriften,* p. 72. Cf. in the same essay, p. 96: "Es ist etwas in dem Staate, das höher ist als Regel und Gesetz."

[66]"Preussen und Deutschland," *ibid.*, pp. 114-116.

[67]Cf. Wolfgang Hock, pp. 150-153.

[68]Quoted in Felix Gilbert (above, n. 64), p. 122.

[69]To Wilhelm Arendt, Jena, December 1, 1851 in *Briefwechsel,* II, p. 11.

[70]Friedrich Meinecke in "Johann Gustav Droysen. Sein Briefwechsel und seine Geschichtsschreibung" in *HZ,* 141 (1930), p. 270. Joachim Wach, too, in his chapter on "Die Lehre vom geschichtlichen Verstehen bei Droysen" in *Das Verstehen,* III, pp. 134-188, tends to overemphasize the role of *Verstehen* in Droysen at the expense of Droysen's systematic views of history. For this reason Sybel may have seemed so much closer to the positivists in Wach's judgment than did Droysen (cf. III, pp. 189-190). A more balanced analysis of Droysen's theoretical notions of history is contained in Ernst Meister, "Die geschichtsphilosophischen Voraussetzungen von J. G. Droysen's 'Historik'," *Historische Vierteljahrschrift,* 23 (1926), pp. 25-63 and pp. 199-221.

[71]"Erhebung der Geschichte zum Rang einer Wissenschaft," reprinted in *Grundriss* (above, n. 52), pp. 41-62, and in *Vorlesungen,* pp. 386-405.

[72]See above, n. 53.

[73]*Vorlesungen,* pp. 12, 22.

[74]*Ibid.,* p. 328. The character of this subject matter is morphological, according to Droysen.

[75]*Ibid.,* p. 10.

[76]*Ibid.,* pp. 22-23.

[77]*Ibid.,* p. 24.

[78]*Ibid.,* p. 24.

[79]*Grundriss,* p. 7; slightly different wording in *Vorlesungen,* p. 326.

[80]*Grundriss,* p. 26.

[81]*Ibid.,* pp. 59-60.

82*Vorlesungen*, pp. 25-26.

83*Ibid.*, p. 287.

84*Ibid.*, p. 97.

85*Ibid.*, pp. 339-344; 348-353.

86*Grundriss*, p. 11, and *Vorlesungen*, p. 330.

87*Vorlesungen*, p. 179.

88Cf. *Ibid.*, pp. 179, 183-184, 202-203.

89*Ibid.*, p. 184.

90*Ibid.*, p. 183.

91*Ibid.*, p. 349.

92*Grundriss*, pp. 30-34; *Vorlesungen*, pp. 202-264.

93*Vorlesungen*, p. 207.

94*Ibid.*, p. 264.

95*Ibid.*, p. 182.

96*Ibid.*, p. 181.

97*Grundriss*, p. 27; *Vorlesungen*, pp. 356-357.

98*Vorlesungen*, p. 352.

99*Ibid.*, p. 262.

100*Ibid.*, p. 261.

101*Ibid.*, p. 352.

102*Ibid.*, p. 261.

103*Ibid.*, pp. 260-261.

104*Ibid.*, p. 266.

105Particularly the lectures "Über die Gesetze des historischen Wissens" of 1864 published in *Vorträge und Aufsätze* (Berlin, 1874), pp. 1-20; "Über den Stand der neueren deutschen Geschichtsschreibung" (1856) in *Kleine historische Schriften*, I, pp. 349-364, and "Die christlich-germanische Staatslehre" (1851), *ibid.*, pp. 365-414. The lectures on politics have not been published, but have been analyzed by Hellmut Seier in his dissertation, *Die Staatsidee Heinrich von Sybels in den Wandlungen der Reichsgründerzeit 1862-71* (Freie Universität Berlin, 1956), and his article, "Sybels Vorlesung über Politik und die Kontinuität des 'staatsbildenden' Liberalismus" in *HZ,* 187 (1959), pp. 90-112.

106In "Über den Stand der neueren deutschen Geschichtsschreibung," Sybel remarks that almost all historians of note in the Germany of that time belong to the "liberal-conservative circle, to that fusion, if we may be permitted parliamentary terminology, of the two centers, of the moderate Whigs and the liberal Tories." Among the historians of this orientation he includes Mommsen, Duncker, Waitz, Giesebrecht, Droysen, and Häusser and, despite slight deviations to the left and right, respectively, resulting from the subject matter with which they were dealing, also Gervinus and Hopfner *(Kleine his-*

torische Schriften, I, pp. 362-363.) On "liberal conservatism," see also above, n. 8. On Sybel; see also Hellmut Seier, *Die Staatsidee Heinrich von Sybels in den Wandlungen der Reichsgründungszeit 1862/1871* (Lübeck, 1961), and Hans Schleier, *Sybel und Treitschke. Antidemokratismus und Militarismus im historisch-politischen Denken grossbourgeoiser Geschichtsideologen* (Berlin, 1965), the latter written from the Marxist position.

[107]Heinrich von Sybel's concern with social forces in his *Geschichte der Revolutionszeit* is particularly stressed by Fueter, pp. 537-538. Sybel's name is closely associated with his controversy with the Catholic Austrian historian Julius Ficker on the character and mission of the Holy Roman Empire in the Middle Ages. Sybel, writing from a *kleindeutsch,* Protestant point of view, condemned the universalistic aspirations of imperial policy, its relations with Burgundy, Italy, and the Papacy as injurious to German national interests. Ficker, judging from a Catholic and *grossdeutsch* position, defended the European concept of the medieval empire. A great deal has been written about the "Sybel-Ficker controversy" which need not concern us here. For a discussion of the controversy, see Heinrich von Srbik, *Geist und Geschichte,* II, pp. 33-34 and Gottfried Koch, "Der Streit zwischen Sybel und Ficker und die Einschätzung der mittelalterlichen Kaiserpolitik in der modernen Historiographie" in Joachim Streisand ed., *Studien über die deutsche Geschichtswissenschaft,* I, pp. 311-336.

[108]"Über die Gesetze des historischen Wissens," pp. 3-6.

[109]*Ibid.,* p. 20.

[110]*Ibid.,* pp. 10-11.

[111]Cf. Wach, *Das Verstehen,* III, pp. 189-205; Heinz-Otto Sieburg, *Deutschland und Frankreich in der Geschichtsschreibung des 19. Jahrhunderts (1848-1871),* (above, n. 2), p. 205.

[112]"Über den Stand . . .," pp. 358-359.

[113]*Ibid.,* pp. 355-356.

[114]Hellmut Seier, *Die Staatsidee* (above, n. 105), pp. 41-42.

[115]"Die christlich-germanische Staatslehre," p. 374.

[116]Hellmut Seier, "Sybels Vorlesung," pp. 103, 105.

[117]"Die christlich-germanische Staatslehre," p. 409.

[118]Hellmut Seier, "Sybels Vorlesung," pp. 98-99.

[119]"Die christlich-germanische Staatslehre," p. 374.

[120]Quoted in Seier, "Sybels Vorlesung," pp. 105-106: "The first requirement always remains that the state . . . possess power; the second, that it use its power rightfully; the third, that it further the unfolding of ethical life and of the spiritual aptitudes of the individuals; the final and supreme requirement is that the state bring about

(*verwirklichen*) ethical life based on the free consent of its members."

[121]*Ibid.,* p. 106.

[122]*Ibid.,* p. 107.

[123]*Ibid.,* pp. 111-112.

[124]Hellmut Seier, *Die Staatsidee,* pp. 51-52.

[125]Cf. H. v. Petersdorff, "Max D. Duncker," *Allgemeine Deutsche Biographie* 48 (Leipzig, 1904), p. 184.

[126]Cf. O. Hintze, "Johann Gustav D. Droysen," *ibid.,* 48, pp. 112-13.

[127]*Preussische Jahrbücher,* XI (1863), 635-36.

[128]*Ibid.,* p. 632.

[129]*Ibid.,* p. 636-37.

[130]Cf. Andreas Dorpalen, *Heinrich von Treitschke* (New Haven, 1957), pp. 77-78. For a discussion of Treitschke's political views, also see W. Bussmann, "Treitschke als Politiker" in *HZ* 177 (1954), pp. 249-79; his article, "Heinrich von Treitschke" in *Die Grossen Deutschen* (Berlin, 1957), V, pp. 368-379, and his *Treitschke. Sein Welt- und Geschichtsbild* (Göttingen, 1952); cf. pp. 367-370 on the Haym-Treitschke controversy; also Treitschke's letters to Haym, Leipzig, July 17 and 19, 1863, in *Heinrich von Treitschkes Briefe* (Leipzig, 1912-1920), III, pp. 273-77, and Treitschke's article, "Das Schweigen der Presse in Deutschland," first published on July 17, 1863, in Gustav Freytag's *Grenzboten,* also in *Historische und politische Aufsätze,* IV (Leipzig, 1897), pp. 126-37. For a Marxist assessment of Treitschke, see Hans Schleier, *Sybel und Treitschke* (above, n. 106).

[131]Cf. P. Bailleu, "Heinrich v. Sybel" in *Allgemeine Deutsche Biographie* 54 (Leipzig, 1908), p. 660.

[132]Berlin, June 12, 1864; Droysen, *Briefwechsel,* II, p. 841.

[133]Bonn, June 19, 1864; *ibid.,* II, 848: "I grant you that the power interests must come first for every state. But I also think that you will admit that they must not be the only thing for a nation. Because they come first, I am glad to make very significant and very painful concessions to them. But since they neither can nor may fill the world by themselves, I cannot extend these concessions to the point at which the principle of justice (*Rechtsprinzip*) is annihilated."

[134]"Der deutsche Liberalismus. Eine Selbstkritik," *Historische und politische Aufsätze und Reden* (Strassburg, 1894); p. 175; written for the *Preussische Jahrbücher,* (1866), pp. 455-515.

[135]"Die Freiheit," *Preussische Jahrbücher,* 7 (1861), pp. 381-403.

[136]*Historische und politische Aufsätze* I (Leipzig, 1867), pp. 596-635. In his "Habilitationsschrift" in *Die Gesellschaftswissenschaft* (1859), Treitschke had argued against the political scientist Robert von Mohl that the science of society cannot be separated from the study of the state or of history.

[137]*Einleitung in die Geschichte des neunzehnten Jahrhunderts* (Leipzig, 1853), p. 13.

[138]*Ibid.,* p. 165.

[139]"Vorwort," *Geschichte der deutschen Dichtung,* 5th ed. (Leipzig, 1871), I, vii.

[140]*Allgemeine Deutsche Biographie* (see above, n. 126), p. 113.

[141]Cf. Andreas Dorpalen, *Treitschke.*

[142]Cf. Hermann Baumgarten (above, n. 34), p. 111.

[143]*Preussische Jahrbücher,* VII (1861), p. 381, 392.

[144]See Dorpalen, *Treitschke,* p. 199.

[145]Cf. Dorpalen. His anti-Semitism led to a vigorous declaration by seventy-five Berlin professors in 1880 and to the essay "Auch ein Wort über unser Judentum" by Theodor Mommsen (Berlin, 1880) also in *Reden und Aufsätze* (Berlin, 1905), pp. 410-426. For a collection of contemporary essays by Treitschke, Mommsen, and others, in the famous controversy on anti-Semitism, see the recently published Insel paperback, *Der Berliner Antisemitismusstreit.* Walter Boehlich, ed. (Frankfurt, 1965).

[146]Reproduced in A. Heuss, *Th. Mommsen,* p. 282, and A. Wucher, *Theodor Mommsen,* pp. 218-219.

[147]"Wie wir wieder ein Volk geworden sind" in *Historische und politische Aufsätze und Reden* (Strassburg, 1894), pp. 276-277. For a discussion of Baumgarten's political ideas, see also the biographical essay by Erich Marks in the volume cited above, and the biography by W. Wiegand in the *Allgemeine Deutsche Biographie,* Vol. 55, pp. 437-451. Also Rudolf Haym, "Hermann Baumgarten," in *Gesammelte Aufsätze* (Berlin, 1903), pp. 609-628.

[148]*Treitschke's Deutsche Geschichte* (Strassburg, 1883).

[149]*Historische und politische Aufsätze und Reden* (above, n. 146), p. cxviii.

CHAPTER VI: THE "CRISIS OF HISTORICISM" I

[1]H. Stuart Hughes, *Consciousness and Society. The Reorientation of European Social Thought, 1890-1930* (New York, 1958); Gerhard Masur, *Prophets of Yesterday. Studies in European Culture, 1890-1914.* (New York, 1961); Arnold Brecht, *Political Theory. The Foundations of Twentieth-Century Political Thought* (Princeton, 1959).

[2]Cf. particularly Arnold Brecht.

[3]"Über den Begriff einer historischen Dialektik, Windelband-Rickert und Hegel" *HZ,* 119 (1919), p. 373.

[4]"Rede zum 70. Geburtstag" in *Gesammelte Schriften,* V (Leipzig, 1924), p. 9.

[5]Cf. Christian Graf von Krockow, *Die Entscheidung. Eine Untersuchung über Ernst Jünger, Carl Schmitt, Martin Heidegger* (Stuttgart, 1958).

[6]Arnold Brecht, p. 9.

[7]Cf. Walter Rohlfing, *Fortschrittsglaube im Wilhelminischen Deutschland.* Unpublished dissertation. (Univ. Göttingen, 1955).

[8]Friedrich Meinecke, *Strassburg, Freiburg, Berlin. 1901-1919. Erinnerungen* (Stuttgart, 1949), p. 123.

[9]Cf. entry "Geschichte" in *Schopenhauer-Lexikon* I, Julius Frauenstadt, ed. (Leipzig, 1871), pp. 266-271.

[10]"Vom Nutzen und Nachteil der Historie für das Leben."

[11]"Einleitung" to *Weltgeschichtliche Betrachtungen in Gesamtausgabe* (Stuttgart, 1929-1934), VII, pp. 1, 3. Cf. Rudolf Stadelmann, "Jacob Burckhardts Weltgeschichtliche Betrachtungen," in *HZ,* 169 (1949), pp. 31-72; Theodor Schieder, "Die historischen Krisen im Geschichtsdenken Jakob Burckhardts" in *Schicksalswege deutscher Vergangenheit* (Festschrift für Siegfried A. Kaehler), Walther Hubatsch, ed. (Düsseldorf, 1950), pp. 421-454.

[12]*Neuer Versuch einer alten auf die Wahrheit der Tatsachen gegründeten Philosophie der Geschichte* (München, 1856; reprinted Wien, 1952).

[13]Cf. *Gesamtausgabe,* VII, p. 9; see also Stadelmann (above, n. 11), pp. 54-55.

[14]"Zur Charakteristik der europäischen Krisis" in *Politische Schriften,* pp. 307-342.

[15]Cf. Koenraad W. Swart, "The Idea of Decadence in the Second Empire," in *Review of Politics,* 23 (1961), pp. 77-92.

[16]Cf. e.g., "Zusätze über Ursprung und Beschaffenheit der heutigen Krisis" in *Weltgeschichtliche Betrachtungen, Gesamtausgabe,* VII, pp. 148-159, especially pp. 156-158, trans. in Jacob Burckhardt, *Force and Freedom, Reflections on History;* James Nichols ed. (New York, 1943), pp. 293-300; letter to Friedrich V. Preen, Basel, July 2, 1871, in *Briefe* (Leipzig, 1935), pp. 338-339. The expression *"terribles simplificateurs"* actually appears later in Burckhardt's letter to Preen, Basel, July 24, 1889, *Briefe,* p. 485. On Burckhardt's reaction to the events of 1870-1871, see also Schieder (above, n. 11), pp. 449-450; also Nichols' Introduction to *Force and Freedom,* especially the section, "Burckhardt as Prophet," pp. 30-49.

[17]Cf. Hans-Heinz Krill, *Die Rankerenaissance, Max Lenz und Erich Marcks.* (Berlin, 1962); also Ludwig Dehio, *Deutschland und die Weltpolitik im 20. Jahrhundert* (München, 1955), translated as *Germany and World Politics in the Twentieth Century* (New York, 1960); see especially Chap., "Ranke and German Imperialism," pp. 38-71.

[18]See Heinrich von Srbik, *Geist und Geschichte vom deutschen Humanismus bis zur Gegenwart,* II (München, 1951), p. 1.

[19]For a discussion of positivism in German historiography, see Heinrich Ritter von Srbik, *Geist und Geschichte vom deutschen Humanismus bis zur Gegenwart,* II, pp. 225-226; on Karl Lamprecht, *ibid.,* II, pp. 227-238.

[20]"Johann Gustav Droysen. Sein Briefwechsel und seine Geschichtsschreibung" in *HZ* 141 (1930), p. 250.

[21]Georg von Below, *Die deutsche Geschichtsschreibung von den Befreiungskriegen bis zu unseren Tagen,* 2nd ed. (München, 1924), p. 64. For Georg von Below 1878 was a turning point in German historiography marked by a rebirth of political historiography (Treitschke), and by the rise of politically oriented economic history. Below links this to the political shift of 1878-1879, to Bismarck's neo-conservative, social policy which he hails. (Cf. p. 84.)

[22]*Theodor Mommsen und das 19. Jahrhundert,* pp. 94-98.

[23]Heinrich Treitschke, *Deutsche Geschichte im 19. Jahrhundert* (Leipzig, 1879-1894), 5 vols.; Karl Lamprecht, *Deutsche Geschichte* (Berlin, 1891-1909), 12 vols.

[24]Hans Gehrig, "Schmoller, Gustav von," *Encyclopedia of the Social Sciences,* XIII (New York, 1934), p. 576.

[25]*Grundriss der allgemeinen Volkswirtschaftslehre* (Leipzig, 1901-1904), II, pp. 652-678. For an affirmation of moral progress, see pp. 677-688.

[26]"Naturrecht und deutsches Recht. Antrittsrede, 15. Oktober, 1882," (Frankfurt a/M, 1883).

[27]Cf. Heinrich Heffter, *Die deutsche Selbstverwaltung im 19. Jahrhundert* (Stuttgart, 1950), pp. 525-530. The term *Genossenschaft* is extremely difficult to translate. Its dictionary definition includes "fellowship," "association," "cooperative society," and the like. Otto von Gierke, Carl Friedrich observes, nowhere defined the term clearly "but traced its evolution in contrast with its antithesis *Herrschaft. Genossenschaft* is found where several human beings realize the ends of the group through some form of cooperation of their several wills, while *Herrschaft* is found where group ends are realized through subordination of the wills of the members under one or several commanding wills." ("Gierke Otto von," *Encyclopedia of*

the Social Sciences, VI (New York, 1931), p. 655. See also Gierke, *Das deutsche Genossenschaftsrecht* I (Berlin, 1868-1913), p. 12.

[28]Cf. Friedmann (above, n. 26), p. 174, cf. p. 172; also Heinrich Heffter, *Die deutsche Selbstverwaltung,* p. 528.

[29]H. A. Hodges analyzes philosophic differences between Dilthey and the Neo-Kantians in *The Philosophy of Wilhelm Dilthey* (London, 1952). There is a large literature on Dilthey. For studies of Dilthey and the Neo-Kantians, see also Pietro Rossi, *Lo Storicismo Tedesco Contemporaneo* (n.l., 1956), and from a Marxist point of view, I. S. Kon, *Die Geschichtsphilosophie des 20. Jahrhunderts. Kritischer Abriss.,* Vol. I (Berlin, 1964); also Frank Fiedler, "Methodologische Auseinandersetzung in der Zeit des Übergangs zum Imperialismus (Dilthey, Windelband, Rickert)," in *Studien über die deutsche Geschichtswissenschaft,* II, Joachim Streisand, ed. (Berlin, 1963-   ), pp. 153-178. Attention is called to the as yet unpublished *Habilitationsschrift* on Dilthey by Dr. Peter Krausser, recently accepted by the Free University of Berlin. Krausser sees a much sharper break with German Idealistic epistemology than much of the literature does, and views Dilthey as a forerunner of modern communication theory.

[30]"Rede zum 70. Geburtstag" in *GS* V (Leipzig, 1922-1936), p. 9.

[31]*Einleitung in die Geisteswissenschaften* in *GS,* I, pp. xv-xvi.

[32]*Ibid.,* I, pp. 27-28, 49.

[33]*Ibid.,* I, p. xvii.

[34]*Ibid.,* I, p. xviii.

[35]*Ibid.*

[36]*Ibid.,* I, p. 394; cf. pp. xix, and 392-393.

[37]*Ibid.,* I, pp. 115-116.

[38]*Ibid.,* I, p. 394; cf. p. xviii.

[39]*Ibid.,* I, p. 92; cf. pp. 81-82; "Every theory grasps only parts (*Teilinhalte)* of complex reality."

[40]*Ibid.,* I, p. 31; cf. p. 124.

[41]*Ibid.,* I, p. 41. But compare his use of the term "Nationalgeist," VII, p. 175.

[42]*Ibid.,* I, pp. 50-51; cf. p. 82.

[43]*Ibid.,* I, p. 82.

[44]*Ibid.,* I, p. 74.

[45]*Ibid.,* I, p. 82.

[46]*Ibid.,* I, p. 385.

[47]*Ibid.,* I, p. 44.

[48]*Ibid.,* I, pp. 384-385. All men have a need to find such contexts. For Dilthey this context is grasped by personal experience (*persönliche Erfahrung).* Dilthey calls it "meta-physical" to distin-

guish it from metaphysics, which seeks to subordinate man's life to an objective higher reality. These 'meta-physical' (as distinct from 'metaphysical') experiences *(Erfahrungen),* Dilthey notes, "are so personal, are so directly part of the will, that an atheist may *live* the metaphysical, while the *idea of God* of a convinced believer may be nothing but an empty shell."

[49]*Ibid.,* I, pp. 78-79; cf. pp. 54-55.

[50]*Ibid.,* I, pp. 113-114. Regarding his confidence in the forces of history in German affairs, see Dilthey's *Die Reorganisatoren des preussischen Staates* (1807-1813) in *GS,* XII, pp. 37-130 (first published in 1872). But in his later writings, he rejects the idea of progress (see "Der Aufbau der geschichtlichen Welt in den Geisteswissenschaften," VII, pp. 172-173), and denies progress in metaphysical concepts see ("Die Typen der Weltanschauungen und ihre Ausbildung in den metaphysischen Systemen," VIII, p. 98).

[51]*Ibid.,* I, p. 113.

[52]*Ibid.,* I, p. 97.

[53]"Die Typen der Weltanschauungen . . .," VIII, p. 78.

[54]"Der Aufbau der geschichtlichen Welt . . .," VII, p. 150.

[55]*Ibid.,* VII, p. 170.

[56]Cf. VII, p. 152. Dilthey does not use the term *Struktur* here.

[57]*Ibid.,* VII, p. 171.

[58]*Ibid.*

[59]*Ibid.,* VII, p. 87; cf. p. 131: "Erlebnis, Ausdruck und Verstehen"

[60]*Ibid.,* VII, p. 151.

[61]*Ibid.,* VII, p. 155.

[62]*Ibid.,* VII, p. 154.

[63]*Ibid.,* VII, p. 157.

[64]*Ibid.,* VII, p. 172.

[65]*Ibid.,* VII, pp. 164-166.

[66]*Ibid.,* VII, p. 173.

[67]*Ibid.,* "Die Typen der Weltanschauungen . . .," VIII, p. 78.

[68]*Ibid.,* VIII, p. 86.

[69]*Ibid.,* VIII, p. 79.

[70]*Ibid.,* VIII, pp. 98-99.

[71]"Das geschichtliche Bewusstsein und die Weltanschauungen," VIII, p. 3; cf. "Der Aufbau der geschichtlichen Welt . . .," VII, p. 86.

[72]"Das geschichtliche Bewusstsein . . .," VIII, p. 8.

[73]"Der Aufbau der geschichtlichen Welt . . .," VIII, p. 78.

[74]"Das Wesen der Philosophie," V, pp. 365-366; cf. *The Essence of Philosophy.* Stephen A. Emory and William T. Emery, trans. (Chapel Hill, 1954), p. 27.

[75]"Der Aufbau der geschichtlichen Welt . . .," VIII, p. 114.

[76]"Plan der Fortsetzung zum Aufbau der geschichtlichen Welt in den Geisteswissenschaften," VIII, p. 278; cf. Hodges (above, n. 29), p. 153.

[77]"Rede zum 70. Geburtstag," V, p. 9.

[78]Cf. Hermann Cohen, *Logik der reinen Erkenntnis* (Berlin, 1902), Part I of *System der Philosophie.*

[79]"Die Geisteswissenschaften und die Philosophie" in *Schriften zur Philosophie und Zeitgeschichte,* I (Berlin, 1928), pp. 520, 522.

[80]I, 525. Cf. *Ethik des reinen Willens (*Berlin, 1907), Part II of *System der Philosophie.*

[81]Cf. Ernst Troeltsch, "Der historische Entwicklungsbegriff in der modernen Geistes- und Lebensphilosophie. II. Die Marburger Schule, die südwestdeutsche Schule, Simmel" in *HZ* 124 (1921), pp. 389-395. Also Simon Kaplan, *Das Problem der Geschichte im System der Philosophie H. Cohens* (dissertation, Univ. Jena, 1930).

[82]"Über das Eigentümliche des deutschen Geistes" in *Schriften,* I, 558. The doctoral dissertation by Walter Schutze, *Die Idee der sozialen Gerechtigkeit im neukantischen und christlichsozialen Schrifttum in der zweiten Hälfte des 19. Jahrhunderts* (Leipzig, 1938), written from a Nazi point of view, does not even mention Cohen.

[83]"Über das Eigentümliche des deutschen Geistes" in *Schriften,* I, p. 570; cf. "Kantische Gedanken im deutschen Militarismus," II, pp. 347-354.

[84]"Kantische Gedanken im deutschen Militarismus," II, p. 348.

[85]For a discussion of the ethical character of the state, see *Ethik* (above, n. 80), *passim.* Interesting is Cohen's qualified defense of eudaemonism, pp. 295-296.

[86]"Das allgemeine, gleiche und direkte Wahlrecht," *Schriften,* II, p. 332.

[87]*Ethik,* p. 255.

[88]Cf. Heinrich Rickert, *Wilhelm Windelband* (Tübingen, 1929), p. 14. On Windelband, see also Ernst Troeltsch, "Der historische Entwicklungsbegriff . . ." (above, n. 81), and "Über den Begriff einer historischen Dialektik. Windelband-Rickert und Hegel" in *HZ,* 119 (1919), pp. 373-426.

[90]"Geschichte und Naturwissenschaft. Strassburger Rektoratsrede, 1894" in *Präludien. Aufsätze und Reden zur Philosophie und ihrer Geschichte,* 7th and 8th eds. (Tübingen, 1921), II, pp. 142-145.

[91]*Ibid.,* II, p. 147.

[92]*Ibid.,* II, p. 148.

[93]*Ibid.,* II, pp. 151-152.

[94]*Ibid.*, II, p. 159.

[95]*Geschichtsphilosophie, Eine Kriegsvorlesung. Fragment aus dem Nachlass.* Edited by Wolfgang Windelband and Bruno Bauch. *Kantstudien,* No. 38 (Berlin, 1916), p. 21.

[96]*Ibid.*, p. 39.

[97]*Ibid.*, p. 40.

[98]*Ibid.*, pp. 43-46.

[99]*Ibid.*, p. 40.

[100]*Ibid.*, pp. 50-51.

[101]*Ibid.*, p. 52.

[102]*Ibid.*, pp. 9-11.

[103]*Ibid.*, pp. 56-57.

[104]*Ibid.*, pp. 57, 63.

[105]*Ibid.*, pp. 11-12.

[106]"Über Friedrich Hölderlin und sein Geschick" in *Praludien,* I, 253-254. Cf. Ernst Troeltsch, "Der historische Entwicklungsbegriff . . .," *HZ,* 124 (1921), p. 408, discusses Windelband's "Kulturpessimismus."

[107]"Fichte's Idee des deutschen Staates" (Freiburg, 1890), p. 8.

[108]*Ibid.*, pp. 23-26.

[109]Brecht, *Political Theory* (above, n. 1), pp. 215-231, includes Heinrich Rickert with Georg Simmel, Max Weber, and the legal theorist and political scientist Georg Jellinek among "the fathers" of "scientific value relativism." Cf. Gerhard Masur, *Prophets of Yesterday,* pp. 172-176. Maurice Mandelbaum, on the other hand, calls Rickert a "counter-relativist" in his *The Problem of Historical Knowledge. An Answer to Relativism* (New York, 1938). On Heinrich Rickert, see especially the two Troeltsch articles mentioned above (notes 68 and 73); also Maurice Mandelbaum; Fritz Kaufmann, *Geschichtsphilosophie der Gegenwart* (Berlin, 1931), pp. 5-42; Willy Moog, *Die deutsche Philosophie des 20. Jahrhunderts* (Stuttgart, 1922). Chap. on "Die logische Wertlehre (Windelband und Rickert)," pp. 235-248.

[110]*Kulturwissenschaft und Naturwissenschaft,* 4th and 5th eds. (Tübingen, 1921), pp. 14-18. Translated as *Science and History,* George Reisman, trans.; Arthur Goddard, ed. (Princeton, 1962).

[111]*Kulturwissenschaft . . .,* p. 81.

[112]*Ibid.*, pp. 35-36.

[113]*Ibid.*, pp. 33-34.

[114]*Ibid.*, p. 95.

[115]*Ibid.*, p. 89.

[116]*Ibid.*, pp. 92-93.

[117]*Ibid.*, pp. 21-23.

[118]*Ibid.*, p. 93 (*Science and History*, p. 83).

[119]*Kulturwissenschaft* . . ., pp. 98-100.

[120]*Ibid.*, p. 88.

[121]*Ibid.*, pp. 110-111; cf. *Science and History*, p. 97.

[122]Cf. also Maurice Mandelbaum's critique of Heinrich Rickert (above, n. 109).

[123]*Kulturwissenschaft und Naturwissenschaft*, pp. 156-160.

[124]*Ibid.*, pp. 109-110; also "Geschichtsphilosophie" in *Die Philosophie im zwanzigsten Jahrhundert*, II (Festschrift für Kuno Fischer). Wilhelm Windelband, ed. (Heidelberg, 1904-1905), pp. 101-102.

[125]*Kulturwissenschaft und Naturwissenschaft*, p. 157; cf. *Science and History*, p. 135.

[126]*Kulturwissenschaft und Naturwissenschaft*, pp. 156-157.

[127]Quoted by Heinrich Rickert, *ibid.*, pp. 165-166.

[128]*Ibid.*, pp. 167.

[129]For Heinrich Rickert's interpretation of Max Weber's theory of value, see Rickert's somewhat biographical and eulogistic article, "Max Weber and seine Stellung zur Wissenschaft" in *Logos*, 15 (1926), pp. 222-237. Rickert maintains that Weber was "far removed from anything one calls relativism today"; that Weber intentionally, for pedagogical reasons, overstated his position on value neutrality in his lecture "Science as a Vocation"; that he was concerned with excluding value judgments from the special sciences, but (p. 235) stood much closer to the scientific philosophy concerned with ultimates (which he seemingly opposed) than he was aware.

[130]*Kulturwissenschaft*, p. 162.

[131]*Ibid.*

[132]*Ibid.*, pp. 165-166.

[133]*Ibid.*, p. 99.

[134]*Die Grenzen der naturwissenschaftlichen Begriffsbildung. Eine logische Einleitung in die historischen Wissenschaften* (Freiburg, 1896), pp. 716-717.

[135]*Ibid.*, pp. 723-724.

[136]*Ibid.*, pp. 722-723.

[137]*Ibid.*, p. 730.

[138]*Ibid.*, p. 742; cf. "Geschichtsphilosophie," II (above, n. 109), p. 117.

[139]"Geschichtsphilosophie," II, p. 117.

[140]Cf. Rickert's *Die Philosophie des Lebens. Darstellung und Kritik der philosophischen Modeströmungen unserer Zeit* (Tübingen, 1920).

[141]*Die Grenzen* (above, n. 116), pp. 736-738. See also

Rickert's protest against Troeltsch's assertion in his article on Windelband and Rickert (see above, n. 73) that for him, Rickert, philosophy of history is strictly "formal," concerned with the logic of
historical knowledge, rather than "material," and with the problem
of the meaning of the historical process: *Kulturwissenschaft und
Naturwissenschaft*, p. 163n.

[142]For discussions of Weber's methodology, see Talcott Parsons,
"Weber's Methodology of Social Science," in Max Weber, *The Theory of Social and Economic Organization*. A. M. Henderson and
Talcott Parsons, trans. (New York, 1947), pp. 8-29; also Talcott
Parsons, *The Structure of Social Action* (Glencoe, Ill., 1949), pp.
579-639; H. Stuart Hughes, *Consciousness and Society* (above, n.
1), pp. 278-335; Carlo Antoni, *From History to Sociology*, pp. 119-
184; Ernst Troeltsch, "Der historische Entwicklungsbegriff" *HZ*, 124
(1921), pp. 415-420; Julius Jakob Schaaf, *Geschichte und Begriff.
Eine kritische Studie zur Geschichtsmethodologie von Ernst
Troeltsch und Max Weber* (Tübingen, 1946); Reinhard Bendix,
Max Weber, An Intellectual Portrait (New York, 1960). There is an
important biography by his wife, Marianne Weber; *Max Weber. Ein
Lebensbild* (Tübingen, 1926).

[143]"Die 'Objektivität' sozialwissenschaftlicher und sozialpoli-
tischer Erkenntnis" (first published in 1904) in *Gesammelte
Aufsätze zur Wissenschaftslehre* (to be henceforth cited as *Wissenschaftslehre)* (Tübingen, 1951), p. 175. Translated as " 'Objectivity' in Social Science and Social Policy" in *Max Weber on the
Methodology of the Social Sciences*, trans. and ed. by Edward A.
Shils and Henry A. Finch (Glencoe, Ill., 1949), p. 76.

[144]*Wissenschaftslehre*, p. 154.

[145]"Wissenschaft als Beruf" (delivered in 1918) in *Wis-
senschaftslehre*, p. 587; cf. "Science as a Vocation" in *From Max
Weber: Essays in Sociology*. Trans. and ed. by H. H. Gerth and C.
Wright Mills (New York, 1946), p. 147.

[146]"Der Sinn der 'Wertfreiheit' der soziologischen und
ökonomischen Wissenschaften" in *Wissenschaftslehre*, p. 517.

[147]"Wissenschaft als Beruf" in *Wissenschaftslehre*, pp. 581-582.

[148]"Politik als Beruf" (first published 1919) in *Gesammelte
politische Schriften*, 2nd ed. Johannes Winckelmann, ed., p. 541; cf.
"Politics as a Vocation" in *From Max Weber*, p. 122.

[149]Hughes, *Consciousness and Society*, pp. 302-303.

[150]"Die 'Objektivität' . . ." in *Wissenschaftslehre*, p. 155.

[151]Cf. Hughes, *Consciousness and Society*, pp. 330-331.

[152]"Die 'Objektivität' . . ." in *Wissenschaftslehre*, p. 160. (cf.
Max Weber on The Methodology . . ., p. 63).

[153]*Ibid.*, p. 182; (cf. *Max Weber on The Methodology* . . ., p. 84).

[154]*Ibid.*, p. 173; (cf. *Max Weber on The Methodology* . . ., p. 74). Cf. "Der Sinn der Wertfreiheit . . ." in *Wissenschaftslehre*, pp. 518-519.

[155]See Weber's discussion of Rickert in "Roscher und Knies und die logischen Probleme der historischen Nationalökonomie (1903-1906)," *Wissenschaftslehre*, pp. 1-145.

[156]"Die 'Objektivität' . . ." in *Wissenschaftslehre*, p. 180; (cf. *Max Weber on The Methodology* . . ., p. 80).

[157]"Roscher und Knies . . ." in *Wissenschaftslehre*, pp. 9-12.

[158]"Die 'Objektivität' . . .," *Wissenschaftslehre*, pp. 178-180; cf. "Roscher und Knies . . .," *ibid.*, pp. 12-13.

[159]"Roscher und Knies . . .," *ibid.*, p. 17.

[160]"Roscher und Knies . . .," *ibid.*, pp. 67, 136-317; "Kritische Studien auf dem Gebiet der kulturwissenschaftlichen Logik; I. Zur Auseinandersetzung mit Eduard Meyer," *ibid.*, pp. 226-227; cf. Hughes, *Consciousness and Society*, pp. 304-305.

[161]"Die 'Objektivität' . . .," *Wissenschaftslehre*, p. 151 (cf. *Max Weber on The Methodology* . . ., p. 54).

[162]"Der Sinn der Wertfreiheit . . .," in *Wissenschaftslehre*, pp. 496-497; cf. "Die 'Objektivität' . . .," *ibid.*, pp. 149-150.

[163]"Politik als Beruf" in *GS*, p. 540. (cf. *From Max Weber*, p. 121).

[164]"Die 'Objektivität' . . .," *Wissenschaftslehre*, p. 197.

[165]*Ibid.*, p. 202 (cf. *Max Weber on the Methodology* . . ., p. 101).

[166]For a discussion of ideal type, cf. *Wissenschaftslehre*, pp. 190-212.

[167]*Consciousness and Society*, p. 287.

[168]*From History to Sociology*.

[169]"Die 'Objektivität' . . .," *Wissenschaftslehre*, pp. 181-182 (cf. *Max Weber on The Methodology* . . ., pp. 170).

[170]*Ibid.*, p. 170.

[171]*Ibid.*, pp. 183-184.

[172]"Politik als Beruf" (above, n. 147).

[173]Cf. "Die 'Objektivität' . . .," *Wissenschaftslehre*, p. 154; "Wissenschaft als Beruf," *ibid.*, p. 587.

[174]"Politik als Beruf" in *GS*, p. 540.

[175]*Ibid.*, p. 536.

[176]*Ibid.*, pp. 539-540.

[177]*Ibid.*, p. 538; "Wissenschaft als Beruf," *Wissenschaftslehre*, p. 588.

[178]"Politik als Beruf," *GS,* p. 545 (*From Max Weber,* pp. 125-126).

[179]"Der Nationalstaat und die Volkswirtschaft" in *GS,* pp. 1-25.

[180]*Ibid.,* p. 12.

[181]*Ibid.,* p. 14.

[182]*Ibid.*

[183]*Ibid.,* pp. 12-13.

[184]Cf. "Parlament und Regierung im neugeordneten Deutschland. Zur politischen Kritik des Beamtentums und Parteiwesens," *ibid.,* pp. 294-431, especially pp. 325-328; "Politik als Beruf," *ibid.,* p. 512; cf. Wolfgang J. Mommsen, *Max Weber und die deutsche Politik, 1890-1920* (Tübingen, 1959), pp. 183-184.

[185]"Der Nationalstaat . . ." in *GS,* p. 15.

[186]*Ibid.,* p. 23.

[187]Wolfgang Mommsen, *Max Weber . . .,* pp. 86-88.

[188]*Ibid.,* pp. 153-206.

[189]*Ibid.,* pp. 324-413. For a discussion of Weber's conception of plebiscitarian democracy, see Gustav Schmidt, *Deutscher Historismus und der Übergang zur parlamentarischen Demokratie* (Lübeck, 1964), pp. 226-306.

[190]In 1919 Weber seriously favored a German *levée en masse* to prevent enforcement of the Versailles Treaty, particularly as it regarded the loss of the Eastern territories. Cf. Mommsen, *Max Weber . . .,* pp. 280-323.

[191]Cf. Carlo Antoni, *From History to Sociology,* pp. 136-137; J. P. Mayer in *Max Weber and German Politics,* 2nd ed. (London, 1956) calls Weber's views "a new Machiavellism of the steel age" (p. 109, cf. p. 117).

[192]Mommsen, *Max Weber . . .,* p. 394.

[193]*Ibid.,* p. 408.

[194]Cf. *Ibid.,* pp. 53-54.

[195]See Max Weber's discussion of "progress" in "Der Sinn der Wertfreiheit . . ." in *Wissenschaftslehre,* pp. 504-516.

[196]"Wissenschaft als Beruf," *ibid.,* p. 577; cf. *From Max Weber,* p. 138.

[197]*Wissenschaftslehre,* pp. 578-579.

[198]*Ibid.,* p. 596.

[199]Cf. Reinhard Bendix, *Max Weber, An Intellectual Portrait* (New York, 1960), pp. 450-459.

[200]Wolfgang Mommsen in "Universalgeschichtliches und politisches Denken bei Max Weber" in *HZ,* 201 (1965), pp. 557-612, points to close similarities in Weber and Nietzsche's concept of history and society. Both see the interaction of two forces in history, the

creative individuals and the process of rationalization. The latter is driven by an inner logic of its own. Weber, like Nietzsche, stresses the role of struggle, despises the *Fachmenschen* or *Ordnungsmenschen,* and rejects the ethics of the Sermon on the Mount as unworthy of human dignity. But while Nietzsche sees the great individual stand above the masses, and apart from them, Weber sees the great man as the charismatic leader of the masses. Weber views history as an open process, but questions whether, at this stage of development, a reversal of the tendencies toward bureaucratic rationalization by the charismatic personality is still possible. There has been an extensive literature on Weber in recent years, particularly on his political views. An important collection of conflicting interpretations by German and non-German social theorists of Weber's contribution to modern sociology and political thought is contained in the proceedings of the 1964 convention of the German Sociological Association, published as *Max Weber und die Soziologie heute* (Tübingen 1965).

CHAPTER VII: THE "CRISIS OF HISTORICISM" II

[1]Otto Hintze, "Troeltsch und die Probleme des Historismus" in *HZ,* 135 (1927), p. 189.

[2]Friedrich Meinecke, "Ernst Troeltsch und das Problem des Historismus" in *Werke,* Vol. IV (Stuttgart, 1959), p. 376.

[3]Ernst Troeltsch, *Der Historismus und seine Probleme* in *Gesammelte Schriften,* III, (Tübingen, 1912-1925), p. 677.

[4]Friedrich Meinecke, "Die Entstehung des Historismus," in *Werke,* III, p. 577.

[5]Meinecke discusses these contacts in his two autobiographical books, *Erlebtes, 1862-1901* (Leipzig, 1941), and *Strassburg, Freiburg, Berlin 1901-1919. Erinnerungen* (Stuttgart, 1949) (hereafter cited as *Erinnerungen*); Troeltsch treats them in his very brief autobiographical sketch, "Meine Bücher" (first published in 1922), in *GS,* IV, pp. 3-18.

[6]Cf. *Erinnerungen* (above, n. 5), pp. 153-161.

[7]For an analysis of Troeltsch, Weber, and Meinecke's political ideas during this period, see Gustav Schmidt, *Deutscher Historismus und der Übergang zur parlamentarischen Demokratie. Untersuchungen zu den politischen Gedanken von Meinecke, Troeltsch, Max Weber* (Lübeck, 1964); also K. Schwabe, "Zur politischen Haltung der deutschen Professoren im Ersten Weltkrieg" in *HZ* 193 (1961), pp. 601-634; Georg Kotowski, "Parlamentarismus und Demokratie im Urteil Friedrich Meineckes" in *Zur Geschichte und Problematik*

der Demokratie. (Festgabe für Hans Herzfeld.) Wilhelm Berges and Carl Hinrichs, ed. (Berlin, 1958); Eric C. Kollman, "Eine Diagnose der Weimarer Republik. Ernst Troeltschs politische Anschauungen" in *HZ*, 182 (1956), pp. 291-319; Ernst Troeltsch, *Spektatorbriefe. Aufsätze über die deutsche Revolution und die Weltpolitik,* 1918/22. Hans Baron, ed. (Tübingen, 1924).

[8]*From History to Sociology,* pp. 41-42. For an analysis of Troeltsch's philosophy of history, see especially Walter Bodenstein, *Neige des Historismus. Ernst Troeltsch's Entwicklungsgang* (Gütersloh, 1959), as well as the essay by Otto Hintze and the chap. by Carlo Antoni, *From History to Sociology, op.cit.;* Pietro Rossi, *Lo Storicismo tedesco contemporaneo* (Torino, 1956), and Walther Koehler, *Ernst Troeltsch* (Tübingen, 1941).

[9]Walther Koehler, *Ernst Troeltsch,* p. 1.

[10]*Vernunft und Offenbarung bei J. Gerhard und Melanchton. Untersuchung zur Geschichte der altprotestantischen Theologie* (Göttingen, 1891); published separately in part also as Troeltsch's dissertation.

[11]"Christentum und Religionsgeschichte" (first published in the *Preussische Jahrbücher,* 1897) in *GS,* II, pp. 328-329, 331-32.

[12]For a discussion of this, see especially Walter Bodenstein, *Neige des Historismus.*

[13]"Christentum und Religionsgeschichte" in *GS,* II, p. 336.

[14]*Die Absolutheit des Christentums und die Religionsgeschichte* (Tübingen, 1902), pp. 48-49.

[15]*Ibid.,* pp. iv-v.

[16]*Ibid.,* pp. 3-4.

[17]*Ibid.,* p. iv.

[18]*Ibid.,* p. 54.

[19]*Ibid.,* pp. 62-64.

[20]*Ibid.,* pp. 64, 68.

[21]*Ibid.,* pp. 80, 81, 94.

[22]"Moderne Geschichtsphilosophie" in *GS,* II, p. 697.

[23]*Die Absolutheit des Christentums . . .,* p. 54.

[24]"Die moderne Geschchichtsphilosophie" in *GS,* II, pp. 676-678.

[25]*Ibid.,* pp. 703, 707.

[26]*Ibid.,* p. 711.

[27]*Ibid.,* pp. 709, 711.

[28]*Ibid.,* p. 727; cf. *ibid.,* p. 724. Rickert, as Troeltsch correctly notes, recognizes a metaphysical element in his theory of history.

[29]*Ibid.,* p. 725; cf. pp. 721-725.

[30]*Ibid.,* p. 726.

[31]*Ibid.*, pp. 712, 726.

[32]*Ibid.*, pp. 721, 724.

[33]*Die Soziallehren der christlichen Kirchen und Gruppen* in *GS*, I; translated as *The Social Teachings of the Christian Churches*. Olive Wyon, trans. (London, 1931), 2 vols.

[34]*Ibid.*, pp. 975-977.

[35]*Ibid.*, pp. 15, 33-49, 967.

[36]*Ibid.*, pp. 49, 975-977.

[37]Cf. *ibid.*, pp. 967 ff., especially p. 976.

[38]*Ibid.*, p. 977.

[39]*Ibid.*, p. 973.

[40]*Ibid.*, pp. 973, 52ff., 532; see also "Das stoisch-christliche Naturrecht und das moderne profane Naturrecht" in *HZ*, 106 (1911), pp. 239-267.

[41]*Soziallehren . . .* in *GS*, I, p. 977.

[42]*Ibid.*, p. 978.

[43]*Ibid.*, pp. 983-86.

[44]The most important of these lectures have been gathered in *Deutscher Geist und Westeuropa. Gesammelte kulturphilosophische Aufsätze und Reden,* Hans Baron, ed. (Tübingen, 1925). See also Schmitt and Schwabe; also G. M. Schwarz, "Deutschland und Westeuropa bei Ernst Troeltsch" in *HZ* 191 (1960), pp. 510-47. Klaus Dockhorn criticizes Troeltsch for his juxtaposition of Western Europe and Germany and his emphasis upon a Calvinistic element in English or American history, and stresses the influence of German historicism on English nineteenth-century thought; see his *Die Staatsphilosophie des englischen Idealismus* (Bochum, 1937); *Der deutsche Historismus in England. Ein Beitrag zur englischen Geistesgeschichte des 19. Jahrhunderts* (Göttingen, 1950); *Deutscher Geist und angelsächsische Geistesgeschichte. Ein Versuch der Deutung ihres Verhältnisses* (Göttingen, 1954).

[45]*Soziallehren,* in *GS* I, p. 532; cf. *ibid.*, pp. 525-605.

[46]Cf. *ibid.,* "Das neunzehnte Jahrhundert" in *GS,* IV, pp. 614-649; "Das Wesen des modernen Geistes," *ibid.,* IV, pp. 297-338; G. M. Schwarz, "Deutschland und Westeuropa bei Ernst Troeltsch," (above, n. 44), pp. 517-521.

[47]"Der Geist der deutschen Kultur" (delivered in 1916) in *Deutschland und Westeuropa,* p. 73.

[48]"Privatmoral und Staatsmoral," *ibid.,* p. 151. The unabridged essay is contained in Ernst Troeltsch, *Deutsche Zukunft* (Berlin, 1916), pp. 61-112.

[49]*Ibid.*, pp. 140-141.

[50]*Ibid.*, p. 166.

[51]"Die deutsche Idee von der Freiheit" (delivered in 1916), *ibid.*, p. 94. (Complete text of lecture is in *Deutsche Zukunft,* pp. 7-60).

[52]*Ibid.*, p. 98.

[53]*Ibid.*, p. 94.

[54]*Ibid.*, p. 103.

[55]Same essay, *Deutsche Zukunft,* pp. 27-28.

[56]"Naturrecht und Humanität in der Weltpolitik," *Deutscher Geist und Westeuropa,* p. 22; cf. "The Ideas of Natural Law and Humanity in World Politics" in Otto Gierke, *Natural Law and the Theory of Society, 1500 to 1800.* Ernest Barker, trans. (Cambridge, 1934), I, p. 216.

[57]"Naturrecht . . ." (above, n. 56), pp. 17-18; cf. "The Ideas of Natural Law . . ." (above, n. 56), I, p. 214.

[58]"Uber die Masstäbe zur Beurteilung historischer Dinge" in *HZ,* 116 (1916), pp. 1-47.

[59]*Der Historismus und seine Probleme. I. Das logische Problem der Geschichtsphilosophie* as Vol. III of *GS.* The announced second part on the material philosophy of history, intended to develop Troeltsch's concept of Europeanism, remained unwritten.

[60]In his essay "Meine Bücher" (above, n. 5), pp. 14-15, Troeltsch observes that he considered his work on historicism and his search for a cultural synthesis necessary steps for completing his philosophy of religion which remained his main concern.

[61]"Das neunzehnte Jahrhundert" in *GS,* IV, p. 628.

[62]"Die Krisis des Historismus" in *Die Neue Rundschau,* 33 (1922), pp. 563-574.

[63]*Ibid.*, p. 584.

[64]*Ibid.*, p. 582.

[65]*Ibid.*, pp. 577-582.

[66]Carlo Antoni, *From History to Sociology,* pp. 76-77.

[67]"Die Krisis des Historismus" (above, n. 62), p. 584.

[68]*Der Historismus und seine Probleme,* p. 68.

[69]"Uber Masstäbe . . ." in *HZ,* 116 (1916), p. 38.

[70]*Ibid.*, p. 32.

[71]*Ibid.*, p. 34.

[72]*Ibid.*, p. 4.

[73]*Ibid.*, p. 12.

[74]*Ibid.*, pp. 26-27.

[75]*Ibid.*, p. 28.

[76]*Ibid.*, p. 29.

[77]*Ibid.*, pp. 32-33.

[78]*Ibid.*, pp. 33-34.

[79]*Ibid.,* p. 36.

[80]*Ibid.,* p. 39.

[81]*Ibid.,* p. 38.

[82]*Ibid.*

[83]As the subtitle, "Erstes Buch: Das logische Problem der Geschichtsphilosophie," indicates, this volume primarily deals with what Troeltsch calls the "formal logic of history." In a second volume, which Troeltsch announced in the preface but had no time to write before his death a few months later, he intended to present a "material philosophy of history" and to find in empirical history the indications of a cultural synthesis for the European world of the future.

[84]*Ibid.,* pp. 234-235.

[85]*Ibid.,* pp. 30-31.

[86]*Ibid.,* p. 38.

[87]*Ibid.,* p. 688.

[88]*Ibid.,* p. 38.

[89]*Ibid.,* pp. 32-42.

[90]*Ibid.,* p. 677.

[91]*Ibid.,* p. 706.

[92]Cf. *ibid.,* pp. 694-730.

[93]*From History to Sociology,* p. 83.

[94]*Der Historismus und seine Probleme* in *GS,* I, pp. 166, 182-192 *et passim.*

[95]"Privatmoral und Staatsmoral" in *Deutsche Zukunft,* p. 75.

[96]See Troeltsch's review of Oswald Spengler's *Der Untergang des Abendlandes* in *GS,* IV, p. 684.

[97]*Der Historismus und seine Überwindung* (Berlin, 1924); English ed., *Christian Thought. Its History and Application. Lectures written for Delivery in England during March 1923* (London, 1923).

[98]Of the two book-length studies of Meinecke, Walther Hofer, *Geschichtsschreibung und Weltanschauung* (München, 1950) is devoted to an analysis of Meinecke's theory of history; Richard W. Sterling, *Ethics in a World of Power* (Princeton, 1958) to an analysis of Meinecke's political ideas.

[99]Cf. Meinecke's account of his early life, *Erlebtes, 1862-1901* (Leipzig, 1941), pp. 86-87, 89, 132. *HZ,* 189 (1959), pp. 1-104.

[100]*Ibid.,* p. 96. Cf. Theodor Schieder, "Die deutsche Geschichtswissenschaft im Spiegel der Historischen Zeitschrift" in *HZ,* 189 (1959), pp. 1-104. Schieder discusses Karl Lamprecht's attempt to gain control of the *HZ* upon Sybel's death and Meinecke's vigorous efforts to prevent this.

[101]Cf. *Erlebtes,* p. 132.

[102]*Ibid.,* pp. 206-207.

[103]*Ibid.,* p. 80.

[104]*Das Leben des Generalfeldmarschalls Hermann von Boyen* (Stuttgart, 1896-1899), 2 vols. Cf. Richard W. Sterling, *Ethics in a World of Power,* p. 21.

[105]"Vorwort" to second edition of *Deutsche Geschichte* (Berlin, 1894), pp. vi, vii. For a discussion of the Lamprecht controversy, see also Theodor Schieder (above, n. 101); Friedrich Seifert, *Der Streit um Karl Lamprechts Geschichtsphilosophie* (Augsburg, 1925), and Henrich von Srbik, *Geist und Geschichte von deutschen Humanismus bis zur Gegenwart,* München, 1951, II, pp. 228-239. On Karl Lamprecht, see also Karl Weintraub, *Visions of Culture: Guizot; Burckhardt; Lamprecht; Huizinga; Ortega y Gasset* (Chicago, 1966).

[106]*Alte und neue Richtungen in der Geschichtswissenschaft* (Berlin, 1896), p. 71.

[107]*Ibid.,* p. 44.

[108]Cf. *Erlebtes,* pp. 204-205; Theodor Schieder (above, n. 101). G. von Below's attacks included a review of the first three volumes of Karl Lamprecht's *Deutsche Geschichte* in *HZ,* 71 (1893), pp. 465-498; review of Lamprecht's article, "Die Herrlichkeit Erpel," in *HZ,* 76 (1896), pp. 478-479; "Die neue historische Methode" in *HZ,* 81 (1898), pp. 193-273 and 82 (1899), pp. 567-568. Max Lenz reviewed the fifth volume of the *Deutsche Geschichte* in *HZ,* 77 (1896), pp. 385-447. Hermann Oncken, Max Lehmann, Hans Delbrück, and F. Rachfahl were also actively engaged, Lehmann alone not negatively in his Leipzig inaugural address of 1893. See the comprehensive bibliography in Siefert (above, n. 106). Meinecke's three main contributions to the controversy began with his obituary article on Heinrich von Sybel in *HZ,* 75 (1895), pp. 390-395. The concluding paragraphs on p. 395, indirectly aimed at Lamprecht, gave occasion to Lamprecht's critique in *Alte und neue Richtungen . . .* (above, n. 107), p. 1. Meinecke, in a brief note in *HZ,* 76 (1896), pp. 530-531, criticized Lamprecht's article, "Die gegenwärtige Lage der Geschichtswissenschaft," which had appeared in Maximilian Harden's *Die Zukunft,* 14 (1896), pp. 247-255. Karl Lamprecht countered in *HZ,* 77 (1896), pp. 257-261, and Meinecke replied on pp. 262-266. Lamprecht took the issue up further in *Die Zukunft,* and Meinecke replied very briefly in *HZ,* 78 (1897), pp. 334-335. See also Meinecke's obituary of Lamprecht in *HZ,* 114 (1915), pp. 696-698. The *HZ* declined to publish Lamprecht's *Die historische Methode des Herrn von Below. Eine Kritik* (Berlin, 1899), written in reply to Below's "Die neue historische, Methode" in *HZ* 81 (1898), pp. 193-273, but agreed to distribute it as a

supplement *(Beigabe)* to Vol. 82. See also Karl Lamprecht, *Zwei Streitschriften den Herren H. Oncken, H. Delbrück, M. Lenz zugeeignet* (Berlin, 1897).

[109]"Die neue historische Method" in *HZ,* 81 (1898), p. 208.

[110]"Über individualistische und kollektivistische Geschichtsauffassung" in *HZ,* 78 (1897), pp. 60-67.

[111]*Die historische Methode des Herrn v. Below* (above, n. 108), p. 15.

[112]*Ibid.,* pp. 16-18.

[113]"Was ist Kulturgeschichte? Beitrag zu einer empirischen Historik" in *Deutsche Zeitschrift für Geschichtswissenschaft,* 7 (1896-1897), p. 83. Cf. "Die Historische Methode . . .," p. 25: "The 'general' is epistemologically *(erkenntnistheoretisch)* considered that which constitutes the 'scientific.' "

[114]"Die historische Methode . . .," p. 16.

[115]"Was ist Kulturgeschichte? . . .," pp. 86-87.

[116]*Ibid.,* p. 83.

[117]*Die historische Methode des Herrn v. Below,* p. 18.

[118]*Ibid.,* pp. 20-22.

[119]"Was ist Kulturgeschichte? . . .," p. 92.

[120]*Ibid.,* p. 96.

[121]*Ibid.,* p. 102.

[122]*Ibid.,* pp. 99-102.

[123]Cf. Karl Lamprecht, *Alte und neue Richtungen in der Geschichtswissenschaft,* pp. 7-8; Friedrich Meinecke, "Erwiderung" in *HZ,* 77 (1896), p. 263.

[124]Cf. Lamprecht in *HZ,* 77 (1896), pp. 259-260; Meinecke on pp. 264-265.

[125]"Heinrich von Sybel" in *HZ,* 75 (1895), p. 395.

[126]Cf. "Griechische Kulturgeschichte in der Auffassung Jakob Burckhardt's" in *HZ,* 85 (1900), p. 396; cited by Theodor Schieder, "Die deutsche Geschichtswissenschaft im Spiegel der Historischen Zeitschrift" in *HZ,* 189 (1959), p. 51.

[127]"Geleitwort zum 100. Bande der Historischen Zeitschrift" in *HZ,* 100 (1908), p. 6.

[128]Preface to second edition (1911) of *Weltbürgertum und Nationalstaat. Studien zur Genesis des deutschen Nationalstaates,* as Vol. V, *Werke* (Munchen, 1962), pp. 1-2.

[129]*Ibid.,* pp. 24-25.

[130]*Ibid.,* p. 391; cf. also Meinecke's critique of Niebuhr, *ibid.,* p. 187.

[131]Cf. *ibid.,* p. 83.

[132]*Ibid.,* p. 94.

[133]*Ibid.,* p. 83.

[134]*Ibid.,* p. 185.

[135]See particularly Book II, Chaps. IV and VI.

[136]*Ibid.,* p. 420.

[137]*Ibid.,* p. 445; for a discussion of Meinecke's attitudes toward parliamentary government, see Schmitt, *Deutscher Historismus . . .* (above, n. 7), and Kotowski, "Parlamentarismus und Demokratie im Urteil Friedrich Meineckes" (above, n. 7).

[138]Cf. *ibid.,* p. 418.

[139]*Ibid.,* p. 379.

[140]*Ibid.,* p. 446. Regarding Meinecke's view of the Bismarckian Constitution, see Schmidt, *Deutscher Historismus . . .;* also Georg Kotowski, "Friedrich Meinecke als Kritiker der Bismarckschen Reichsverfassung" in *Forschungen zu Staat und Verfassung.* (Festgabe für Fritz Hartung). Richard Dietrich and Gerhard Oestreich, eds. (Berlin, 1958), pp. 145-162.

[141]*Ibid.,* p. 438.

[142]*Ibid.,* p. 446; cf. pp. 491-492 of first edition (1908).

[143]"Der Sinn unseres Wahlkampfes" (first published in 1912) in *Politische Schriften und Reden,* Vol. II of *Werke,* pp. 51-52. Regarding Meinecke's concept of a plebiscitarian dictatorship, see Schmidt and Kotowski (above, n. 7).

[144]*Erinnerungen,* p. 137.

[145]*Ibid.,* p. 193.

[146]Stuttgart, 1914.

[146]On Meinecke's ideas on war aims in the early phases of the war, see particularly his letters in *Ausgewählter Briefwechsel* (Stuttgart, 1962), published as *Werke,* Vol. VI, to Walter Goetz (Berlin-Dahlem, May 5, 1915), pp. 58-59; to A. Dove (Dahlem, May 23, 1915), p. 61 and (Berlin-Dahlem, July 31, 1915), p. 65; and to W. Goetz (Berlin-Dahlem, October 22, 1915), p. 74. See also "Präliminarien der Kriegsziele (1915)" in *Politische Schriften und Reden, Werke,* II, 101-113, and his disassociation from an annexationist memorandum, *ibid.,* II, 125. In 1917 Meinecke still urged a negotiated exchange of Russian and German populations, *ibid.,* II, 191.

[147]Cf. Meinecke's letters in *Ausgewählter Briefwechsel;* the extensive account of his war-time political activities in his *Erinnerungen;* his journalistic contributions reprinted in *Politische Schriften und Reden, Werke,* Vol. II, and Georg Kotowski's introduction to this volume, as well as Richard W. Sterling, *Ethics in a World of Power;* Gustav Schmidt, *Deutscher Historismus . . .;* Schwabe, "Zur politischen Haltung der deutschen Professoren . . .;" Georg Kotowski, "Parlamentarismus und Demokratie . . ." (above, n. 7).

[148]"Nationalismus und nationale Idee" in *Werke,* II, p. 86. (The essay had actually been written shortly before the outbreak of the war and first published in *Die Deutsche Erhebung von 1914.*) Cf. also "Kultur, Machtpolitik und Militarismus" in *Deutschland und der Weltkrieg.* Edited by Otto Hintze *et al.,* pp. 617-643.

[149]"Politik und Kultur" (written a few days after the outbreak of the war) in *Werke,* II, pp. 80-81.

[150]Letter to Willy Andreas, Berlin, November 7, 1915, in *Werke,* VI, p. 76.

[151]"Die deutsche Geschichtswissenschaft und die modernen Bedürfnisse" in *Die Hilfe,* 22 (1916), p. 225.

[152]"Demobilmachung der Geister" in *Werke,* II, p. 198.

[153]Cf. Walter Hofer's "Einleitung" to *Die Idee der Staatsräson in der neueren Geschichte* (München, 1957) in *Werke,* I, p. 1.

[154]*Erinnerungen,* pp. 191-194.

[155]*Die Idee der Staatsräson* (first published in 1924) in *Werke,* I (München, 1957), p. 1. Translated as *Machiavellism. The Doctrine of Raison d'Etat and Its Place in Modern History.* Introduction by W. Stark; Douglas Scott, trans. (New Haven, 1957).

[156]*Ibid.,* p. 22.

[157]*Ibid.,* p. 5; cf. *Machiavellism,* p. 5.

[158]*Ibid.,* pp. 4-5, 13.

[159]*Ibid.,* p. 13; cf. *Machiavellism,* p. 11.

[160]*Ibid.,* p. 14.

[161]*Ibid.,* p. 25.

[162]*Ibid.,* p. 10.

[163]*Ibid.,* pp. 403-404.

[164]*Ibid.,* p. 241.

[165]*Ibid.,* pp. 365-366; 407-408.

[166]Cf. *ibid.,* p. 245.

[167]Cf. *ibid.,* p. 427.

[168]*Ibid.,* p. 411; *Machiavellism,* p. 350; cf. pp. 432-433.

[169]*Ibid.,* p. 443.

[170]*Ibid.,* pp. 458-459.

[171]*Ibid.,* p. 449; *Machiavellism,* p. 383; cf. Ranke, *Über die Epochen der neueren Geschichte in Weltgeschichte,* 9. Teil, 2. Abt. (Leipzig, 1888), p. 7.

[172]*Idee der Staatsräson, Werke,* I, p. 452; cf. Ranke, "Politisches Gespräch" in SW 49/50, p. 327.

[173]*Idee der Staatsräson, Werke,* I, p. 459; *Machiavellism,* p. 391.

[174]*Ibid.,* pp. 475-477.

[175]*Ibid.,* pp. 481-499.

[176]*Ibid.,* p. 477; cf. *Machiavellism,* pp. 405-406.

[177]*Ibid.,* p. 499; cf. *Machiavellism,* p. 424.

[178]*Ibid.,* p. 502.

[179]*Ibid.,* p. 501; cf. *Machiavellism,* p. 426.

[180]*Ibid.,* p. 503.

[181]*Ibid.,* p. 504; cf. *Machiavellism,* p. 428.

[182]*Ibid.,* p. 494; cf. *Machiavellism,* p. 420.

[183]*Ibid.,* p. 497.

[184]*Ibid.,* p. 1.

[185]*Ibid.,* pp. 15-17.

[186]"Kausalitäten und Werte in der Geschichte" (written in 1925) in *Werke,* IV, p. 85.

[187]*Erinnerungen,* p. 192.

[188]"Kausalitäten und Werte . . ." in *Werke,* IV, p. 85.

[189]"Ernst Troeltsch und das Problem des Historismus" in *ibid.,* IV, p. 378. Meinecke criticizes Troeltsch for having required a practical cultural program from historical scholarship.

[190]*Ibid.,* p. 372; cf. *Die Entstehung des Historismus, Werke,* III, p. 1.

[191]"Ernst Troeltsch . . ." in *Werke,* IV, pp. 373-374.

[192]*Ibid.,* p. 374.

[193]*Ibid.,* p. 376.

[194]"Geschichte und Gegenwart" (delivered in 1930), *ibid.,* pp. 98-99.

[195]Cf. Walter Bussmann, "Politische Ideologien zwischen Monarchie und Weimarer Republik. Ein Beitrag zur Ideengeschichte der Weimarer Republik" in *HZ,* 190 (1960), pp. 55-77, but especially Gustav Schmidt, *Deutscher Historismus* . . . (above, n. 7) and the two essays by Georg Kotowski (above, n. 7 and 140).

[196]Cf. "Ernst Troeltsch . . ." in *Werke,* IV, p. 378.

[197]"Über Spengler's Geschichtsschreibung," a review of *Das Untergang des Abendlandes* first published in 1923, in *ibid.,* IV, p. 188.

[198]"Kausalitäten . . ." in *ibid.,* IV, p. 76; cf. his distinction between spirit *(Geist)* and psychological functions, p. 75.

[199]*Die Entstehung des Historismus, Werke,* III, p. 4.

[200]Cf. the excellent essay by Ernst Schulin, "Das Problem der Individualität. Eine kritische Betrachtung des Historismus-Werkes von Friedrich Meinecke" in *HZ,* 197 (1963), pp. 115-116.

[201]Meinecke distinguishes between two lines of development in German thought of which only one directly prepared the way for German historicism; the other line, of which Lessing, Winckelmann, Schiller, and Kant are the main representatives, led into an "ideal-

izing" rather than "individualizing direction" *(Entstehung . . ., Werke,* III, pp. 287-288.)

[202]*Ibid.,* III, p. 346.

[203]Cf. III, pp. 423-425. Meinecke considered Herder's *Ideen* a "step backward" *(Ibid.,* p. 425) from *Auch eine Philosophie der Geschichte.*

[204]*Ibid.,* III, p. 580.

[205]Cf. Ernst Schulin, "Das Problem der Individualität" (see above, n. 200), p. 117.

[206]Cf. *Entstehung des Historismus, Werke,* III, p. 504.

[207]Meinecke discusses Goethe's negative attitude toward history at length, *ibid.,* III, pp. 504-523, and in "Goethes Missvergnügen an der Geschichte" in Preussische Akademie der Wissenschaften, Philosophisch-historische Klasse, *Sitzungsberichte,* (1933), pp. 178-194.

[208]*Entstehung des Historismus, Werke,* III, p. 580; for a discussion of Goethe's relationship to Enlightenment thought, see *ibid.,* pp. 499-504.

[209]*Ibid.,* pp. 503, 577.

[210]*Ibid.,* p. 579.

[211]Cf. *ibid.,* III, p. 584; Goethe occupied "the most elevated position on history which is perhaps possible." See also p. 581.

[212]*Ibid.,* III, p. 577.

[213]*Ibid.*

[214]*Ibid.,* III, p. 584.

[215]*Ibid.*

[216]*Ibid.,* III, p. 589.

[217]*Ibid.,* III, p. 4.

[218]*Ibid.,* III, p. 2.

[219]Cf., III, pp. 17-18, 602, *et passim.*

[220]*Strassburg, Freiburg, Berlin, 1901-1919; Erinnerungen,* p. 192.

[221]Cf. Ernst Schulin, "Das Problem der Individualität . . .," p. 121; see also Meinecke's letter to S. A. Kaehler (Berlin, October 8, 1935), regarding his assurances to the publisher that the *Entstehung des Historismus* will not be politically embarrassing.

[222]Cf. Golo Mann's critique of Meinecke's continued faith in the reason of state in the review written in 1938 of *Die Entstehung des Historismus* in *Geschichte und Geschichten* (Frankfurt, 1961), pp. 40-46.

[223]April 7, 1938, *Werke,* VI, p. 180.

[224]To G. Mayer (Berlin-Dahlem, June 13, 1938); *ibid.,* p. 180.

[225]To Carl Rabl (Wernigerode, June 12, 1940); *ibid.,* p. 192.

[226]Berlin-Dahlem, July 8, 1940; *ibid.,* pp. 193-194.

[227]*Ibid.,* p. 194.

[228]To W. Goetz (Berlin-Dahlem, May 18, 1943); *ibid., p.* 216. Also, *ibid*.: "I would not be opposed to a fusion with certain elements of National Socialist ideology, presupposing, however, that the golden threat of German and Western spirit regain its importance." The editors, at this point, refer to Chap. IX, "The Positive Elements of Hitlerism" in *Die deutsche Katastrophe.* Regarding the cultural danger of Bolshevism, see letter to W. Goetz (March 22, 1943); *ibid., p.* 214; also to Heinrich von Srbik (April 15, 1944); *ibid., p.* 222; need to resist to the last, cf. to Sabine Rabl (Dahlem, October 26, 1944); *ibid., p.* 226; to her (Dahlem, March 5, 1945); *ibid., p.* 237.

[229]To S. A. Kaehler (Dahlem, June 2, 1944); *ibid., p.* 453.

[230]To S. A. Kaehler (Dahlem, December 31, 1942); *ibid., p.* 411.

[231]*Die deutsche Katastrophe. Betrachtungen und Erinnerungen* (Wiesbaden, 1946), p. 10. Translated as *The German Catastrophe,* Sidney B. Fay, trans. (Cambridge, Mass., 1950), p. 1.

[232]Cf. Chap. VIII, "Der Zufall und das Allgemeine," *ibid.,* pp. 87-104 ("Chance and General Tendencies." pp. 56-70).

[233]*Ibid., p.* 21.

[234]Cf. *ibid.,* pp. 10-18; also Chap. VII, "Der Massenmachiavellismus" ("Mass Machiavellism").

[235]*Ibid., p.* 19.

[236]*Ibid., p.* 23.

[237]*Ibid.,* pp. 21-22, 27-28.

[238]*Ibid.,* pp. 44-45.

[239]*Ibid., p.* 154.

[240]*Ibid., p.* 159; cf. *German Catastrophe,* p. 109.

[241]*Ibid., p.* 161.

[242]*Ibid., p.* 173; cf. *German Catastrophe,* p. 119.

[243]"Ranke und Burckhardt" in *Deutsche Akademie der Wissenschaften zu Berlin, Vorträge und Schriften,* Heft 27 (Berlin, 1948). Translated as "Ranke and Burckhardt" in *German History. Some New German View.* Hans Kohn, ed. (London, 1954), pp. 142-156.

[244]"1848; eine Säkularbetrachtung" (Berlin, 1948), pp. 8-9.

[245]"Irrwege in unserer Geschichte?" in *Werke,* IV, p. 205.

[246]*Ibid.,* pp. 206-207.

[247]*Ibid., p.* 207.

[248]*Ibid.,* pp. 209-210.

[249]*Deutsche Katastrophe,* p. 29 *(German Catastrophe,* p. 15).

CHAPTER VIII: THE DECLINE OF THE GERMAN "IDEA" OF HISTORY

[1]"Die deutsche Geschichtsschreibung der Gegenwart" (first published in 1924) in *Historiker meiner Zeit* (Köln, 1957), p. 419.

[2]The book reviews of Meinecke's *Idee der Staatsräson* offer an interesting barometer of the political climate among German scholars in the 1920's. Even a historian who made his peace with the Weimar Republic, such as Hermann Oncken in the *Deutsche Literaturzeitung,* NF 3 (1926), pp. 1304-1315, bitterly rejected the idea that German thought or policy had placed an undue value on power in the past. Carl Schmitt in the *Archiv für Sozialwissenschaft,* 56 (1926), pp. 226-234, rejects Meinecke's dualism of ethics and power. More sympathetic is Gerhard Ritter's review in *Neue Jahrbücher für Wissenschaft und Jugendbildung,* I (1925), pp. 101-114.

[3]Cf. Hans Kohn, *German History, Some New German Views, op.cit.,* p. 33; Franz Schnabel, *Deutsche Geschichte im neunzehnten Jahrhundert,* I (Freiburg i.B., 1929), pp. 100-101.

[4]"Staat und Nation in der deutschen Geschichtsschreibung der Weimarer Zeit" in *Ausgewählte Aufsätze* (Berlin, 1962), p. 51.

[5]Troeltsch, *Spektatorbriefe, op.cit.,* pp. 68, 69, 153, 159, 165-166, 172; cf. E. C. Kollman, "Eine Diagnose der Weimarer Republik" in *HZ,* 182 (1956), p. 303.

[6]Hans Herzfeld, "Die deutsche Geschichtsschreibung" (above, n. 1), p. 55.

[7]Cf. Hermann Oncken, "Der Sinn der deutschen Geschichte" (delivered in 1924) in *Nation und Geschichte. Reden und Aufsätze, 1919-1935* (Berlin, 1935), pp. 15-44, especially p. 36.

[8]Ludwig Dehio, "Ranke und der deutsche Imperialismus" in *HZ,* 170 (1950), pp. 307-328, discusses Max Lenz, Hans Delbrück, Otto Hintze, Hermann Oncken, Erich Marcks, and Friedrich Meinecke. Hans-Heinz Krill, *Die Rankerenaissance. Max Lenz und Erich Marcks. Ein Beitrag zum historisch-politischen Denken in Deutschland, 1880-1935* (Berlin, 1962).

[9]Cf. Krill (above, n. 8), p. 4.

[10]Cf. the volume, *Deutschland und der Weltkrieg,* edited by Otto Hintze, Friedrich Meinecke, Hermann Oncken, and Hermann Schumacher (Berlin, 1915), which contains essays on this subject by Hintze, Troeltsch, Delbrück, Marcks, Meinecke, and others; also K. Schwabe, "Zur politischen Haltung der deutschen Professoren im Ersten Weltkrieg" in *HZ,* 193 (1961), pp. 601-634; see also Henry Cord Meyer, *Mitteleuropa in German Thought and Action 1815-1945, op.cit.* On Delbrück, see also Annelise Thimme, *Hans Delbrück als Kritiker der Wilhelminischen Epoche* (Düsseldorf, 1955).

[11]Meinecke, "Die deutschen Universitäten und der heutige Staat" (delivered in 1926) in *Werke,* II, p. 407; cf. Troeltsch, *Spektatorbriefe,* pp. 305-306; see also Waldemar Besson, "Friedrich

Meinecke und die Weimarer Republik," *Vierteljahrshefte für Zeitgeschichte,* 7 (1959), pp. 113-29 and Kollman (above, n. 5).

[12]Meinecke, "Verfassung und Verwaltung der deutschen Republik" (written in November 1918) in *Werke,* II, p. 281.

[13]*Ibid.,* p. 282; cf. Waldemar Besson (above, n. 11).

[14]Walter Götz, "Die deutsche Geschichtsschreibung der Gegenwart" (above, n. 1), p. 421.

[15]For a discussion of the Bismarck literature of the 1920's, see the bibliographical article by Lawrence D. Steefel, "Bismarck" in *Journal of Modern History,* 2 (1930), pp. 74-95; also G. P. Gooch, "Revisionism in Germany" in *Times Literary Supplement,* Jan. 6, 1956. Eyck, however, wrote his important work on Bismarck, *Bismarck, Leben und Werk,* only after 1933 and it was published in exile (Zürich, 1941-1944). Cf. Richard H. Bauer, "Veit Valentin, 1885-1947" in *Some 20th-Century Historians,* S. William Halperin, ed. (Chicago, 1961), pp. 103-141, and William H. Maehl, "Erich Eyck, 1878- ," *ibid.,* pp. 227-253. Among works critical of Bismarck, Johannes Ziekursch, *Politische Geschichte des neuen deutschen Kaiserreiches,* 3 vols. (Frankfurt, 1925-1930) is cited; also Arthur Rosenberg, *Die Entstehung der deutschen Republik, 1871-1918* (Berlin, 1928), translated as *The Birth of the German Republic, 1871-1918,* Ian F. D. Morrow, trans. (New York, 1931); H. Kantorowicz, *Bismarck's Werk im Lichte der föderalistischen Kritik* (Ludwigsburg, 1921).

[16]*Gesammelte Abhandlungen zur allgemeinen Verfassungsgeschichte,* 3 vols. Fritz Hartung, ed. (Leipzig, 1941-1943). A more inclusive edition of Vol. I, *Staat und Verfassung,* was edited by Gerhard Oesterreich (Göttingen, 1962). See also Vol. II, *Soziologie und Geschichte* (Göttingen, 1964) and Vol. III, *Regierung und Verwaltung,* (Göttingen, 1967).

[17]Fritz Hartung wrote a biographical essay in *Ges. Abhandlungen* (above, n. 16), I, pp. 5-23, and an obituary in *Forschungen zur brandenburgischen und preussischen Geschichte,* 52 (1941), pp. 199-233, reprinted in Hartung, *Staatsbildende Kräfte der Neuzeit. Gesammelte Aufsätze* (Berlin, 1961), pp. 496-520. More perceptive is H. O. Meisner, "Otto Hintzes Lebenswerk" in *HZ,* 164 (1941), pp. 66-90, except for the unfortunate last few sentences which tend to distort Otto Hintze's position on the Weimar Republic to please the Nazi regime.

[18]Berlin, 1916. For a complete bibliography of Hintze's writings, see *Ges. Abhandlungen,* I, pp. 460-468.

[19]"Antrittsrede" *(Kön. Preussische Akademie der Wissenschaften)* in *Sitzungsberichte* (1914), pp. 745-746.

[20]"Über individualistische und kollektivistische Geschichtsauffassung" in *HZ,* 78 (1897), pp. 60-67.

[21]"Troeltsch und die Probleme des Historismus" in *HZ,* 135 (1927), pp. 188-239; cf. esp. pp. 200-201, 226-227.

[22]Cf. Gerhard Oestreich, "Otto Hintzes Stellung zur Politikwissenschaft und Soziologie" in *Otto Hintze, Soziologie und Geschichte,* 2nd. ed. (see above, n. 16).

[23]"Wesen und Wandlung des modernen Staats" *(Preussische Akademie der Wissenschaften, Philosophisch-Historische Klasse)* in *Sitzungsberichte* (1931), p. 790.

[24]"Soziologische und geschichtliche Staatsauffasung. Zu Franz Oppenheimers System der Soziologie" in *Zeitschrift für die gesamte Staatswissenschaft,* 86 (1929), pp. 38-39; cf. Herzfeld, "Deutsche Geschichtsschreibung . . .," p. 59.

[25]"Wesen und Wandlung . . ." (above, n. 22), p. 792; Review of Rudolf Smend, *Verfassung und Verfassungsrecht* in *HZ,* 139 (1929), p. 561.

[26]"Der moderne Kapitalismus als historisches Individuum. Ein kritischer Bericht über Sombarts Werk" *(Das Wirtschaftsleben im Zeitalter des Hochkapitalismus)* in *Ges. Abhandlungen,* II, pp. 71-123, and "Wirtschaft und Politik im Zeitalter des modernen Kapitalismus," *ibid.,* II, pp. 124-149.

[27]"Troeltsch und das Problem des Historismus" in *HZ,* 135 (1927), pp. 188-239, esp. pp. 209-214, 233-234.

[28]*Ibid.,* pp. 219, 229-230.

[29]*Ibid.,* p. 207.

[30]Cf. "Kelsens Staatslehre" in *HZ,* 135 (1927), p. 75; review of Carl Schmitt, *Verfassungslehre* in *HZ,* 139 (1929), p. 564.

[31]Review of Rudolf Smend, *Verfassung und Verfassungsrecht* in *HZ,* 139 (1929, p. 562; "Wesen und Wandlung . . ." (above, n. 22), p. 809.

[32]"Wesen und Wandlung . . .," pp. 804-806.

[33]"Wirtschaft und Politik . . .," (above, n. 25), pp. 130-32.

[34]Eckart Kehr, "Neuere deutsche Geschichtsschreibung" in *Der Primat der Innenpolitik,* Hans-Ulrich Wehler, ed. (Berlin, 1965), p. 259.

[35]Georg von Below, a highly conservative historian, and L. M. Hartmann, who in 1901 joined the Social Democratic Party, were joint editors. Early contributors to the *Viertelsjahrschrift,* founded in 1903, and its predecessor, the *Zeitschrift für Social-und Wirtschaftsgeschichte* included Theodor Mommsen, Karl Lamprecht, Kurt Breysig, Georg von Below, and Werner Sombart, For the early history of the journal, see Hermann Aubin, "Zum 50. Band der Viertelsjahr-

schrift für Sozial- und Wirtschaftsgeschichte," *ibid.*, 50 (1963), pp. 1-24.

[36]Kurt Breysig, *Kulturgeschichte der Neuzeit; Vom geschichtlichen Werden; Vom deutschen Geist und seiner Wesensart; Die Geschichte der Menschheit; Der Stufenbau und die Gesetze der Weltgeschichte.*

[37]"Neuere deutsche Geschichtsschreibung," (above, n. 34), p. 259.

[38]*Schlachtflottenbau und Parteipolitik 1894-1901. Versuch eines Querschnitts durch die innenpolitischen, sozialen und ideologischen Voraussetzungen des deutschen Imperialismus* (Berlin, 1930).

[39]For a brief biography of Eckart Kehr, see Hans-Ulrich Wehler's "Einleitung" to *Der Primat der Innenpolitik* (above, n. 34), pp. 1-29.

[40]See Wehler's "Einleitung," *ibid.*

[41]"Neuere deutsche Geschichtsschreibung," *ibid.*, p. 261.

[42]Among sociologists who returned from exile, e.g., Theodor Adorno, Max Horckheimer, Helmuth Plessner, among political scientists Ernst Fraenkel and Ossip Flechtheim are democratically oriented.

[43]Cf. Fritz Stern, *The Politics of Cultural Despair, A Study in the Rise of the Germanic Ideology* (Berkeley, 1961); Georg Lukacs, *Die Zerstörung der Vernunft* (Berlin, 1954), a challenging Marxist interpretation of nineteenth and twentieth-century irrationalism as "an international manifestation of the imperialist period." Of writers treated in this book, Lukacs deals especially with Wilhelm Dilthey, Oswald Spengler, Max Weber, Martin Heidegger, and Carl Schmitt.

[44]See discussion of the intellectual temper of 1911 in H. Stuart Hughes, *Oswald Spengler. A Critical Estimate* (New York, 1952).

[45]Cf. Walter Rohlfing, *Fortschrittsglaube im Wilhelminischen Deutschland, op.cit.*

[46]*Geschichte als Sinngebung des Sinnlosen,* 2nd ed. (München, 1921).

[47]See Theodor Lessing's critique of his critics, written in 1927, in "Vorrede" of *Geschichte als Sinngebung des Sinnlosen* (Hamburg, 1962), pp. 9-28. Although Lessing considers any reconstruction of historical development myth-building, he is willing to admit the objectivity of bare event, but does not consider this history (cf. pp. 22-23).

[48]"Über Masstäbe zur Beurteilung historischer Dinge" in *HZ,* 116 (1916), pp. 1-47.

[49]Troeltsch's review of Oswald Spengler's *Der Untergang des Abendlandes* in *Gesammelte Schriften,* IV, p. 684.

⁵⁰*Die Krisis des Historismus* (Tübingen, 1932).

⁵¹"Die 'Objektivität' . . .," *op.cit.,* p. 155; cf. *The Methodology of the Social Sciences,* p. 58.

⁵²"Historismus," *Archiv für Sozialwissenschaft und Sozialpolitik,* 52 (1924), pp. 1-60.

⁵³"Kulturzyklentheorie und das Problem des Kulturzerfalls," *Geisteskultur,* 38 (1929), pp. 65-90.

⁵⁴*Einleitung in die Geisteswissenschaften* (Tübingen, 1920); *Logik und Systematik der Geisteswissenschaften* (München, 1926).

⁵⁵*Logik und Systematik der Geisteswissenschaften.*

⁵⁶Cf. Christian Graf von Krockow, *Die Entscheidung. Eine Untersuchung über Ernst Jünger, Carl Schmitt, Martin Heidegger* (Stuttgart, 1958).

⁵⁷Part I, 6th ed. (Tübingen, 1949). Part I was first published in 1927; a second part never appeared; translated in English as *Being and Time,* John Macquarrie and Edward Robinson, trans. (London, 1962).

⁵⁸*Verlust der Geschichte* (Göttingen, 1959).

⁵⁹*Das Interesse an der Geschichte* (Göttingen, 1959), p. 97.

⁶⁰*Ibid.,* p. 95.

⁶¹"Gegenwartsaufgaben der Geschichtswissenschaft" in *Kapitulation vor der Geschichte?* (Göttingen, 1956), pp. 54-55.

⁶²"Grundfragen der neueren deutschen Geschichte" in *HZ,* 192 (1961), p. 4; cf. "Erneuerung des Geschichtsbewusstseins" in *Staat und Gesellschaft im Wandel unserer Zeit* (München, 1958), pp. 188-207; cf. Werner Conze, "Die Strukturgeschichte des technisch-industriellen Zeitalters für Forschung und Unterricht" in *Arbeitsgemeinschaft für Forschung des Landes Nordrhein-Westfalen. Geisteswissenschaften,* Heft 66 (Cologne, 1957); cf. Fritz Wagner, "Begegnung von Geschichte und Soziologie bei der Deutung der Gegenwart" in *HZ,* 192 (1961), pp. 607-624; also "Rankes Geschichtsbild und die moderne Universalhistorie," *Archiv für Kulturgeschichte,* XLIV (1962), pp. 1-26, and *Moderne Geschichtsschreibung. Ausblick auf eine Philosophie der Geschichtswissenschaft* (Berlin, 1960). The last title acquaints Germans with trends in French, American, and British social history.

⁶³"Eine neue Kriegsschuldthese? Zu Fritz Fischers Buch Griff nach der Welmacht" in *HZ,* 194 (1962), p. 668.

⁶⁴"Aufgaben des Geschichtsschreibers" in *HZ,* 174 (1952), pp. 251-268.

⁶⁵*Die Wiedererweckung des geschichtlichen Bewusstseins* (Heidelberg, 1956), p. 79; cf. *Wege und Irrwege des geschichtlichen*

Denkens (München, 1948), *Geschichtswissenschaft und Geschichtsphilosophie* (München, 1950).

[66]"Die dogmatische Denkform in den Geisteswissenschaften und das Problem des Historismus" *(Akademie der Wissenschaften und der Literatur in Mainz)* in *Abhandlungen geistes- und sozialwissenschaftlicher Klasse* (1954), No. 6 (Wiesbaden, 1954), p. 32; cf. Rothacker's brief autobiography in *Philosophen-Lexikon* (Berlin, 1950), II, pp. 375-382.

[67]*Wahrheit und Methode* (Tübingen, 1960); cf. "Hermeneutik und Historismus" in *Philosophische Rundschau,* 9 (1961-62), pp. 241-276; the article "Geschichtlichkeit" in *Religion in Geschichte und Gegenwart,* II (1958), pp. 1497-1498. The *Historische Zeitschrift* published a long review on *Wahrheit und Methode* by H. Kuhn; see "Wahrheit und geschichtliches Verstehen. Bemerkungen zu H. G. Gadamers philosophischer Hermeneutik," 193 (1961), pp. 376-389. Other discussions of the concept *Geschichtlichkeit* occurred in Gerhart Bauer, *Geschichtlichkeit: Wege und Irrwege eines Begriffs* (Berlin, 1963); Hermann Noack, "Probleme der Geschichtlichkeit" in *Studium Generale,* 15 (1962), pp. 373-389; August Brunner, *Geschichtlichkeit* (Bern, 1961) which questions the absolute historicity of values and truths, and Walther Brühning, *Geschichtsphilosophie* (Stuttgart, 1961).

[68]Martin Heidegger apparently modified his earlier philosophic position. Some of his disciples began to speak of a "turn" *(Wende)* in his thought after World War II from his radically existentialist position in *Being and Time* to the recognition of the reality of an essence transcending the existing individual. Cf. Krockow, *op.cit.,* Chap. iii.

[69]*Geschichte zwischen Philosophie und Politik. Studien zur Problematik des modernen Geschichtsdenkens* (Basel, 1956), p. 10; cf. "Geschichte und Politik" in *HZ,* 174 (1952), pp. 287-306; *Geschichtsschreibung und Weltanschauung. Betrachtungen zum Werk Friedrich Meineckes* (München, 1950). In addition to his studies of historicism, Walther Hofer made important contributions to the study of Nazism and the origins of World War II; cf. his *Die Entfesselung des 2. Weltkrieges* (Stuttgart, 1954).

[70]Cf. "Geschichte und Politik," *op.cit.*

[71]"Die Geschichte im Denken der Gegenwart" in *Wissenschaft und Gegenwart,* No. 16 (Frankfurt, 1947); cf. *Geschichte und Tradition* (Stuttgart, 1948).

[72]"Die Dynamik der Geschichte und der Historismus," *Eranos-Jahrbuch,* 221 (1952), p. 252.

[73]Chicago, 1949, p. 5.

[74]"Die Dynamik der Geschichte . . .," *op.cit.,* p. 247.

[75]Chicago, 1953, p. 18.

[76]*Ibid.,* pp. 23-24.

[77]Cf. Ernst Topitsch, "Zum Problem des Naturrechts" in *Der Staat,* 1 (1962), pp. 225-234.

[78]Historismus und Naturrecht" in *Geschichte und Wissenschaft,* XII (1961), pp. 353-381.

[79]"Zeitgeschichte and the New German Conservatism" in *Journal of Central European Affairs,* 20 (1960), p. 156. Cf. Hans Mommsen, "Politische Wissenschaft und Geschichtswissenschaft" in *Vierteljahrhefte für Zeitgeschichte,* 10 (1962), pp. 341-372.

[80]"Einleitung" in *Propyläen-Weltgeschichte,* VIII (Frankfurt, 1960-   ), p. 14. In striking contrast to the historicist position that man has no nature but only a history stand the three lengthy introductory essays to the new ten-volume *Propyläen-Weltgeschichte.* Man's "intrahuman structure" cannot be perceived from a history of evolution, Alfred Heuss observes in the Introduction to the first volume (p. 19). Through more than fifty pages, the philosopher Helmuth Plessner searches for the *"Conditio Humana,"* the specific, constant human element which appears in all historical change (*ibid.,* I, pp. 33-86).

[81]*Vom Ursprung und Ziel der Geschichte* (Zürich, 1949); English translation (New Haven, 1953).

[82]"Schlussbetrachtungen" in *Propyläen-Weltgeschichte,* X, pp. 623-625.

[83]"Grundfragen der neueren deutschen Geschichte" in *HZ,* 192 (1961), p. 3. Interest in world history has found expression in the journal, *Saeculum. Jahrbuch für Universalgeschichte,* founded in 1950, and edited by Oskar Köhler. One of the co-editors, Joseph Vogt, professor of ancient history at Tübingen, recently published the paperback, *Wege zum historischen Universum: Von Ranke bis Toynbee* (Stuttgart, 1961). Othmar Anderle, formerly at the Institute for European History in Mainz, has founded an Institute for Theoretical History at Salzburg. Strongly influenced by Oswald Spengler, when he contributed to the *Zeitschrift für Geopolitik* in the 1930's, Anderle became a disciple of Toynbee in the postwar period. His institute and the International Society for the Comparative Study of Civilizations is dedicated not merely to the comparative study of institutions, but to the propagation of the view that a morphology of history is possible, that there are self-contained civilizations, and that Russia represents a civilization distinct from the Christian West, a position which contains strong political undertones. Pieter Geyl strongly criticizes Anderle in "Othmar F. Anderle, Un-

reason as a Doctrine" in his *Encounters in History* (Cleveland, 1961), pp. 328-330.

[84]"Das Faktum und der Mensch," *HZ,* 185 (1958), p. 68.

[85]"Gegenwärtige Lage und Zukunftsaufgaben deutscher Geschichts-schreibung" in *HZ,* 170 (1950), p. 9.

[86]"Gegenwartsaufgaben der Geschichtswissenschaft," *op.cit.,* p. 63.

[87]"Der Typus in der Geschichtswissenschaft" in *Staat und Gesell-schaft im Wandel unserer Zeit* (München, 1958), p. 172.

[88]Cf. Werner Conze, "Die Strukturgeschichte . . .," *op.cit.,* p. 18.

[89]"Ranke und Burckhardt" *(Deutsche Akademie der Wis-senschaften zu Berlin), Vorträge und Schriften,* Heft 27 (Berlin, 1948); English translation in *German History. Some New German Views,* Hans Kohn, ed. (Boston, 1954), pp. 141-156.

[90]"Rankes Geschichtsbild und die moderne Universalhistorie" in *Archiv für Kulturgeschichte,* 44 (1962), pp. 6-7.

[91]Dietrich Gerhard divided his duties between the *Amerika-Institut* at the University of Cologne, and the Washington University of St. Louis; later he directed the modern European history section of the *Max-Planck-Institut für Geschichte* in Göttingen until his re-tirement in the summer of 1967, while continuing to teach in St. Louis. Hans Rosenberg has been a visiting professor at the Free University in Berlin. Golo Mann returned from the United States and became a professor at the *Technische Hochschule* in Stuttgart but has since then left Germany for Switzerland. For a Communist inter-pretation of postwar German historiography, see Gerhard Lozek and Horst Syrbe, *Geschichtsschreibung contra Geschichte* (Berlin, 1964).

[92]E.g., Friedrich Meinecke, "Irrwege in unserer Geschichte" in *Werke,* IV, p. 205. For East German discussions of trends in West German historiography since 1945, see Werner Berthold, Gerhard Lozek, and Helmut Meier, "Grundlinien und Entwicklungstendenzen in der westdeutschen Geschichtsschreibung von 1945-1964" in *Wis-senschaftliche Zeitschrift der Karl-Marx-Universität Leipzig,* 14 (1965), pp. 609-622; Gerhard Lozek and Horst Syrbe, *Geschichts-schreibung contra Geschichte* (Berlin, 1964); and Werner Berthold, ". . . grosshungern und gehorchen" (Berlin, 1960).

[93]Stuttgart, 1950.

[94]*Die Tragödie des deutschen Liberalismus* (Stuttgart, 1953).

[95]*Europa und die deutsche Frage. Betrachtungen über die geschichtliche Eigenart des deutschen Staatsdenkens* (München, 1948); a revised version appeared in 1962 under the title *Das deutsche Problem. Grundfragen deutschen Staatslebens gestern und heute* (München, 1962), published in English as *The German Prob-lem: Basic Questions of German Political Life, Past and Present* (Co-

lumbus, Ohio, 1965). For a Communist interpretation of Ritter, see Werner Berthold, ". . . *grosshungern und gehorchen"*, (above, n. 92).

[96]*Deutsche Katastrophe, op.cit.*, p. 154; cf. *The German Catastrophe, op.cit.*, p. 105.

[97]*Staatskunst und Kriegshandwerk* (München, 1954-   ), I, p. 23.

[98]Friedrich   Meinecke,   "Ranke   und   Burckhardt,"   *op.cit.;* Gerhard Ritter, *Vom sittlichen Problem der Macht,* 2nd ed. (Bern, 1961), p. 101.

[99]*Friedrich der Grosse. Ein historisches Profil* (Leipzig, 1936).

[100]*Friedrich der Grosse. Ein historisches Profil* (Heidelberg, 1953); see especially p. 8.

[101]Cf. "The Fault of Mass Democracy" in *The Nazi Revolution, Germany's Guilt or Germany's Fate?* John L. Snell, ed. (New York, 1959), p. 81; also *Carl Goerdeler und die deutsche Widerstandsbewegung* (Stuttgart, 1955), p. 92.

[102]*German Catastrophe,* p. 63.

[103]"Das Problem des Militarismus in Deutschland" in *Historische Zeitschrift,* 177 (1954), pp. 21-48; similar sentiments are expressed throughout *Europa und die deutsche Frage* (above, n. 95).

[104]*Europa und die deutsche Frage,* Chaps. IV and V.

[105]"Das Problem des Militarismus in Deutschland" in *HZ,* 176 (1954), pp. 21-23.

[106]*Ibid.,* pp. 23-26.

[107]*Ibid.,* p. 26.

[108]*Ibid.,* pp. 27-28.

[109]*Ibid.,* pp. 35-37.

[110]*Ibid.,* p. 44.

[111]*Ibid.,* p. 46.

[112]"The Prussian Army and Politics" in *Journal of Central European Affairs,* 15 (1954-1956) pp. 400-405.

[113]*The German Opposition to Hitler,* rev. ed. (Chicago, 1962), p. 41. Similarly, Gerhard Ritter sees Nazism as a European phenomenon, as an aspect of "an epoch of general cultural decay, lack of faith, and nihilism"; see *Europa und die deutsche Frage,* p. 199.

[114]*Ibid.,* p. 24.

[115]See *ibid.,* pp. 45-48.

[116]*Ibid.,* p. 155.

[117]*Ibid.,* p. 101.

[118]*Op. cit.* (above, n. 101).

[119]*Ibid.,* p. 90.

[120]*Ibid.;* see also Das deutsche Problem (above, n. 95), p. 194.

[121]*Carl Goerdeler und die deutsche Widerstandsbewegung,* p. 11.

[122]*Ibid.*, p. 103.

[123]Cf. *Gleichgewicht oder Hegemonie* (Krefeld, 1948), translated as *The Precarious Balance. Four Centuries of the European Power Struggle* (New York, 1962), and *Deutschland und die Weltpolitik im 20. Jahrhundert* (München, 1955), translated as *Germany and World Politics in the Twentieth Century* (New York, 1960).

[124]"Preussisch-deutsche Geschichte, 1640-1945. Dauer im Wechsel" in *Das Parlament* (Beilage, Jan. 18, 1961), pp. 25-31; cf. "Deutschland und die Epoche der Weltkriege" in *HZ,* CLXXIII (1952), pp. 77-94.

[125]Cf. Erich Marcks and Walther Hubatsch, *Hindenburg,* Vol. 32 of *Persönlichkeit und Geschichte* (Göttingen, 1963). See also Walter Hubatsch, *Hindenburg und der Staat. Aus den Papieren des Generalfeldmarschalls und Reichspräsidenten von 1878 bis 1934* (Göttingen, 1966), especially Marcks's Introduction, p. 1. For other works of Hubatsch, see *Eckpfeiler Europas. Probleme des Preussenlandes in geschichtlicher Sicht* (Heidelberg, 1953); cf., e.g., *Das Problem der Staatsräson bei Friedrich dem Grossen* (Göttingen, 1956); *"Weserübung;" die deutsche Besetzung von Dänemark und Norwegen* (Göttingen, 1960); *Germany and the Central Powers in the World War 1914-1918.* Oswald P. Backus, ed. (Lawrence, 1962). Trans. from *Handbuch der deutschen Geschichte,* IV, Part II (Koblenz, 1955); *Hohenzollern in der Geschichte* (Frankfurt a/M, 1961).

[126]*Eckpfeiler Europas,* p. 130.

[127]London, 1961.

[128]*Der erzwungene Krieg; die Ursachen und Urheber des 2. Weltkriegs* (Tübingen, 1961).

[129]*Deutsche Geschichte. Schicksal des Volkes in Europas Mitte* (Gütersloh, 1961).

[130]"Der polnische Grenzstreifen—Wilhelminische Expansionspläne im Lichte heutiger Geschichtsforschung" in *Der Monat,* Heft 171 (Dec. 1962), p. 58.

[131]*Ibid.*

[132]*Bismarck: Leben und Werk,* 3 vols. (Zürich, 1941-1944); a shortened English version, *Bismarck and the German Empire* (London, 1950); published as paperback (New York, 1964).

[133]Quoted in Hans Kohn, "Rethinking Recent German History" in *German History. Some New German Views.* Hans Kohn, ed. (Boston, 1954), p. 35.

[134]Cf. Walter Bussmann, "Zur Geschichte des deutschen Liberalismus im 19. Jahrhundert" in *HZ,* 186 (1958), pp. 527-557; Werner Conze, *Die deutsche Nation* (Göttingen, 1963); Hans

Rothfels, "Zum 150. Geburtstag Bismarcks" in *Vierteljahrshefte für Zeitgeschichte* 13 (1965), pp. 329-343. On the reassessment of Bismarck in German historiography since 1945, see especially Otto Pflanze's Introduction "The Bismarck Problem" to his *Bismarck and the Development of Germany: The Period of Unification, 1815-1871* (Princeton, 1963); also Andreas Dorpalen, "The German Historians and Bismarck" in *Review of Politics,* 15 (1953), pp. 53-67, and various contributions to *German History. Some New German Views* Hans Kohn, ed. (Boston, 1954).

[135]Werner Conze, *Die deutsche Nation.* Conze, like Theodor Schieder in *Das Kaiserreich von 1871 als Nationalstaat* (Köln, 1961), recognizes inadequacies of Bismarck's state, both in its failure as a completed national state and in its undemocratic constitution.

[136]Martin Göhring, *Bismarcks Erben, 1890-1945. Deutschlands Weg von Wilhelm II bis Hitler* (Wiesbaden,1959).

[137]"Bismarck und das 19. Jahrhundert" in *Schicksalswege deutscher Vergangenheit. Festschrift für Siegried Kaehler.* Walther Hubatsch, ed. (Düsseldorf, 1950), p. 247.

[138]"Der Typus in der Geschichtswissenschaft" in *Staat und Gesellschaft im Wandel unserer Zeit* (München, 1958).

[139]Cf. *ibid.,* p. 177; cf. also Werner Conze, "Die Strukturgeschichte . . .," *op.cit.,* p. 18.

[140]Cf. Fritz Wagner, "Begegnung von Geschichte und Soziologie bei der Deutung der Gegenwart" in *HZ,* CXCII (1961), pp. 607-624.

[141]"Rankes Geschichtsbild und die moderne Universalhistorie" in *Archiv für Kulturgeschichte,* XLIV (1962), pp. 1-26.

[142]Theodor Schieder, "Strukturen und Persönlichkeiten in der Geschichte" in *HZ,* CXCV (1962), pp. 265-296.

[143]Cf. Hans Freyer, *Theorie des gegenwärtigen Zeitalters,* 3rd ed. (Leipzig, 1934).

[144]"Zum Problem der historischen Wurzelns des Nationalsozialismus," *Politik und Geschichte,* 13 (1963), No. 5, pp. 19-27.

[145]E.g., Conze's *Die deutsche Nation* (above, n. 134). On the other hand, in the collective volume edited by Conze, *Staat und Gesellschaft im deutschen Vormärz* (Stuttgart, 1962), Conze, Schieder, Brunner and others attempt structural history.

[146]See also Dietrich Gerhard's essay "Vergleichende Geschichtsbetrachtung und Zeitgeschichte" in the collection of his essays, *Alte und Neue Welt in vergleichender Geschichtsbetrachtung* (Göttingen, 1962), pp. 89-107.

[147]The expression "unbewältigte Vergangenheit," approximately translated as "unmastered past," refers to Germany's Nazi past and its antecedents.

[148]Manfred Schlenke, "Geschichtsdeutung und Selbstverständnis

im 19. und 20. Jahrhundert" in *Haltungen und Fehlhaltungen in Deutschland. Ein Tagungsbericht.* Hermann Glaser, ed. (Freiburg i. Br., 1966), p. 75.

[149]Cf. Hans Rothfels's introductory article to the first issue, "Zeitgeschichte als Aufgabe" in *Viertelsjahrhefte für Zeitgeschichte,"* 1 (1953), pp. 1-8; see also Robert Koehl, "Zeitgeschichte and the New German Conservatism" (above, n. 79).

[150]"Zeitgeschichte als Aufgabe," (above, note 149), p. 8.

[151]"Antidemokratisches Denken in der Weimarer Republik" in *Viertelsjahrhefte für Zeitgeschichte,* 5 (1957), pp. 42-62; also Sontheimer's *Antidemokratisches Denken in der Weimarer Republik. Die politischen Ideen des deutschen Nationalismus zwischen 1918 und 1933* (München, 1962).

[152]For a critical discussion of this literature, see Robert Koehl, "Zeitgeschichte and the new German Conservatism" (above, n. 79).

[153]Cf. Hans Maier, "Zur Lage der Politischen Wissenschaft in Deutschland" in *Vierteljahrshefte für Zeitgeschichte,* 10 (1962), pp. 225-249; also Hans Mommsen, "Das Verhältnis von politischer Wissenschaft und Geschichtswissenschaft in Deutschland," *ibid.,* 10 (1962), pp. 341-372.

[154]*Die Auflösung der Weimarer Republik. Eine Studie zum Problem des Machtverfalls in der Demokratie* (Villingen, 1955).

[155]Karl Dietrich Bracher, Wolfgang Sauer, Gerhard Schulz, *Die nationalsozialistische Machtergreifung. Studien zur Errichtung des totalitären Herrschaftssystem in Deutschland* (Köln, 1962).

[156]Cf. "Die Auflösung einer Demokratie. Das Ende der Weimarer Republik als Forschungsproblem" in *Faktoren der Machtbildung* (Berlin, 1952), II, pp. 39-98. Waldemar Besson criticizes Bracher's attempt to apply models to historical situations as contrary to the historian's interest in the particular in the "Einleitung" to his *Württemberg und die deutsche Staatskrise, 1928-1933* (Stuttgart, 1959), but later withdrew this criticism. See also Werner Conze's review of *Die Auflösung der Weimarer Republik* in *HZ,* 183 (1957), pp. 378-382.

[157]"Der Griff nach der Weltmacht" in *Die Kriegszielpolitik des kaiserlichen Deutschland, 1914-1918,* 3rd ed. (Düsseldorf, 1964). English translation, *Germany's Aims in the First World War* (New York, 1967).

[158]Cf. "Weltpolitik, Weltmachtstreben und deutsche Kriegsziele" in *HZ* 199 (1964), pp. 275-278.

[159]*Griff nach der Weltmacht,* p. 12.

[160]*Ibid.*

[161]*Ibid.,* p. 24.

[162]"Eine neue Kriegsschuldthese" in *HZ* 194 (1962), p. 668.

[163]A collection of significant articles on the Fischer book is contained in the Ullstein paperback, *Deutsche Kriegsziele 1914-1918*. Ernst W. Graf Lynar, ed. (Berlin, 1964).

[164]E.g., Vol. 199 (1964) with articles by Fischer and E. Zechlin.

[165]Helmuth Böhme, *Deutschlands Weg zur Grossmacht. Studien zum Verhältnis von Wirtschaft und Staat während der Reichsgründerzeit* (Köln, 1966).

[166]*Der Primat der Innenpolitik* (see above, n. 34).

CHAPTER IX: CONCLUSION

[1]Cf. *Die Soziallehren der christlichen Kirchen und Gruppen in G.S.,* I, pp. 534-548; translated as *The Social Teaching of the Christian Churches, op.cit.,* II, pp. 528-539.

[2]"Das politische Gespräch" in *SW*, 49/50, p. 329; translated in Theodore Von Laue, *Leopold Ranke, The Formative Years, op.cit.,* pp. 168-169.

[3]*Weltbürgertum und Nationalstaat* in *Werke, op.cit.,* V, p. 83.

[4]*Liberalism* (New York, n.d.), p. 158.

[5]Ernest Barker, "Translator's Introduction" to Otto Gierke, *Natural Law and the Theory of Society, 1500-1800* (Cambridge, 1934), I, p.xv-lxxxvii.

[6]"Principles of Political Obligation" in *Works,* II (London, 1911), p. 339.

[7]*Ideen zu einem Versuch die Grenzen der Wirksamkeit des Staates zu bestimmen* in *G.S.,* I, p. 109.

[8]*Der Historiker und die Weltgeschichte* (Freiburg i.B., 1965).

[9]W. H. Walsh, *An Introduction to Philosophy of History* (5th ed., London, 1958), 107. For a similar line of reasoning, see E. H. Carr, *What Is History?* (New York, 1963), pp. 122-123.

[10]Karl Popper, *The Open Society and Its Enemies,* (London, 1945), II, p. 265.

[11]*Einleitung in die Geisteswissenschaften* in *G.S. op.cit.* (Leipzig, 1922-1936), I, 97

[12]*The Origin and Goal of History* (New Haven, 1953).

[13]*What is History?* (New York, 1963).

[14]Cf. E. A. Arab-Ogly, "Filosofiya Istoria Arnolda J. Toynbee," *Voprosy Filosofii,* 1955, no. 4, pp. 113-21. See also Ernst Bloch, "Differenzierungen im Begriff Fortschritt," *Sitzungsberichte der Deutschen Akademie der Wissenschaften. Klasse für Philosophie, Geschichte, Staats-, Rechts-und Wirtschaftswissenschaften,* 1955, no. 5, pp. 1-44.

Suggested Readings

[The following bibliography is not intended to be complete. The listing of the secondary literature is selective. Primary works discussed in this book are not included here unless they themselves are histories of historiography or historical thought.]

There are a number of histories of historiography which contain lengthy discussions of the German development. These include Eduard Fueter, *Geschichte der neueren Historiographie,* 3rd ed. (München, 1936); James Westfall Thompson, *A History of Historical Writing* (New York, 1942), 2 vols.; Moriz Ritter, *Die Entwicklung der Geschichtswissenschaft an den führenden Werken betrachtet* (München, 1919); Harry Elmer Barnes, *A History of Historical Writing,* 2nd. ed. (New York, 1962); Matthew A. Fitzsimons *et al., The Development of Historiography* (Harrisburg, Pa., 1954); George P. Gooch, *History and Historians in the Nineteenth Century* (London, 1914; reprinted Boston, 1959). Only Fitzsimons and Barnes have even brief treatments of twentieth-century German historians, exceedingly brief in Barnes. The best bibliography on German historiography is contained in Fritz Wagner, *Geschichtswissenschaft* (Freiburg i. Br., 1951), an anthology of historical writings.

There have been only two recent comprehensive studies of German historiography in German, none in English. One of these, Heinrich von Srbik's *Geist und Geschichte vom deutschen Humanismus bis zur Gegenwart,* 2 vols. (München, 1950-1951) was written by an Austrian advocate of a Greater Germany, a historian still steeped in German Idealistic traditions. The other, *Studien über die deutsche Geschichtswissenschaft,* ed. Joachim Streisand, 2 vols. (Berlin, 1963-1965), is a collection of essays by East German Marxist historians. Both works include discussions of twentieth-century German historians. Older works include Franz X. von Wegele, *Geschichte der Deutschen Historiographie seit dem Auftreten des Humanismus* (München, 1885) which deals primarily with pre-Rankean historiography but includes a brief section on nineteenth-century historians; Ottokar Lorenz, *Die Geschichtswissenschaft in Hauptrichtungen und Aufgaben,* 2 vols. (Berlin, 1886-1891), a broad history of German historiography in the nineteenth century with particular emphasis on Ranke; and Georg von Below, *Die deutsche Geschichtschreibung von den Befreiungskriegen bis zu unseren Tagen* (Leipzig, 1916), also a

349

broad treatment of German historiography since Herder, emphasizing the role of Romanticism, Ranke, and the Prussian School but also dealing with cultural history, economic history, and the role of Marxism in German historiography. Antoine Guilland, *L'Allemagne nouvelle et ses historiens. Niebuhr—Ranke—Mommsen—Sybel—Treitschke* (Paris, 1899), appeared in English as *Modern Germany and Her Historians* (London, 1915). Good discussions of German historians are also contained in Heinz-Otto Sieburg, *Deutschland und Frankreich in der Geschichtsschreibung des 19. Jahrhundert,* 2 vols. (Wiesbaden, 1954-1958), which covers the years from 1815 to 1871. On conflicting political and national aims of German historians, see Gustav Wolf, Dietrich Schäfer, and Hans Delbrück, *Nationale Ziele der deutschen Geschichtschreibung seit der französischen Revolution* (Gotha, 1918). There has been no comprehensive work on philosophy of history in Germany since Robert Flint, *The Philosophy of History in France and Germany* (Edinburgh, 1874).

For a discussion of the meanings of the term "historicism," see Dwight E. Lee and Robert N. Beck, "The Meaning of 'Historicism'," *American Historical Review,* 59 (1953-1954), pp. 568-77; also Karl Heussi, *Die Krisis des Historismus* (Tübingen, 1932), especially pp. 1-21. On the *Verstehen* theory of knowledge in the nineteenth century, see Joachim Wach, *Das Verstehen. Grundzüge einer Geschichte der hermeneutischen Theorie im 19. Jahrhundert,* 3 vol. (Tübingen, 1926-1933); also Erich Rothacker, *Einleitung in die Geisteswissenschaften* (Tübingen, 1920); and Hans-Georg Gadamer, *Wahrheit und Methode* (Tübingen, 1960).

On the varieties of historicism, German and non-German, in the eighteenth and nineteenth centuries, see especially, Carlo Antoni, *Lo Storicismo* (Roma, 1957), translated into French as *L'Historisme* (Génève, 1963). On the roots of German historicism in seventeenth- and eighteenth-century European thought see Friedrich Meinecke, *Die Entstehung des Historismus,* vol. III of *Werke* (München, 1959). The early history of German historicism into the mid-nineteenth century is discussed in Friedrich Engel-Janosi, *The Growth of German Historicism* (Baltimore, 1944). A broad historical survey of German historicism is contained in Maarten Cornelis Brands, *Historisme als Ideologie. Het 'Onpolitieke' en 'Anti-Normatieve' Element in de duitse Geschiedwetenschap* (Assen, 1965).

For a discussion of German historical science in the eighteenth century, see Andreas Kraus, *Vernunft und Geschichte. Die Bedeutung der deutschen Akademien für die Geschichtswissenschaft im späten 18. Jahrhundert* (Freiburg i. Br., 1963). Herbert Butterfield,

Man on His Past. A Study of Historical Scholarship (Boston, 1960) discusses the transition from the concern of the Göttingen historians with universal history in the eighteenth century to the Rankean historiography of the nineteenth century. On eighteenth-century German historical thought, see Joachim Streisand, *Geschichtliches Denken von der deutschen Frühaufklärung bis zur Klassik* (Berlin, 1964).

There is an extensive literature on Herder, including several works in English. On Herder's conception of history, see especially Rudolf Stadelmann, *Der historische Sinn bei Herder* (Halle, 1928). See also Wilhelm Dobbek, *Johann Gottfried Herder* (Weimar, 1950); Robert Reinhold Ergang, *Herder and the Foundations of German Nationalism;* F. M. Barnard, *Herder's Social and Political Thought. From Enlightenment to Nationalism* (Oxford, 1965); Robert Clark, *Herder, His Life and Thought* (Berkeley, 1955); G. A. Wells, *Herder and After* ('s Gravenhage, 1959). On Herder in the general intellectual setting of his time, see also Roy Pascal, *The German Sturm und Drang* (Manchester, 1953) and especially H. A. Korff, *Geist der Goethezeit,* 4 vols. (Leipzig, 1923-1958), particularly vols. I and II.

On German thought in the period of the French Revolution and Napoleon, see Reinhold Aris, *History of Political Thought in Germany from 1789 to 1815* (London, 1936); G. P. Gooch, *Germany and the French Revolution* (London, 1920); and Jacques Droz, *L'Allemagne et la Révolution Française* (Paris, 1949). For two very different approaches to the emergence of German nationalism, see Friedrich Meinecke, *Weltbürgertum und Nationalstaat,* vol. V of *Werke* (München, 1962) and Eugene N. Anderson, *Nationalism and the Cultural Crisis in Prussia, 1806-1815* (New York, 1939).

On Wilhelm von Humboldt, see especially Siegfried Kaehler, *Wilhelm von Humboldt und der Staat* (München, 1927); also Eduard Spranger, *Wilhelm von Humboldt und die Humanitätsidee* (Berlin, 1909); Bruno Gebhardt, *Wilhelm von Humboldt als Staatsmann,* 2 vols. (Stuttgart, 1896-1899); and Friedrich Schaffstein, *Wilhelm von Humboldt, Ein Lebensbild* (Frankfurt, 1952).

There is an immense literature on Ranke. For a discussion of this literature, see Georg G. Iggers, "The Image of Ranke in American and German Historical Thought," *History and Theory,* II (1962), 17-40. On Ranke's conception of history, see particularly Theodore Von Laue, *Leopold Ranke, The Formative Years* (Princeton, 1950); Carl Hinrichs, *Ranke und die Geschichtstheologie der Goethezeit* (Göttingen, 1954); Gerhard Masur, *Rankes Begriff der Weltgeschichte* (München, 1926) published as *Beiheft* 6 of the *Historische Zeitschrift;*

Ernst Simon, *Ranke und Hegel* (München, 1928), *Beiheft* 15 of the *Historische Zeitschrift;* on Ranke's political views, Wilhelm Mommsen, *Stein, Ranke, Bismarck* (München, 1954); on his conception of society, Rudolf Vierhaus, *Ranke und die soziale Welt* (Münster, 1957).

There is no comprehensive work on the Prussian historians. On the political views of the Prussian historians in the years preceding and following the 1848 Revolution, see Wolfgang Hock, *Liberales Denken im Zeitalter der Paulskirche. Droysen und die Frankfurter Mitte* (Münster, 1957). There are a number of monographs on individual historians: on Droysen, Günter Birtsch, *Die Nation als sittliche Idee* (Köln, 1964); on Dahlmann, an essay in Hermann Heimpel, *Zwei Historiker. Friedrich Christoph Dahlmann. Jacob Burckhardt* (Göttingen, 1962); on Sybel, Hellmut Seier, *Die Staatsidee Heinrich von Sybels in den Wandlungen der Reichsgründungszeit* (Lübeck, 1961); on Sybel and Treitschke, a Marxist interpretation, Hans Schleier, *Sybel und Treitschke. Antidemokratismus und Militarismus im historisch-politischen Denken grossbourgeoiser Geschichtsideologen* (Berlin, 1965); on Treitschke, especially Andreas Dorpalen, *Heinrich von Treitschke* (New Haven, 1957); also Walter Bussmann, *Treitschke: Sein Welt und Geschichtsbild* (Göttingen, 1962); on Theodor Mommsen, Alfred Heuss, *Theodor Mommsen und das 19. Jahrhundert* (Kiel, 1956); Albert Wucher, *Theodor Mommsen, Geschichtschreibung und Politik* (Göttingen, 1956) and the projected three-volume biography, Lothar Wickert, *Theodor Mommsen, Eine Biographie* (Frankfurt, 1959-   ), of which two volumes have appeared.

There is an extensive literature on the thinkers—Dilthey, Windelband, Rickert, Max Weber, Ernst Troeltsch—who are discussed in chapters VI and VII. See Carlo Antoni, *From History to Sociology* (Detroit, 1960); Pietro Rossi, *Lo Storicismo Tedesco Contemporaneo* (n.1., 1956); H. Stuart Hughes, *Consciousness and Society. The Reorientation of European Social Thought 1890-1930* (New York, 1958); Gerhard Masur, *Prophets of Yesterday. Studies in European Culture, 1890-1914* (New York, 1961); I. S. Kon, *Geschichtsphilosophie des 20. Jahrhunderts,* translated from Russian, 2 vols. (Berlin, 1965), especially vol. I. A more technical, philosophic analysis of their views is contained in Maurice Mandelbaum, *The Problem of Historical Knowledge, An Answer to Relativism* (New York, 1938).

On Dilthey, see H. A. Hodges, *The Philosophy of Wilhelm Dilthey* (London, 1952); Jean-François Suter, *Wilhelm Dilthey, Essai sur le problème de l'historicisme* (Basel, 1960); Hellmut Diwald, *Wilhelm Dilthey, Erkenntnistheorie und Philosophie der*

Geschichte (Göttingen, 1963). Otto Friedrich Böllnow, *Dilthey, Eine Einführung in seine Philosophie* (Leipzig, 1936) deals extensively with Dilthey's theory of *Verstehen* but only marginally with his philosophy of history.

The literature on Max Weber has grown immensely during the past years. There is an important biography by his wife, Marianne Weber, *Max Weber. Ein Lebensbild* (Tübingen, 1926). See also Reinhard Bendix, *Max Weber. An Intellectual Portrait* (New York, 1960). On Weber's politics, see especially Wolfgang J. Mommsen, *Max Weber und die deutsche Politik, 1890-1920* (Tübingen, 1959); J. P. Mayer, *Max Weber and German Politics,* 2nd ed. (London, 1956); and Karl Loewenstein, *Max Webers staatspolitische Auffassungen in der Sicht unserer Zeit* (Frankfurt, 1965). Mommsen's book led to considerable controversy. See the proceedings of the 1964 meeting of the German Sociological Association devoted to a reassessment of Max Weber, published as *Max Weber und die Soziologie heute* (Tübingen, 1965). On Weber's conception of history, see Wolfgang J. Mommsen, "Universalgeschichtliches und politisches Denken bei Max Weber," in *Historische Zeitschrift* 201 (1965), pp. 557-612; and Günter Abramowski, *Das Geschichtsbild Max Webers. Universalgeschichte am Leitfaden des okzidentalen Rationalisierungsprozesses* (Stuttgart, 1966). Karl Jaspers essay, *Max Weber. Politiker. Forscher. Philosoph* (Bremen, 1946) should be mentioned.

Carlo Antoni, *From History to Sociology,* mentioned above, contains an important essay on Troeltsch. See also Walter Bodenstein, *Neige des Historismus. Ernst Troeltschs Entwicklungsgang* (Gütersloh, 1959); Wilhelm Kasch, *Die Sozialphilosophie von Ernst Troeltsch* (Tübingen, 1963); E. Lessing, *Die Geschichtsphilosophie Ernst Troeltschs* (Hamburg, 1965). See also the essay by Otto Hintze, "Troeltsch und das Problem des Historismus," *Historische Zeitschrift,* 135 (1927), 188-239.

Meinecke's autobiography, *Erlebtes, 1862-1919* (Stuttgart, 1964), re-creates a good deal of the intellectual and political atmosphere in German academic circles. There are two major works on Meinecke: Walther Hofer, *Geschichtsschreibung und Weltanschauung* (München, 1950) is devoted to an analysis of Meinecke's theory of history; Richard W. Sterling, *Ethics in a World of Power* (Princeton, 1958) is an analysis of Meinecke's political ideas. An excellent critical analysis of Meinecke's conception of individuality is contained in Ernst Schulin's article "Das Problem der Individualität. Eine kritische Betrachtung des Historismus-Werkes von Friedrich Meinecke," in *Historische Zeitschrift,* 197 (1963), pp. 115-116. See also the introductions to the various volumes of Meinecke's *Werke.*

On the political opinions of German historians and social theorists in the transition from the Wilhelminian period to the Weimar Republic, and on the impact of World War I on the political thought of the historians, see Gustav Schmidt, *Deutscher Historismus und der Übergang zur Demokratie. Untersuchungen zu den politischen Gedanken von Meinecke, Troeltsch, Max Weber* (Lübeck, 1964); also K. Schwabe, "Zur politischen Haltung der deutschen Professoren im Ersten Weltkrieg," in *Historische Zeitschrift*, CXCIII (1961), pp. 601-634. On the Neo-Rankeans, see Hans-Heinz Krill, *Die Rankerenaissance. Max Lenz und Erich Marcks. Ein Beitrag zum historisch-politischen Denken in Deutschland, 1880-1935* (Berlin, 1962); and Ludwig Dehio, "Ranke and German Imperialism" in his *Germany and World Politics in the Twentieth Century,* tr. Dieter Pevsner (New York, 1967), pp. 38-71. On Hans Delbrück, see Annelise Thimme, *Hans Delbrück als Kritiker der Wilhelminischen Epoche* (Düsseldorf, 1955). See also Horst Schallenberg's analysis of school textbooks in the Wilhelminian Era and the Weimar Republic, *Untersuchungen zum Geschichtsbild der Wilhelminischen Ära und der Weimarer Zeit* (Düsseldorf, 1964).

On historians in the Weimar republic, see Walter Götz, *Historiker meiner Zeit* (Köln, 1957). S. William Halperin, ed., *Some 20th-Century Historians* (Chicago, 1961) contains an essay by Richard H. Bauer on Veit Valentin and one by William H. Maehl on Erich Eyck. For a brief biography of Eckart Kehr, see Hans-Ulrich Wehler's "Einleitung" to Eckart Kehr, *Der Primat der Innenpolitik* (Berlin, 1965), pp. 1-29. A brief biography of Otto Hintze by Fritz Hartung is contained in Otto Hintze, *Staat und Verfassung,* vol. I of *Gesammelte Abhandlungen,* ed. Gerhard Oestreich (Göttingen, 1962), pp. 7-33. On Arthur Rosenberg, see Helmut Schachenmayer, *Arthur Rosenberg als Vertreter des historischen Materialismus* (Wiesbaden, 1964). On German historians and the Nazi regime, see Helmut Heiber, *Walter Frank und sein Reichsinstitut für Geschichte* (Stuttgart, 1966).

The problem of the revision of German historiographical traditions after the catastrophes of Nazism and World War II is raised in the essays in Hans Kohn, ed., *German History. Some New Views* (Cambridge, Mass., 1954). See also the essays by Hans Buchheim, Ludwig Dehio, Theodor Schieder, and Karl Buchheim in Karl Forster, ed., *Gibt es ein deutsches Geschichtsbild?* (Würzburg, 1961); and Adolf Grote, *Unangenehmne Geschichstatsachen. Zur Revision des neuen deutschen Geschichtsbildes* (Nürnberg, 1960). No extensive study of trends in West German historiography since 1945 has appeared in West Germany. There are several East German studies, among which the most useful is probably Werner Berthold, Gerhard Lozek, and Horst Syrbe, "Grundlinien und Entwicklungs-tendenzen in der westdeutschen Geschichtsschreibung von 1945-1964," in *Wissenschaftliche Zeitschrift der Karl-Marx-Universität Leipzig,* XIV (1965), pp. 609-622. For other East German Communist discussions of trends in West German historiography see Gerhard Lozek and Horst Syrbe, *Geschichtsschreibung contra Geschichte* (Berlin, 1964) and Werner Berthold, ". . . grosshungern und gehorchen" (Berlin, 1960), the latter a critique of Gerhard Ritter. A critique of Lozek and Syrbe's attempt to interpret West German historiography almost exclusively as a function of the cold war is contained in the well balanced essay by the Czechslovak historian Bedřich Loewenstein, "Zur Kritik am Nationalgedanken in der westdeutschen Geschichtsschreibung," in *Der Antikommu-nismus in Theorie und Praxis. Zur Auseinandersetzung mit der im-perialistischen deutschen Geschichtsschreibung,* ed. Leo Stern *et al.* (Halle, 1963). See also Jaroslav Kudrna, *Historie, filosofie, politika v N.S.R.* (Praha, 1964). For bibliographical references to Soviet studies of German historiography, see Werner Berthold and Günter Katsch, "Zentren historiographischer Forschung in der UdSSR. Zur Bedeutung der sowjetischen Historiographie für die Erforschung der Geschichte der Geschichtsschreibung der DDR und Westdeutsch-lands," in *Zeitschrift für Geschichtswissenschaft,* XV (1967), 478-485. A series of articles by different authors on recent German historical scholarship, East and West, on various epochs of German history, "L'Historiographie Allemande Depuis la Guerre," began in *Annales. Économies. Sociétés. Civilisations,* XXI (1966), pp. 1402-1409, with an article by P. Aycoberry, "Histoire de l'Allemagne au XIXe siècle." On West German historiography, see also Hans Herz-feld, "Germany: After the Catastrophe", in *Journal of Contemporary History,* II (1967), no. 1, pp. 79-92.

Dietrich Fischer, *Die deutsche Geschichtswissenschaft von J. G. Droysen bis O. Hintze in ihrem Verhältnis zur Soziologie. Grundzüge eines Methodenproblems* (Köln, 1966) and Karl Ferdinand Werner, *Das NS—Geschichtsbild und die deutsche Geschichtswissenschaft* (Stuttgart, 1967) came to my attention too late to be used in this study.

Index

Acton, John Dalberg, Lord, 6, 11
Adams, Brooks, 63
Adams, George Burton, 64
Adams, Henry, 63
Adams, Herbert Baxter, 63
Adorno, Theodor, 337
Alexander the Great, 96, 105
Ancillon, Johann Peter Friedrich, 71
Anderle, Othmar, 340
Annales, Économies, Sociétés, Civilisations, 262
Anti-Semitism, 122, 123, 304, 311
Antoni, Carlo, 6, 32, 33, 166, 176, 189, 194, 286
Aquinas, Thomas, 273
Arndt, Ernst Moritz, 41
Arnold, Gottfried, 32, 34, 219
Aubin, Hermann, 336
Augustine, Saint, 77
Auschwitz, 263

Baumgarten, Hermann, 23, 91, 120, 122, 123
Beard, Charles, 286, 287
Beethoven, Ludwig von, 127
Below, Georg von, 14, 131, 197, 198, 199, 229, 230, 327, 336
Bentham, Jeremy, 38, 274
Berkeley, George, 145
Berliner Politisches Wochenblatt, 70, 71
Bernstorff, Christian Günther, Count von, 70, 71
Bethmann-Hollweg, Theobald von, 255, 267
Bismarck, Otto, Prince von, 11, 23, 24, 86, 92, 94, 119, 120, 122, 123, 169, 170, 171, 176, 196, 201, 202, 204, 206, 214, 224, 229, 230, 232, 253, 254, 255, 256, 259, 261, 335

Bloch, Marc, 262
Böckh, August, 65, 66
Böhme, Helmut, 268
Bopp, Franz, 66
Bosanquet, Bernard, 274
Boyen, Hermann von, 196, 197
Bracher, Karl Dietrich, 250, 266
Bradenburg, Erich, 229
Braudel, Fernand, 262
Brecht, Arnold, 124, 126
Breysig, Kurt, 236, 336
Brunner, Otto, 263, 264
Buckle, Henry Thomas, 63, 109, 111, 130, 164, 239, 280
Büchner, Karl, 239
Burckhardt, Jacob, 4, 11, 12, 129, 130, 151, 172, 182, 200, 207, 225, 226, 239, 245, 252, 259, 279, 280
Burke, Edmund, 6, 32, 33, 76, 101, 116, 219
Bussmann, Walter, 92, 261
Butterfield, Herbert, 65

Calvinism, 33, 183, 185, 186
Carlyle, Thomas, 6, 129
Carr, Edward Hallett, 282
Catholicism, Roman, 33, 184
Center Party, 267
Charles X, King of Sweden, 256
Cohen, Hermann, 128, 144–147, 148, 151, 152, 161, 205
Cohen, Morris, 286
Communism, 223–224, 243, 257
Comte, Auguste, 6, 36, 63, 130, 135, 138, 140, 164, 198, 239, 242, 280, 282
Condillac, Étienne Bonnot de, 38
Condorcet, Jean Antoine, Marquis de, 146, 241, 280, 282, 283
Conservative Party, 196
Constant, Benjamin, 6

Conze, Werner, 245, 261, 262, 263, 264, 265, 268
Coulanges, Numa Denis Fustel de, 11
Craig, Gordon, 257
Croce, Benedetto, 285, 286

Dahlmann, Friedrich Christoph, 22, 91, 93, 100–102, 108, 203
Danilevskii, Nikolai, 129
Danton, Georges Jacques, 254
Darwinism, 206
Dehio, Ludwig, 230, 250, 259, 260, 263, 268, 334
Delbrück, Hans, 15, 176, 196, 231, 327, 328, 334
Descartes, René, 31, 34, 219
Dilthey, Wilhelm, 1x, 10, 91, 109, 111, 124, 125, 126, 127, 133, 134-144, 155, 160, 161, 173, 196, 239, 240, 242, 243, 244, 279, 337
Döllinger, Johann von, 4
Droysen, Johann Gustav, 9, 21, 22, 65, 91, 93, 95, 104–119, 120, 121, 127, 129, 133, 135, 138, 139, 140, 171, 195, 196, 201, 202, 203, 232, 286, 308
Duncker, Max, 91, 119, 308

Eichhorn, Johann Albrecht, 70
Eichhorn, Karl Friedrich, 65, 66
Eisler, Rudolf, 287
Emerton, Ephraim, 64
Engels, Friedrich, 11
Ernst August, King of Hanover, 91
Eschenburg, Theodor, 250, 265
Eyck, Erich, 25, 232, 253, 261, 335

Fascism, 235
Febvre, Lucien, 262
Feuerbach, Ludwig, 239
Fichte, Johann Gottlieb, 11, 39, 41, 42, 152, 201, 202
Ficker, Julius von, 4, 369

Fischer, Fritz, 246, 267–268
Fiske, John, 63
Flechtheim, Ossip, 337
Fraenkel, Ernst, 337
Frederick II, King of Prussia, 19, 210, 254, 255, 256, 259, 273
French Revolution, 6, 7, 20, 21, 33, 36, 40, 44, 47, 72, 85, 86, 96, 97, 98, 102, 106, 108, 116, 224, 256, 263
Freud, Sigmund, 124, 125, 126, 161
Friedmann, Wolfgang, 133
Friedrich, Wilhelm IV, King of Prussia, 85, 91, 121, 203, 204
Fueter, Edward, 86

Gadamer, Hans-Georg, 247
Gagern, Max Joseph Ludwig, 201, 203
Gagern, Wilhelm Heinrich August, 201, 203
Geiss, Immanuel, 260
Gentz, Friedrich, 44
Gerhard, Dietrich, 264, 341
Gerlach, Ernst Ludwig von, 70
Gerlach, Leopold von, 70
Gervinus, Georg, 91, 92, 93, 102–103, 109, 121
Geschichtlichkeit, 243–244, 246, 247, 248, 339
Geyl, Pieter, 340
Gibbon, Edward, 7, 29, 31, 219
Gierke, Otto von, 131, 132 133
Giesebrecht, Wilhelm von, 308
Gneisenau, Neithardt, Count von, 7
Goerdeler, Carl Friedrich, 258, 259
Goethe, Johann Wolfgang, 11, 32, 37, 38, 42, 44, 45, 52, 53, 127, 216, 217, 219, 220–222, 224, 225
Goetz, Walter, 26, 229, 232, 261
Green, Theodore H., 274, 275

Häusser, Ludwig, 91, 308
Haller, Johannes, 229, 261

Haller, Karl Ludwig von, 41, 70, 74, 75, 201
Hamann, Johann Georg, 34
Harden, Maximilian, 327
Hardenberg, Karl August, Prince von, 20, 40, 44, 52, 97
Hartmann, L. M., 336
Hartung, Fritz, 237
Haym, Rudolf, 91, 119–120
Heffter, Heinrich, 253
Hegel, Georg Wilhelm Friedrich, 9, 11, 32, 36, 39, 40, 41, 42, 65, 66, 67, 69, 77, 80, 82, 85, 89, 95, 96, 101, 102, 104, 105, 114, 118, 129, 130, 132, 133, 137, 139, 153, 174, 179, 180, 182, 186, 198, 201, 202, 208, 210, 211, 218, 234, 239, 282, 285, 287
Hegelianism, Left, 22, 47
Heidegger, Martin, 25, 243, 244, 245, 247, 248
Heimpel, Hermann, 245, 251
Herder, Johann Gottfried, 9, 11, 30, 33, 34–38, 41, 42, 43, 45, 57, 72, 102, 173, 201, 216, 219, 220, 222, 239, 276, 277
Herzfeld, Hans, 230, 238, 250, 252, 259, 263, 265, 268
Heuss, Alfred, 131, 245, 340
Heussi, Karl, 241
Hindenburg, Otto von, 224, 254, 259–260
Hintze, Otto, 11, 26, 174, 176, 198, 206, 229, 230, 231, 232–236, 251, 261, 262, 280, 334
Historisch-Politische Zeitschrift, 70–84
Historische Zeitschrift, 196, 197, 200, 223, 230, 245, 246, 259
Hitler, Adolf, 223, 224, 228, 254, 255, 257, 259, 267
Hobbes, Thomas, 273
Hobhouse, Leonard T., 274
Hochschule für Politik, 266
Hock, Wolfgang, 103–104

Hölderlin, Friedrich, 151
Hofer, Walther, 247, 250
Hoggan, David, 260
Holborn, Hajo, 18, 20, 223, 238
Hollowell, John, 16
Horckheimer, Max, 337
Hubatsch, Walther, 259–260
Hughes, H. Stuart, 124, 160–161, 165
Humanitätsideal, 37, 38, 44, 45, 52
Humboldt, Wilhelm von, ix, 3, 4, 7, 9, 10, 11, 13, 16, 20, 37, 38, 39, 40, 41, 42, 44–62, 72, 74, 75, 85, 97, 102, 103, 105, 109, 110, 127, 137, 153, 173, 201, 216, 234, 240, 246, 270, 271
Hume, David, 31, 38, 125

Institut für Zeitgeschichte, 265

Jaspers, Karl, 250, 251, 282
Jefferson, Thomas, 96
Jellinek, Georg, 182
Jesus, 168, 177, 183, 184
Jews, 223, 228, 240
Jünger, Ernst, 26, 243, 245, 271
Jung, Carl Gustav, 124

Kaehler, Siegfried, 46
Kahler, Erich, 287
Kant, Immanuel, 11, 39, 47, 54, 102, 127, 133, 135, 136, 139, 140, 143, 144, 146, 157, 158, 177, 187, 206, 213, 251, 282, 331
Kathedersozialisten, 122
Kehr, Eckart, 24, 236, 237–238, 268
Kelsen, Hans, 16, 233
Kierkegaard, Søren, 280
Koehl, Robert, 250
Kohn, Hans, 253
Krieger, Leonard, 19, 93
Krill, Hans-Heinz, 230
Krüger, Gerhard, 248, 249

Lachmann, Karl, 66
Lafayette, Marie Joseph, Marquis de, 102
Lamprecht, Karl, 4, 11, 25, 130, 131, 197–200, 205, 231, 233, 239, 262, 280, 327, 328, 336
Lasaulx, Ernst von, 129
Laue, Theodore von, 84
Leber, Julius, 258
Lehmann, Max, 9, 327
Leibniz, Gottfried Wilhelm, 32, 34, 68, 174, 194, 216, 219
Lenin, Vladimir Ilyich, 254
Lenz, Max, 130, 197, 229, 230, 327, 328, 334
Leo, Heinrich, 67–69, 105
Lessing, Gotthold Ephraim, 331
Lessing, Theodor, 240
Litt, Theodor, 246, 247
Locke, John, 16, 38, 45, 98, 135, 274
Löwith, Karl, 249
Louis XIV, King of France, 256
Ludendorff, Erich von, 256
Lukacz, Georg, 17, 337
Luther, Martin, 33, 34, 146, 185, 270
Lutheranism, 14, 33, 71, 184, 185, 186, 270

Macaulay, Thomas Babington, 6
Machiavelli, Niccolò, 9, 42, 67, 68, 171, 202, 207, 210, 211, 224, 254
Maistre, Joseph de, 129
Mann, Golo, 238, 251, 332, 341
Mannheim, Karl, 241–242, 243, 285, 331, 334
Marcks, Erich, 14, 130, 229, 230, 260, 334
Marx, Karl, 11, 36, 183, 239, 241, 282, 283
Marxism, 18
Masur, Gerhard, 124
Maximilian, King of Bavaria, 70, 85

Max-Planck-Institut für Geschichte, 264
Meinecke, Friedrich, ix, 5, 6, 9, 10, 12, 13, 15, 16, 17, 21, 25, 26, 30, 31, 32, 33, 34, 39, 47, 62, 127, 128, 130, 131, 174–177, 195–228, 229, 230, 231, 232, 235, 237, 247, 250, 252, 253, 254, 256, 257, 259, 261, 263, 264, 270, 271, 285, 286, 287
Melanchton, Philipp, 177
Menger, Carl, 287
Meyer, Edward, 206
Meyerhoff, Hans, 287
Michelet, Jules, 6, 8
Mill, James, 38, 274
Mill, John Stuart, 94, 96, 121, 129, 135, 198, 241, 274, 280
Militarism, 224, 225, 226, 253–257, 258
Möser, Justus, 33, 34, 201, 219
Mommsen, Hans, 264
Mommsen, Theodor, 23, 91, 93, 121, 122–123, 131, 308, 311, 336
Mommsen, Wolfgang, 321
Montesquieu, Charles de Secondat, Baron de, 31, 97, 219
Müller, Adam, 201
Mussolini, Benito, 254

Napoleon I, Bonaparte, Emperor of France, 7, 20, 21, 40, 44, 52, 96, 98, 108, 256
National Liberal Party, 120, 122, 127, 129–130
Natorp, Paul, 128, 144, 147, 148
Naumann, Friedrich, 12, 15, 123, 127, 168, 170, 175, 176, 189, 196, 204, 207, 225, 231
Nazism, 27, 223, 225, 228, 246, 254, 255, 257, 258, 260, 263, 264, 265,
Neo-Platonism, 31, 219, 222
Neo-Rankeans, 89, 130, 199, 230
Neumann, Carl, 200

Newton, Sir Isaac, 34, 125, 220
Niebuhr, Barthold Georg, 65, 66, 71
Nietzsche, Friedrich, 4, 12, 124, 129, 156, 173, 239, 321
Novalis, 201

Oncken, Hermann, 130, 230, 236, 237, 261, 327, 328, 334
Oppenheimer, Franz, 233
Orwell, George, 173, 283
Otto-Suhr-Institut, 266

Pan-Germans, 206, 231, 255, 267
Paul, Saint, 34, 270
Perthes, Friedrich, 70, 71, 105
Pestalozzi, Johann Heinrich, 52
Peter the Great, 256
Pfizer, Paul Achatius, 99–100, 102
Pietism, 31, 34, 37, 219
Plato, 58, 248
Platonism: *see* Neo-Platonism
Plessner, Helmuth, 337, 340
Popper, Karl, 286, 287
Positivism, 124, 125, 126, 127, 130, 135, 239
Preuss, Hugo, 271
Preussische Jahrbücher, 91, 92, 94, 119, 120, 121, 196, 224
Progress Party, 119, 120
Proust, Marcel, 124

Quinet, Edgar, 94

Rachfahl, Felix, 130, 327
Radowitz, Joseph Maria von, 70
Ranke, Leopold von, ix, 3, 4, 8, 9, 10, 11, 12, 13, 14, 17, 39, 40, 42, 61–91, 94, 95, 106, 109, 110, 117, 123, 127, 129, 130, 131, 137, 138, 140, 153, 173, 174, 179, 182, 184, 186, 189, 190, 193, 195, 197, 198, 201, 202, 208, 210, 211, 212, 216, 217, 221, 222, 225, 230, 233, 234, 242, 246, 248, 252, 259, 262, 270, 276, 277, 279

Ranke-Renaissance: see Neo-Rankeans
Rathenau, Walther, 176
Raumer, Friedrich von, 70
Renouvier, Charles, 274
Resistance against Nazis, 257–259, 265
Revolution of 1848, 22, 24, 85, 91, 92, 93, 104, 108, 109, 116, 226, 232
Rickert, Heinrich, 127, 133, 134, 144, 148, 152–160, 161, 162, 173, 174, 175, 178, 180, 181, 182, 193, 197, 198, 233, 240, 244, 252
Rintelen, Karl Ludwig, 250
Ritschl, Albrecht, 177
Ritter, Gerhard, ix, 13, 17, 238, 246, 251, 252, 253–257, 258–259, 261, 263, 265, 267, 268, 334
Robespierre, Maximilien, 7, 97
Robinson, James Harvey, 64
Rochau, August Ludwig von, 121, 122
Roessler, Hellmuth, 260
Rosenberg, Arthur, 25, 232
Rosenberg, Hans, 21, 23, 238, 253, 341
Rote, Kapelle, 259
Rothacker, Erich, 242, 243, 246, 247, 287
Rothfels, Hans, 238, 250, 252, 253, 257, 258, 259, 261, 263, 265, 268
Rotteck, Karl von, 41, 91, 97, 98–99
Rousseau, Jean-Jacques, 97, 98, 99, 273
Ruggiero, Guido, 286

Saint-Simon, Claude Henri, Comte de, 36, 107, 280
Savigny, Friedrich Carl von, 41, 48, 65, 66, 70, 71, 72, 85, 94, 95, 132
Schäfer, Dietrich, 229, 230, 261

Scharnhorst, Gerhard Johann
    David von, 7, 20, 140
Schelling, Friedrich Wilhelm
    Joseph, 39, 198
Schieder, Theodor, 245, 246, 251,
    262, 263, 264, 265, 268
Schiller, Friedrich, 37, 42, 44, 45,
    50, 331
Schlegel, Friedrich, 201
Schleier, Hans, 87
Schleiermacher, Friedrich, 10, 66,
    71, 234, 240
Schlenke, Manfred, 264
Schlieffen Plan, 255
Schlosser, Friedrich Christoph,
    105, 117
Schmitt, Carl, 25, 233, 243, 245,
    271, 334, 337
Schmoller, Gustav von, 12, 122,
    130, 131, 132, 232, 233, 236,
    262, 287
Schnabel, Franz, 4, 229
Schoeps, Hans Joachim, 238
Schopenhauer, Arthur, 4, 129
Schulin, Ernst, 85
Sell, F. C., 253
Shaftesbury, Anthony Ashley
    Cooper, Earl of, 219
Simon, Ernst, 238
Smend, Rudolf, 233
Social Democratic Party, 205, 238,
    267
Sombart, Werner, 233, 236, 280,
    336
Sontheimer, Kurt, 265
Spencer, Herbert, 6, 94, 275, 280
Spengler, Oswald, 194, 195, 199,
    217, 236, 240, 241, 243, 245,
    271, 280, 337, 340
Spinoza, Benedict, 194
Spranger, Edward, 242, 246, 247
Srbik, Heinrich Ritter von, ix, 130,
    223
Stalin, Joseph, 283
Stein, Heinrich Friedrich Karl
    Freiherr vom und zu, 7, 20, 22,
    40, 44, 52, 55, 74, 97, 108

Stein, Lorenz von, 4, 11
Stoecker, Adolf, 123
Strauss, Leo, 249
Streisand, Joachim, ix
Strukturgeschichte, 262, 263, 264
Sybel, Heinrich von, 12, 88, 91,
    95, 116–119, 120, 121, 123,
    176, 186, 189, 196, 198, 199,
    200, 201, 239, 308, 309, 327

Tacitus, 32
Taylor, Alan John Percivale, 260
Thierry, Augustin, 6
Tirpitz, Alfred von, 170
Tocqueville, Alexis de, 11, 129,
    245
Tönnies, Ferdinand, 280
Toynbee, Arnold, 282, 340
Treitschke, Heinrich von, 14, 16,
    88, 91, 96, 120, 121, 122, 123,
    131, 171, 176, 186, 196, 198,
    201, 211, 230, 271, 311
Troeltsch, Ernst, 5, 12, 15, 16, 26,
    28, 33, 125, 127, 128, 173,
    174–195, 196, 199, 205, 206,
    216, 217, 224, 227, 228, 230,
    231, 233, 234, 235, 239, 240,
    241, 242, 244, 270, 271, 285,
    287
Turner, Frederick, 11, 64

Vagts, Alfred, 286, 287
Valentin, Veit, 25, 232, 335
Varnhagen von Ense, Karl August,
    71
Verein für Sozialpolitik, 122, 132
Versailles, Treaty of (1919), 230,
    235, 236, 255
Vico, Giambattista, 30, 33, 219,
    287
Vierhaus, Rudolf, 87
Vierteljahrschrift für Sozial- und
    Wirtschaftsgeschichte, 236
Vierteljahrschrift für
    Zeitgeschichte, 250, 265
Voltaire, 7, 29, 31, 32, 219
Wagner, Adolf, 287

Wagner, Fritz, 245, 262, 263, 268, 276
Waitz, Georg, 91, 252, 308
Walsh, William Henry, 278
Wars of Liberation, German (1813–1815), 7, 11, 20, 21, 43, 53, 106, 205, 206, 229, 253
Webb, Walter Prescott, 64
Weber, Max, ix, 11, 12, 15, 111, 126, 127, 128, 134, 140, 153, 156, 159–173, 174, 175, 176, 182, 182, 184, 187, 196, 204, 206, 215, 227, 228, 233, 234, 239, 241, 244, 251, 252, 262, 272, 280, 281, 318, 321, 337
Weimar Republic, 231, 235, 236, 237, 238, 253, 261, 265, 271, 336
Welcker, Karl Theodor, 91, 92, 97, 98
Werner, Karl, 287
Westphal, Otto, 261

White, Andrew, 63
Wilhelm I, King of Prussia, Emperor of Germany, 91
Wilhelm II, Emperor of Germany, 128, 170, 196, 253
Winckelmann, Johann Joachim, 37, 38, 52, 331
Windelband, Wilhelm, 126, 127, 133, 134, 144, 147–152, 153, 161, 175, 197, 239, 244
Wittram, Reinhard, 245, 251
Wolf, Friedrich August, 65
Wolff, Christian von, 34
World War I, 128, 205–207, 211, 225, 231, 235, 238, 239, 244, 255, 256, 259, 261, 267, 336
World War II, 223–224, 259, 267

Young Germany, 22

Zeitgeschichte, 250, 264, 265–266
Ziekursch, Johannes, 232, 335

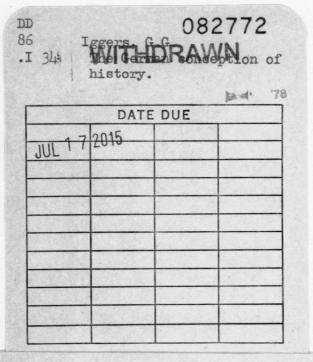